W9-CBU-328

The Mission
of an
Evangelist

The Mission
of an
Evangelist

Amsterdam **2000**

WORLD WIDE PUBLICATIONS
Minneapolis, MN 55403

ACKNOWLEDGEMENTS

Bible quotations marked KJV are taken from the King James Version of the Bible. Bible quotations marked NIV are taken from the The Holy Bible, New International Version. Copyright © 1973, 1978, 1984 International Bible Society. Used by permission of Zondervan Publishing House. All rights reserved. Bible quotations marked RSV are taken by permission from the Revised Standard Version Bible. Copyright © 1946, 1952, 1971, 1973. National Council of the Churches of Christ in the U.S.A., New York. Bible quotations marked NASB are taken from the New American Standard Bible. Copyright © 1960, 1962, 1963, 1968, 1971, 1972, 1973, 1975, 1977 The Lockman Foundation. Used by permission. Bible quotations marked NLT are taken from the Holy Bible, New Living Translation. Copyright © 1996. Used by permission of Tyndale House Publishers, Inc. Wheaton, Illinois 60189. All rights reserved. Bible quotations marked TLB are taken from The Living Bible © 1971. Used by permission of Tyndale House Publishers Inc., Wheaton, IL 60189. All rights reserved. Bible quotations marked NKJV are taken by permission from The Holy Bible, New King James Version. Copyright © 1979, 1980, 1982 Thomas Nelson, Inc. Bible quotations marked NEB are taken from the New English Bible, © 1961 Oxford University Press, Cambridge University Press. Bible quotations marked NRSV are taken from the New Revised Standard Version Bible. Copyright © 1989 by the Division of Christian Education of the National Council of the Churches of Christ in the United States of America.

PUBLISHER'S NOTE

The Amsterdam 2000 Conference of Preaching Evangelists offered 22 plenary sessions which were attended by all the participants, eight seminars in different Conference languages (there were 29 official languages), and over 220 workshops in various languages. All the plenary messages, with other plenary program elements, all the seminar topics, and a limited selection of workshops are included in this Compendium. In most cases, for length and consistency, we have been obliged to edit, condense or include only extracts of the presentations. Our thanks to Dr. Roger Palms for his excellent edits. We have sought to include photos of all the speakers; our apologies for the cases in which we were unable to secure photographs.

The Amsterdam 2000 Conference is reported to have drawn together the largest number of Christian leaders ever assembled, from the widest national, ethnic, linguistic, cultural and denominational backgrounds. All the speakers were asked to base their presentations on the Bible, and to respect the Statement of Faith of the Billy Graham Evangelistic Association. While these parameters were clearly established, there remained significant liberty for speakers to represent varying viewpoints according to their diverse backgrounds, thoughts and experiences.

This Compendium of the Amsterdam 2000 Conference seeks to represent fairly the wonderful diversity of thinking in the Church worldwide on various aspects of evangelism. At the same time, we hope that readers will understand that the viewpoints expressed by the many speakers at the Conference do not necessarily represent the policies, procedures and doctrines of the Billy Graham Evangelistic Association.

Published by World Wide Publications, 1303 Hennepin Avenue, Minneapolis, Minnesota 55403, U.S.A.
Paperback ISBN: 0-89066-323-8
Hard Cover ISBN: 0-89066-324-6

Printed in the U.S.A.

Table of Contents

*Plenary messages

Amsterdam 2000 Workshops

The Personal Life of the Evangelist

The World Around Us

Evangelistic Methods and Strategies

The Theology of an Evangelist

Amsterdam 2000 Documents

Editorial Preface

The Amsterdam 2000 Conference of Preaching Evangelists follows in the rich train of earlier conferences, namely, Berlin 1964, Amsterdam 1983 and Amsterdam 1986, in which the key focus was the message, the messengers and the methods of evangelism. Other international conferences also prepared the way for Amsterdam 2000.

Some have asked, "Why another conference on evangelism?" The message has not changed, and messengers are still needed; but the world has changed dramatically with the overwhelming shift to post-modern thinking—so there was an urgent need to explore how methods may need to be adapted to convincingly reach contemporary men and women. This presented a formidable challenge in the development of a conference program, since not all the world is currently affected by the same philosophies, but Christians believe that people of all the world need to hear and to respond to the Gospel of God's love in Christ. A Program Planning Committee drawn from Christian leaders in nine countries met repeatedly to lay out the themes and topics of the conference, and there were thousands of contacts with Christian leaders around the world, who made very valuable recommendations as the program developed. Thanks are due to the Program Staff, who worked long and hard to bring the conference to fruition.

Although he was unable to attend the conference due to the recommendation of his doctors, Dr. Billy Graham was deeply involved in the conference preparations, and his passion throughout the process was to learn from, to help and to encourage evangelists in every country on earth.

The conference program was aimed to meet the opportunities and challenges faced by preachers who (1) tell the Gospel story (as defined in 1 Corinthians 15 and other Bible passages), (2) urge people to trust Christ as their Savior, and (3) exercise their ministry in relationship to the local church.

Many of the messages presented in this Compendium were transcribed from taped presentations, and while we have made our best effort to faithfully reflect the speakers' messages, we ask their forgiveness if we have gotten details wrong.

This book has been published due to the encouragement of Dr. John Corts, President of the Billy Graham Evangelistic Association and General Director of Amsterdam 2000; Dr. John Akers, Chairman of the Program Planning Committee of the conference; and staff of the Billy Graham Evangelistic Association who labored joyfully to encourage more people to begin or to continue the wonderful and eternally productive ministry of bringing others to Jesus.

—*William W. Conard, Program Director, Amsterdam 2000*

Billy Graham's Opening Greetings

You are gathered in Amsterdam from over 200 countries. Some of you have traveled thousands of miles and at great sacrifice. Why are you all in that beautiful city? What is the purpose of all the planning, the work, the travel, the price that we have paid? We have come together to discover how the evangelical church worldwide can further the Kingdom of God by the proclamation of the Gospel. To this end we will commit ourselves during the entire conference.

Several years ago there was a movie entitled *Back to the Future.* The actors in the movie traveled back in time, enabling them to understand the future. I suggest that we do that as well during this conference, but not in fantasy. We must go back and search the Word of God to discover what we need to do for the extension of the Kingdom in our day. That is the reason we have convened this conference. We must go back 2000 years to discover the future.

The most important passage of Scripture that we can study together is Acts 1 and 2. There we see how God, by the Holy Spirit, launched the church. The principles that surrounded that dramatic day will give us concepts of how we can be used by the Spirit to evangelize and to disciple people today. The way God started it all is the way that He will carry it on today. So this week we will go back in time to see what the Bible has to say, so as to be more useful in the future for God.

One thing remains certain. If we are to see our task of evangelism fulfilled and to enter the next generation without disappointment, we must have the power of God manifested and the overwhelming presence of the Holy Spirit. Without power there will be no major world evangelistic thrust.

Some of you may have heard of the beautiful Yosemite National Park in California in the United States. I remember a tremendous spectacle called "The Firefall," which was put on years ago every night during the summer. A huge fire was kindled on Inspiration Point high above the floor of the valley where people gathered to watch this great sight. When the flames reached their most majestic peak, a dramatic voice pierced the clear night air saying, "Let the fire fall." At that moment a tremendous waterfall of glowing embers poured down the granite cliff. It was a never-to-be-forgotten sight to any who saw it.

In an age given over to cynicism, coldness and doubt, and in which the fire and the warmth of God is conspicuous for its absence in the world, my heart cry is, "Let the fire fall!" And during these days of Amsterdam 2000, when we refocus on the blueprint of the early church for evangelism so we can be more useful in the future, may that too be our prayer. "O God, let the fire of Your Holy Spirit fall on us!" God bless you all!

Billy Graham

Dr. Graham was reared in Charlotte, North Carolina, U.S.A. At the age of 16 he made a personal commitment to Christ and was ordained as a young man. He graduated from Wheaton College in Illinois. He founded the Billy Graham Evangelistic Association in 1950, which headquarters in Minneapolis, Minnesota, U.S.A. Dr. Graham and his wife, Ruth, have three daughters, two sons, 19 grandchildren and numerous great-grandchildren. The Grahams make their home in North Carolina (U.S.A.).

The Motives for Evangelism

Billy Kim

Two thousand years ago Jesus Christ was killed outside the walls of Jerusalem. Today half of the world has yet to hear the news of the Savior's death on the Cross of Calvary.

Jesus spoke about world evangelization at least five times after He was resurrected from the dead. The first time, Matthew 28:18–19, He said, "All power is given unto me in heaven and in earth. [You go] therefore, and teach all nations, baptizing them in the name of the Father, and of the Son, and of the Holy Ghost" (KJV).

The second time Jesus spoke about world evangelization is in Mark 16:15 when Jesus said, "[You go] into all the world, and preach the gospel to every creature" (KJV).

The third time He spoke about world evangelization is recorded in Luke 24:47, "And that repentance and remission of sins should be preached . . . among all nations, beginning at Jerusalem" (KJV).

The fourth time that Jesus spoke about world evangelization is in John 20:21 when He said, "As my Father hath sent me, even so send I you" (KJV).

And the fifth time Jesus spoke about world evangelization, just before He ascended to heaven, was in Acts 1:8, "[You] shall receive power, after that the Holy Ghost is come upon you: [you] shall be witnesses unto me both in Jerusalem, and in all Judaea, and in Samaria, and unto the uttermost part of the earth" (KJV).

That was 2,000 years ago. Paul declares, "Woe is unto me, if I preach not the gospel!" (1 Corinthians 9:16, KJV). Do we have the same burning determination? If so, we can evangelize the world for Jesus Christ.

Lawlessness Demands Evangelism

Why do we evangelize? Why is evangelism so urgent? First, the lawlessness of our world demands evangelism. Scripture tells us, "As it is written, There is none righteous, no, not one: There is none that understandeth, there is none that seeketh after God" (Romans 3:10–11, KJV).

Jesus said, "Repent or perish" (see Luke 13:3). The United Nations cannot stop the lawlessness in our world. Education cannot stop the lawlessness. All of the armies in the world cannot stop the lawlessness in our society. Lawlessness demands evangelism in our world. Only the power of the Gospel of our Lord Jesus Christ can stop the lawlessness of our world! Therefore, we must preach the Gospel at all costs.

The Lostness of Mankind Urges Evangelism

Secondly, the lostness of mankind urges evangelism. Scripture tells us, "For all have sinned, and come short of the glory of God" (Romans 3:23, KJV). "Wherefore, as by one man sin entered into the world, and death by sin; . . . so death passed upon all men, for that all have sinned" (Romans 5:12, KJV).

A primary motive for evangelism is the lostness of a person without faith in Jesus Christ. We cannot evangelize aright until we believe that the person outside of Jesus Christ is lost and undone, without hope in this world or the one to come.

J. Wilbur Chapman said that a man is an evangelist who realizes that men are lost without Christ, and that the Gospel is the only way of salvation.

May we pray and weep over the lost and join God's searching party, seeking to find them and bring them home!

Charles Spurgeon was asked if the heathen would be saved if Christian people did not preach the Gospel to them. His answer: "The question is, Are *we* saved if we do not preach the Gospel to them?"

Jesus said, "For the Son of man is come to seek and to save that which was lost" (Luke 19:10, KJV).

A minister said that he never knew what it meant for a person to be lost until a little girl was lost in a town where he pastored. This child and her little brother went out into the country to look for the cows. They did not find them. When nightfall overtook them, they got into an argument as to which way led to their home. Neither one would give in. They went their own ways. When the little boy arrived home a little after dark, his mother asked, "Son, where is your sister?" He replied, "She said I was lost and would not come home with me. She went the other way."

The news went out for miles around. Neighbors gathered to help search for the child. Women prayed with the mother while men searched the woods. It was understood that if anyone would find her, he would fire a gun.

The next morning about daylight, the crack of a rifle was heard resounding over the wooded area. Everyone rushed back to the home and learned that the child had been found alive. The preacher said that strong men put their arms around each other and wept with joy. No one went to work that day. Plows stood still; stores were unopened. People gathered at the village church, rang the bell, sang praises, rejoiced that the child who was lost had been found.

The minister said he rejoiced with them and then began to think, "We spent all night searching for this child and now we are rejoicing that she has been found. Yet there are millions of lost souls around us. We have spent no sleepless nights in prayer for those who are lost. May God forgive us for not being deeply concerned over lost, hell-bound souls. May we pray and weep over the lost and join God's searching party, seeking to find them and bring them home!"

All without Christ are lost. "For as by one man's disobedience many were made sinners, so by the obedience of one shall many be made righteous" (Romans 5:19, KJV).

Looking back upon the past, every person except the sinless Christ must say what Pharaoh said, "I have sinned" (Exodus 9:27, KJV); what Achan said, "I have sinned" (Joshua 7:20, KJV); what King Saul said, "I have sinned" (1 Samuel 15:24, KJV); what David said, "I have sinned" (1 Chronicles 21:8, KJV); what the prodigal son said, "I have sinned" (Luke 15:21, KJV).

The lostness of mankind urges that we evangelize the world for Jesus Christ. There is only one way for God to banish the darkness of sin, to remove the degradation of sin, to heal the disease of sin, to cleanse the defilement of sin, to abolish the death of sin, to pay the debt of sin. This God has done in the redeeming work of our blessed Lord Jesus Christ on the Cross. He paid the debt. He died the death. He cleansed from defilement. He removed the degradation. He healed the disease. He is the life.

How I Heard the Gospel

For 17 years I had never heard the Gospel story. No one ever told me that He was wounded for my transgressions and He was bruised for my iniquities. I had never heard John 3:16, "For God so loved the world, that he gave his only begotten Son, that whosoever believeth in him should not perish, but have everlasting life" (KJV).

But during the Korean War when the American soldiers came over, one of the army camps moved near my home. Some of us boys went over there, hoping to get some chocolate candy bars. My school was bombed, and I couldn't go to school. So I decided to work for the American soldiers—shined their shoes, hung their blankets out in the sun, washed their mess kits, heated some water so they could shave.

One day I met Sergeant Carl Powers from Virginia, U.S.A. He asked me a question. He said, "Would you like to go to America?" I told him I did not want to go. But every excuse that I offered, Sergeant Powers would not accept.

He came back again. I saw tears. Some strange feeling came to my heart that I should go to the United States. I did not know what it was then. Now I know it was the providential hand of God working in his life as well as in my own life. I told him I would go. He got permission from my mom. We began to do the paperwork. I got my passport and my visa. Sergeant Powers paid my boat fare from Pusan to San Francisco. The Powers family helped me.

In Greenville, South Carolina, I was all alone on campus. I couldn't understand English. I got homesick. I was so lonely; I wished I had never left home. One day a college student came to my dormitory room with a black book. He opened it to John 3:16 and read, "For God so loved the world, that he gave his only begotten Son, that whosoever believeth in him should not perish, but have everlasting life" (KJV).

He asked, "Would you like to receive Christ as your personal Savior?" I said, "Would it take away my homesickness and loneliness?" He said, "He'll not only take away your homesickness and loneliness, but He'll give you peace, joy and happiness, and purpose in life." I told him I would like to receive Christ as my Savior. He said, "Let's kneel down and pray to receive Christ." So we knelt down. He asked me to pray. "I've never prayed in my life. I don't know how to pray." He said, "Can you try it in Korean?" I said, "I will." "O God, I'm a sinner. Please forgive my sins. Come into my heart."

When I finished praying in Korean, he prayed in English. When he finished, he put his arms around me. He said, "I didn't understand a word you said, but we have a God who understands Korean as well as English."

That summer I went back to Sergeant Powers' home. After we mowed the lawn we sat on the porch. I told Sergeant Powers something wonderful happened to me at school: I received Christ as my own personal Savior. Tears began to trickle down his cheek. He said, "You know, I have never trusted Christ as my Savior." That afternoon Sergeant Powers received Christ as his personal Savior.

Only the Gospel of the Lord Jesus Christ will bring lost sinners into the glorious conversion experience. Let us evangelize the world!

We Evangelize Because the Love of Christ Constrains Us

Thirdly, the love of God should be the motivating factor for evangelism. "For God so loved the world, that he gave his only begotten Son, that whosoever believeth in him should not perish, but have everlasting life" (John 3:16, KJV).

Why should we evangelize? What is our theological rationale for making Christian disciples? We evangelize because the love of Christ constrains us! The New English Bible translation reads, "For the love of Christ leaves us no choice" (2 Corinthians 5:14). Precisely what is this love of Christ which leaves us no choice but to engage in the ministry of reconciliation and evangelization?

When Sam James was serving as a missionary in Vietnam, someone broke into his house and stole some toys. Later that day James got into a taxi and struck up a conversation with the driver. The cab driver, realizing that James spoke his language, asked him how long he had been in Vietnam. Then he said, "You must really love the Vietnamese very much. What do you love about them?" The question kept nagging at James all day, into the night. "What do you love about them?" James couldn't sleep. He went into his study and began to pray. As he talked with God he realized that he really did not love the Vietnamese, and confessed it to Him. Then it seems as though God was speaking to James saying, "Sam, I didn't send you here because *you* love the Vietnamese. I sent you here because *I* love them and I want to love them through you."

"For God sent not his Son into the world to condemn the world; but that the world through him might be saved" (John 3:17, KJV). There is no higher motive for evangelization than the love of God. It was *agape* love which moved God to send His only begotten Son into the world.

The Bible is a book of love. There is much about the love of God in the Old Testament as well as in the New. In Psalm 136 the psalmist tells us, "His love endures forever" (NIV). John 3:16, which has been called the "little Gospel," says, "For God so loved the world, that he gave his only begotten Son" (KJV). Those two verbs, *love* and *gave,* go together. They belong to each other. You cannot have one without the other because love always gives. It is God's love which motivates us to evangelize the world. We have a story which must be told to the world!

The Samaritan woman had five husbands and was an outcast in the society. But when she met Jesus, she was wonderfully changed. "Jesus said to her, 'Go, call your husband. . . .' The woman . . . said, 'I have no husband.' Jesus said to her, 'You have well said, "I have no husband," for you have had five husbands, and the one whom you now have is not your husband.' . . . The woman then left her waterpot, went . . . into the city, and said to the men, 'Come, see a Man who told me all things that I ever did. Could this be the Christ?'" (John 4:16–18, 28–29, NKJV).

> **Jesus is ... the beauty of God's holiness, the purity of God's nature, the reality of God's love, the majesty of God's power, the ocean of God's matchless grace. That is why we must evangelize the world!**

Dr. Robert G. Lee said, "At Calvary the greatest problem of human sin and degradation is solved. At Calvary all human sorrows hide in His wounds. At Calvary the fires of the law are extinguished. Our condemnation is lifted. Our death sentence is revoked. At Calvary the door of heaven is opened. At Calvary the fountain of salvation is unsealed. At Calvary the bitterness of life is sweetened." And Calvary still echoes, "For God so loved the world, that he gave his only begotten Son."

Who was this Jesus who was willing to go to Calvary and pay the debt? When we read the well-known *One Solitary Life* we see that He was born in an obscure village. He worked in a carpenter's shop. He was an itinerant evangelist. He never held an office. He never owned a house. He didn't attend college. He had no credentials except Himself. He was only 33 when the public turned against Him and crucified Him. Nineteen centuries have come and gone. Today He is the central figure of the human race. All of the armies that ever marched, all of the navies that ever sailed, all of the kings that ever reigned, all of the parliaments that ever met have not affected the lives of men as much as that One Life, our Lord Jesus Christ.

Jesus is the verity of God's truth, the beauty of God's holiness, the purity of God's nature, the reality of God's love, the majesty of God's power, the ocean of God's matchless grace. That is why we must evangelize the world!

Only perfect love comes from God. "Herein is love, not that we loved God, but that he loved us, and sent his Son to be the propitiation for our sins"

(1 John 4:10, KJV). Only that unselfish love can change the world. We have received the love of God freely; we must give freely to those who need it.

A young man in Korea killed 17 people. He was arrested, tried and sentenced to execution. While he was waiting on death row, a Christian woman visited this young man. At first he did not respond to her visit. However, when he was hungry she sent him food. When he was cold she sent him warm clothing. When he wanted some candy she sent him chocolate. During the Christmas season she sent him a beautiful card to express her care and love for him.

Finally, one day he broke down and received Christ as his own personal Savior. Before he went to the gallows, he wrote 11 letters to this Christian lady stating that he believed that God had forgiven him, that he had trusted Christ as his own personal Savior. Just before he was executed, officials asked if he had any final words. He said, "Gentlemen, I have accepted Christ as my Savior. Today I'm going to meet my Savior, the Lord Jesus Christ. I long to see you trust Christ as your personal Savior, so that we can meet in heaven." He was able to evangelize many prison guards and inmates.

If the love of God can change a murderer, He can change my family, my neighborhood, my community, my nation and my world! "For God so loved the world, that he gave his only begotten Son, that whosoever believeth in him should not perish, but have everlasting life" (John 3:16, KJV).

Let us evangelize, evangelize, evangelize the whole world with the Gospel of our Lord Jesus Christ! Amen and amen!

Billy Kim

Dr. Billy Jang Hwan Kim is a pastor, evangelist and broadcaster. Currently he serves as the senior pastor of the 13,000-member Suwon Central Baptist Church in Suwon, Korea. In addition, Dr. Kim is the president of Far East Broadcasting Company in Korea, and was elected to serve a five-year term as president of the Baptist World Alliance. Dr. Kim has been awarded numerous honorary doctorates. He and his wife, Trudy, have three children and several grandchildren. The Kims reside in Seoul, Korea.

The Gift and Calling of the Evangelist

Video: Haje Andraus, Brazil
Petrus Octavianus

We are not in this to build a name for ourselves or to build an empire. An evangelist is a person who loves Jesus, who loves the souls of lost people and wants to be faithful in preaching the Gospel, bringing people to Christ. I didn't ask the Lord to give me the gift of an evangelist. He made that decision and made me an evangelist. But now He holds me accountable to be faithful to my call.

Haje Andraus and Petrus Octavianus
Rev. Haje Andraus is an evangelist from Brazil who holds meetings in many countries of the world. Dr. Petrus Octavianus is an evangelist from Indonesia who has worked in many countries of Asia.

The Gift and Calling of the Evangelist

Ulrich Parzany

How do I know or discover if God has called me to be an evangelist? What is the unique gift of the evangelist? What limits does this calling imply? How much more, beyond my calling, can I incorporate into my ministry? What if I realize I don't have the gift?

I will try to answer these questions as well as I can, and may the Lord help me. Let me start with some personal remarks about my own experience. I will tell you how the Lord led me to become an evangelist.

The Way the Lord Has Led Me

My conversion as a teenager was connected with the immediate beginning of an evangelistic outreach to my peers. We did it in different ways—sport activities, home visits, youth club activities—building relationships with them.

There was a strong example in my life. The German pastor Wilhelm Busch, youth pastor and evangelist, had a great impact on me. He helped me and others to become involved as volunteers in evangelistic activities. I have to confess that I never could imagine myself doing full-time ministry. So the Lord had to overcome me in this, and He did. I well remember there was a Bible study on Moses in Hebrews 11. When God overcame my resistance against full-time ministry and called me into that, my focus first was the ordinary work of a pastor. I am a Lutheran, and I was excited by the evangelistic possibilities of a mainline church. That was my focus.

During my university studies of theology, a friend of mine challenged me to get involved in campaign evangelization. He recommended me to a local church that did not know me but, on his recommendation, they invited me to preach during a week of evangelistic meetings. Well, it would take an hour or two to tell you the stories of my experiences during that week, but by these the Lord assured me that He wanted me to do this kind of work.

During all of my life I have been called by Christian leaders into different ministries which I had not looked for. In fact, at first I resisted these callings for different reasons. I struggled and prayed, and finally I had to admit that the Lord was calling me through these leaders. When I became obedient to the call, I received peace within me about the new placement. We have to be obedient.

There are always two components in God's call into a special ministry: There is the strong challenge and invitation of Christian leaders. And then the other side is the inner assurance and peace received through struggle and prayer.

Itinerant evangelism has been part of my ministry beside my local ministry as a youth pastor since the '60s, and it has been a priority for me as National General Secretary of the German YMCA. Although I always had a strong desire to reach as many people as possible with the Gospel of Jesus Christ, I have not been led into full-time evangelistic preaching. It was and it is my conviction that churches and Christian leaders are to decide whether or not they want to make use of my gift of evangelistic preaching.

You may wonder why I am so reluctant and hesitating. Is it a lack of trust and obedience to the Lord? Is it due to the fact that evangelistic preaching in the mainline churches of Europe has been very controversial and under suspicion? I have to admit that I am still struggling, and I leave it to my Lord to judge. But I am ready to serve Him with all my life as long as He gives me the work to do.

Now I try to avoid the mistake of making my own experiences normative for others. But as your steward, I wanted to share my testimony with you. Now, let's go to work. It is of great importance to learn from the Holy Scriptures how God calls His evangelists into the ministry.

The New Testament Calling of Evangelists

Looking to the New Testament, I see the Lord using different ways of calling people into the ministry of evangelization. At first the apostles were filled with the Holy Spirit on Pentecost and immediately started presenting Jesus Christ as Lord and Savior, publicly calling people to conversion (see Acts 2:4–40).

When we go on in Acts, we find that Stephen and Philip had been appointed to be deacons of the church in Jerusalem to care for the social welfare within the first congregation. But both of them had a specific and strong ministry of evangelistic preaching in different situations. The Lord definitely had called and guided them to do the work of evangelists, besides their other responsibilities (see Acts 6:8). Then the Lord turned the most dangerous human enemy into the world's most influential evangelist: that was Paul (see Acts 9).

So why shouldn't God do that again today? Be careful, all these enemies today may be God's evangelists tomorrow! We pray for that.

Then we read about prophets and teachers in the church of Antioch who received the guidance from the Holy Spirit to call out Barnabas and Paul for the work of evangelization (see Acts 13:1–3). We learn about Timothy, whom Paul involved in his ministry (see Acts 16:1–3). He must have received the gift of evangelization, besides other gifts through prophecy and the laying of hands on him by the elders (see 1 Timothy 4:14) and through Paul himself (see 2 Timothy 1:6). Paul encouraged him to "do the work of an evangelist" (2 Timothy 4:5). Obviously Paul was a leader of the church. He was in charge of placing members into different positions of responsibility. This may not always go along with the gift of evangelization.

There is no one single method by which the Lord calls people to be evangelists. But we observe two lines more or less intertwined: The Lord calls through the leaders of His church, and He speaks to the person.

In the New Testament the ministry of the evangelists was confirmed and backed by the church. Obviously this is important, because evangelists are called by the Lord to contribute to the building of the Body of Christ, as we read in Scripture (see Ephesians 4:11–12). This immediately leads to the painful question: What will happen if the Church forgets about the necessity of evangelization?

This seems to be a major issue in today's church in some parts of the world. As a result, the gift of evangelization, which the Lord has given to some people, may not be discovered, may not be used and developed. Fewer people will hear about Jesus. Or independently operating evangelists will not effectively contribute to building the church because of lack of cooperation with the other gifts and ministries within the Body of Christ. It is a most important task of the Church to carefully watch to see to whom God has given the gift to become an evangelist.

The Unique Gift of the Evangelist

What is the unique gift of the evangelist? I see eight different factors which constitute the gift of an evangelist.

First, the evangelist is determined by the urgency of love for the lost. Scripture says, "Since, then, we know what it is to fear the Lord, we try to persuade men" (2 Corinthians 5:11, NIV). What the lost people do not realize, the Word of God has revealed: it is a matter of eternal life for each person to know Jesus and to accept Him as Lord and Savior. The love of God has been poured into the hearts of evangelists. They have a strong concern for the lost.

Second, the evangelist has a strong desire to communicate Christ to nonbelievers. Of course much time and effort goes into preaching to Christians, to the church. That is not wrong. There is an ongoing demand for teaching, encouraging, admonishing the believers. But each local church will have members who fervently plead for a stronger commitment to nonbelievers in public preaching and in private, personal communication as well. These are the evangelists. God, through the Holy Spirit, has implanted into them the sensitivity and concern for God's beloved people who do not yet trust Him. Evangelists have a strong desire to communicate Christ to nonbelievers.

Third, the evangelist is able to listen and understand what nonbelievers are thinking and feeling in relation to the Gospel. He or she obviously has a keen interest in the thinking and the attitude of nonbelievers. This is not to affirm it, but to understand it in order to respond to it. God has entrusted to us the one and eternal Gospel. We are dealing with the human predicament of sin, which means separation from God and eternal death. This affects each person. In addition, each individual is positioned in a special time, a culture, a society. His or her life is designed by special attitudes and convictions. The evangelist has an ability to understand these special conditions and to communicate the message about Jesus Christ to the people of today.

Fourth, the evangelist has the ability to speak a language understood by the people addressed—to communicate with people who do not believe in Christ. The people, of course, need to understand. But before that, we need to get people's attention. They should be attracted to listen. They should become curious to know more about it. An evangelist has a concern and a gift to communicate with people who do not believe in Christ and may not be interested in Him.

Fifth, the evangelist is confirmed by the power of the Holy Spirit to lead people to Christ. As we read, "The Lord's hand was with them, and a great number of people believed and turned to the Lord" (Acts 11:21, NIV). Love urges us to do our best in terms of methods and techniques in communicating the Gospel. But it does not depend on techniques of communication whether a person accepts Jesus as Lord. There is always a temptation to believe in methods and techniques. But it is the Holy Spirit who makes people understand. The Holy Spirit must convince people of their sin and of their need to be reconciled to God. We as evangelists are not in control of this. God may use us as His instruments. If He does not, all that we do will be in vain. God must do it, and He has promised to use us as His instruments. So evangelists are people who are confirmed by the power of the Holy Spirit to lead people to Christ.

> An evangelist has a concern and a gift to communicate with people who do not believe in Christ and may not be interested in Him.

Sixth, the evangelist has a God-given ability to call people to make a decision for Christ. I remind you of Pentecost, "What shall we do?" asked the people. "Repent and be baptized, every one of you, in the name of Jesus Christ for the forgiveness of your sins" (Acts 2:37–38 NIV). The work of the evangelist is like that of a midwife. While only the Holy Spirit creates the new life, the evangelist is God's instrument in helping the new birth to happen. Therefore, the evangelist has the authority to call people to respond to the invitation and to make a decision for Christ. The decision of a person is always a response to the stronger decision that God in Jesus Christ has made for us. Salvation is based on God's decision, which calls people and enables them to commit themselves to Jesus. Because of that, we call people to a decision.

Seventh, the evangelist is flexible in terms of methods. "I have become all things to all men so that by all possible means I might save some," says Paul (1 Corinthians 9:22, NIV). Driven by love, we want to reach the hearts of the people. People are so different, although they all are lost without Jesus and they all need Him as their Savior.

There is no single method of evangelization. Jesus is the unique and only way of salvation, but there are hundreds of ways to approach people with the

Good News. In the New Testament we observe different ways of evangelistic preaching. Paul seems to have had a different way of preaching than Apollos, while Stephen, for example, was very strong in reasoning with opponents, as we read in Acts 6 and 7.

It is the love of the Creator which teaches us a variety of ways. We must faithfully stick to the truth of the Gospel. But we enjoy a great variety of styles and methods which are used by evangelists to address people. This is due to the various cultural and social settings.

Eighth, the evangelist, by obedience to the calling of the Lord, is determined to do evangelistic preaching. "Yet when I preach the gospel, I cannot boast, for I am compelled to preach. Woe to me if I do not preach the gospel!" (1 Corinthians 9:16, NIV). There may or may not be a positive response of the audience. Success never can be the reason for proclaiming the Gospel. Paul went through both extremely negative and extremely positive experiences. He saw many people coming to Christ, but he was beaten and driven out of town as well. We are to do the work of evangelists "in season and out of season" (2 Timothy 4:2, NIV).

There is always a temptation to spoil the Gospel of Jesus by stressing much more of what people are to do than of what God has done for us through Jesus.

The Specific Task of the Evangelist

What, then, is the specific task of the evangelist? The ministry of the evangelist is mostly related to the special gift of public evangelistic preaching. But as we learn from the New Testament, evangelistic work does not depend on crowds of listeners. Philip spoke to the Samaritan crowds and afterwards to an individual, the Nubian minister of finance (see Acts 8). Paul spoke to a small group in Philippi (see Acts 16) but to a crowd in Lystra as well (see Acts 14).

The specific task of the evangelist is, first, to preach the basics of the Gospel to nonbelievers. The teachers of the church have a much broader range of biblical topics than the evangelist. Basic or elementary preaching means to make Jesus known to the people who do not know Him and do not believe in Him. Some of us are preaching to people who know about Jesus but do not know Him. They do not have a personal relationship with Him. Others are preaching much more to people who do not know about Jesus at all. The main task is to tell about Jesus. The four evangelists of the New Testament are the real models for preaching Jesus to people who do not know Him.

We have to keep in mind that only the Gospel of Jesus crucified and risen will bring people to a saving knowledge of Him. This includes the message that salvation comes by grace and through faith only. We must take care of the truth of the Gospel as Paul reminds us in his letter to the Galatians (see 1:6–10).

There is always a temptation to spoil the Gospel of Jesus by stressing much more of what people are to do than of what God has done for us through Jesus. So we preach the basics of the Gospel.

Second, we give a clear invitation. It is the specific task of evangelists to extend a clear invitation to their listeners, to show them how to turn around and commit themselves to Jesus Christ as Lord and Savior. The evangelist must offer some way of responding. Again, there are a variety of ways to do it. Different ways are helpful to different people.

Very important is the *why* of doing it. Jesus promised His disciples, "He who listens to you listens to me" (Luke 10:16, NIV). Jesus identifies with us. His words always do what they say. He called Lazarus to come out of the grave. To what extent is a corpse free to decide? Has a dead person a free will? It was not the freedom of Lazarus which he had by himself, but it was the freedom the word of Jesus created in him that enabled him to get up and walk out of the tomb (see John 11:1–44).

We depend on the complementary ministries of the other members of the church.

It is the same power of Jesus that set the lame people free, enabling them to get up and walk when Jesus told them to do so (see Matthew 15:30–31). It is the same power that enabled Levi to leave his money table and business and follow Jesus (see Mark 2:14). It is the same power that gives freedom to people today who hear the evangelist's invitation. Don't put your trust in qualifications that people may or may not have. You may get confused. You may try to put psychological pressure on the audience. Or you may not dare to extend an invitation at all. It is God by Himself who creates our willingness and our ability to do His will, as we see in Philippians 2:13. Therefore we can call people to respond to the invitation that we bring to them in the name of the Lord Jesus Christ.

So, first is to preach the basics of the Gospel. Second is giving a clear invitation. And third, we explain that conversion is the beginning of discipleship. We should never forget that conversion is the beginning of a way to go. It is not an end in itself. It doesn't make sense to overemphasize the importance of a birth without explaining that the purpose of a birth is the life that now begins. New birth is the starting point of a development that will not end until we see the Lord in His glory.

Let me conclude. Evangelists are to do the specific work that Jesus has entrusted to them. Therefore, they must not try to take over tasks and responsibilities which are not theirs. They are to respect the leaders of the church. They are to respect teachers and counselors and whatever gifts and tasks God has given through His Holy Spirit to any member of the Body of Christ.

We are to honor others even as they are to respect the ministry of the evangelist. By this cooperation we are enabled to concentrate on the task the Lord has given to us as evangelists.

Let us hear what God told Timothy: "In the presence of God and of Christ Jesus, who will judge the living and the dead, and in view of his appearing and his kingdom, I give you this charge: Preach the Word; be prepared in season and out of season. . . . For the time will come when men will not put up with sound doctrine. Instead, to suit their own desires, they will gather around them a great number of teachers to say what their itching ears want to hear. They will turn their ears away from the truth and turn aside to myths. But you, keep your head in all situations, endure hardship, do the work of an evangelist" (2 Timothy 4:1–5, NIV).

People are dying without knowing Jesus as their only Savior. We have to encourage each other, and dedicate ourselves again to Jesus our Lord and to the ministry He has called us to do.

Ulrich Parzany
Reverend Ulrich Parzany is the General Secretary of the German National YMCA. In addition to ministering in numerous countries, Rev. Parzany was also the director of ProChrist in 1995 and 1997, and continues in that responsibility, with international evangelistic outreaches in Europe. He was also a key leader in the Christian project at Expo 2000 in Hanover (which ran concurrently with Amsterdam 2000). Rev. Parzany and his wife, Regine, are the parents of three children and live in Germany.

The Content of the Gospel

J. I. Packer

I am a teacher. I teach theology; that's my job. But inside some teachers of theology there is a Bible teacher trying to get out, and inside some Bible teachers there is a preacher of the Gospel trying to get out. And that is who I am. So please think with me as we explore the theme of "The Content of the Gospel."

In a court of law, certainly in Britain and North America, before you give evidence you are required to swear that you will tell the truth, the whole truth and nothing but the truth. If you are not going to tell the whole truth, you will mislead the court. And if the court is misled, injustice may be done. So it is very important that in communication the whole truth be told.

My point is that this is just as true in the matter of godliness, knowing and honoring and serving the Lord. This is something which I want to press because there is, I think, a danger that some of us who are called to be evangelists may not take it as seriously as we should. We have to tell the whole story.

Not Just Half the Story, the Whole of It

Paul, the master evangelist, is the model for us at that point. As he said to the elders of Miletus, "I am innocent of the blood of all of you, for I did not shrink from declaring to you the whole counsel of God" (Acts 20:26–27, RSV). He is saying that if he had not told people the whole of the story, he could not have a clear conscience about having discharged his responsibility to them. He is saying, however, that he did tell them the whole story and so he was innocent of their blood. That is how seriously he took it.

In the same way, it is the evangelist's task today to set forth the whole counsel of God. How are we to understand this phrase, "the whole counsel of God"? Well, counsel means plan, purpose, intention. What Paul has in view here is the whole of what we call the plan of salvation, God's plan whereby He brings people out of darkness into the light, out of death into life, and leads us through this world to the glory that He has in store for us. It is the evangelist's business to tell that whole story. So let us make sure that we have a conscience about this just as Paul did.

When Paul evangelized, when he began to preach the Gospel to those who did not yet know it, he talked about their need and God's grace, blessing them with salvation through Jesus our Lord. But when Paul "did" theology, as we see from the letters that he wrote to his converts, what bubbled out of his heart was simply the truth about Jesus: King Jesus; glorious Jesus; Jesus the divine Savior; Jesus head of the Church; Jesus Lord of the angels; Jesus our prophet, priest and king; Jesus the one through whom all grace comes to us from God; Jesus whose praise we are called to give in this life and to go on giving through all eternity; Jesus our joy. Paul talks about these things endlessly, showing that for him Jesus is the focus. The greatness and the glory of Jesus is the center. Jesus is all in all to the apostle Paul. And he wants Jesus to be all in all to Christians.

Two Halves: Evangelizing and Discipling

I don't think we ought to separate the two halves of Paul's ministry: Paul evangelizing those who don't yet know Jesus, and Paul discipling those who have begun to know Jesus. It is one ministry; it is one Gospel. Here is Paul, the master evangelist and the master pastor. We who are called to be evangelists have something of that pastoral responsibility that we must discharge, too. Says Paul, "I didn't shrink from sharing with you the whole counsel of God." Again I say, brothers and sisters, that must be the model for us. That is the way we, too, must go.

I want to warn you, friends, that there is a danger of our stumbling at the first step. You say, "What do you mean?" I mean this: that if the question in your mind is, "How little need I say?" when preaching the Gospel rather than, "How much ought I to say in preaching the Gospel?" you and I are going to stumble. In this age when quick results are what everybody hopes for, the danger of reducing the Gospel to the minimum is, I think, a real danger to everyone who preaches it.

Oh, you can't say everything in one sermon. I know that. And if you are an evangelist speaking to people who know nothing about Jesus as yet, at your first presentation you can't deal with all those themes that Paul deals with in his letters. I know that too. But my purpose when I preach the Gospel—and yours, too, I hope—is to tell the whole story just as soon as I can, just as fully as I can, so that people moving into the life of discipleship know what they are in for. They are not misled by thinking that they know the whole story when I've only told but half of it.

A Gospel Too Small and Too Fuzzy

I take my cue from a book written by a man in England named J. B. Phillips. J. B. Phillips wrote this little book under the challenging title, *Your God Is Too Small.* May it never be said either of myself or of you that our Gospel is too small. I'm going to ask some questions which I trust will help us to enlarge our own thinking about that whole story that we have to tell. And so we'll make certain that from now on our Gospel will not be too small.

I should tell you that not very long ago in North America a number of evangelical leaders became aware that in many quarters people were preaching and settling for too small a Gospel and too fuzzy a Gospel. Things on which evangelical believers yesterday had been very clear were not now so clear in people's minds. The connection, for instance, between the substitutionary death of Jesus on the Cross and the gift of righteousness—justification to us sinners whereby we are forgiven and accepted and set before our heavenly Father as if we were no less righteous than Jesus Himself—was not always being clearly explained.

That is just one example of where fuzziness had come in. Well, these leaders in North America were troubled. A group of them got together and labored for months to produce a statement which should clarify and unify at these points where fuzziness had come in, and not enough was being said to achieve clarity in the minds of those being evangelized. This statement was produced under the title "The Gospel of Jesus Christ: An Evangelical Celebration."

I was one of those involved in producing the statement. I believe that by the grace of God we did a good job. I am glad to celebrate the statement and to recommend it to you. I hope that you will find in that statement help for clarity and fullness in your own preaching of the Gospel.

Well, I have said I am going to ask questions which, I trust, will help us to achieve clarity and fullness in the Gospel we preach. And here I start.

The Whole Scriptural Story

First, I ask you: Do we tell the whole scriptural story about our God, the God who is Father, Son and Holy Spirit; three persons in one divine being; the God of whom our Savior is the second person?

We are evangelists, certainly. Stating the Gospel is our business, definitely. But that requires us to affirm the Trinity, for the Gospel is precisely the story of the three persons—Father, Son and Holy Spirit—working together for the salvation of needy human beings. I know that for many in the churches the Trinity as a doctrine—the thought that God is three in one—is just so much lumber for the mind, orthodox truth which you keep in a cupboard at the back of your mind. For many folks, the truth of the Trinity isn't relevant at all. But for us evangelists, the truth of the Trinity is vital. Three coequal persons, always under the leadership of the Father, work together as a team for our salvation. The Father sent the Son; the Father and the Son send the Spirit.

As Jesus told Nicodemus in His evangelistic conversation, if people are going to enter the Kingdom of God, the Kingdom of the Father, they must be born again of the Holy Spirit (see John 3:5). If they want to be born again of the Holy Spirit, they must listen to the teaching of Jesus Christ. They must understand that as Moses lifted up the snake, says Jesus to Nicodemus, so the Son of Man must be lifted up. It is clear that the Son of Man is Jesus speaking of Himself—the Son of God come in human form to save us. The Son of Man, says Jesus, must be lifted up that whoever believes in Him will have eternal life (see John 3:14–15).

In that message—the message that leads on to the best-known verse in the Bible, John 3:16—is a message about the Father, the Son and the Spirit together. Through the atoning work of the Son believed in—and it is the Holy Spirit, of course, who leads people to faith—folks come out into the life of new birth. In that life of new birth they find they are in the Kingdom of the Father. The fullness of new life and hope is theirs. I say that to underline that we have got to tell the truth about the Trinity as part of our message.

Since Jesus our Savior is the second person of the Godhead, we need to be able to tell people, if they are not clear, that Jesus exists from eternity to eternity in the manner of God; that is, He exists in self-sustaining divine life as do the Father and the Holy Spirit. That was pictured for Moses by God Himself when Moses was confronted with a bush. It burned and it burned, and it was still there (see Exodus 3:2). That for Moses was a picture of the life of God, the triune God, who says, "I am who I am, and I will be what I will be" (see Exodus 3:14).

> **We live in dependence on God. God lives in dependence on no one. He is the self-sustaining Lord. So Jesus Christ ... is the same yesterday, today and forever. We must all be clear on that, and so must those to whom we preach.**

We live in dependence on God. God lives in dependence on no one. He is the self-sustaining Lord. So Jesus Christ who exists and lives that way is the same yesterday, today and forever. We must all be clear on that, and so must those to whom we preach.

God's way, the way of the Father and the way of the Holy Spirit along with the Son, is to act as Jesus acted. God is "Jesus-like" in all His ways. And it is in terms of Jesus' likeness that we ought to explain what God said to Moses as the people were traveling from Egypt to the Promised Land. This word of God to Moses came at a time when Moses was praying to God that He would have mercy on the people for their sin with the golden calf. God said, "I'll tell you My name," and "name" in Scripture always means the nature and the place of the person whose name it is. The name is a revelation. God said to Moses, "This is My name." And instead of saying, "My name is Jehovah" (or Yahweh), God tells Moses His character. Every bit of it is to be explained in terms of the character of Jesus, God come in the flesh. For God was, is and always will be "Jesus-like" in His character and His ways.

God said, "I am Yahweh, a God merciful and gracious, slow to anger and abounding in steadfast love and faithfulness, forgiving iniquity and transgression and sin," but who will by no means clear the guilty. That means the people who hold on to their sins. There will be retribution for them. But for those who turn from sin and humble themselves before Him, He is a God merciful and gracious, slow to anger, abounding in steadfast love and faithfulness, forgiving iniquity, transgression and sin. That is our Jesus. That is our Father. That is the Holy Spirit. That is the way of God. This is the greatness of the mercy of the Holy Three. We ought to emphasize these things. These are glorious things for which we, the evangelists, and those who hear our words ought to be praising God forever.

The Depth of Our Real Need

And now a second question: Do we tell the whole Scripture story about ourselves, our natural human condition and the depth of our real need as we stand before God, the way that we are when we are born into this world? Here again I think we who preach the Gospel don't always say enough, because we stop short at people's felt needs. We say, "You feel weak. You feel sad. You feel ashamed. You feel guilty. You feel miserable. Jesus Christ will change all that." True. But friends, there is more that we need to tell them than that "the Lord Jesus meets your felt needs when you put your life in His hands."

The real need is something about which most people, when first they hear of it, are simply in denial. It is that we have bad hearts, that we who were made to love and serve and praise and honor and exalt the God who made us, are self-absorbed, self-centered and, as far as God is concerned, unbelieving of things that He tells us. We are not inclined to praise Him, wanting rather to keep Him at a distance so that He does not control our lives. We want to have the reins, the driving wheel of our life in our own hands.

We are just like Adam and Eve in the Garden of Eden, not believing God but wanting things that God has warned us against, resolving to have them, never mind what God might think (see Genesis 2 and 3). We have lived that way right from the start. And most of us have not faced the fact that that is how we are living. We haven't faced the insult to God that that sort of life represents. This is the bad news: We need new hearts.

The glorious Good News of the Gospel includes the promise that we shall be given new hearts in the new birth. That means that, once again, we find that the deepest desire at the depths of our being is to honor and serve and love and adore and praise and glorify our Father, and with Him the Son, and with them the Holy Spirit. Once again we are back in the posture of praise, and praise becomes the source of strength and the source of delight and the source of triumph and the source of strength and stability.

We who are Christ's know that. It has happened to us. Those to whom we preach can't imagine it. We have to tell them that this is what God will do for them, this and nothing less. If we don't tell them that, we are not telling them the whole story about God's salvation. We are not telling them the whole story of the glory of the grace of Jesus Christ our Lord.

The Story About God's Kingdom

I ask a third question: Do we tell the whole Scripture story about God's Kingdom? We think of ourselves as evangelists charged to extend God's Kingdom. But are we clear that God's Kingdom means His plan for exercising His kingship, establishing His rule over human lives up to the point where—and this will only happen when Jesus returns, but it will happen then—every knee bows at Jesus' name, every tongue confesses that Jesus is Lord to the glory of God the Father? And so the whole world of human kingdoms has become the Kingdom of our

God and of His Christ. God is going to bring that to pass!

Oh, there will be opposition, and there will be battles and conflicts, and there will be moments when the Church is being rolled back rather than advancing. But we are on the victory side, brothers and sisters. The triumph of our God is assured. That is the message of the Kingdom in the service of which we work as evangelists. That is something which we ought to tell the folk to whom we preach the Gospel. People often are running scared of all kinds of evil powers in their own life situation—demonic powers, political powers, the pressures of poverty, and all kinds of other evils which seem to threaten their very existence. Those who put their hands in the hand of Jesus are on the victory side. They are in the Kingdom, and the Kingdom will triumph. That should be said. Everyone needs to hear it!

> Those who put their hands in the hand of Jesus are on the victory side. They are in the Kingdom, and the Kingdom will triumph. That should be said. Everyone needs to hear it!

Real Faith, Real Repentance

My fourth question: Do we tell the world all we need to say about the way of salvation? Two specifics: Do we tell people that repentance is the measure of the reality of faith? It's very easy to tell people, "Believe that Jesus died for your sins and you're in the Kingdom." But Scripture says that real faith brings forth real repentance, turning from sin, going the opposite way to the way you were going, accepting the new life in which you're changed. The word at the heart of the Greek for repentance means "change." Do we make that clear to people? If we don't, we are not telling them the whole story about the Gospel invitation.

And the second point is: When we are seeking to counsel people, do we make clear to them that they must from the heart be trusting Jesus, not because we the evangelists want them to but because they, as needy souls standing before God guilty, condemned and lost, have been brought to the point where they want to? The Holy Spirit does this in His own way, and we as evangelists are the midwives there to help the birth process happen. But just as a premature birth isn't always a healthy birth, so pushing people into a decision they don't fully understand as yet, and don't fully desire from their own hearts, doesn't always produce a healthy Christian life.

The Story of Our Family Fellowship

Question number five: Do we tell folk the whole story about being born again into a family fellowship which is going to be our family fellowship for the rest of our days and on to eternity? In this sense, the Church, the fellowship of the Lord's people, is part of the Gospel. People today are lonely and bewildered and need that message, "Come into the family." It's part of the attraction of the

Gospel to so many in our time. And, of course, we need the Church for our nurture. Let us see that we say it.

Tell About the Christian Hope

The sixth and last question: Do we tell people all we should about the Christian hope, the hope of glory beyond this world, reserved for all of us? It is there on just about every page of the New Testament. Why isn't it there in just about every Gospel sermon that we preach? It should be!

Many of those who come to Christ are going to have a hard life, in which the hope of heaven ought to mean a great deal to them. In this world many of us are going to suffer disappointments. At times of disappointment we shall need the hope of heaven to uphold us. Jesus our Savior is called in the New Testament not only "Christ our life" but also "Christ our hope." Let us see to it that that message of hope—not just or even primarily in this world, but hope for that final glory of supreme joy—is our constant theme in our evangelistic preaching.

Briefly Stated

So, then, there are key points that must be communicated in a complete declaration of the Gospel message.

In the Bible, the Gospel is the entire saving plan of God, all revolving around the person, the place and power of our Savior Jesus Christ—the incarnate, crucified, risen, reigning, returning Lord.

Preaching the Gospel requires us to show how Jesus Christ relates to every part of God's plan, and how every part of it relates to us who are savingly related to the living Christ through faith. Evangelism involves explaining life in Christ, as well as inviting sinners to Him. To summarize, this means dealing with six main topics, as follows:

1. **The Truth About God.** The one God who made and rules everything is revealed as three persons through His plan of salvation. The Father, the Son and the Holy Spirit love us and work together to save us from sin and to make us holy. Jesus Christ, God the Son incarnate, is Lord over all the powers of evil. Any other view of God is *idolatry.*
2. **The Truth About Ourselves.** We were made for God, to bear His image and be like Him in moral character, but sin controls and spoils us so that we need to be brought back to God to be forgiven and remade. Jesus Christ, who brings us back, is Himself the model of true godliness. Any other view of Him or of us is *deception.*
3. **The Story of God's Kingdom.** Step by step, as Scripture tells, God has been working to establish His Kingdom in this fallen world. Jesus Christ is the King, and our lives are to be His Kingdom. King Jesus is also the Judge, and those who have not bowed to His kingship here will not share His joy

hereafter. Trusting, loving and honoring Jesus, and serving others for His sake, is true godliness at its heart. Any other form of religion is *error*.

4. **The Way of Salvation.** Jesus Christ, our Sin-Bearer on the Cross, now from His throne reaches out to rescue us who are lost in the guilt and shame of sin. He calls for faith (trust in Him as Savior) and repentance (turn to Him as Master). He sends His Holy Spirit to change us inwardly so that we hear His call as addressed to us personally and respond wholeheartedly to it. Thereupon we are forgiven and accepted (justified); received as God's children (adopted); made to rejoice at our peace with Him (assurance); and made to realize that now we are living a new life in Christ (regeneration). Any other view of salvation is *deficient*.

5. **The Life of Fellowship.** Christians belong in the Church, the family of God, sharing its worship, work, witness and warfare, and enjoying its worldwide brotherhood in Christ. Any other view of the Christian calling is *sectarian*.

6. **Walking Home to Heaven.** Helped by the ministry in the Church of word and sacrament, prayer and pastoral care, spiritual gifts and loving support, Christians live in our constantly hostile world as travelers, heading for a glorious destination. Led and inspired by their Savior through the Holy Spirit, they seek to do all the good they can as they go, and to battle all forms of evil that they meet. Any lesser view of the Christian life is *worldly*.

Let us not tell half the story. Let us learn to proclaim the whole counsel of God. And may God bless us as messengers and others through our message. To Him be the praise. Amen.

J. I. Packer

Dr. J. I. Packer was born in Gloucestershire, England, and studied at Oxford University, earning degrees in classics and theology, and a D.Phil. Since 1996, Dr. Packer has been Board of Governors Professor of Theology at Regent College in Vancouver, British Columbia, Canada. He is the author of numerous books, and a frequent contributor to theological periodicals. Dr. Packer and his wife, Kit, are the parents of three children.

The Preparation of an Evangelistic Message

Gottfried Osei-Mensah

Fellow evangelists, before you sit down to prepare your message, you must remember that you are a servant of Almighty God. He is sending you to take His message to a particular people, to call them back into a right relationship with God through the Lord Jesus Christ. This fact carries important implications.

Prayer and Personal Holiness

First and foremost, the evangelist is called to be a man or woman of God. "But just as he who called you is holy, so be holy in all you do; for it is written: 'Be holy, because I am holy'" (1 Peter 1:15–16, NIV).

To be holy is to be totally devoted, set apart for God. The model set before God's people is the Lord Jesus Christ Himself. Our Father's purpose for us is "to be conformed to the likeness of his Son" (Romans 8:29, NIV). Therefore to be holy is to be like Christ. Robert Murray McCheyne said, "It is not great gifts that God blesses, as it is great likeness to Christ. A holy person is an awesome weapon in the hand of God."

You must wait on God for a fresh mandate and message, for a clearer insight into humanity's bad news, and a deeper appreciation of God's Good News. You must pray that the Lord will prepare you and make you His effective messenger (see Jeremiah 23:21–22). You should continue in this attitude of prayer through all the stages of preparation.

Knowing Your Listeners

You must find out as much as you can about the people to whom God is sending you to speak. For example, if you are preparing to speak to college students on campus, you will want to read a selection of their bulletins or use a questionnaire to find out the latest assessment of their concerns, attitudes and opinions. Then you can prepare a message relevant to their situation.

Knowledge of your intended audience is an important factor in selecting the Scripture on which to base your message. For example, if your intended listeners are mostly young people who show all the marks of being separated from God—feeling restless, empty, bored, without hope or even showing a tendency to suicide—the parable of the lost son (Luke 15) may be an appropriate basis for your message.

On the other hand, if you are speaking to people who live in constant fear of demonic spirits, a message based on Christ's victory over these powers could "open their eyes and turn them from darkness to light, and from the power of

Satan to God, so that they may receive forgiveness of sins and a place among those who are sanctified by faith in [Christ]" (Acts 26:18, NIV; see also Colossians 2:13–15; Hebrews 2:14–15).

> The purpose of the evangelistic message is to flesh out this heart of the Gospel so that our hearers ... turn to Him in repentance and faith through our Lord Jesus Christ.

The Heart of the Gospel

The heart of the Good News we are sent to proclaim is the death and resurrection of our Lord Jesus Christ. The apostle Paul wrote, "For what I received I passed on to you as of first importance: that Christ died for our sins according to the Scriptures, that he was buried, that he was raised on the third day according to the Scriptures, and that he appeared to Peter, and then to the Twelve" (1 Corinthians 15:3–5, NIV).

Paul affirms that this is what he and the other apostles preached as of first importance; it is what the Corinthians and all other Christians believed for salvation. In this alone stood their assurance and hope of heaven (see 1 Corinthians 15:1–2, 11, 20). That remains true today.

Scripture says, "He was delivered over to death for our sins and was raised to life for our justification [that is, to put us right with God]" (Romans 4:25, NIV). "For God so loved the world, that he gave his only begotten Son, that whosoever believeth in him should not perish, but have everlasting life" (John 3:16, KJV).

The purpose of the evangelistic message is to flesh out this heart of the Gospel so that our hearers can see clearly the relevance of what God has done for them and turn to Him in repentance and faith through our Lord Jesus Christ.

Studying Your Bible Text

The simplest way to study your Bible passage is to read and re-read it. Break it up into its main thoughts and use discovery questions (who, what, where, when, how, why) to bring out the facts. Underline key words and phrases and use questions to bring out their meaning and to aid understanding (i.e., What does ... mean?). Use cross-references, concordances and Bible dictionaries to help you. Finally, draw out the plain application of the passage for the listener's obedience.

To illustrate, let us apply this method of study to the parable of the lost son in Luke 15. In verses 11–13, the younger son chose to be independent of his father and to live his life as he wanted to, away from home. How would you describe the attitude of the younger son? Was he selfish, self-centered, self-seeking, despising his relationship with his father?

In verses 14–16, we read that his happiness and pleasures did not last. What were the results of his chosen way of life? He had no money and he was starving. He was now worse off than the pigs! In verses 17–20, we read, "He came to his senses" (v. 17, NIV). What does this mean? A change of mind (v. 17)—he recalled that even his father's hired men were better fed and far happier than he! A change of direction (v. 18)—he resolved to return home to his father. A change of heart [attitude] (v. 19)—"I have sinned . . . I am no longer worthy to be called your son" (vv. 18–19, NIV).

In verses 20–24, we see the father's love for his returning son. How is the father's love for his returning son described? He longed for his return—he saw him while he was still a long way off (v. 20). He was filled with compassion for him (v. 20). He ran to meet him, embraced and kissed him (v. 20). He restored his son's dignity, inheritance and honor (v. 22). He celebrated his son's safe return to him (v. 24; see also vv. 7, 10, 32).

Constructing the Message

When we are constructing our message, we know that the Holy Spirit is the supreme evangelist (see John 15:26–27). Without His partnership our witness to Christ will be fruitless. It is He who lifts up and unveils Christ through the message, convincing the minds of our hearers with the truth of God's Word, melting their hearts in repentance, and persuading their wills to turn in faith and commitment to the Lord (see John 16:8–15; 1 Thessalonians 1:5, 9). Therefore we must seek His help in putting together our message if it is to be an effective tool in His hand.

Choose a message title that sums up what you want to say. This will make your message stick in your hearers' minds. For example: The parable of the lost son was the last of three parables on the theme of "lost and found" told by our Lord Jesus Christ (Luke 15). He was responding to the complaint of the Jewish religious leaders: "This man welcomes sinners and eats with them" (v. 2, NIV). What they said in contempt is indeed the Good News! "I have not come to call the righteous, but sinners to repentance" (Luke 5:32, NIV; see also 1 Timothy 1:15). Each of the three parables ends with the statement that there is rejoicing in heaven over one sinner who repents. Therefore a suitable title for our message could be: "Return to a Joyful Welcome!"

> Arrange your material logically and persuasively, highlighting the Lord Jesus Christ and what God has done through Him for our salvation. In your message, present Christ as the only way back to God.

Arrange your material logically and persuasively, highlighting the Lord Jesus Christ and what God has done through Him for our salvation. In your message, present Christ as the only way back to God from the dark paths of sin. Through His death on the Cross as our Sin-Bearer, there is forgiveness, cleansing and a joyful welcome to the Father's love for the returning sinner. Truly, our risen Savior still "welcomes sinners and eats with them" (Luke 15:2, NIV; see also

Revelation 3:20). Find suitable illustrations for your main points. Finally, write down your message in full, and pray over it.

Application Exercise

Here is an exercise for people preparing an evangelistic message: First, read Jeremiah 23:16–22. Next, ask yourself, "What is the difference between a false prophet and a true one?" Then, in reference to verses 18, 21 and 22, write down at least five marks of a true messenger of God.

Here is another exercise. Based on the Lord Jesus' conversation with Nicodemus (John 3:1–16), prepare an evangelistic message aimed at respectable churchgoers who nevertheless do not know the Lord Jesus as their personal Savior. First, what needed to happen to Nicodemus (see vv. 3–8)? Second, what does it mean to be "born of water and of the Spirit" (see v. 5)? [See also Ezekiel 36:25–27 and Titus 3:5–7.] Third, what did Nicodemus have to do (see vv. 11–13)? [See also John 1:12.] Fourth, what illustration did the Lord Jesus use to help Nicodemus (see v. 14)? [See also Numbers 21:6–9.] Finally, select a title for your message, and list the main points of your message.

Follow-Up Assignment

Complete the preparation of two evangelistic messages based on Luke 15:11–24 and John 3:1–16. Aim to use these messages in preaching or witnessing within the next three months.

Gottfried Osei-Mensah

Reverend Gottfried Osei-Mensah serves as Chairman of the International Partnership Board of African Evangelistic Enterprise, an evangelistic ministry in Africa with many styles of outreach. He is formerly a special representative on the staff of the Billy Graham Evangelistic Association and served as the first Executive Secretary of the Lausanne Committee for World Evangelism. A citizen of Ghana, Rev. Osei-Mensah was trained as a chemical engineer and worked in the industry for five years before being called into full-time Christian service. Rev. Osei-Mensah and his wife, Audrey, have two grown children and make their home in Reading, United Kingdom.

Preaching in the 21st Century

Video

At a quick glance, one might be led to believe that we are on a collision course to self-destruction. The world where Paul once walked is now a fast-paced global community that is confused with a distorted view of who God is.

One hundred years ago there were two billion people on the planet. Today there are over six billion. Almost half of the people who ever walked on the earth are alive today, and half of those are children and young people.

Centuries ago we were not dealing with the AIDS epidemic, nuclear threats or continuing changes in the global economy that have brought more problems to an already complex situation. Crime, homelessness, unemployment have risen, and the satisfaction of the people has declined. Constant screams of powerfully misleading ideals are infiltrating society from all angles. Greed, self-indulgence and disease affect all levels of society.

Is there room for evangelism in the 21st century? It is important to remember that the Gospel is just as powerful today as it was 2,000 years ago. We as evangelists must thrust ahead, recognizing opportunities for evangelistic outreach throughout the world. Today we have more tools to reach people with the message of Christ than at any other time in history.

Amid the layers of noise and confusion, God hears the prayers of those who seek Him. He sees the work of His people. He has provided us with an unprecedented opportunity to reach all nations with the love of Christ. This is the 21st century, our opportunity!

Evangelistic Preaching in the 21st Century

Ravi Zacharias

When Dr. Graham gave me the honor of addressing this subject, I paced the floor for a little while because the subject is very daunting: evangelism in the new millennium, or in the 21st century. Those of you who are communicators of the Gospel know very well indeed how tough it is to even understand the moment, let alone attempt to understand days, weeks, months and years ahead. And yet we are called to be prepared, aren't we? And as I bowed my head in prayer, thinking of what it might mean to put a message like this together, the theme came in these words: barriers of the mind, and hungers of the heart.

We are in a time of change. You are aware of it and I am aware of it. New words now enter our dictionaries. One of the most startling new terms to come in is the term *post-modern*. If we do not understand what is being said to us in this worldview, people will not understand what we are trying to say to them in an ancient message that is timely and timeless.

Post-modernism is a chronological term in time. It is moving beyond the ideas of what was called "the modern world," in which the scientific world of exactitude reigned supreme. With mathematical certainty, truth by measurement, the age of technology dawned upon us. We were going to conquer new worlds, expand our horizons. There was a pattern of exactness that modernity was offering to us.

What a Huge Chasm the Gospel Has to Cross

Post-modernism has come on the scene to tell us that there is no such thing as *absolute truth,* no such thing as a point of reference for *meaning* and no such thing as *certainty.* No truth, no meaning, no certainty. If you remember that statement, you can understand what a huge chasm the Gospel has to cross because it affirms the *truth,* offers the only *meaning* that is worthy of being had, and gives certainty of the *hope* offered in Jesus Christ.

According to post-modernism we do not know who we are as human beings, and we do not know where we are in a gradation of progress. Try and understand that and come to grips with it. No voice from outside, no units to measure; we don't know where we are and we don't know who we are.

A few years ago a man in his mid-thirties, a medical doctor and a friend of mine, suffered a major heart attack. As we sat talking, he looked at me and he said, "Ravi, I want to tell you what it is like to have a heart attack. As a medical man, I had never understood what actually happens." He said, "You see, with every pain your body experiences you sort of detach yourself from it and say something like this: 'My foot is hurting, my hand is hurting, my head is hurting.' It is as if you stand outside the pain to talk about the pain." He continued, "When my heart was pulsating and threatening my very life, the only description I could give of what I was experiencing is that I was in the pain. I could not talk from outside of it, for the organ intended to pump life was instead pulsating agony, excruciating agony, so that I was trying to stretch my body just to accommodate the convulsing pain."

Ladies and gentlemen, we are not outside of post-modern culture looking in. We are in it. And if you don't believe me, sit down next to your children someday and ask them some questions. You will be surprised at what surprises them—and doesn't surprise them.

No voice from outside, no units to measure; we don't know where we are and we don't know who we are.

I remember my son asking me to see a movie that he thought I would thoroughly enjoy. His hook always is, "Dad, you'll get some good illustrations from this movie; it's very philosophical." So he took me to see it, and suddenly a few minutes into the movie a rather obnoxious word was used. My son knows my sensitivity and sensed me squirm. Then, thoroughly embarrassed, he said, "Dad, I'm awfully sorry. To be honest with you, when I saw this before I never even noticed it." See, they are in a world where they hear this kind of thing all the time. They are in it; they are immersed in it. You and I are part and parcel of this post-modern world whether we like it or not.

The Bold Face of Atheism

I want to underscore five changes that have brought us to this point and three responses we must make. Change number one is the strident, unblushing assertion of atheism and its ramifications. Oh, we have lived for centuries with atheism around us, but something has happened now that I believe is dynamically and drastically different.

The German philosopher Friedrich Nietzsche was the son of a pastor, and both of his grandfathers were in the Christian ministry. But Nietzsche, for some reason, lost his faith in God. He is the one who popularized the phrase, "God is dead," and he wrote essays on it. But there is something that must be commended about Nietzsche: He realized that if that positioning of the death of God was true, then the ramifications were dire. He used metaphors like this: "Who gave us as humanity the sponge to wipe away the horizon?" "What sacred games will we need to invent?" "Is there any up or down left?" "Must we light lanterns in the morning hours?" Do you see what he is saying? No point of reference. We have wiped away the horizon. Even daylight offers no glimpse of reality. How will we cope with this? We must remember that ideas have consequences.

I was doing a series of lectures at Oxford University, and at the end of one of those lectures a whole group of students stormed toward the front. The man who was going to engage me was the most vocal of them all. He said to me, "Dr. Zacharias, I do not believe for a moment that objective values actually exist, that there is an absolute good or absolute evil." I said, "Can I ask you a question? If I were to put a live baby on this platform and chop it into pieces with a butcher knife, would I have done anything morally wrong?" You will be shocked to hear his response. He paused, looked at his foot for a moment and then said to me, "I would not like what you did, but I could not honestly say that what you did is morally wrong."

G. K. Chesterton said it well, "The tragedy of disbelieving in God is not that a person ends up believing in nothing; alas, it is much worse. A person may end up believing in anything." That is what the stridency of atheism has done.

The Growing Impact of Eastern Spirituality

The second change is the growing impact of Eastern spirituality. What has now happened as time has gone by is the inflow of the idea that each life is a payment for a previous life. All of these thoughts that are steeped in an Eastern worldview are wrapped up in the pantheistic idea that you are ultimately one with the universe. These ideas are sweeping across our world.

May I suggest to you one of the main reasons is because the underlying hook is this: that you can still be good without there being a God. That is what carries the wind of such an idea. And I say to you, it is important that we face this and understand it as the cultures mix and we learn to respect cultures, accept our differences and know that these are different ideas in an intermix. We must still bear in mind something important.

All along through history in the East, religion and culture were interwoven. You cannot separate the two. Ask a Hindu, ask a Buddhist; they will tell you that religion and culture are interwoven—religion is the essence of culture; culture is the dress of religion. Eastern culture has prided itself in its age, in its values and in its sense of spirituality. With such confidence it now seeks to live within a Western context which has evicted Christianity as a dominant factor. It is not just a culture that is imported; it is a worldview that brings not just culture in the midst of other cultures, but it brings the religious focus that carries that culture.

The psalmist warns us that "the idols of the nations are silver and gold, made by the hands of men. They have mouths, but cannot speak, eyes, but they cannot see; they have ears, but cannot hear, nor is there breath in their mouths. Those who make them will be like them, and so will all who trust in them" (Psalm 135:15–18, NIV). So we see the amalgam of cultures, part of which has as its central focus a religious worldview, moving into cultures where Christianity has been evicted, and culture has become a catch-all for anything that can be absorbed.

The Dominance of the Visual

Third is the dominance of the visual. William Blake spoke of seeing with and not through the eye. "This life's dim window of the soul distorts the heavens from pole to pole, and goads you to believe a lie, when you see with and not through the eye." We are meant to see through the eye with the conscience. Modern-day communication is drawing us into seeing with the eye devoid of a conscience.

How can you reach a generation so soaked in the visual? Our Lord reminded us to let your eye be single because the eye is the lamp of the body, and if the light within you becomes darkness, how great is the darkness indeed (see Matthew 6:22–23).

Malcolm Muggeridge tells of the time when some political prisoners were about to be executed. The soldiers came with their guns, an officer shouted the command, "Ready! Aim!" . . . when all of a sudden one cameraman shouted, "Stop, my battery is dead." So the execution was stopped until he could go and get a new battery pack and was ready to roll again. "Ready! Aim!" Bang, bang! And the political prisoners fell to the ground. Muggeridge makes this astute comment, "Some future analyst may ask, 'Wherein lay the greatest barbarism? Was it on the part of the executioners, or on the part of the viewers?'"

We must understand that there is a capacity here, an immense capacity, to assault the imagination. I can only say this to you. I came to know Christ when I was 17 years old in the city of Delhi. My life was a tangled mess. I just wonder what I would have done if my imagination had been assaulted the way the modern day teenager's imagination is assaulted. With all the drives and the passions, it is hard enough to lead a life of integrity and truthfulness and moral commitment. With all these pictures bombarding you and assaulting the imagination, making you think there is something in there when there isn't, this world has become lonelier than ever before because each thrill has a shorter shelf life.

The implications here are extremely important. For decades science has been seen as an exacting discipline of the intellect, and the arts as a free-floating realm of the imagination. With the advance of computers the two disciplines will converge, and the imagination may place demands upon the sciences till a free-floating technological power will play the role of a creator of people's fantasies. The intellect will be seduced by the imagination. The Tower of Babel could well be built with one language, only it will be in pictures accessed by buttons.

But let me say this. Just because young people are exposed to the visual, let us not forget that they still think seriously about issues. My son Nathan, when he was in high school, phoned home one day and said, "Mom, I'm going to be about an hour late coming back from school." So my wife asked, "Are you going somewhere, Son?" And he said, "Yes." She said, "Can you just tell us where you're going so we know where you are?" He replied, "Well, I'm afraid if I tell you, you won't like it." That, of course, made it all the more important that she find out where he was going. She said, "Where are you going?" He answered, "Well, I'm going to the mall." "Why?" He said, "I want to buy a chain to put around my neck, and I want to get a pendant with the number 13 on it. Will you let me do that, Mom?" It suddenly dawned on my wife why he was doing it. Just a few days before, one faculty member and twelve students had been murdered at Columbine High School in Littleton, Colorado. Nathan was so deeply moved by it, he now wears that chain with 13. You will never see it; it is under his shirt. He said, "I want this to remind me of the courage of those young people, especially the ones who were willing to pay with their lives for their commitment to the Lord Jesus Christ." I would never have thought in those terms, but he did. Our expression is in words. For young people it is the visual, the symbols.

The Increasing Power of a Youth–Dominated World

Fourth, the world is shaped by the young. A Western diplomat was sitting at a table with former Chinese premiere Chou En-lai years ago, and he didn't know what conversation to make. Knowing of Chou En-lai's love for history he said, "What do you think of the French Revolution?" Chou En-lai looked at him and said, "It's too soon to tell." For one man the French Revolution was archaic; for another it was just in the recent past. How is a young world that lives for the moment going to cope with the past?

A Lost Center for Cultural Molding

Fifth, there is a lost center for cultural molding. We celebrate diversity. There is no one single point of reference for truth, no one single source from which life gains its coherence, no single source of authority. The result is an accepted disconnectedness, a built-in fragmentation. God reminds us that we need a light for our path and a lamp for our feet (see Psalm 119:105).

How do you reach a generation that listens with its eyes and thinks with its feelings? We can be assured of at least two things. Number one, as Malcolm Muggeridge used to say, "All new news is old news happening to new people." While the outward signs may change, the inner hunger remains consistent. The second is that the Word of God stands forever. We know that to be true.

Proclamation That Is Not Only Heard but Seen

How then do we respond? First, *we need to have a proclamation that is not only heard but is also seen.* Why is it that a community that talks so much about supernatural transformation shows so little of that transformation?

We will have to be men and women who embody the message that we are preaching, whose lives are faithful to the claims we are making, whose love is shown as the love of God, whose kindness and gentleness is present even in the midst of such diversity—so that men and women will see. If our proclamation is to reach a generation, we will have to live lives that make the Gospel visible. Jesus said, "Let your light shine before men, that they may see your good deeds and praise your Father in heaven" (Matthew 5:16, NIV).

Mahatma Gandhi once said, "I like their Christ. I am not sure about their Christians." It was Nietzsche who said, "I want to see a little more of the redeemed if I am to believe in their Redeemer." Gypsy Smith said, "There are five Gospels: Matthew, Mark, Luke, John and the Christian. And some people will never read the first four." We must be letters read and known of all men and women (see 2 Corinthians 3:2), a message that is not only heard but is also seen.

Proclamation That Is Not Merely Argued but Felt

Second, *we will need a proclamation that is not merely argued but is also felt.* The greatest search in philosophy has always been one thing: How do you find unity in diversity? The only way we can find unity in diversity is if we first find unity in the diversity within ourselves. How do we find unity in the diversity of our passions?

We will have to be men and women who embody the message that we are preaching. . . . We will have to live lives that make the Gospel visible.

Post-modernism longs for community. It may be that the most powerful evangelism of the next century will be a community in worship. Men and women must understand how the Gospel not only saves in an eternal sense but binds together in the temporal sense, bringing all of our senses into one composite expression.

Archbishop William Temple defined worship in these words, "Worship is the submission of all of our nature to God. It is the quickening of conscience by His holiness; nourishment of mind by His truth; purifying of imagination by His beauty; opening of the heart to His love; and submission of will to His purpose. All this gathered up in adoration is the greatest expression of which we are capable."

Watch young people singing where every sense is involved. Is that any different than when we bow before the table and take the bread and drink the cup, where history is brought into focus and everything we do is brought into balance in coherence?

The last book of the Old Testament, Malachi, is on worship. In the last book of the New Testament, the glimpse is of worship. The conversation with the woman at the well ended in worship (see John 4:1–42). The conversation about the woman with the alabaster ointment focused on worship (see Matthew 26:6–13). What a moment we have in a fractured world to show people a community of believers worshiping the living God, the greatest expression of which we are capable.

Not Only the Ends of the Gospel; Also the Means

Lastly, *we must rescue not only the ends, the goal of the Gospel, the transformation of a life, but the means of the Gospel, the very words that we use.* The Bible does not say, "In the beginning was video." The Bible says, "In the beginning was the

Word" (John 1:1, KJV). There is a propositional nature to truth. Let us not get so gobbled up by thinking we can do it with pictures that we forget we have a responsibility to rescue language as well. I have seen many pictures of the miracle of Cana at Galilee, artists' ideas of the conversion of water into wine. Not one of them did for me what Alexander Pope's one sentence did. About the miracle he said, "The conscious water saw its Master and blushed."

Our task in this generation is hard. One of the disciplines will be that of learning to speak words that stir the imagination and demand the attention. In the beginning God spoke. Throughout history He has spoken. He reminds us that it is His Word that abides forever.

Let me tie it together now. The Gospel must not only be heard but seen, not only argued but felt; we rescue not only the ends but also the means.

How do you reach a culture that hears with its eyes and thinks with its feelings, a culture where life and feeling are synonymous? We reach them with a life that is synonymous with the Word, one in which the Word and life are identical. Let us not break our commitment to be honest communicators and livers of the truth, then we put our lives in our hands. And when they see our lives consistent with what we say, they will see the Word that could not be broken. Times are changing; His Word does not. His Word abides forever.

Sir Robert Bold wrote the play *A Man for All Seasons* about Thomas More. Thomas More was put in jail because he did not support the king in an immoral decision the king was making. So More was put into prison. And his daughter came to him one day and said, "Dad, why don't you just say the words? You don't have to mean them. Just say the words as if you support him. In your heart you do not have to mean them." He looked at her and said, "Meg, Meg, you've got it all wrong." Please listen now. He said, "When you give your word to anybody, it is like taking your life and putting it into your hands. And if you go back on that word, it will fall through and you shall look down and not find yourself there again."

Do you see what he is saying? When you give your word, you are putting your life in your hands. And if you break your word, your life will fall through. And when you look down, you shall not find yourself there again. Let us never forget this, all of us who are called to be evangelists in this generation.

Ravi Zacharias

Dr. Ravi Zacharias was born in India. He received his M.Div. from Trinity Evangelical Divinity School. Dr. Zacharias has received honorary Doctor of Divinity degrees from Houghton College and Tyndale College and Seminary, and a Doctor of Laws degree from Asbury College. He is president of Ravi Zacharias International Ministries, which headquarters in Atlanta, Georgia, U.S.A., with additional offices in Canada, India and the United Kingdom. Dr. Zacharias and his wife, Margaret, have three children and reside in Atlanta, Georgia, U.S.A.

The Bible-Based Message

Video: Billy Graham

Our authority comes from the Bible, the Word of God. When our message is based on the Word of God, just quoting from Scripture gives an authority. The Bible has its own built-in power. That's the reason I use the phrase, "The Bible says." When I say, "The Bible says," I notice there's a new attention from the audience.

I did struggle before we held our Los Angeles Crusade in 1949. We were high up in the mountains at a little conference center called Forest Home. I was there as a speaker, and I was the youngest speaker there. Several students there were from one of the most prestigious seminaries in the country, and they believed that I was very naïve in accepting the Bible as the Word of God. They were sort of making fun of me. I felt discouraged.

So one moonlit night I went out into the woods. I had my Bible. There was a tree stump there. I opened the Bible and laid it down. Tears were coming down my cheeks. I said, "Lord, there's a lot in the Bible that I don't understand. But I accept this as your authoritative Word from one end to the other." And from that moment on, I've never had a doubt about it. I can't prove it all, but I accept it by faith as the Word of God.

Billy Graham
Dr. Graham founded the Billy Graham Evangelistic Association in 1950, which headquarters in Minneapolis, Minnesota, U.S.A. Dr. Graham and his wife, Ruth, make their home in North Carolina, U.S.A.

The Evangelist's Message Is Bible-Based

John R. W. Stott

Our topic is a fine statement or affirmation. It is this: "The Evangelist's Message Is Bible-Based." Indeed, the Bible is the only basis on which the authentic evangelist can build his or her message. The Bible is indispensable to true evangelism. Without the Bible, evangelists would have nothing to say, nothing worth listening to and no hope of success. But if the message is based on the Bible, then it is radically different.

First, it has rich Gospel content, for it is God's Good News for sinners. It concentrates on salvation through the atoning death and glorious resurrection of our Lord and Savior Jesus Christ. Second, it breathes an authority which compels attention and even assent. It rings true. And third, it has liberating and transforming power. It sets people free.

Now, these three features of the Gospel—its content, its authority and its power—all come from the Bible, which is the Word of God.

The Bible Gives the Evangelist's Message Its Content

First, the Bible gives the evangelist's message its content. Biblical content is essential to true evangelism—for evangelism, at its very simplest, is the communication of the Gospel. And the Gospel has God-given content. I want to emphasize two points about the Gospel.

First, the Gospel comes from God. The Gospel is God's Good News for the world. It is not a human invention. It is not a human speculation. It is a divine revelation. If God had not taken the initiative to make Himself known, then He would have remained forever unknown. All the altars in the world, like that altar which the apostle Paul discovered outside Athens, would be inscribed "To an unknown god" (Acts 17:23, RSV).

The fact is that we cannot even read each other's minds, let alone the mind of God. If I were to stand here silent, you would not know what I was thinking. Try it. . . . What is going on in my mind? . . . You don't know, so I'll tell you: I was climbing the Eiffel Tower in Paris. But you had no idea. You couldn't read my mind. I cannot read your minds. And if we cannot read each other's minds, how much less can we read the mind of God? Unless God should speak, we would never know what was in His mind.

Let me remind you of what is written in Isaiah 55:8–9. God is speaking, and He says, "My thoughts are not your thoughts, neither are your ways my ways, saith the LORD. For as the heavens are higher than the earth, so are my ways higher than your ways, and my thoughts than your thoughts" (KJV). And so,

God's thoughts are as much higher than our thoughts as the heavens are higher than the earth, which is infinity.

How then can we possibly know God's mind? We cannot. It is altogether beyond and above us. There is no ladder by which we can climb up into the infinite mind of God. There is no way to bridge the gulf, the chasm that yawns between Him and us. We could never understand His mind, never understand His saving purpose in the Gospel, if He had not spoken. But God has spoken! His Word has come down to us!

Let me read again from Isaiah 55, this time verses 10 and 11, "As the rain and the snow come down from heaven, and . . . water the earth" (Isaiah 55:10, RSV)—notice the repetition of the heaven and the earth. As His Word comes—as the rain and the snow come down to us from heaven—so His Word has come down to the earth. "So is my word that goes out from my mouth: It will not return to me empty" (Isaiah 55:11, NIV). His Word comes out of His mouth, and it will not return to Him empty. It will accomplish what He desires and achieve the purpose for which He sent it.

> Since salvation is in Christ alone, by grace alone, through faith alone, Scripture focuses on Christ, in whom salvation is found. Christ crucified, Christ risen, Christ reigning and coming again!

God Has Clothed His Thoughts in Words

So, you see, God has clothed His thoughts in words. At this moment, as I am speaking, you know what I am thinking, because I am speaking. I am communicating the thoughts of my mind in the words of my mouth. And that is exactly what God has done. Thank God for the Bible! God has clothed His thoughts in words—supremely in the incarnate Word, our Lord Jesus Christ, but also in the written Word of Scripture which bears witness to Christ. He has disclosed His mind. He has revealed His message for the world.

So the Gospel comes from God. It has come down from God by revelation. Let's hold on to this truth and never forget it.

Second, the Gospel that comes from God focuses on Christ. You remember what Paul wrote to Timothy, "From infancy you have known the holy Scriptures, which are able to make you wise for salvation through faith in Christ Jesus" (2 Timothy 3:15, NIV). That is to say, the Bible is essentially a book of salvation. Its chief purpose is to teach us the way of salvation. And since salvation is in Christ alone, by grace alone, through faith alone, Scripture focuses on Christ, in whom salvation is found: Christ crucified, Christ risen, Christ reigning and coming again! And Scripture urges us to put our trust in Christ as the one and only Savior.

Now Jesus Himself was quite clear about this, that Scripture focuses on Himself. "The Scriptures bear witness to me," He said. "Moses wrote about me."

And "he explained to them what was said in all the Scriptures concerning himself" (Luke 24:27, NIV). So then, as we read Scripture we need to look for Christ. As the great fifth-century church father Jerome wrote, "Ignorance of Scripture is ignorance of Christ." Whereas we could say conversely, knowledge of Scripture is knowledge of Christ.

We Worship the Christ of the Bible

Now this explains why we love the Bible. Evangelical believers are sometimes accused of being "bibliolaters," that is, "Bible worshipers." But it's simply not true. It is a slander. We do not worship the Bible; we worship the Christ of the Bible. The reason we love the Bible is that it focuses on Christ. The Bible speaks to us of Him.

For example, it occurs to me that there may be somebody, a young man perhaps, in this great assembly who is in love. Because you are in love, you keep in your pocket a picture of your beloved. And sometimes when nobody is looking, you take the picture out of your pocket and you give it a surreptitious or secret kiss. But kissing the picture is a poor substitute for the real thing! The reason you love the picture is that it speaks to you of her. And the reason we love the Bible is that it speaks to us of Him, of Christ.

But, if we love the Bible because we love Christ, other people love neither. On the contrary, they are hostile to Christ. So if in our evangelism we focus faithfully on Christ, on the authentic Christ of the New Testament witness, I'm afraid we are bound to suffer for it. What is it then, I often ask myself, about the Gospel of Christ which arouses people's hostility? Why is it that they hate the Bible and they hate the Gospel? There seem to be three main reasons.

The first concerns the uniqueness and finality of Christ and of the Gospel. In our increasingly pluralistic cultures, our insistence on Jesus as the only saving name causes great offense, and I fear that the offense is going to increase as pluralism spreads throughout the world.

Secondly, there is the freeness of the Gospel of Christ. Proud human beings would give anything to be able to earn their own salvation; or if they cannot earn their salvation, at least contribute to it. When they are told that salvation and eternal life are a noncontributory gift of God—that is to say, absolutely free and utterly undeserved—they are offended because it is extremely humiliating to people's arrogant self-confidence. Jesus says to us from the cross, "I am here because of you. If it were not that you were sinners, hell-deserving sinners, I would not be here." This is the stumbling block of the cross.

Thirdly, there are the high moral standards of the Gospel of Christ, and they are another stumbling block. People love their own sinful ways. They want to be left alone in their own self-centeredness, and they resent the Gospel which calls us to holiness and to surrender to the lordship of Jesus Christ.

If then we are faithful to Christ in these ways—affirming the uniqueness and the freeness and the high moral standards of the Gospel—I'm afraid we are sure to suffer. And if we compromise less, we will undoubtedly suffer more.

So with regard to the content of the Gospel, we affirm that the Gospel comes from God and focuses on Christ. And in these ways the Bible gives the evangelist's message its rich content.

The Bible Gives the Evangelist's Message Its Authority

Secondly, the Bible gives the evangelist's message not only its content but its authority. The word *authority* is increasingly unpopular and distasteful to many people today. They are looking for freedom, they say, not authority. And they assume that authority and freedom are mutually incompatible, which they are not. For it is not in throwing off the yoke of Christ that we find freedom. It is in submitting to His yoke, that is, His authority. You remember what He said, "Come unto me, all ye that labor and are heavy laden, and I will give you rest. Take my yoke"—a symbol of submission to authority—"take my yoke upon you, and learn of me . . ."—let Me be your teacher—". . . and ye shall find rest unto your souls" (Matthew 11:28–29, KJV). Rest is under the yoke of Christ. It is not in discarding His yoke.

Ever since the 1960s the world has been in revolt against all forms of authority—against the authority of the State and of the Church, against the authority of school and college, against the authority of the family and of the Bible. Yet it is a psychological truth that adults, like adolescents, crave the very authority they say they resent. So whatever people may say to the contrary, human beings are longing for a word of authority, a word they can trust. And the only word that is unconditionally trustworthy is not a human word. It is the Word of God.

Authentic evangelists are not apologetic about the Gospel. We are not ashamed of the Gospel. On the contrary, we believe it to be truth from God, and so we proclaim it with clarity, with conviction and with courage. In our post-modern era in which the very possibility of truth is being denied, it is wonderfully refreshing to read the Bible and to sense the strong assurance of the biblical authors, and to communicate their message with their authority to the world. Wise evangelists stick to the Bible because they know that there is authority in God's Word.

So the Bible gives us our content; it gives us our authority. Yet in saying this I've made it sound a bit too simple. Honesty compels me to add two important qualifications about the Word of God.

The first qualification is that the Word of God does not include everything we would like to know. We human beings, of course, are restlessly inquisitive. We are always asking questions, and we demand answers to our questions. But God has not revealed everything to us. He is not wanting to answer all our questions. In this respect, Deuteronomy 29:29 is a verse that we all ought to know by heart. I hope we do. It's a very important text, and this is how it goes: "The secret things belong to the LORD our God, but the things revealed belong to us and to our children forever, that we may follow all the words of this law" (NIV).

So in this verse truth is divided into two categories: the secret things which belong to God, and the revealed things which belong to us. In other words, some truths have indeed been revealed and we wouldn't know them if they had not been revealed, while other truths have not been revealed but have been kept secret by God.

For this reason Christian believers are an unusual combination of the dogmatic and the agnostic. We are dogmatic about those truths which are plainly revealed in the Bible, but we are agnostic about those things which have not been clearly revealed or have been kept secret. About the secret things it is right for us to say, "I don't know," because God has not revealed them. But about the revealed things we are able to say, "I know," because God has revealed them.

So we need to keep these two things separate. Indeed, many of our problems arise from a failure to observe this distinction. It is equally as foolish to allow our dogmatism to trespass into the secret things as it is to allow our agnosticism to trespass into the revealed things. And among us evangelical Christians the former, I think, is the more common fault. That is, we tend to be overly dogmatic, more so than Scripture itself permits, and then we cause offense by our arrogance.

> **Some truths have indeed been revealed and we wouldn't know them if they hadn't been revealed, while other truths have not been revealed but have been kept secret by God.**

We need to remember the modesty of the apostles of Jesus Christ. The apostle John wrote of our future state that we do not yet know what we shall be, but we know that when Christ comes, we shall see Him and we shall be like Him (see 1 John 3:2). But we don't know more than that. Here is an apostle who says, "I don't know," because it has not been revealed. And the apostle Paul writes in 1 Corinthians 13, "Now I know only partially, but then when Christ comes again, I shall know as fully as I am already known" (see verse 12). If two of the leading apostles acknowledged their partial ignorance, it is only right that we should do the same.

More Evangelical Confidence, More Evangelical Humility

I confess, sisters and brothers, that I would love to see among us more evangelical confidence in the Gospel, and at the same time more evangelical humility about what God has not yet clearly revealed. To maintain this distinction in our evangelism would commend our Gospel for its honesty. The Word of God does not include everything that we would like it to or that we would like to know.

The second qualification is that the Word of God needs to be interpreted. To be sure, we believe in what the sixteenth-century Reformers called the "perspicuity" of Scripture. That is to say, it is perspicuous, it has a see-through or transparent quality. But the Reformers were referring to the way of salvation in Christ by grace through faith. That is as plain as day in Scripture. Even the uneducated, even little children, can understand the essence of the Gospel.

But not everything in Scripture is equally perspicuous. The apostle Peter confessed that some things in Paul's letters were "hard to understand" (2 Peter 3:16, NIV). If one apostle could not always understand another apostle, it would hardly be modest for us to claim that we can.

The main reason why some parts of Scripture may be obscure and difficult to understand concerns the problems of culture. God did not shout culture-free truths to us out of the clear blue sky. On the contrary, God revealed Himself within the cultures of the human race and of the human authors, and these may be quite alien to us in our particular cultures. Indeed, one of the great glories of God's revelation is that He has condescended to come down to our level and to speak to us within our own cultures and in our own languages. No word of God was spoken in a cultural vacuum. Every word of God was spoken in a cultural context.

So in consequence of that, we cannot avoid the task of building bridges between the ancient cultures of the Word of God and the cultures in which we are living and working today. I beg you not to resist this task. I beg you not to avoid the hard sweat of study, of interpretation and of application. We need to repent of our tendency to evangelical laziness, behaving as if Scripture would yield up its treasures to those who do not dig for them. We need to explore the Word of God and we need to cry to the Holy Spirit to increase our understanding. God said to Daniel, "Since the first day that you set your mind to gain understanding and to humble yourself before your God, your words were heard" (Daniel 10:12, NIV). Humility and industry go together, as do prayer and study.

So not everything has been revealed in Scripture. And although what has been revealed is not always easy to understand, yet Scripture has a unique authority in evangelism. We come to Scripture with confidence. We study it with painstaking care. We humble ourselves before it, and we pray for the illumination of the Holy Spirit. We determine to proclaim its sacred teaching with conviction. I sometimes wonder if anything is more necessary for the health and growth of the church today than a recovery of conscientious biblical preaching, both by evangelists and by pastors. So the Bible gives us the content and the Bible gives the evangelist's message its authority.

The Bible Gives the Evangelist's Message Its Power

Third, the Bible also gives the evangelist's message its power. It is important to distinguish between authority and power. In the context of evangelism, authority is largely subjective, the conviction with which we preach; whereas power is objective, the effect that God's Word has on those who hear it. True Gospel preaching combines authority and power. As the apostle Paul wrote to the Thessalonians, "Our gospel came to you not simply with words, but also with power, . . . and with deep conviction" (1 Thessalonians 1:5, NIV).

It is the Holy Spirit who gives us both conviction and power in our evangelism. We long that our message, which is often spoken in great human weakness, will be carried home with divine power to the mind, the heart, the conscience and the will of the hearers. There is power in the Gospel. I trust we can all echo the apostle Paul's resounding affirmation, "I am not ashamed of the gospel of Christ: for it is the power of God unto salvation to every one that believeth" (Romans 1:16, KJV).

Scripture emphasizes the power of the Word of God by the use of rich imagery or pictures. The Word of God is like fire; it burns up the rubbish. The Word of God is like a hammer; it breaks the rock in pieces. It is like seed; it germinates and bears fruit. It is like food; it nourishes us. It is like good pasture in which the sheep may safely graze. And, above all, it is like a sword. In fact, it is "the sword of the Spirit, which is the word of God" (Ephesians 6:17, KJV).

Never, then, should we separate the Word from the Spirit or the Spirit from the Word. Some Christians have great confidence in the Holy Spirit, which is wonderful, but they neither study nor expound the Word of God. Others make the opposite mistake. They are great students of the Word; their desk is piled high with study books. But they seldom, if ever, fall on their knees and humble themselves before the Scripture and cry to God for light and the power of the Holy Spirit.

Why must we always polarize? Why must we always separate what God has joined—the Word and the Spirit? The Word without the Spirit lacks power. The Spirit without the Word lacks His weapon. So we must keep the two together. They belong together in evangelism.

Because the Bible is the Word of God, we should read it as we read no other book. We should read it on our knees, in prayerful humility before God, looking to Him for light. But because the Bible is the Word of God through the words of the human authors, we should read it as we read every other book, paying careful attention to both the text and the context. It is the double authorship of the Bible—divine and human—that necessitates the double authority, the double approach to the Bible: humble and studious at the same time.

Evangelism without the Bible is inconceivable, even impossible. For without the Bible the evangelist's message lacks content, authority and power. It is the Bible that gives our message its *content*—Christ crucified, risen and reigning. It is the Bible that gives our message its *authority* so that we proclaim it with deep conviction. And it is the Bible that gives the message its *power,* as the Holy Spirit reinforces the Word in the experience of the hearers.

This is the Trinitarian shape of all authentic evangelism. It is the Word of God the Father, that focuses upon the death and resurrection of Christ, in the power of the Holy Spirit. May God keep us true to this Trinitarian evangelism.

John R. W. Stott
The Reverend Dr. John Stott, well-known evangelist, preacher, biblical scholar and author, is rector emeritus of All Souls Church, Langham Place, London, England. Dr. John Stott was appointed a chaplain to the Queen of England in 1959, serving in that capacity until 1991 when he was appointed an extra chaplain. He has written more than 40 books, including Bible expositions, and his recent book Evangelical Truth. He has participated in many evangelistic university missions. Dr. Stott makes his home in London (UK).

Studying the Bible

Video: Michael Songyemba, Uganda
Cliff Barrows, Billy Graham Evangelistic Association

All Scripture is God-breathed and is useful for teaching, rebuking, correcting and training in righteousness, so that the man of God may be thoroughly equipped for every good work" (2 Timothy 3:16–17, NIV). An evangelist who is deeply rooted in the knowledge of the Scriptures has the ability to communicate the message more effectively. It is necessary to take advantage of the wealth of study aids, books and materials to help interpret the Scripture accurately.

Michael Songyemba: "The Bible is the manual for my daily walk. It is very important that anybody who wants to be used of the Lord gets time on a daily basis to study and reflect on what the Word of God is saying. One needs to study the Bible, trying to understand the context and how that message can apply to the people. One needs to fall in love with the Bible and with the author, the God of the Bible."

Cliff Barrows: "It is very easy to become distracted, to lose focus. And one of the greatest enemies is activity. When we realize that, and each day cultivate a personal relationship with the living Christ, the Holy Spirit comes in our quiet time and in our meditation on His Word."

Cliff Barrows and Michael Songyemba
The Reverend Cliff Barrows is the Music and Program Director for the Billy Graham Crusade Team. Bishop Michael Songyemba is a bishop in the Anglican Church in Uganda.

Cliff Barrows   Michael
Songyemba

The Evangelist and the Bible

Anne Graham Lotz

In the year 741 B.C. the nation of Judah was in such moral and spiritual decline that she was provoking the judgment of God. It was in that setting that God raised up a man who was a good preacher. He had a head knowledge of God's Word. This man was in ministry for several years when he had a fresh vision of Jesus. When he received a fresh vision of Jesus, the knowledge of God's Word that was in his head went to his heart and he became the greatest of the Old Testament prophets. His name is Isaiah.

I believe that today you and I are living in a world that is also provoking the judgment of God. Many of you are good preachers and you have God's Word and God's truth in your heads. But I believe God is calling you and me to have His Word in our heads *and* in our hearts.

My challenge to you is what I believe God is calling us to. It's a call to greatness. The difference between a good preacher and a great preacher is basically 18 inches. It's the distance from your head to your heart.

Living in a Changing World

Would you open your Bible to Isaiah 1. We're going to look together at Isaiah's personal testimony. In Isaiah 1:1 he says this: "The vision concerning Judah and Jerusalem that Isaiah son of Amoz saw during the reigns of Uzziah, Jotham, Ahaz and Hezekiah, kings of Judah" (NIV). That verse reveals to you and me that Isaiah was living in a changing world. One king was giving way to another.

You and I also live in a changing world. One king gives way to another, one government gives way to another. We have changes in technology, changes in the environment. We have changes in our own lives.

Isaiah was living in a changing world, and he understood what the basic problem was. Do you? When we look at our world today, what is the basic problem? Do we think the basic problem is a post-modern era and a dominance of the youth culture and bold atheism? Do you think the primary problem in your country, in your city, in your world is poverty or human rights abuse or drugs or AIDS? Isaiah understood that the basic problem in his world was *sin*.

Preach the Word

He said, "Ah, sinful nation, a people loaded with guilt, a brood of evildoers, children given to corruption!" (Isaiah 1:4, NIV). Isaiah pinpointed the basic problem in his world. Would you acknowledge that the basic problem in our world today is just sin? We have to acknowledge the basic problem before we can come to the basic solution. And if the basic problem is none of those things I listed, then the solution isn't going to be those things. The solution will not be more money or more education or more anything. The solution is a Savior.

"'Come now, let us reason together,' says the LORD. 'Though your sins are like scarlet, they shall be as white as snow'" (Isaiah 1:18, NIV). Isaiah, from an Old Testament perspective, preaches the Gospel. He knows that the Gospel is the solution to the problem in his world. Isaiah in a changing world understood the basic problem, understood the basic solution. Therefore, he was committed to the Word of God. Isaiah preached the Word. The apostle Paul says God's Word is like our schoolteacher. God's Word teaches us that we're sinners. God's Word reveals to us our Savior. So Isaiah preached the Word.

Look with me at Isaiah 1:2, "Hear, O heavens! Listen, O earth! For the LORD has spoken" (NIV); Isaiah preaches the Word. Look at verse 10, "Hear the word of the LORD" (NIV); Isaiah preaches the Word. Look at verse 24, "Therefore the Lord, the LORD Almighty, the Mighty One of Israel, declares" (NIV); Isaiah preaches the Word. He's not preaching books *about* the Word. He's not preaching videos or drama or entertainment or music. He's preaching the Word of God.

> I pray to God we had more good preachers who would preach the Word.

When you preach, what do you preach? Preach the Word. Preach the Word. Preach the Word! Isaiah was a good prophet. He was a good preacher. He preached the Word. I'll tell you something: I pray to God we had more good preachers who would preach the Word—who understand the problem, understand the solution, and preach the Word.

God was calling Isaiah to greatness. Isaiah had an experience that made the transition of his knowledge of God's Word from his head to his heart. Turn with me to Isaiah 6. Isaiah experienced three things that caused him to make the transition from his head to his heart.

His life was shaken. "In the year that King Uzziah died" (v. 1, NIV). In the year King Uzziah died, Isaiah was shaken in three ways, I believe. Because we think that Isaiah was a relative of the king, I'm going to assume Isaiah was shaken *personally* because his loved one had just died and he was grieving.

Isaiah was also shaken *financially*, because I'm assuming that if he had a need he went to the king and the king met his need. But now the king is dead, and Isaiah is suddenly cut off from his financial resources. And Isaiah was shaken *mortally* as he stood at the grave of his loved one and realized that death is just a breath away, eternity is just a breath away. Isaiah was shaken.

In what way are you being shaken? When our lives are shaken, look up!

Maybe God is allowing you and me to be shaken so that we will look up.

A Fresh Vision of the Power of Jesus

"In the year that King Uzziah died, I saw the Lord" (Isaiah 6:1, NIV). Isaiah's eyes were opened when his life was shaken. His eyes were opened to a fresh vision of Jesus. John 12:41 tells us that Isaiah saw the glory of Jesus Christ. This vision, in Isaiah 6, is a vision of the preincarnate Son of God. Isaiah says, "I saw the Lord seated on a throne" (v. 1, NIV). He had a fresh vision of the *power* of Jesus Christ. Jesus was seated on the throne, meaning He was in absolute authority of all that was taking place. He was in control.

What has caused you to doubt that Jesus is in control? Is it when God hasn't answered your prayer? Is it when nobody responds to your Gospel message? Is it when some tragedy happens to your child or another loved one? And you say, "Jesus, are You on the throne?"

Isaiah said, "In the year that King Uzziah died, I looked up and I saw the Lord, and He was seated on the throne." Looking at the end of human history, in Revelation 4 the apostle John said, "I also saw heaven opened, and I saw Jesus still seated on the throne" (see vv. 1–2). Isaiah's eyes were opened to a fresh vision of the power of Jesus. He is in control!

A Fresh Vision of the Position of Jesus

Isaiah's eyes were opened to a fresh vision of the *position* of Jesus. He says He is high. No one is higher than Jesus. I don't know who is higher than you are. Perhaps your board of deacons, or you have a boss, and perhaps there's a governor and maybe a king or a president. We have rulers and authorities in this world. All have different heights in their position. But there's no position of authority in all of the universe that is higher than Jesus. He is the highest!

Ephesians 1 says that when God raised Jesus from the dead, He raised Him up through all those principalities and powers in the seen world and the unseen world and seated Him at the right hand of the Father and put all authority under His feet (see vv. 20–23). He is high!

A Fresh Vision of the Person of Jesus

Isaiah's eyes were opened to a fresh vision of the *person* of Jesus. He is exalted. No one is greater than Jesus. I know many of you face in a very real way demons and evil spirits and principalities and powers in the unseen world and people who persecute the church and persecute God's people. You face evil and wickedness. But listen to me. It doesn't matter who you face or what you face, whether they're visible or invisible—none is greater than Jesus. He is exalted! He is above all!

A Fresh Vision of the Presence of Jesus

Isaiah's eyes were opened to a fresh vision of the *presence* of Jesus. "The train of his robe filled the temple" (Isaiah 6:1, NIV). Isaiah had a fresh vision of what it would be like if the temple of his body was filled with the Spirit of Jesus. What would it be like if your church and your ministry and your city and your country and the world were filled with the presence of Jesus? Isaiah's eyes were opened with a fresh vision of what it would be like if Jesus filled everywhere and everyone.

A Fresh Vision of the Praise of Jesus

Then his eyes were opened to a fresh vision of the *praise* of Jesus. The angels gathered together and they were calling to each other, "'Holy, holy, holy is the LORD Almighty; the whole earth is full of his glory.' At the sound of their voices the doorposts and thresholds shook and the temple was filled with smoke" (vv. 3–4, NIV). That smoke is not smoke from a fire. That's the glory of God come down. That's the Shekinah glory that came down.

When we praise Jesus—never mind whether He answers our prayer or not, never mind if anybody ever responds to our message or not, never mind if He ever heals our disease or not, never mind if He never gives us our money or if He never solves our problem or reconciles that person—we just praise Jesus for who He is. When we praise Jesus, things happen! The church moves. The glory of God comes down.

A Fresh Vision of the Purity of Jesus

Isaiah's eyes were opened to a fresh vision of the *purity* of Jesus. "Holy, holy, holy." Because Jesus is absolutely pure in His motives, absolutely pure in His methods, absolutely pure in His words, absolutely pure in His thoughts, absolutely pure in His deeds, absolutely pure in His decisions, He is holy, holy, holy. And God says, "Be ye holy, as I am holy" (see Leviticus 19:2). He demands holiness from His people, especially the leaders of His people.

A Fresh Vision of the Holiness of Jesus

Isaiah's eyes were opened to a fresh vision of the *holiness* of Jesus. Do you need a fresh vision of Jesus? Then look up. When your life is shaken, ask God to open your eyes. The apostle John on the Isle of Patmos—suffering for the Word of God and the testimony of Jesus Christ—looked up and had a fresh vision of Jesus. Isaiah had a fresh vision of the holiness of Jesus Christ.

The Helplessness of His Own Condition

Then his eyes were opened to the *helplessness* of his own condition. Turn with me to Isaiah 5. This is a sermon Isaiah was preaching when he was a good preacher with the knowledge of God's Word in his head: "Woe to you who add house to house and join field to field" (Isaiah 5:8, NIV). "Woe to you." Now turn to Isaiah 5:11, "Woe to those who rise early in the morning to run after their drinks." Verse 18, "Woe to those who draw sin along with cords of deceit." Verse 20, "Woe to those who call evil good and good evil." Verse 21, "Woe to those who are wise in their own eyes." Verse 22, "Woe to those who are heroes at drinking wine." Isaiah is preaching a sermon, pointing his finger at everybody in the audience, "Woe to you, woe to you, woe to you." Isaiah was right. He was convicting them of their sin.

But what does he say when his eyes are opened to the holiness of Christ? In Isaiah 6:5, he says, "Woe to me!" (NIV). Isaiah sees the helplessness of his own condition. He recognizes that he himself is responsible for sin in his life. He wasn't a victim. He was a sinner.

Did you think that because you're in ministry somehow you sin less or somehow God lets you get by with it? It doesn't matter as much? Have you been blaming your sin on a spouse or lack of education or the way you were brought up or your culture? Isaiah had to confess before God, "Woe to me. I'm responsible for sin in my life." Then he said, "I am ruined!" (v. 5, NIV). Isaiah knew the sin in his life ruined him as a person. I believe he stood there in the light of the holiness of Jesus and he lost all of his self-confidence. He lost all of his pride. Isaiah just crumbled in the light of who Jesus is. "I am ruined!" he said.

Not only ruined himself, he's ruined in service. "I am a man of unclean lips" (v. 5, NIV). Isaiah was a preacher. He served God with his lips. He's saying, "I'm ruined. My lips are unclean. I am not worthy to be in ministry. I am not worthy to be a preacher."

Then he says, "I live among a people of unclean lips" (v. 5, NIV). "I am no better than the people to whom I've been preaching. And I've been pointing my finger at these people, and I'm no better than they are. How can I be in ministry? How can I be a preacher?" Isaiah acknowledged that he was responsible for sin in his life; he was ruined by it. Have you accepted responsibility for the sin in your life? Have you confessed that you're ruined by it? That there's nothing you can ever do to serve God in yourself, no way you can ever be in ministry in yourself?

The Hope of the Cross

Praise God! Isaiah's eyes remained open, and he saw not only the *holiness* of Jesus Christ and the *helplessness* of his own condition, but he saw the *hope* of the Cross. "One of the seraphs flew to me with a live coal in his hand, which he had taken with tongs from the altar. With it he touched my mouth and said, 'See, this has touched your lips; your guilt is taken away and your sin atoned for'" (6:6–7, NIV). There's only one altar I know of where you can have your guilt taken away and your sin atoned for; it's the altar of the Cross.

In an Old Testament sense, Isaiah was coming back to the Cross. The angel took that burning coal and pressed it on Isaiah's lips. That hurt. That was painful. I expect his lips blistered, and he talked differently after that.

When God convicts you and me of sin, it hurts, doesn't it? Especially when we're in ministry and we're preaching to others. When God convicts me of my sin it hurts. But it cleanses. When we're convicted, when we come to the Cross and confess, and the blood of Jesus is applied to our lips, we're cleansed.

Do you need the blood of Jesus applied to you, applied to your lips and what you've been saying, applied to your ears and what you've been hearing, applied to your eyes and what you've been seeing, applied to your mind and what you've been thinking, applied to your heart and what you've been feeling, applied to your hands and what you've been doing, applied to your feet and where you've been going? Do you need to be cleansed by the blood of Jesus? It hurts, but it makes a huge difference. We don't talk the same way after that, we don't walk the same way, we don't think the same way, we don't feel the same way. When we've been cleansed by the blood of Jesus, we are cleansed!

Isaiah, whose eyes were opened to the holiness of Christ and the helplessness of his own condition and the hope of the Cross, came back to the Cross. The Cross he'd been preaching to them was for him. He knew that if God ever called him to service it would not be because he'd been to Amsterdam 2000, it would not be because he'd been to seminary, it would not be because he could dissect the Word of God. It would be because of God's grace extended to him at the Cross.

**Do you need
to be cleansed by
the blood of Jesus?
It hurts, but it makes
a huge difference.**

The Cry of a Broken Heart

Isaiah's heart was broken. I believe his heart was broken when he heard God crying. He heard God crying out from a broken heart, "Whom shall I send? And who will go for [Me]?" (Isaiah 6:8, NIV). The fields are white unto harvest, but the laborers are few (see John 4:35 and Matthew 9:37). People all around are dying and going to hell.

I think Isaiah timidly raised his hand, "God, here I am. You remember me, God. My life has been shaken.

My eyes have been opened; I've seen Jesus in a fresh way. I've seen myself, God. You remember I'm responsible for my sin and I'm ruined by it; I'm no better than the people I'm preaching to. But, God, I've been to the Cross and my guilt has been removed and my sin has been atoned for. God, if You can use me, I'm available." Would you be willing to say, "God, I'm available; I'll go where You send; I'll say what You tell me; I'll do what You want; I'm available"?

God said to Isaiah, "Go and tell this people" (Isaiah 6:9, NIV). "Give out My words." Isaiah asked how long he would be preaching. God said, "Isaiah, you're going to preach until judgment comes or until I take you to heaven. You preach until the day you draw your last breath" (see vv. 11–12). The rest of the book of Isaiah gives testimony to Isaiah's obedience to that command.

Look with me at chapter 7. Do you remember in chapter 1 and 2 when Isaiah, as a good preacher with head knowledge of God's Word, was preaching

God's Word? He said, "Thus says the Lord, thus declares the Lord," and he gave out God's Word? Look at the difference. "Then the LORD said to Isaiah" (Isaiah 7:3, NIV). Isaiah received God's Word personally, and then he gave it out. "The LORD said to me" (Isaiah 8:1, NIV). Again, Isaiah received God's Word personally in his heart, and then he gave it out. "The LORD said to me" (Isaiah 8:3, NIV). Isaiah received God's Word personally in his heart, and then he gave it out, "The LORD spoke to me again" (Isaiah 8:5, NIV). Isaiah received God's Word personally in his heart, and then he gave it out. "The LORD spoke to me with his strong hand upon me" (Isaiah 8:11, NIV). Isaiah received God's Word personally in his heart, and then he gave it out.

See the Difference?

Do you see the difference? It's no longer just, "Thus says the Lord, because I know what the problem is and I know what the solution is." Now it's in his heart, and he himself understands by his own experience what the problem is: he is a sinner. And he understands by experience what the solution is because he has a Savior who has taken away his guilt and atoned for his sin at the Cross. The Word of God now comes into Isaiah's heart, and he becomes the greatest of the Old Testament prophets.

Would you choose to be great in God's eyes? Would you choose to repent of your sin? Would you choose to return to the Cross of Jesus Christ? Would you choose to recommit yourself to preaching God's Word from your heart?

Sin in the Camp

I want to tell you a story from the Old Testament. Joshua was raised up by God to lead God's people out of the wilderness, where they were going nowhere, and to lead them into the Promised Land, that they might possess all He had for them. The first thing they faced in the Promised Land was Jericho, an enemy stronghold. In the power of God they overcame. The walls came down. They were victorious. Then they came to a little town called Ai, just a small town. Joshua sent his troops to Ai, and Ai defeated Joshua's army.

Joshua fell on his face before God. He said, "God, have you saved us just to cause us to live in defeat? You saved us from Egypt and bondage to slavery. Is it so that we might live in defeat?" God said, "Joshua, this is not a time to pray. This is a time to repent of your sin. There is sin in the camp."

Joshua had to get up off his face and search the camp. The sin wasn't obvious. It had been buried under the tent of one man. Nobody even knew it was there except that one man. They had to dig it out and then put it out of the camp before they could go back to Ai and have victory (see Joshua 5–8).

This is my point: Sin in the camp, sin in your heart, sin in your life, buried down deep—nobody knows it's there—will cause you to be defeated in your ministry. It will cause you to be defeated in your preaching. You're not going to have the power to bring people to Christ as God wants. You won't have power to bear much eternal fruit. You'll not be pleasing to God, and you know it. When you put your head on the pillow at night and everything is silent and still, does a memory of some sin fester in your heart—some habit of sin, sinful thoughts, an attitude of sin?

God is saying to you right now, "Repent, confess your sin." Is it jealousy of somebody else's ministry? Is it unbelief? You don't believe God can really use you to bring people to Christ. Is it unforgiveness toward someone who has wronged you? Is it bitterness toward someone who has harmed your family? Is it an unforgiving spirit toward someone who has hurt you? Is it selfishness? Is it pride? Is it lustful thoughts? Is it anger? Is it a critical spirit? Name your sin and confess it before God.

Prayer of Recommitment

Would you in your spirit get alone with God right now? Pray with me:

God, would you take away our superficiality, our shallowness? We don't even know we're sinners, for our pride is keeping us from confessing it before You. God, would You bring to our conscious minds the sin that's buried down deep? Holy Spirit, convict us. And, God, we want to thank You for Your promise that if we confess our sin, if we say the same thing about it that You say, if we stop pretending it's not there, if we stop giving it a different name to make it seem less like sin, but if we confess honestly, sincerely, our sin, You, O God, are faithful and just to forgive us our sin and to cleanse us of all unrighteousness. O dear God, thank You for the blood of Jesus. Thank You for the Cross of Jesus. It's not just for them, it's for me.

I pray You would take us gently by the hand and lead us back to the Cross, and that our experience at the Cross would transform us from being just good preachers who have a head knowledge of Your Word to being great preachers who know Your Word in our hearts, experiencing its power for ourselves.

And so, God, having been to the Cross and having been cleansed of our sin, I pray You would lead us in a deep recommitment to preach Your Word and serve You with all of our hearts. We love You. We commit the thoughts in our minds, the emotions in our hearts, and the decisions that we make with our wills to You in the name of the One who is the Lord, seated on the throne, high and exalted, whose presence fills this place, the angels crying, "Holy, holy, holy." It's in Jesus' name that we pray. Amen.

Anne Graham Lotz

Mrs. Anne Graham Lotz, the second daughter of Billy and Ruth Bell Graham, was born and reared in Montreat, North Carolina, U.S.A. In 1988, Mrs. Lotz established AnGeL Ministries. In 1991, she received an honorary Doctorate of Humanities from King College. She also serves on the Board of Directors for the Billy Graham Evangelistic Association and speaks in many international gatherings. Mrs. Anne Lotz is the wife of Dr. Dan Lotz and the mother of three children.

The Delivery of an Evangelistic Message and the Invitation

Bill Newman

We are here to talk about the delivery of the evangelistic address and the invitation. I love this passage of Scripture: "In the presence of God and of Christ Jesus, who will judge the living and the dead, and in view of his appearing and his kingdom, I give you this charge: Preach the Word" (2 Timothy 4:1–2, NIV). Indeed, it is a solemn charge to preach the message of the Gospel.

We Need Biblical, Positive, Direct Preaching

What sort of preaching is evangelistic preaching? First, preaching in evangelism should be biblical preaching—based on the Word of God. Unless we are preaching the Word of God, we are just another religion in the world.

I remember one time we went into the Central City Lockup in Sydney—that is the jail. There was this young man who was swearing at us, and he didn't want to hear what we had to say. But I got alongside him, and I had my Bible. I said, "Look, would you please read this verse?" So he read it: "For all have sinned, and come short of the glory of God" (Romans 3:23, KJV). I asked, "Does that mean that I've sinned?" He said, "Certainly." I said, "Well, does that mean that you've sinned?" He had to acknowledge he was a sinner. And I showed him one verse after another. A little while later, there we were kneeling down in this cell, with the other guys looking from the other cells, and he was giving his life to Jesus Christ. Why? It was because of the power of the Word of God. We need to be preaching the Word of God.

It is the Word of God that convicts (see Hebrews 4:12). It is the Word of God that enlightens (see Psalm 119:18). It is the Word of God that generates faith in people (see Romans 10:17). It is the Word of God that converts (see Psalm 19:7 and 1 Peter 1:23). It is the Word of God that changes people's lives. It is the Word of God that strengthens and builds people. It is the Word of God that preserves from error, both doctrinal and personal (see 2 Timothy 3:16). "I charge you, before God: Preach the Word" (see 2 Timothy 4:1–2). We need to be preaching the Word of God.

Second, evangelistic preaching needs to be positive preaching. What do we mean by that? As you preach the Word of God, never negate the power of the Word of God. That is why I encourage you to study the Word of God diligently. Don't leap out of a text, but leap into a text. As you are studying that passage of Scripture you are seeing why the Spirit of God put that passage into that context. When you understand that, as you preach the Word of God, you are preaching with the Holy Spirit, because that is the message that the Holy Spirit wants conveyed through that passage. That is why we must diligently study the Word of God. But make it positive preaching.

Third, we need direct preaching. In Australia we like direct preaching. I think that would be the same in your culture as well. We want people to be direct in their preaching, straight to the heart. In Acts it says, "When they heard these things, they were cut to the heart, and they gnashed on him with their teeth" (Acts 7:54, KJV). That is certainly direct preaching. We need to be direct in our preaching.

We Need Sympathetic, Heart-Reaching, Clear Preaching

Fourth, evangelistic preaching must be sympathetic preaching. When Dwight L. Moody was converted to Christ, he used to pack a church pew. Every Sunday he would invite people that he met on the streets, and he would pack another pew. Now it doesn't say this in any of the books, but what I feel is this: Moody might have been sitting down there in the congregation with his friends listening to the preacher. He was thinking, "They wouldn't understand that," or, "That wouldn't get through," or, "That's not communicating." I believe that made him the great preacher that he became, because he was sympathetic to the people he was with.

Fifth, preaching needs to be directed to the heart. In Scripture it says, "Which show the work of the law written in their hearts, their conscience also bearing witness, and their thoughts the mean while accusing or else excusing one another" (Romans 2:15, KJV). That word *conscience* is the human being's heart. You have got to reach the heart, and the evangelistic preacher goes for the heart. You see, the teacher says, "Let us look into the Word." The evangelist goes through the Word to the person's heart. Unless you can reach the hearts of people, you can't fully touch them for Jesus Christ.

Sixth, it must be clear preaching. Study to be clear. Paul says, "That I might preach clearly" (see Ephesians 6:19). Someone said about Billy Graham's messages, "Oh, he's so simple. Anybody could preach that." I said, "Well, have you ever tried?" He studied to be simple. Jesus said, "Feed my sheep" (John 21:16, KJV). Bring it down to where people can feed off it. We need to be absolutely clear in our preaching.

John Wesley would preach to one of the young women who worked for them in their home. He would say, "Now, listen. When I say a word you don't understand, tell me." That is how he learned to preach simply and clearly. And it was the same thing with R. A. Torrey. He had a brilliant brain but he preached clearly and simply. Charles Finney would outline his message to make sure that people heard the message clearly. So preach it clearly.

Preach With Illustrations and Intensity, as Called Evangelists

Seven, preach the Word of God with illustrations. Use word pictures. More and more these days I am taking a story from the Scriptures and progressing through the story, illustrating the Gospel in that way. The Latin word for illustrating is "to let light shine in." That is what an illustration does. I encourage you to develop your illustrations. You will be talking to people and they may just float away a little bit. Bring them back with an illustration, and they will grasp the Word of God. Let them see it in their minds.

Eighth, good evangelistic preaching is intensive preaching. Intensiveness is getting through to people's hearts. Richard Baxter said, "I preach as a dying man to dying men." There can be humor in your message, but people have to sense that there is seriousness too. I love that little saying, "We are proclaiming a living Christ to a dying world." There must be intensity to what we are saying.

> Get aside with God. Get down on your knees. He will place urgency within your heart, a fervent desire to preach the Word of God.

Ninth, evangelistic preachers are preachers called by God. The prophet could say, "The hand of the LORD was upon me" (Ezekiel 37:1, KJV). Men and women used of God have a sense of destiny, of purpose, of meaning to their lives. They know that God is calling them. Get aside with God. Get down on your knees. He will place urgency within your heart, a fervent desire to preach the Word of God. Paul says, "Woe is unto me, if I preach not the gospel!" (1 Corinthians 9:16, KJV).

Preach Spirit-Controlled, Brief Sermons With Authority and Repetition

Tenth, evangelistic preachers are controlled and led by the Holy Spirit. They are sensitive to the Holy Spirit as they preach the Word of God. That is important today. Look at Philip going to meet the man from Ethiopia (see Acts 8:26–39). I was in Ethiopia, and the church is alive and well in Ethiopia today. Philip was led by the Holy Spirit to speak to the Ethiopian.

Eleventh, evangelistic preaching is brief preaching. Get a good start, get a good ending, and keep them as close together as you possibly can. Practice to be succinct. Don't paddle around. As we develop our sermons they tend to get longer and longer. Strive to crystallize what you are saying.

Twelfth, preach with the authority of God. Jesus Christ spoke "as one having authority, and not as the scribes" (Matthew 7:29, KJV). In Australia people are looking for leaders with authority, politicians that sound as if they know where they are going. People want to have a sense of purpose and authority in their lives. When we preach the Word of God we are preaching with authority, because it is the declaration of the Word of God.

The last point about evangelistic preaching is that it must be repetitive preaching. The good preachers know how to say something again and again in different ways. That is the skill that you must develop. How many times did you hear the Gospel, or did I hear the Gospel, before the penny dropped? First you come in this way, then you back out and go in another way. You are bringing the Gospel in through different ways.

Sixty-two percent of all ideas are accepted only after they are presented the sixth time. So here is what happens to an idea without repetition: After 24 hours, 25 percent have forgotten it; after 48 hours, 50 percent have forgotten it; after four days, 85 percent have forgotten it; after 16 days, 98 percent have forgotten it. That is why it is good to have illustrations. I like drama because people can see what is being acted out, and it stays in their minds. Preach in a repetitive way.

Developing an Evangelistic Message

I believe the simplest way to prepare an evangelistic sermon is this: *state, illustrate, apply.* State, say what you're going to say; illustrate; and then apply that to the hearts of people. Here's the best way: introduction; point one—state, illustrate, apply; point two—state, illustrate, apply; point three—state, illustrate, apply; then conclusion and invitation. That is the simplest way you can make a message, but it is probably one of the best.

Here are some keys to developing and organizing your evangelistic message.

Number one: *Does it exalt Jesus Christ?* Always ask that question. "And I, if I am lifted up . . . will draw all peoples to Myself" (John 12:32, NKJV). So we must be exalting the wonderful, precious person of the Lord Jesus Christ.

Number two: *Is the message scriptural?* Start memorizing Scriptures. Bind your message to the Word of God.

Number three: *Is the message soul searching?* Does it really meet human need? Is the message getting through to their hearts?

Number four: *Is the message logical?* Think it through in your own mind before you actually preach it.

Keep it simple. I remember going to Vanuatu to preach. I had worked on my messages. My interpreter said, "Bill, throw out that illustration." I said, "Why?" He said, "Bill, they do not have trains in Vanuatu. That won't work." I said, "Well, it's a good illustration." He said, "Throw it out. It won't work." He kept saying, "Throw that out. Throw that out." After we had been through all my messages, all I had left was the simple impact of the Gospel message. But two-and-a-half thousand people came to Jesus Christ. It taught me the greatest lesson: the power of the Word of God and the impact of the simple Gospel. Dear brothers and sisters, what we must get back to in our preaching is the simple Gospel of Jesus Christ.

When you make it logical and keep it simple, ask the question, "Does it work?" Is this message really working in people's lives? Thank God, the Gospel works. In the hearts and lives of families coming back together, people coming off drugs, the Gospel works. Preach for a verdict. Make sure your message demands that verdict.

Preparing and Delivering an Evangelistic Message

Here are some general suggestions for preparing and delivering an evangelistic address. First, develop your resources by gathering information. Build your library. Read good newspapers. Develop your resources; get material from the Internet. Keep reading all the time. Find out what is the latest situation in the world. Know how you can apply that.

Second, I would encourage you to read the book of Romans. If you want to do the work of an evangelist, know the book of Romans. It is Paul's great treatise on the Gospel.

Third, give your messages good titles. The title is a hook.

Fourth, study doctrine. That is important. A lot of evangelistic preaching is tissue-thin on doctrine. We need to study doctrine.

Fifth, use a little humor. When you go into a different culture, tap into that culture and find out what is humorous in that culture. I am finding it very difficult here because I can't use a lot of my good Aussie jokes! We have people here from other cultures. But use humor.

Sixth, study the sermons of others. Look for other sermons and see what those preachers communicate.

Seventh, preach with enthusiasm. Get excited about what you preach. If you are not excited, nobody else will be. You are serving the Lord! Get excited about it!

Eighth, preach with rhetoric—say different things different ways.

Ninth, find an effective way to keep your notes together. I have my notes in folders, and I use big type. If I go into a situation where there is just a stand and a microphone, with no place to put my notes, I can use little stick-on papers and have a message in my Bible. People think I'm preaching without notes; but the notes are right there, attached to the page of my Bible.

In addition, use tabs in your Bible. As you are moving through your Bible trying to find a verse, you are wasting everybody's time. So use little techniques—it could be slide pins or something else—but be practical with your preaching.

Prepare yourself. Spend time with God. Pray the sermon through on your knees before you get out and preach. Visualize yourself preaching. Listen to tapes of your own preaching. You will hate it, but you are hearing things you are saying which aren't coming over. Get other people to critique you as well. Listen to the tapes and videos of other preachers. Speak to the children. If you can't hold children, you can't hold anybody.

Then study the place where you are going to preach. Make sure the light is on your face and people can see you. A lot of lighting is bad. I came up here earlier, and I moved this stand. It rocks, so I made sure I knew that. I had to prepare things, otherwise I would have gotten up here and been fumbling around, trying to get everything ready. Get a good sound check as well, before you get up to preach.

Prepare yourself. Get serious about preaching, because we are preaching the Word of God. If athletes prepare themselves and discipline themselves, how much more should we, as preachers of the Gospel of Jesus Christ.

Ways to Give an Invitation

Now for the invitation. God's favorite word is *come*. "Come, for all things are now ready" (see Matthew 22:4). "Come now, and let us reason together, saith the LORD" (Isaiah 1:18, KJV). "Come unto me, all ye that labor and are heavy laden, and I will give you rest" (Matthew 11:28, KJV). "The Spirit and the bride say, Come" (Revelation 22:17, KJV). *Come*—that is God's favorite word. C is for children. O is for the old-timers. M is for the middle-aged. And E is for everyone. God wants people to come, so He gives out the invitation.

There are many ways to give an invitation to come forward at the end of a meeting. There is the invitation to the inquiry room, used by C. H. Spurgeon, Moody and others: "The door is open. The light is on and I'll be waiting inside." Or, "Come and see me afterwards. I'll be waiting at the back of the church. I'll have this bit of literature. It tells you how to become a Christian." Or, "Ask me about this card to fill out." Or you can pray with a person where that person is sitting. Just say, "Raise your hand; somebody will come and join you." Make sure that you have some sort of invitation.

I gave my life to Jesus Christ because of an invitation. Did I go forward that night? No. But the preacher gave an invitation and several people responded. I didn't know much about the Gospel of Jesus Christ. But for one week I couldn't sleep at night because it was yes or no—until, at the end of the week, I sought out some people and I gave my life to Jesus Christ. Give the invitation.

We read about Peter preaching, "When the people heard this, they were cut to the heart and said to Peter and the other apostles, 'Brothers, what shall we do?' Peter replied, 'Repent and be baptized, every one of you'" (Acts 2:37–38, NIV). Peter went straight to the point: Repent! Get baptized! Do it now! That was an invitation, and that is what we need to be doing.

How do you give the invitation? I do it this way: I ask people to pray a prayer of commitment after me, while their heads are bowed. I lead them in that prayer, phrase by phrase. I say, "You don't have to pray it out loud. The Bible says, 'Let the words of my mouth, and the meditation of my heart, be acceptable in thy sight, O LORD' (Psalm 19:14, KJV). So God understands what you're praying from your heart." I say, "Pray this prayer after me."

Then, based on the commitment that they have made in their heart, I ask them to make a public declaration. I use Scriptures to back up what I am saying. Jesus said, "If you confess Me before men, I'll confess you before My Father who is in heaven. If you deny Me before men, I'll deny you before My Father who is in heaven" (see Matthew 10:32–33). "Let the redeemed of the LORD say so" (Psalm 107:2, KJV). So it is important to give the invitation clearly.

Be Clear and Courageous With the Invitation

Give the invitation clearly. You must be crystal clear. Give an absolute—don't be hazy in what you are saying to people. Also, the invitation should be given with compassion. Before every meeting I pray for people. I say, "God, help me to love these people. I love them in Jesus Christ." When I get up to preach, that love of Jesus Christ will come through the message as I am preaching to people.

Give the invitation with confidence. You are representing the Lord Jesus Christ. We are His ambassadors. Give the invitation with conviction, courageously. Some preachers will not give invitations because they are afraid nobody will respond. If nobody responds, it doesn't matter. You are not there to produce and manufacture results. It is the work of the Holy Spirit. You are there as a servant of Jesus Christ. So give the invitation with courage!

The invitation should be given courteously. No undue pressure should be brought to bear upon individuals, making them incapable of reaching a rational decision on the basis of their own volition. Respect people. Don't use psychological tricks, but depend on God and the power of the Holy Spirit. Say, "Lord, work through me, please, as I give this invitation."

> **You are not there to produce and manufacture results. It is the work of the Holy Spirit. You are there as a servant of Jesus Christ. So give the invitation with courage!**

Give the invitation earnestly. I find that the average Australian is totally defenseless against someone who is sincere. Give it earnestly, from your heart. You believe it—that is coming through. Give it with empathy—realizing where they are. Here is a man whose marriage has just split up. Here are young people on drugs. Give the invitation with empathy.

Give the invitation with expectancy, too. The angels are standing back with bated breath. "According to your faith be it unto you" (Matthew 9:29, KJV). A man came up to Charles Spurgeon one time and said, "Mr. Spurgeon, how come people don't come to Christ when I preach but they come to Christ when you preach?" Spurgeon replied, "Surely, young man, you don't expect people to come to Christ every time you preach, do you?" The young man replied, "Well, no I don't." Spurgeon said, "Well, that's the very reason." Give the invitation expectantly. You are trusting that God is going to work, and people are going to come to Christ.

Give the Invitation with Integrity

The invitation should be given firmly—no fumbling or timidity. Give it straight, but give it in a friendly manner, gently. The invitation should be given honestly. Don't say, "Now we're going to sing another six verses," after you have said you are going to conclude.

The invitation should be given with absolute integrity. Be clear with them. Say, "I'm going to ask you to come down one of these aisles and stand facing the platform." Go through what you are going to do. For example, say, "Some of our Christian workers will come and stand with you," so they know that people are going to be coming. "I'll have a short word of prayer with you. We won't keep you long." Get rid of the problems that are in their minds: "But I've come on a bus." Tell them, "The people that you've come with, they'll wait for you." Get rid of anything in their minds which may hinder them from coming. Make sure that your building is set up so people can respond easily. I go to an auditorium early and make sure we don't have big, long rows, which make it difficult for people to get out of their seats to an aisle and walk forward. Make sure it is easy for them to respond.

Give the invitation with honesty. Give it with absolute integrity. Give it naturally. Give it optimistically. You are trusting God for things to happen. In addition, give it in a pleading sense. Paul says, "We beg you, we urge you. Be reconciled to God" (see 2 Corinthians 5:20). The invitation should be given positively—not, "If there's someone here present, perhaps you would like to come," but, "Now, as we sing this song, people are praying; I'm going to ask you right now to come down here and stand for Jesus Christ."

The invitation should be given prayerfully. Ask people to pray as you give the invitation. We, in our ministry, have intercessors praying behind the platform. They are covering us with prayer, and we are praying as we give that invitation.

Then, too, in a gentle sense, give the invitation repeatedly. You may have to explain it again. You don't have to give it the same way every time. Be resourceful as you give the invitation. Quote a Scripture here and there. Give it thoroughly. Sometimes we stop too soon. Be sensitive to the Holy Spirit. There is urgency to the Gospel. Give the invitation vigorously. Be your best physical self when you are giving the invitation.

Sometimes you might give the invitation, too, for those who are Christians but need to be brought closer to the Lord. I think there are about 40 people on the mission field today because of the Crusades along the northwest coast of Tasmania where they made a recommitment to the Lord Jesus Christ. After Billy Graham preached in Sydney, the numbers going through theological college and others that went into the ministry were incredible.

So, my friends, preach a living Christ to a dying world.

Bill Newman

Dr. Bill Newman is an Australian evangelist who brings over 20 years of experience in preaching the Gospel. He is the president of Bill Newman International and is the author of several books on evangelism and Christian living. As an interdenominational preacher working with leaders of many churches, Dr. Newman has become a world-renowned Christian statesman endorsed by many government and civic leaders. Dr. Newman and his wife, Dorothy, have two sons and live in Queensland, Australia.

Preaching Christ
in a Broken World

Video: Rosario Rivera, Peru, and Sukrit Roy, India

They walk among us. Their eyes tell of pain and hopelessness, emptiness and broken promises. These are the people of our society who are lost. God has called the evangelist to preach the Good News to all people so that they may be healed from brokenness. In Lima, Peru, Rosario Rivera has devoted her life to helping the poor and needy in her country.

But Rosario used to live a different life. Years ago she was a member of a violent revolutionary group in South America. After hearing Luis Palau preach and through reading portions of the Bible, this hardened soldier put down her weapons and took up the Cross. Rosario could no longer deny the truth of the Gospel, and she embraced the love of God. Today Rosario helps the less fortunate in Peru, knowing that Christ is the most powerful One in her life.

She tells us: "I was a revolutionary. I remember what our leader told us: 'Be honest, be loyal, and above everything else be revolutionaries. If you seek the truth, the truth will find you.' I remembered those words. That is what I lived by. And when I read the Bible for the first time, God used my own words as ammunition. Some say that a terrorist or a revolutionary will not be dissuaded. The only weapon that can dissuade him is the Christian faith and the love that a Christian is willing to give."

In Calcutta, India, 15 million people crowd the busy streets. Although this is a place where major religions converge and coexist, Calcutta is also symbolic of a world broken without Christ.

In Calcutta, the compassion of Christ's love is expressed through Sukrit Roy. He says, "In India there are so many people who don't even know what a church is. When you go to a village and say, 'Is there any church?' people think it is a hospital or something else. They don't know. They do not even hear the name of Jesus. If nobody goes to preach the Gospel, how will they hear? If they don't hear, how will they believe? Calcutta is an unreached city. Fewer than 0.7 percent of the people know the Lord.

"But in this city people are eager to listen. There is a search for divine things. If we go with the Gospel, I believe that hunger will be met. The Lord has given me a definite call to take this Gospel to our people that they may know the Lord and they may come to the house of the Lord. We need prayer so we can give them the Gospel, so we can do outreach programs on the street corners and also personal evangelism. Through that we can reach them. Today we see the

Gospel going to different corners. Men and women are coming to the Lord. New churches are being planted."

Rosario Rivera and Sukrit Roy

Rosario Rivera was formerly a terrorist/revolutionary in Peru. Since becoming a Christian she has devoted her life to the poor and needy in Lima, Peru. Rev. Sukrit Roy directs a multi-faceted mission in India that uses many different methods to reach people for Christ.

Rosario Rivera   Sukrit Roy

Preaching Christ in a Broken World

George Carey

My theme is "Preaching Christ in a Broken World." You know, I find it ironic and deeply relevant that we are meeting in Amsterdam. Many of you know that Albert Camus' great book *The Fall (La Chute)* is set here in this city, and it is a disturbing book. It opens in a bar in a murky harbor area of Amsterdam, amidst an atmosphere of total despair. The central character, Jean-Baptiste Clamense, a self-described "judge-penitent," tells the story of guilt, of humankind and his own guilt, because he was able to stop a woman from committing suicide in the Seine, but he didn't. One thing that Camus was quite convinced about was the fallenness of humankind and the helplessness of everybody.

Yet Albert Camus tries to find the reason for it by stressing the value of morality in the face of weakness, of human weakness. Jean-Baptiste Clamense, addressing his friend, says, "For anyone who is alone, without God and without a master, the weight of days is dreadful."

That is Camus' conclusion. For the fascinating and disturbing thing about Camus' book is this: Accurate though his description of the brokenness and fallenness of humankind is, he has no real answer because for him there is no savior, no redeemer, no solution to the weight of guilt and the burden of despair. Camus is not alone in seeing the human condition in that way. That is why, in this address, we must give due weight to the two poles of the title: preaching Christ and broken world.

Definitely Fallen but Always Loved

So let's look, first of all, at our world. It is a wonderful world. It is a beautiful world. It is God's world. And no true Christian ever despises the world. We love it. We exult in it. We cherish it. And we love humanity made in the image and likeness of God. Fallen? Yes, definitely fallen, but always loved by almighty God and, therefore, humanity should be loved by us as well—always open to new possibilities, always open to redemption and God's surprises.

But alongside the beautiful world that God has created, we know the world is broken. We know it, and the most skeptical and irreligious person alive knows it too. Not for nothing did that brilliant man Sir Isaiah Berlin speak of "the broken timber of humanity." He knew that the magnificent capabilities of human nature had been shattered as he surveyed the world around him. But he, too, had no answer. All that he could say, in an affirmation of agnostic liberalism, was that no one discipline, no one religion had the answer. Yet from a

Christian perspective, that analysis is deeply flawed because the brokenness of our world goes much deeper than that.

Three Graphic Pictures

Romans 5 speaks of sin and the depths of sin, the brokenness and despair of sin, and at the same time God's amazing answer in Jesus Christ, His gift. Sin is described by Paul in three graphic pictures: sin enslaves, sin kills and sin reigns. In fact, the verb *basileuo*, meaning to reign, occurs five times in this passage. Three times it is used of the reign of sin, a tyrant, holding mankind subject. And twice it is used of the reign of God's people, reigning in life through Christ's victory on the Cross. The Kingdom language that Paul uses depicts a world in which evil is triumphant. It reigns as a tyrant unless Christ's victory is known and accepted and received.

So as we look at the world around us, we are in no doubt whatsoever about the destructive power of sin. We look around and we see sin's enslaving, reigning and death-producing power. Well did the Catholic writer G. K. Chesterton once say that of all doctrines "the doctrine of original sin is the only directly observable Christian doctrine." You can see it all around us. It is self-evident.

Yet, the reign of sin disguises itself and seeks to shift the center of attention elsewhere. So while the predicament of human nature is so clearly shown in our powerlessness over wrongdoing, we try to shift the blame. We try to find saviors elsewhere, but they are no substitutes for Christ. They are false gods.

As I see it, my culture, Western culture, is obsessed with three alternative "saviors": therapy, education and wealth—among many others—none of which can provide a lasting solution to our broken world.

Three Alternative "Saviors"

Let's look at them. First is therapy. Our society is fascinated by the healing of the body and the mind. The unspoken assumption is that if we keep in tune with the well-being of our inner selves, all will be well. Now, let me make this clear: There is nothing wrong with many therapeutic practices. After all, Christ is the supreme example of a whole person, at one with Himself. Yet therapy easily fails to face up to the reality of sin in our lives.

When therapy replaces faith and when therapeutic techniques are seen as the total answer to humanity's needs, another idolatry is introduced. That idolatry reveals itself when it replaces the Gospel by focusing on *my* needs, *my* happiness, *my* desires, *my* fulfillment. Christ the Savior is replaced by Christ the counselor. Listen to many sermons today and you will find, almost innocently, a therapeutic approach replacing a savior. Missing is that true understanding of the holiness of God that Romans 5 talks about, and our need for salvation.

The second idol that our world introduces is that of education to somehow answer the brokenness of our world. Now, there is a very proper focus on education in all our societies, and we agree. Throughout the world today the Christian church is entering into education and providing resources, as we have done for hundreds of years. But when education is seen as the answer to the problems of the human race, then very serious troubles and questions begin.

Indeed, we ask: Why is it that in spite of universal education in many countries today there is still such crime, vandalism and a breakdown of family life? Why is it that so many terrible atrocities have occurred in advanced societies? Why is it that education does not meet the loneliness of the human heart and the feelings of guilt? When education is introduced as an alternative to the Gospel, it introduces a different kind of savior—an enlightened teacher—and the early church knew all about that. It was called gnosticism. It was as imperfect then to address the true nature of the human heart as it is today.

What about the other pseudo savior: wealth? I don't want to be heard as denying the obvious benefits of wealth and of what riches bring. After all, without wealth-creation, societies cannot prosper. Without wealth-creation, poorer countries cannot receive. But neither should we underestimate the power of money to corrupt. It is a false god when wealth, riches and temptations become the ultimate aims of life. And, you know, in church life we know of the insidious temptation of money. Think of the number of televangelists for whom the lure of money has become an inescapable part of the Gospel. Think of the rise of prosperity "gospels" which have lured poor people to a false faith based on the promise of a good life or riches. It is called a "cargo gospel" in some parts of the world—"If you believe in Jesus, you, too, will be prosperous and will succeed." And it may sound like good news, but the Good News we preach is good news in which a Cross is central. Despite the attractions of wealth, it cannot solve the problem of humanity, the problem of the human heart. We need a better savior.

> **Our task is to address this world with a true analysis of its problems, and to enable our fellow human beings to discover a true solution found in Jesus Christ.**

Change the Human Heart

The three gods I have mentioned—therapy, education and wealth—are but three of the powerful defenses that human nature sets up to avoid the reality of brokenness, which the Bible calls sin—sin which enslaves, sin which kills, sin which reigns. The human heart must be changed.

Yet even in the Church we shy away from that analysis. If we consider our world at the beginning of the 21st century, our world seems out of tune with the Christian analysis of the human condition. You will find people agreeing with you in your societies, "Yes, no one is perfect. All are weak. We all fall short of our ideals." Everyone will agree with that. But people want to find solutions elsewhere. Man has put his trust in man and seemingly has not been disappointed. He trusts in wealth or in health. He believes that through universal education all our problems will be eradicated. That is a road to nowhere other than despair.

You see, our task is to address this world with a true analysis of its problems, and to enable our fellow human beings to discover a true solution found in Jesus Christ. So if we are going to preach Christ to an oh-so-broken world, then we need to ask two further questions: What kind of savior does this world need? And, secondly, what kind of church can bring this savior to our world?

What Kind of Savior?

What kind of savior does our world need? It could easily be deduced that the only savior that Christians can bring to our multicultural, many-religioned world is our contribution to the marketplace of religions—an understandable Christ, a tolerant Christ, a cheerful Christ who doesn't make too many demands on people, a Christ who simply came to make a "contribution to the religious storehouse of mankind," as Visser't Hooft once described such pluralism.

But that is not the kind of Christ described in Romans 5. Paul speaks in the most outrageous terms of Christ—as the universal Savior from sin, as God's gift to us all, and as the One through whom a new reign has begun. The relevance, my brothers and sisters, of the Christian Gospel lies not simply in the experience of renewal—because, you know, many, many other philosophies offer that—but in the incomparable person of Jesus Christ. There must be no apology for preaching what the theologian Hans Frei refers to as the "unique identity" of Jesus Christ. Churches fail and preachers fail when we cease speaking of what the theologians call the singularity of Christ or the "scandal of particularity": that in this man Jesus Christ, God has appeared for all humankind.

I want to state this in even stronger terms. When Christians and churches depart from a committed faith in Christ, who was not only an incomparable teacher and visionary leader, but the One whom God raised from the dead and who is the only Lord and only Savior—when we depart from that, we depart from the throbbing heartbeat of authentic Christian faith, earthed in the New Testament and anchored in the creeds of the church.

This is the Savior who came to our world two thousand years ago. And this is the Savior that our world needs to hear afresh today.

I come as a person born and bred in a working-class district of East London. My parents had nothing to do with the Christian faith. But God broke into our family in a most remarkable way. That testimony continues to this day. And as Archbishop, I am privileged to see God at work in so many different parts of the world as well as in my own country. Every week people tell me of how God has come into their lives. One is humbled by such testimonies of God's love, pointing to the Savior our world so desperately needs.

The Christ We Follow

But it would be wrong to conclude that this emphasis upon the particularity of the Gospel, on this person who is God's unique revelation to us, leads to a bigoted, narrow and dogmatic message that we thrust down people's throats. Of course not. The Christ we follow is One who allows people to think, argue, dispute and doubt. Authentic Christianity is not afraid of scholarship or the critical study of Scripture. The true evangelist, the devoted pastor, has everything to gain by helping people to explore their questions. We know the lasting benefit that comes from listening and wrestling with difficulties, because a strong faith has deep foundations.

Max Warren was one of the great English missionary leaders, and his words still ring true today. He said, "If the Cross stands at the center of history, as Christians believe, if it is the central key to understanding the nature of God, the dilemma of man, the mystery of life and death, then we have to expound its meaning as the way in which all men are meant to live and die."

So what kind of savior does our world need? The same One whom the apostles wondered about and the church has taught down the centuries: the Christ who saves us, liberates us and reigns in us. If your church or my church departs from that faith and that Gospel, then that church might as well shut up shop at once because it will have no Good News to share.

What Kind of Church?

But the second question is, What kind of church can bring such a savior to our world? The first World Council of Churches met here in Amsterdam in 1948. And we have made much ecumenical progress since then. Of course, there are still many differences that keep us apart. How we long to see churches transformed into authentic bodies reaching out in love and service and witness to the world around us. How can we work in unison with the Holy Spirit to revitalize our churches? I want to offer you four points.

Partnerships Based on a Common Faith

First, we must welcome and accept new ecumenical partnerships based on a common faith. I have been struck during my time as Archbishop that the real fissures, the real chasms, that seem to run through all mainstream churches today are fissures not of churchmanship but of belief. And indeed, the real dividing line has to do with the Savior we proclaim.

Do we or do we not truly believe in a God who has revealed Himself as Father, Son and Holy Spirit? Do we or do we not believe that the Christian revelation is for everybody? Do we or do we not believe that the Scriptures are God's timeless revelation of His love? Do we or do we not believe that the same Scriptures declare to us God's moral demands about how we should live and conduct ourselves?

My tradition has always given a welcome place to a godly liberal tradition that accepts the faith of the Church. But I believe that the truly worrying dilemma today is a radical liberalism that denies the truth the Church has borne witness to down the centuries. That is an enemy to us all. Such an approach denies or undermines the authority of the Scriptures, which for two thousand years has been the base of historic Christianity. Those same Scriptures contain the foundational truths of our faith, and we depart from them at our peril. To make human judgment the arbiter of whether or not we accept the faith of Jesus Christ is, in my view, to cut oneself adrift from authentic Christianity.

But this is not to retreat into a dogmatic, anti-intellectual fundamentalist creed. I am all for biblical scholarship. I am all for the need to wrestle with intellectual questions. If Christ is the truth, then His followers have nothing to fear from truth. Nevertheless, our commitment to the authority of Scripture as an indispensable and reliable witness to God's will, and His definitive revelation in Jesus Christ is a fundamental plank in not only evangelical Christianity but historic and traditional Christianity as well. That is why I want to say to evangelicals, "Let's seek new partners in the vital struggle to share a common faith to our world."

> Scriptures contain the foundational truths of our faith. . . . To make human judgment the arbiter of whether or not we accept the faith of Jesus Christ is, in my view, to cut oneself adrift from authentic Christianity.

Understand Our Cultures

My second point is this: We must seek to promote an effective evangelism rooted in the culture of those to whom we speak. Churches die, and even evangelists die, when they lose touch with the communities in which they are situated. So I believe that you and I need to understand our cultures, to find what makes them tick, what they value most, what they are most concerned about, what they fear most in life.

In England a recent television survey revealed that the majority of people in Britain these days do not describe themselves as religious but they describe themselves as spiritual. The majority say they believe in God and they pray. And this finding has been echoed in a report I read in *Le Monde* that says that on the Internet there are no less than 170,000 pages—note the word *pages*—170,000 pages which contain the word *God* and offer spiritual guidance. That does indicate we are living at a very interesting time in world history.

I find the confession by so many people in my country that they are "spiritual" very interesting and hopeful, because in one sense I am not particularly religious. There is much in institutional religion that makes me impatient. I, too, am a spiritual person for whom Christianity is more than a religion. It is a way of life. It is a philosophy of life. It is following a Savior. It is walking with Him. And He takes us into risky situations. Yes, we know that a lot of people are put off by institutional religion. It doesn't seem to offer a way in for them. Their interests—our friends out there in the world—their interests lie in sport and fun and art and theatre and nature and books and good food. And as I read that out, there is nothing in that list which is alien to me or to you.

I don't plead for a religionless Christianity, but I do plead for a rooted faith, an incarnational faith which is in touch with life, which endeavors to understand the concerns and interests and needs of the people we serve, and which can make the Christian faith accessible.

While church life must be rooted in culture lest it run the risk of irrelevancy, we must never be taken over by our culture and controlled and shaped by it. The Gospel challenges sinful structures, evil and wrong structures, and the Gospel seeks to shape culture according to the values and norms of the Christian faith. There are times—and perhaps this is true of your situation and your culture, but I believe it is going to be increasingly true of my country and the Western world—when the Church will seem to be increasingly an alternative culture to those around us.

Related to the Whole of Life

My third point is a development of the last one: Effective evangelism is related to the whole of life. I believe we need to foster patterns of church life that can help evangelism to take place. In my country, for much of this century, evangelicals have been accused of neglecting social and political concerns. Well, now, that is a very surprising and sad criticism when you think that many of the reformers, such as Wilberforce and Shaftesbury and others, were actually evangelical.

If, as Christ said, "By their fruits they will be known" (see Matthew 7:16–20), then authentic witness is as much communicated by loving, faithful action as it is by loving, faithful preaching. Now the word *relevance* has to be used with care. But I believe that if a local church is not relevant to the culture and community in which it is set, then we are falling a long way short of Christ's desire for His people.

Evangelism and Worship

The fourth thing is that if we're thinking of ways in which the church can be changed to be more effective in proclaiming our Savior, then I need to touch on worship. Evangelism at its very heart is the natural response of believers and congregations in love with and on fire for Jesus Christ. Such joy and enthusiasm, when it is reflected in worship, is one of the most potent channels of evangelism. It should never be said of church worship that it is boring. Christ was never boring!

Those of us who come from traditions where liturgy has a central place must pay particular attention that liturgy doesn't become a straitjacket that confines our worship. Liturgy can become a framework that stops the Holy Spirit working in His people.

But let me add another health warning. Nonliturgical worship has its problems in a different kind of repetition. It may lead to a different kind of deadness. I mean, after all, a hymn sandwich is not necessarily any more attractive than a Eucharist or morning and evening prayer.

But this is the point I want to make: Where churches come to life, worship comes to life. And through passionate preaching, through joy and testimony and wonderful singing—hymns ancient and modern—others may be brought to faith.

Thrilling Times for Any Christian

We live in very uncertain times, but I believe they are thrilling times for any Christian to be alive. The Christian faith is as relevant today as it has ever been, and the need for a Savior is more urgent than ever.

The first Archbishop of Canterbury, Augustine, was a missionary. He came to the English shores in 597 with a group of 40 other monks. He didn't want to come to evangelize the English. He was afraid of them. Sometimes it can be a dreadful thing, and he backed away at one particular point. But he came and he stayed and he prayed, and he saw God at work.

My brothers and sisters, God has called you. God has named you. God has blessed you. And now it is our exhilarating task to be faithful to Him and to share His liberating, life-transforming message with others. May God bless you in that task.

George Carey

The Most Reverend and Right Honorable Dr. George Carey has been Archbishop of Canterbury (Anglican Church) since 1991. Born in Bow, London, England, he was educated at London College of Divinity and Kings College, London, England. He is the author of numerous books, and the contributor to several journals and publications. Dr. Carey and his wife, Eileen, are the parents of four grown children, and they live near London, UK.

The Invitation
Video: Billy Graham

"For God so loved the world, that he gave his only begotten Son, that whosoever believeth in him should not perish, but have everlasting life. For God sent not his Son into the world to condemn the world; but that the world through him might be saved" (John 3:16, KJV).

God has not come to condemn us. He's come to save us because He loves us. We need to open our hearts to Him. When my two sons were little, I was walking along the road with one of them, and we stepped on an anthill. We looked down and there were a lot of little ants crawling around. Some of them were wounded, many of them had died, and my son said, "Wouldn't it be wonderful if we could go down and help those ants, rebuild their little house that we destroyed?" I said, "It would, but we're too big and they're too little! We couldn't communicate with them."

He thought about that a moment, then I tried to give him a spiritual lesson from the Bible. I said, "God looks at us, and we're just little ants crawling around on this little dust out here in space called the 'earth.' And God wanted to communicate with us that He loved us, that He was willing to pay a price in order for us to be saved to spend eternity with Him, and to change our lives here and give direction to us, and bring a joy and a peace and a happiness to our lives."

You know what God did? God became a man. And that's who Jesus Christ was—the Son of the Living God, born of the virgin Mary. God took the initiative in giving Christ. Christ took our sins on the Cross. The Bible says that Jesus was made to be sin for us.

Think of it, Jesus was made to be sin! He became guilty of adultery. He became guilty of murder. He became guilty of everything that you and I have ever done or ever thought. "The LORD hath laid on him the iniquity of us all," the Scripture says (Isaiah 53:6, KJV). First Peter 2:24 says, "Who his own self bare our sins in his own body on the tree" (KJV). Peter says Christ also suffered for sins, the just for the unjust. He took your place and He took my place. I deserve hell. I deserve to go to the judgment, but I'll not be there. Don't look for me because my judgment was taken by Christ on that Cross.

Jesus didn't stay on the Cross. They brought Him down from the Cross and they buried Him, but on the third day He rose from the dead. He said, "I am the resurrection, and the life: he that believeth in me, though he were dead, yet shall he live: and whosoever liveth and believeth in me shall never die" (John 11:25–26, KJV). The Bible says, "If thou shalt confess with thy mouth the Lord Jesus, and shalt believe in thine heart that God hath raised him from the dead, thou shalt be saved" (Romans 10:9, KJV). Have you done that? Are you sure of it?

The Bible also says that Jesus Christ is coming back to this earth again. Someday we're going to have universal peace. All the armies and all the armaments will be gone. Christ will reign and you and I will reign with Him and with the angels of heaven, if we know Christ.

Billy Graham

Dr. Graham founded the Billy Graham Evangelistic Association in 1950, which headquarters in Minneapolis, Minnesota, U.S.A. Dr. Graham and his wife, Ruth, make their home in North Carolina, U.S.A.

The Evangelist Proclaims That Jesus Christ Is the Only Way and Calls for a Response of Faith

Ajith Fernando

The question of the uniqueness of Christ is a very important topic because there is much hostility to this doctrine in the church and outside. Pluralism is the dominant approach to religion in most countries of the world today. And according to pluralism, all religions are more or less equal, and you cannot say that one way is supreme and the only way to salvation.

In many countries, when we talk about the uniqueness of Christ, people remember the colonial era when so-called Christian countries said that they were unique and supreme and they dominated us. Now, when we are being involved in evangelism, people are saying that a new colonialism has come and people are trying to dominate again.

And then there is what people are calling "fundamentalism" among Buddhists, Hindus and Muslims. For them—for the fundamentalists of those other religions—evangelism is dangerous and must be stopped. In fact, even in the church some people are embarrassed by the claim that Christ is unique. So it seems as if much of the world is hostile to this doctrine.

A Doctrine That Shines Through the New Testament

This is, of course, a very wide topic. There's a lot that can be said. But I want to highlight a few important issues that affect us as we share the Gospel of Jesus Christ. First, I want to give you three very common texts. Now this is not to say that the doctrine of the uniqueness of Christ is built on just a few texts. It is a doctrine that shines through the New Testament. Almost on every page you see this doctrine presented.

But the three passages I want to read are John 14:6, "I am the way and the truth and the life. No one comes to the Father except through me" (NIV); Acts 4:12, "Salvation is found in no one else, for there is no other name under heaven given to men by which we must be saved" (NIV); and 1 Timothy 2:5, "There is one God and one mediator between God and men, the man Christ Jesus" (NIV).

The Only Way to Fulfillment

John 14:6 gives us a comprehensive case for the uniqueness of Christ. He is the *way*. And as the way, He is unique because only through Him and His work can we find salvation. He is the *truth*, and as the truth He is unique because He alone is absolute truth. In other religions there are truths; there are all sorts of ways that have truths in them. But Jesus alone is absolute truth. He is the *life*. And as the life, He is unique because He opens up for us the way to have life to the full, to experience the purpose for which God made us. He is the only way to fulfillment!

And yet this belief is under fire today. We have a big challenge because there is a different approach to truth in many countries. In most countries, because pluralism is so important, the pluralists say that there is no such thing as absolute truth. What do I mean by absolute truth? What I mean is that there is a truth that is so perfect and so complete that all people everywhere need to submit to it. Absolute truth is for everyone.

But the pluralist says, "No, there is no such thing as absolute truth." We say this is objective truth—that is, I read the Bible; the Bible is the object, I am the subject. And it is objective truth in that it has been revealed by God to us through Jesus, and it is up to us to accept it and to submit to it.

Instead, people are saying that truth is personal; it is subjective. For us Christians, at the heart of truth is the fact that God has revealed something that is outside of us. It is an object that we respond to. So they say that truth is subjective; it has to do with my experience. This was an idea that was very common in the East, but now it is also coming to the West in this post-modern era.

"You Have Your Truth; I Have My Truth"

People are revolting against the idea of having to submit to things outside of themselves, such as scientific laws and the Bible and God. They say that it makes machines and slaves out of us. So they say, "We want to be free." What is important is me, the subject, not things outside of me like the Bible or God. So truth is subjective, they say. It is "personal to my experience. You have your truth; I have my truth. If your truth is good for you, great. My truth is good for me. There is no need to convert others. Don't thrust your religion upon other people." That is what we are hearing today.

But in this environment Jesus says He is absolute truth. All people everywhere need to come to Him and submit to Him. Now Jesus knew that many would not accept what He says. So in John, chapter 14, Jesus gives reasons as to why we can believe that He is absolute truth. He says, as we read in verse 7, "If you really knew me, you would know my Father as well. From now on, you do know him and have seen him" (NIV). What He is saying is that He is equal to God.

Right from the first chapter of John you will find this truth presented: "In the beginning was the Word, and the Word was with God, and the Word was God" (verse 1, NIV). And this is the God who created the universe. He is absolute, God Himself, the creator of everything. Surely then He must be absolute truth if He is absolute God Himself.

Claims That Only God Could Make

Of course, some people object to that statement, and Jesus knew that, too. So He gave evidence as to why we can believe that He is equal with God. In John 14:10, He says, "Don't you believe that I am in the Father, and that the Father is in me? The words I say to you are not just my own. Rather, it is the Father, living in me, who is doing his work" (NIV).

In other words, Jesus is saying, "When you hear Me speak, you should realize that it is God speaking." So when Jesus spoke, His words were divine. He made claims that only God would make. And there is an amazingly large amount of these claims in the Bible, claims that only God could make—that He is the Savior of the world, that He is the judge of the eternal destinies of people, that He is the one who forgives us of sin, that He is absolute Lord.

There was an Asian student who was studying English using the New Testament, and the class was reading the Gospel of John. In the middle of this English class, this student suddenly got up and walked up and down the room. He said, "These are not the words of a man; these are the words of God." When we read the words of Jesus, we realize that it is God Himself who is speaking.

But Jesus knew that some people would reject His claims. In anticipation of that He responded by saying, "Believe me that I am in the Father and the Father is in me; but if you do not, then believe me because of the works themselves" (John 14:11, NRSV). "If you can't believe My words," Jesus is saying, "look at My works." Look at His spotless life. Look at His miracles that are given to prove who He is and the claims that He makes. The supreme miracle, of course, is the resurrection of Jesus.

He Is Who He Claims to Be

When Jesus makes statements that He is absolute Lord of the universe, then, as someone once said long ago (and it has become very popular today), "One who makes such claims should be a liar, a lunatic, or someone who is mistaken, hopelessly deluded. Or He is who He claims to be." As you look at the life of Jesus, you can't say that He is a liar. You can't say that He is deluded, or a lunatic.

The life of Jesus presents us convincing evidence that we should take His words seriously. Today there is a universal recognition that Jesus is a wonderful example for people. If so, we should take seriously what He says. But what is happening is that people simply want to live the life of Jesus apart from the words of Jesus, because they say that although He lived a wonderful life, they don't accept that He is absolute Lord. But you can't separate these two, because He says—not once or twice, but so many times—that His message is an integral part of His life. His life forces us to take His words seriously. There are many people who don't make that connection.

"I'd Better Do Something About This Life"

There was a devout Buddhist in Sri Lanka. After his retirement he would go to the public library in his town to borrow books. Once he borrowed a book about the life of Jesus. After reading that book he realized that this is a life that is unparalleled in history. He knew that he needed to do something about this life. He came to the city of Colombo, which is the capital of Sri Lanka, and across from the railway station in Colombo was a Christian bookstore. He went to that bookstore and said, "I have read about the life of Jesus. It's an amazing life. I want to know more." This man became a Christian. He realized that the life of Jesus was so amazing that "I'd better do something about this life."

The Bible is so clear that Jesus is the absolute truth. How is it that people are rejecting it today?

The Bible is so clear that Jesus is the absolute truth. How is it that people are rejecting it today? I can say many things, but I just want to give you one reason why people reject it. They say that what the Gospels record as the statements of Jesus are not necessarily what Jesus said. They say the Gospels are only what the Church believed about Jesus. The Church believed that Jesus was unique and wonderful, so they put words into the mouth of Jesus. They said, "My Jesus is the only way," so they put words into the mouth of Jesus saying, "I am the way." They said, "Jesus is God," so they put those words into the mouth of Jesus.

In other words, what they are saying is that the Gospels are not historical documents. They say this especially of the Gospel of John, which is such a theological book. They say that because it is so theological, it is not historical. Therefore, they dismiss the statements of Jesus regarding the uniqueness of Christ. They say those words were not spoken by Jesus.

Eager to Write What Really Happened

But if you read the Gospels, you realize that the writers of the Gospels were eager to write what really happened, not just what the Church believed. For example, look at the start of the Gospel of Luke. In Luke 1:1–4, Luke says, "Since many have undertaken to set down an orderly account of the events that have been fulfilled among us, just as they were handed on to us by those who from the beginning were eyewitnesses and servants of the word, I too decided, after investigating everything carefully from the very first, to write an orderly account for you, most excellent Theophilus, so that you may know the truth concerning the things about which you have been instructed" (NRSV). Luke took pains to find out and write what Jesus really said and did.

You know, some people say that the Gospel of John is not a historical book.

But of the four Gospels, John is the one that has the most details about geography, about time, about social and political conditions. Where those details can be checked they have been found to be correct. John was certainly interested in historical detail. In fact, recently some liberal scholars are realizing that John was writing history.

So people say the Gospels do not give us what Jesus said. But the Gospels were written as history. Also, the memory powers of people in those days were much better than ours, because the system of education they had was rote memorizing. So they would memorize whole chunks of material, unlike us, because we are used to television and we have books with us. They considered Jesus' teachings very important, so they would have been careful to memorize what Jesus really said.

People Would Have Known What He Said

The Gospel writers wrote a short time after the events took place. And Jesus was a very controversial figure. A lot of people would have known what He said, and His ministry was done in public, not in secret. If what they wrote was wrong, people would have contested it.

But the debate in the early Christian church was not about what Jesus taught but about the significance of what He taught. They accepted that this is what Jesus taught. The early Christians were very committed to truthfulness. When they wrote the Gospels so soon after Jesus had gone to heaven, surely if there were false teachings people would have said, "This is wrong." But they didn't.

So the way they wrote, the commitment they had, was such that we can believe that they wrote what really happened. What they are saying is that Jesus claimed to be absolutely unique, and He backed that claim with His words. It is wise, therefore, for us to accept that this was truly what Jesus said.

The Doctrine of the Uniqueness of Christ Did Not Develop in the West

Some people are saying today that the doctrine of the uniqueness of Christ was held in the West because the West had only Christianity for so many centuries, and they would hold this doctrine. They are saying now that since other religions have come to the West, Christianity is no longer the only religion there, so you can't hold this doctrine anymore. Therefore, we have to adopt the pluralistic stand.

Well, it may be true that the West had only Christianity for a long time, but the doctrine of the uniqueness of Christ did not develop in the West. It developed in the first-century Roman Empire where, except for the Jews, all people were pluralists. In that pluralistic environment, the early Christians taught the doctrine that Jesus was absolutely unique.

And how about our societies in Asia? We live surrounded by other religions. Where I grew up as a boy, within three houses right around our home there was a Buddhist home, there was a Hindu home, there was a Sunni Muslim home, and there was a Shi'ite Muslim home. All were our neighbors, and we were friendly with these people. But we were faced with the unmistakable teaching of the Bible that Jesus is the only way, and we accepted it. Why did we accept it? Because we believed the words of Jesus.

We Call People to Respond

The Bible says that Jesus is the only way to salvation. If that is true, we should make it our goal to persuade people about the truth of Jesus Christ. In the book of Acts the word *persuade* is used at least eight times in connection with evangelism. What it meant was that you reason with people until their minds are changed and they leave their old ways and come to Christ. Therefore, we call people to respond to the message and come to Jesus.

> Where I grew up as a boy, within three houses right around our home there was a Buddhist home, there was a Hindu home, there was a Sunni Muslim home, and there was a Shi'ite Muslim home.

There are seven evangelistic messages in the book of Acts, and all of them have something about a response to the message—except one which was in Lystra where Paul couldn't finish his message because the people came and gave him problems (see Acts 14:15–19). All the others have something of response. There is a warning, there is a calling to respond in repentance and faith. Twice, even before the call was given the people responded—with Philip and the eunuch (see Acts 8:26–39) and in the home of Cornelius (see Acts 10). We need to call people to respond.

When I was a theological student, I went with my missions professor for a weekend preaching trip. After I finished preaching, my professor told me something that I will never forget. He said, "Ajith, whenever you preach, you must preach for a verdict."

The truth is so important that we must call people to respond, and so we preach for a verdict. What is the verdict that we want? What is the response that we want? The Bible calls it faith. And included, of course, in faith is repentance, turning from our past and entrusting ourselves to God.

In the book of Acts, we read that Peter asked people to "call on the name of the Lord" (Acts 2:21, KJV). In Acts, Paul says to the jailer, "Believe on the Lord Jesus, and you will be saved" (Acts 16:31, NRSV).

You know, I think today in the Church people are getting a little soft on insisting that people have to respond to the Gospel for salvation. People are beginning to say, even in evangelical circles, that people can be saved another way. But Paul is very clear on this issue. He says in Romans 10:13–14, "'Everyone who calls on the name of the Lord will be saved.' . . . How can they believe in the one of whom they have not heard? And how can they hear without someone preaching to them?" (NIV). We must take the Gospel to the world so that people can believe in Jesus.

Now people are asking, "Why is belief so important for salvation? Why is it that calling on the name of the Lord is what brings salvation?" Well, the reason it is so important is that it brings us to the heart of the sin question. Adam and Eve ate of the fruit of the tree of the knowledge of good and evil. When they ate of that tree, what they were saying was, "*We* will be like God. *We* will decide what is good and evil. *We* will save ourselves" (see Genesis 2–3).

The Only Way to Erase the Guilt of Sin From Us

And that is what sin is at the heart. It is independence from God. But we know that we cannot save ourselves. And because we cannot save ourselves, we are headed for judgment, for eternal punishment. But God, in His grace, has provided us a way through the work of Christ. God is offering salvation as a gift. When we accept it, we can be forgiven. We can be justified—just as if we had never sinned—and we can find salvation. And that is the only way to erase the guilt of sin from us. We must accept the message. In other words, whereas once we were independent from God, trying to save ourselves, now we must entrust ourselves to God and say, "God, I can't save myself. You save me. I want to leave my past. Save me."

When we exercise faith, when we believe, we are reversing what happened in the Garden of Eden. We are giving back the fruit of the tree of the knowledge of good and evil. We are saying to God, "You be my Lord. I am tired of running my own life." So faith is the key to salvation. We give up trying to save ourselves. We trust God to do what we cannot do. This is why the Gospel is Good News. Jesus did for us what we cannot do.

The Gospel Says, "It Is Done"

Another important aspect of the uniqueness of Christ is this: Jesus is the only way of salvation. Oh, there are many good things in other religions, but they will not save. As someone has put it, "Religion says, 'Try,' the Gospel says, 'Trust.' Religion says, 'Attain,' the Gospel says, 'Abstain.' Religion says, 'Attempt,' the Gospel says, 'Accept.' Religion says, 'Do this,' the Gospel says, 'It is done.'"

And so we have a message to give to this world: Jesus is the only way to salvation. But we face a major objection when we go to do this. People today say we are being arrogant: "How dare you claim that your way is better than our way," they say. "How dare you say that your ideas are better than our ideas."

Well, I must say, in the first place, that these are not our ideas. This is not just our conviction; Christ is confronting us with it. He presents Himself as absolute, as Lord of the universe. And He is calling us to respond to that truth. The real arrogance is for us humans to reject what the Lord of the universe says about Himself.

It is like an employee coming to work in an office and refusing to accept that the managing director is really the managing director. It's just like that. Who are we to reject what Christ says, so that we can fit Christianity to the mood of our society?

Now I suppose we can understand non-Christians coming up with understandings like that because they don't know. But when we see this coming into the Church, I think it is very serious business. Yet the charge is made that we are being arrogant, and we must respond to it.

It Is Impossible for Us to Be Arrogant

The very nature of the Gospel shows that it is impossible for us to be arrogant. In Ephesians 2:8–9, we are told that "by grace you have been saved, through faith—and this not from yourselves, it is the gift of God—not by works, so that no one can boast" (NIV). Christians are people who have accepted that they cannot save themselves. But they are amazed by the fact that God has had mercy on them. Even our ministry is a result of mercy, not because we deserve to be in the ministry. You see, when we realize this, there is so much amazement that with gratitude we turn our attention away from ourselves to God.

Arrogance focuses on self. Gratitude focuses on another. When we are grateful to Christ for saving us, we can't be arrogant. The Gospel and arrogance are incompatible. But we are thrilled! We are thrilled that God has saved us! We are full of gratitude, so we are excited and we want to share this Gospel with others.

Peter and John said to the Sanhedrin, "We cannot help speaking about what we have seen and heard" (Acts 4:20, NIV). In Romans 1:14–15, Paul says he is a debtor to the Greeks and to the non-Greeks, to the wise and to the foolish. Therefore, he says, "I am so eager to preach the gospel also to you who are at Rome" (NIV).

Why is he so eager? He says, "I am not ashamed of the gospel, because it is the power of God for the salvation of everyone who believes" (Romans 1:16, NIV). He says, "I am not ashamed." Let's put it positively. "I am excited, and that's why I want to preach the Gospel," says Paul. "It's the power of God; it changes people." It is not arrogance that causes us to share the Gospel. It is our excitement over the truth of the Gospel!

That's Not Arrogance. That's Excitement!

Many years ago there was a young, poor boy in a village in England. His father had died; his mother was very poor. The boy had a clubfoot deformity, and it was very difficult for him to walk.

But a friend of theirs in England was a rich man who heard about a doctor who was performing surgery to correct this kind of deformity. So this friend said to the boy's mother, "You hand over your son to me. I will take him to London, and we will look after him. We'll have the operation and have him safely brought back home." And so he went.

She got letters saying that the operation was successful. Finally she received a telegram saying, "Your son is coming on this train at this time." She eagerly went to the station. When her son came down from the train, he said, "Mother, I . . . ." The mother said, "Son, don't say a word. Just walk up and down the platform so that Mother can see you walking like any other boy." So he walked up and came back. His mother said, "Son, one more time, I want to see you walking." So he went up and came back, and now she was ready. The son was able to say what he had wanted to say. And this is what he said, "Mother, I will never be satisfied until you meet that doctor in London. He's the most wonderful man in the world!"

My dear friends, that's not arrogance. That's excitement! God has done something in us, and because He has done something in us, we want to share this Gospel with others.

A Humble and a Holy Life

When we share this Gospel, some people are not going to be convinced. But however difficult they find it to believe in the Gospel, one thing they cannot answer is a humble and a holy life. I feel there is a great call today for us to live holy and humble lives in the world.

The Bible is very clear: Our message is that Jesus is Lord. But the messenger is a servant. Paul says, "We do not preach ourselves, but Jesus Christ as Lord, and ourselves as your servants for Jesus' sake" (2 Corinthians 4:5, NIV). In 1 Corinthians 9:19 Paul says, "Though I am free and belong to no man, I make myself a slave to everyone, to win as many as possible" (NIV).

Jesus Himself was presented as one who took upon Himself "the very nature of a servant" (Philippians 2:7, NIV). I think this is a very important message for us today. It is very powerful in this particular environment. If people see us as servants, it will be difficult for them to attack us when challenged to consider the Gospel.

What if large numbers of Christians adopt a style of loving servanthood? Oh, at first people may laugh at us. In fact, they may exploit us. But soon they will be forced to take note. They will note the power of this life, and their hostility will be reduced. And they will become more receptive to the Gospel. Jesus says, "Let your light shine before men, that they may see your good deeds and praise your Father in heaven" (Matthew 5:16, NIV).

We Have Found the Answer. Now We Have to Share It

Once I was traveling by train to a Buddhist village. I was seated next to a Buddhist, and he knew I was going to preach the Gospel. He said, "Why do you people try to change our religion? Why can't you help Buddhists to be good Buddhists and Christians to be good Christians?" I said, "We believe that there is the God who made this world and that this God loves the world. He knows that the world is in a mess, and He has provided an answer to the problems of this world. We have found the answer. Now we have to share it."

If we don't share it, we will be selfish. It would be wrong for us. There is no choice left for us. The Creator has acted to save the world. We have found the message. People without Christ are lost, lost eternally.

We have been entrusted with the message. Let us be faithful! God bless you.

Dr. Ajith Fernando

For more than 20 years, Dr. Ajith Fernando has served as the national director of Youth For Christ in Sri Lanka. In addition to directing the organization in its outreach to young people, he is also responsible for the pastoral care of the ministry's leaders. He presently leads their ministry with drug addicts. Internationally influential on theological issues, Dr. Fernando's responsibilities have taken him to the far reaches of the world; yet, he remains committed to serving in the leadership of a local church. Dr. Fernando and his wife, Nelun, have one daughter and one son. The family resides in Sri Lanka.

How to Effectively Reach People

Video: K. P. Yohannan, India, and Billy Graham

K. P. Yohannan: "The basic element of communicating the Gospel is, first of all, to understand your audience, to whom you are talking. Are you talking to Muslims? Buddhists? Tribal people? Are you talking to people who have a certain type of job, like fishermen? Understand the need of the people, what they believe, their cultural background and their condition. The felt need of people is basic in communicating effectively with people.

"Second, understand your message. Put it in such a way that you don't dilute the beauty of the Gospel, yet you are able to say it in a way that they'll understand. Use the simple, common, down-to-earth language of the people. Read chapter four of John's Gospel. Jesus is talking to this one woman, understanding her need, her situation, not imposing on her, not manipulating her, but basically talking to her as one individual talks to another. Find illustrations from the culture of the people with whom you are trying to communicate. If it's fishermen, talk about fish. If it's people working in the field, talk about the crops. If you are dealing with taxi drivers, find a way to talk about their world. Jesus talked to people using illustrations that they understood. When we run into illiterate people we use flip charts, the life of Jesus made into pictures. And people are able to understand the message."

"The key to communicating the message is the heart. In your mind and heart you need to know where you want people to go and what you want them to be. That is, they need to follow Jesus as Lord, commit their lives to Christ, walk away from everything they are holding on to, and become followers of Christ. You take the elements, feelings, emotions, stories or their felt need, and then use that as a bridge to explain how Jesus is able to meet their need, forgive them, heal them and make them better. Once you do that, then you can say, 'You can ask Jesus to come into your heart.' "

Billy Graham: "I'm always searching for new ways to approach the same message. For example, let's say that I preached a message 40 years ago. I can still preach that same message today but I need a new outline, I need new illustrations. I'm always asking my team members and my friends to please help me with these illustrations. I like illustrations that are fresh and up-to-date. I like to use something that was in the newspaper today or yesterday, or on television, or something that will illustrate the Gospel better. I'm always looking for that."

K. P. Yohannan and Billy Graham
Rev. K. P. Yohannan is the founder and president of Gospel for Asia, which supports over 10,000 church planters in the heart of the 10/40 window. Dr. Graham founded the Billy Graham Evangelistic Association in 1950, which headquarters in Minneapolis, Minnesota, U.S.A. Dr. Graham and his wife, Ruth, make their home in North Carolina, U.S.A.

The Evangelist Communicates Effectively

Gerald O. Gallimore

M ay I ask you to turn with me to 2 Timothy 4: "I charge you therefore before God and the Lord Jesus Christ, who will judge the living and the dead at His appearing and His kingdom: Preach the word! Be ready in season and out of season. Convince, rebuke, exhort, with all longsuffering and teaching. For the time will come when they will not endure sound doctrine, but according to their own desires, because they have itching ears, they will heap up for themselves teachers; and they will turn their ears away from the truth, and be turned aside to fables. But you be watchful in all things, endure afflictions, do the work of an evangelist, fulfill your ministry" (2 Timothy 4:1–5, NKJV).

In these verses, the apostle Paul sets out for us the enormous responsibility and awesome privilege that we have as evangelists. We are called upon to preach the Word, to announce to lost humanity the only saving message, and to be a vital part of preparing the world for the imminent return of the One who will judge the living and the dead. We are to preach the Word in season and out of season. And we are to do that even more urgently because Paul's prophecy has come to pass in our time. The time of unsound doctrine is here and now.

The Same Compelling, Authoritative Marching Orders

The devil has an army of influencers out there promoting unbiblical falsehood on the airwaves, in the classrooms, in the printed media, on the Internet and in the cinemas. I believe, therefore, that the Lord of the church would give to us the same compelling, authoritative marching orders that He gave to the first 11 evangelists. "All authority," He says, "is mine in heaven and on earth. Therefore, go and preach the Gospel to all the world" (see Matthew 28:18).

Just as He sent those 11 back then to change what was happening in their society and to counteract deception and falsehood with the message of His Gospel, so He sends us today with the great liberating truths of the Gospel. You and I are called upon to share the Good News with people so that the power of sin is broken and the promoter of sin and rebellion is defeated. The price of redemption has been paid. Therefore we are called upon to promote the liberating truth that the way to heaven and to peace with God is open, that salvation full and free is available to everyone, and that the grave is no longer a dead-end street but it has become a drive-through.

This, then, is our message. This is the great, exciting, awesome, wonderful, life-changing message that you and I must convey to this post-modern, cyber-surfing, spiritually lost generation. If the 11 were able to do it back in their day, so must we today. If without radio or television or public address systems, or any of the fancy gadgets, motorcars or airplanes available to us today, they were able to evangelize their generation, then so must we. We are called upon to share the message of Jesus Christ.

The Biblical Message That We Must Proclaim

My theme is "The Evangelist Communicates Effectively." In a nutshell, my thesis would be that when, under the power of the Holy Spirit, the message is conveyed by a messenger with credibility and in a manner that is correct, then effective communication will take place. Communication begins with the message. So I want to call your attention to the biblical message that we must proclaim.

This message is the same message that the 11 disciples proclaimed. It is the message of the atoning, redemptive, substitutionary, once-and-for-all work of Jesus Christ, the Son of God, upon the Cross 2000 years ago. You and I have no liberty in the 21st century to change that message, to water it down or to substitute anything that makes it more palatable to modern man. We have one obligation, and that is to proclaim that message. And we must preach it, lest the curse which is there in Galatians 1:8 fall upon us.

It is imperative that you and I come to know this message and know it well. We are to know it in all its fullness. For in this discipline, like any other, competence is vital for credibility and effectiveness. I am not aware of any easy, cheap, instant packaging to competence. We need to remember that the 11 disciples, the early evangelists, spent three years of intense training under the tutelage of the Master. He had classroom instructions as well as on-the-job missions practicum. They followed Him to the Cross, they experienced the resurrection, and they were filled with the Holy Spirit. You and I cannot expect to make an impact on our generation with any lesser qualifications.

We have to spend time with God and time in the Word. For it is time with Jesus and time in the Word that will help us to come to the right diagnosis of the societies that you and I are called upon to serve. Man is lost in his sin. He is groping in darkness, and he is suffering from his estrangement from God.

If we are going to be true to the biblical message in our time, we have to preach the lostness of humanity. And we have to preach further that humanity in its lostness faces great peril. But that is not all we are called upon to preach, for our Gospel is a Gospel of Good News. It is a Gospel of the life-changing, peril-averting, destiny-changing hope in Jesus Christ, and in Him alone.

In my part of the world, as in your part of the world, this kind of narrow concept is unpalatable to modern man. We want to feel that there are many ways to God. But Jesus says He is the way. He is not one among many. He doesn't sit on the same platform with other prophets of the world. He is the only way, and we must not equivocate on this. We must not waffle on this. You and I must proclaim urgently and lovingly, but uncompromisingly, just as Peter did, "There is no other name under heaven given among men by which we must be saved" (Acts 4:12, NKJV). This is the message that we must proclaim. Communication begins with that message.

The Biblical Integrity That We Must Possess

But communication does not end there. It begins with the message. But it must also continue in the life of the messenger. So we look at the biblical message we must proclaim, but also at the biblical integrity that we must possess. The message must be right, but, equally important, the messenger must be righteous. There is no way that we can separate the message from the messenger. If something is deficient in either of these, then we are not going to have effective communication.

You and I have to regretfully and shamefacedly confess that if there is one crisis facing the church today, it is the crisis of integrity. Not too many of us can look at the news on the airwaves or in the printed media or in the magazines that we get without blushing at so many of the accounts of brothers and sisters of great standing who have crumbled because their spiritual innards were eaten out by termites.

Walk Worthy of the Name

There is a great responsibility, for you and me as evangelists, for our lives to line up with the Word of God and with the message that we preach. We have a real crisis here. And I can hear the apostle Paul pleading with us, "I beseech you, walk worthy of the name and the calling that we have" (see Ephesians 4:1). And Peter comes right behind him and says, "Be holy, for the one we serve is a holy God" (see 1 Peter 1:16).

Fundamental to the integrity that we must possess is the fact that we must be converted to Jesus Christ. I hope I don't embarrass any of you to raise something so basic and simplistic, but how are we going to introduce anyone to Jesus Christ if we do not ourselves have a personal experience of His saving grace? No course in theology or in homiletics, no matter how prestigious the institution, will replace this need. No ordination, however elaborate and ceremonial, will replace this need. You and I need to be born again. Jesus said it to a religious leader (see John 3:7). We need to be born again!

I just wonder, could there be somebody like a John Wesley or a Martin Luther here who is ordained yet hasn't come to that place of personal surrender to Jesus Christ? If your heart is not yet surrendered to Jesus, then may I invite you to find somebody and let that person lead you to a saving knowledge of the Lord Jesus Christ.

The biblical integrity that we must have begins with the fact that we must be converted to Jesus Christ. But secondly, we must be committed to Jesus Christ and the cause for which He died. This commitment must be a present-day, living reality in our lives.

I meet too many people for whom it appears that evangelism is kindergarten stuff that they have graduated from. You did that when you were in Bible school, but now you have gone to seminary. You don't bother with this anymore. My brothers and sisters, we need a present commitment to Jesus Christ and to evangelism, not some past tense of what we used to do or what we used to be when we were active in leading people to Jesus Christ. Go back home and be engaged in the ministry of evangelism. Give leadership to the ministry of evangelism. It is the cause for which Jesus died!

Integrity requires not only conversion to Jesus Christ and a commitment to His cause but also it requires that we be constrained by His love. Our strongest motivation must be our love for Jesus Christ. The love of Jesus displayed in His coming from heaven to earth in search of unworthy sinners like ourselves, dying upon that cruel Cross, is that love that must constrain us as we go out to witness to the Gospel of Jesus Christ. Or has something less worthy captured our hearts? Maybe, for instance, it is an infatuation with ourselves, a love of the limelight and hearing the applause of people. Could it be vainglory? Could it be money or self or something else? Are we servants or are we showmen?

This Bible, when studied under the guidance of the Holy Spirit, will reveal to us certain things about communicating the Gospel effectively. You and I need to go back to the Gospels and observe the master communicator, Jesus Christ Himself.

I think about the words of that famous hymn by Isaac Watts, "When I survey the wondrous cross on which the Prince of Glory died, my richest gain I count but loss, and pour contempt on all my pride. Were the whole realm of nature mine, that were a present far too small; love so amazing, so divine, demands my life, my soul, my all." That's it. The love of Jesus must constrain us. It must consume us.

A Biblical Strategy That We Must Pursue

There is a biblical message that we must proclaim and there is the biblical integrity that we must possess. But I submit that there is also a biblical strategy that we must pursue. Gospel communication that is effective requires biblical orthodoxy and a servant who is authentic, with biblical integrity and credibility. But we may have these two pillars and yet fail to communicate effectively.

You see, my brothers and sisters, we have a responsibility to ensure that we convey the message to our audiences in terms understandable to them. We must communicate where they are, in their culture and their circumstances. We must know the political situations and the social realities which are theirs, the national events that are shaping them, their thinking and lives at that moment. We have a responsibility to share the Good News in such a way that it communicates to their hearts.

Communication is more than mere proclamation. As much as you and I are able so to do, we have a responsibility under God to be sensitive to the people where they are. For we have not communicated until we have delivered the message we intended in a way that they understand, thereby giving the Holy Spirit adequate material to speak conviction to their hearts and their lives.

Where can we find the kind of training that will equip us to be good communicators? There are lots of training vehicles available. But I would like to suggest that we hold in our hands a textbook on effective communication. This Bible, when studied under the guidance of the Holy Spirit, will reveal to us certain things about communicating the Gospel effectively. You and I need to go back to the Gospels and observe the master communicator, Jesus Christ Himself. Reach into the book of Acts, look at the epistles, and see the experiences of those that Jesus used to turn the world upside down in that first century. There you and I will learn some important communication principles. One of those principles we will learn is that we need to be creative.

Some of Us Missed the Train Into the 20th Century

May I remind us that one of the names of the God we serve is Creator! When He made us, He gave us a little vestige of Himself. And He has put some creativity in us. Creativity is demanded in every generation. When you look at the world, everything seems to be up for grabs. Few things stay in place for any length of time. Information flows at a rapid pace. By the time technology meets the marketplace, it is already becoming obsolete because some new thing has been invented. You and I must face the fact that if we are going to make an impact on this world, we have to become more creative in our approach.

And that is a real problem, because some of us missed the train into the 20th century. A number of us will have to change a resistant mindset that we have and begin to catch up with reality. Try as hard as we may, we will never turn the world back to the horse-and-buggy days. We have to face it. We are living in a real world where things are happening at an alarming pace.

We Have Got to Be Creative, Contextual, Cooperative and Compelling

If we are going to communicate effectively, we must become *creative* in our communication. We have got to begin to look at what is happening around us so that we can come up with things we might use. New things are not demons for us to exorcise. They are gifts of God for us to use creatively in the ministry of Jesus Christ.

If we are going to communicate effectively, we must be creative. But also we must be *contextual*. Everything gets its meaning within a certain context. It is the context that gives the particular meaning and color to our words and our gestures. When we use words, metaphors, expressions, we may unwittingly be alienating and even frightening some people if our speech is out of sync with the culture and the reality and the circumstances of the people to whom we minister.

We have to learn a new kind of language. Some of us will have to find a whole new vocabulary for the theological expressions that we love to use, like glorification and sanctification and all of those nice-sounding, important theological words. We are going to have to change the Christianese, the evangelical clichés and the churchy jargon that we use if we are going to communicate to the pagans of this world. We need to remember we are not in business to impress the saints. We are in business to communicate to pagans. We have to speak in the language of the people, in the circumstances of the people, bearing in mind where they are spiritually, emotionally and socially, if we are going to communicate eternal truth to their souls.

Jesus Christ is the master at this. Watch Him as He recruits disciples. He says to them, "I will make you fishers of men" (Matthew 4:19, NKJV). Now I can tell you, I'm a fisherman, and that kind of language resonated with those Galilean fishermen. Jesus goes to speak to a group of farmers. He talks to them about sowing and reaping; He speaks about weeds and wheat. He speaks to the woman at the well and talks to her about water. He speaks to Zacchaeus and He uses business terms. He talks to Pilate and He uses political terms. Jesus uses terms that the people He is speaking to are familiar with so that He can communicate with them. And if we want to communicate effectively, we must follow Jesus' example of using language and imagery with which our audience is familiar.

> We have to speak in the language of the people, in the circumstances of the people, bearing in mind where they are spiritually, emotionally and socially, if we are going to communicate eternal truth to their souls.

Watch the apostle Paul on Mars' Hill. He learned something about the culture so that he could find common ground with the people. He even quoted some of their poets. Watch Peter on the day of Pentecost. People were saying, "That's a bunch of drunks; that's what they are." Do you notice how beautifully Peter began with their accusation of drunkenness to teach them lessons about intoxication under the power of the Holy Spirit and then share with them the great Good News of the message of Jesus Christ?

We've got to be creative. And we've got to be contextual. But, my brothers and sisters, it is also true that if we are going to be effective in evangelizing our nations and our communities, we need to be *cooperative* in our evangelism. Jesus had 12 men, and for three years they worked together. Jesus knew the importance of unity. He spoke about it. He prayed in that high priestly prayer that we would be one (see John 17).

We will do more with cooperation than with isolation, more with cooperation than with competition. We need to follow the pattern of the early church. As they were united together, they were able to evangelize Jerusalem and Judea and Samaria and the rest of the world. Together they touched the world. If we are going to have an effective witness, we need to learn the principles of working together.

They Must Sense a Passion

One last thing. If we are going to be effective—creative, contextual and cooperative—we must also be *compelling* in our presentation. We must give evidence of the reality of our concern and the reality of that message by the intensity of our words and our gestures. Men and women need to sense from us that we really believe we are facing eternal peril; we really believe that this Gospel of Jesus Christ is our only means of salvation. They must sense a passion and an urgency coming from our hearts. If we are going to preach this Gospel effectively, we must preach it compellingly. We must teach it with passion and soul-stirring zeal.

I call our attention to the preacher John the Baptist. He was a blazing torch to his generation. No harmless homilies for him; no politically safe message for him. John the Baptist was an exciting, penetrating, pointed preacher as he called men and women to repentance.

Watch the apostle Peter on the day of Pentecost. He was bold and passionate in his presentation. He called men and women to repentance. He told them about Jesus Christ crucified, buried, raised again from the dead.

When you preach the Gospel of Jesus Christ with passion, people will ask, "What must we do to be saved?" I believe that this kind of preaching allows the Holy Spirit to be able to convince men and women that this message is urgent, this message is important and this message is consequential.

But to be this kind of preacher, we have got to spend time with the Master. We must spend time in His Word. And we need the anointing of the Holy Spirit. There is a human-divine drama going on whenever you and I stand up to proclaim the Gospel of Jesus Christ. The Word of God is eternal, but we are dying people speaking to dying people. The Holy Spirit must be involved to take the truth that we proclaim and move it into the hearts and minds of men and women.

I beg of us, before we ever go on the platform to proclaim that Word, could we take time to seek God? Ask Him to touch our lives and give us a new, fresh infilling of the Holy Spirit? Before we ever go on that platform, will we spend time with God? If you are not going to be this kind of preacher, then please get out of the way and leave the pulpit open for somebody who will! I believe before we go on that platform, we must allow the message to flow over our souls until it does something for our hearts. And then, as the recipients of His grace and a channel for His mercy, we can go into that pulpit to share the Good News of the Gospel of Jesus Christ.

If we are going to be effective, communication begins with the message. There is a biblical message that we must proclaim. If we are going to be effective, there is a biblical integrity that we must possess. And if we are going to be effective, there is a biblical strategy we must pursue.

Call for a Verdict

What then must we do to be effective? We must be very clear about our biblical mandate. We must be faithful to the biblical message. We must be holy in our personal lives. We must be cooperative in our evangelistic endeavors. And we must call for a verdict.

We must call for a verdict because there is nothing that keeps our preaching so focused as when we know where we are leading men and women, where we hope to see them go, what we hope to see the Holy Spirit do with their lives. Nothing is so compelling as preaching for a verdict, and no verdict is so compelling as calling men and women to salvation in Jesus Christ.

God help us, then, as we go out, that when the message is conveyed by a messenger with credibility, in a manner that is correct, we will have communication that the Holy Spirit can use to bring conviction to the hearts of men and women and the spiritual results that God intended.

May God bless us and help us to be these kinds of people in the days ahead.

Gerald O. Gallimore

Gerry Gallimore is a 32-year veteran of Youth For Christ International and currently serves as International Ambassador for the organization. In addition to this responsibility, he is pastor of the Metropolitan Baptist Church of Miami, Miami, Florida, U.S.A. A native of Jamaica, Dr. Gallimore left a promising career in business to answer the call of God to full-time Christian service. Dr. Gallimore's speaking gifts and ministerial responsibilities have taken him to over 90 countries; he and his wife, Sonia, are the parents of three children.

Presenting the Gospel to Different Audiences

Robert Cunville

During this seminar on "Presenting the Gospel to Different Audiences," we will seek to find out how to become more effective in communicating the essential principles of the Gospel to the people to whom we witness in our ministries. Although not all of us are involved in worldwide evangelistic outreach, we know that even in a village setting, because of the migration of people from one place to another, the audiences we encounter are made up of different groups. If you are an itinerant evangelist, then you know that your audiences differ from one place to another.

A Look at the Early Church

I want to go back to the Word of God and look at the primary audience of the early Church. In the early days of the Church, Christians were under the impression that only Jews could become members of the Kingdom of God. In Acts 9:20 we read, "And straightway he"—that means Saul—"preached Christ in the synagogues, that he is the Son of God" (KJV). And in verse 22, "But Saul increased the more in strength, and confounded the Jews which dwelt in Damascus, proving that this is very Christ" (KJV). And Peter said, "Ye know how that it is an unlawful thing for a man that is a Jew to keep company, or come unto one of another nation" (Acts 10:28, KJV).

So the Gospel in the early days of the Church was presented to one particular kind of audience, namely the Jewish people. The target audience for presenting the Gospel was very narrow indeed. Had this persisted, it would have been a great tragedy for the nations of the world.

But God redefined the audiences of the early Church. God broadened the target audience for the presentation of the Gospel when He gave Peter the vision that is recorded in Acts 10. The apostles should not have been surprised, for we read that God had already prophesied that the Messiah would be a light of the Gentiles. "I the LORD have called thee in righteousness, . . . and give thee for a covenant of the people, for a light of the Gentiles" (Isaiah 42:6, KJV). This promise of a broad audience for the Gospel of Jesus Christ was given even in the Old Testament. And God brought about the fulfillment of His eternal plan to include even the Gentiles.

This expansion of the presentation of the Gospel to different audiences was also in keeping with the commandment of Jesus Christ to His disciples when He said, "Go ye into all the world, and preach the gospel to every creature" (Mark 16:15, KJV). Later on we find that Paul said, "Is he the God of the Jews only? Is he not also of the Gentiles? Yes, of the Gentiles also" (Romans 3:29, KJV). So as we look to the Bible, which is the authority of our presentation of the Gospel of Jesus Christ, we find that the original target audience was one. But then God, in His omnipotent wisdom, expanded that audience to include the Gentiles.

The Disciples Had to Adapt

As we include the Gentiles, the broad-based target audience, how do we adapt the presentation of the Gospel of Jesus Christ? We begin to notice a difference in the presentation of the Gospel. It was now presented in a way that could be understood meaningfully by the Gentiles. The early disciples had to adapt this change because the Jews had some knowledge of the Bible, while most of the Gentile world had little or no knowledge of the Bible. So the disciples had to adapt to this new phase of presenting the biblical message. In the early presentation, as they presented the Gospel to the Jews the point of contact was this: "The God of glory appeared to our father Abraham" (Acts 7:2, NIV). That presentation of the Gospel was understood by Jewish audiences.

We are taught from the Word of God that as we present the Gospel to various audiences, we have to change the way we present it to have a point of contact.

Later on, as the Gospel was presented to non-Jewish audiences, the point of contact changed. At Lystra, confronted by a totally Gentile audience, Paul spoke only of "the living God, which made heaven, and earth, and the sea, . . . who in times past suffered all nations to walk in their own ways" (Acts 14:15–16, KJV). Paul had to change his point of contact as he preached to the Gentiles in Lystra. And when Paul preached the famous sermon on Mars' Hill in Acts 17, he changed his point of contact so the audience could identify and understand the Gospel. We are taught from the Word of God that as we present the Gospel to various audiences, we have to change the way we present it to have a point of contact.

The Kinds of Audiences in the World Today

I think it is good for us to try and find out the kinds of audiences we have in the world today. Today the Gentile world has become a very complex world. Gentiles belong to different religious and cultural groups. The task today, therefore, has become more difficult. The different audiences we encounter today are religious groups and cultural groups.

Nominal Christians are a chunk of the audiences that we must reach with the Gospel of Jesus Christ. Islam is a large target audience. Buddhism now has a large following. In the land I come from, Hinduism is the dominant religion. Confucianism is found mainly in China and Korea. People who call themselves animists, who live in remote areas of the world, are some of the most receptive people to the presentation of the Gospel of Jesus Christ.

So that is the first chunk of the different audiences that we can divide religiously. Second, we have the cultural groups of people.

Young people are a different cultural group by themselves. Because this audience is very large and vibrant, special attention has to be given to them. This is the first cultural group that we have to face, no matter where we're preaching the Word of God. The second cultural group that we have to face is the secular person. Most of the audiences that we encounter today are made up of persons who either have no idea of God or do not care about their spiritual lives. The secular mind is not against religion. The secular mind leaves God out of religion. That is the difference. Around the world people are religious, but religious without God. That's why we find so many kinds of teachings in the world today.

Then, there are other cultural groups that anthropologists would identify, such as tribal groups or little pockets that are special cultural groups. There are many groups that are unique to certain areas of the world. In India we had a national strategy meeting. One of our brothers got up to give his testimony of what God is doing. He is working with the prostitutes in Bombay. They are one cultural group. There are people who are working with slum dwellers. In South India, there's a brother who's working with the fishermen. They are a particular group of people.

Wherever we are going, we have to adapt to reach out to these cultural groups. That is the scenario of reality around the world. Now, how do we go about it? How do we present the Gospel to these various audiences?

Presenting the Gospel to Various Audiences

I remember the advice I received from an old pastor who has gone to be with the Lord. He said, "Just preach the simple Gospel. That is all you need to do, and you will never go wrong." And, my dear friends, I heed that simple advice every time I stand before people to present the Gospel. The Bible says, "How then shall they call on him in whom they have not believed? and how shall they believe in him of whom they have not heard? and how shall they hear without a preacher?" (Romans 10:14, KJV). There is no doubt that the preaching of the Cross is the power of God (see 1 Corinthians 1:18).

When we look at the life of Paul, we find that he always preached the simple Gospel, and as he did so he explained the Gospel according to the audiences that he encountered. That's why Paul said, "Unto the Jews I became as a Jew, that I might gain the Jews; . . . to them that are without law, as without law, . . . that I might gain them that are without law" (1 Corinthians 9:20–21, KJV). He adapted his presentation. As we proclaim the Gospel, we will have to adapt our presentation of the simple Gospel according to the types of audiences we face.

What Is Heard Is Also Important

So now, how do we communicate the Gospel? As we seek to communicate the Gospel to various audiences, although what we say is important, we must realize that if we are really going to make an impact, what is heard by them is very important. In other words, the presentation of the Gospel is not a one-way street.

My friends, through bitter experience I've learned that we cannot presume that the Gospel we present is heard by our audience and understood by them as we ourselves understand it. So many times we make that mistake. Sometimes we think we must, if we are going to be good evangelists, shout and speak with speed. It is not true. It is not only what we say that is important, but also how our audience hears that is important.

We sometimes have to be prepared to break out from the traditional way of preaching to meaningfully communicate the Gospel to a particular audience. I'll give you an example. George was an Indian Christian who moved from his home in the south of India, where he had many Christian friends and relatives, and went to a northern city in India where perhaps only five or ten people among the half million living in that city were Christians. George, being the fervent missionary that he was, month after month tried to interest his neighbors in Jesus Christ. George told of Christ's atoning death, of the new life that all who believe in Him can receive. But no one responded to his invitation, to his call.

But he did not want to give up. So George decided that he should present the Gospel as simply as possible. He decided that he would select one point and then stress that one point until it was understood. "And only then," he said, "will I move on to another point of the teaching of the Gospel." His beginning point was the new birth. He said, "I'm going to work on that and tell it to my neighbors until they understand the new birth."

What did he do? He invited some of his new friends to a Bible study in his home. And being interested in religion, his friends—though they were Hindus and Muslims and other religions—gladly came to George's house to talk with him about God. George taught "You must be born again" (John 3:7, NKJV). He went on stressing that until he was interrupted by a loud objection from a Hindu friend. His Hindu friend told George, "You Christians—you teach us what we already know. That's exactly the trouble. We know that we must be born again, and we don't want that. We want to be freed from being born again and again and again. You are telling us what we already know and we fear!"

Do you see the point? George was teaching about new life that was eternal. But his Hindu friend heard the condemnation that he was doomed to live on this earth over and over again, reincarnated in different forms.

Same Sermon, Different Impact

Let us be sensitive to the target audience we are trying to reach, and let us try to communicate the Gospel in the way that they will understand. As preachers of the Gospel, we must constantly ask ourselves, "How can I teach the truth so that it will be understood by the audience?" The same sermon can have a different impact on different audiences.

Forgive me for giving an example from my own ministry. I had preached in one place in Indonesia and the response was great. However, I preached the same sermon in another place in Wales and it just seemed as if it fell on stony ground. Why? What went wrong? As I reflected, I realized that I had not taken into consideration the fact that the meetings in Wales were held in a church building. In Indonesia it was held in a soccer field. In the church building the audience was mainly older folks from a closely knit, churchgoing people who were well known to each other. In Indonesia, 75 percent of the people who attended the Crusade were below 35 years of age. In Wales I should have used illustrations that older folks would have identified with. And I should have invited them to a recommitment to the Lord, rather than asking them to come forward, openly repenting before the Cross of Jesus Christ.

Take Time to Know Your Audience

We have to adapt how we present the Gospel and how we give the invitation. We have no control of the audience, but we can certainly control the way we present the Gospel of Jesus Christ.

Take time to know your audience. The best communicators are the ones who make an effort to learn about the audience. If we as preachers never listen, how will we know what to say and how to present the Gospel effectively?

I still remember when we invited Dr. Billy Graham to come to Nagaland in 1972 to preach the Gospel of Jesus Christ. When Dr. Graham came, he knew all about the Nagas. He had read about the Nagas. He knew what we thought. He knew everything about the Nagas. He took time to understand the audience.

When we are aware of our audiences—their needs, their viewpoints and their experiences—then we will know when it is necessary to express the same truth in different ways. God Himself was aware of His audiences. We find in the Bible that different words are used for salvation for different audiences. The new birth, redemption, deliverance, atonement, ransom, reconciliation, are different terms used for different audiences in the Word of God. Although different words were used to suit the various cultural backgrounds of the audiences, the truth of salvation did not change.

The vast majority of Indians are outside the influence of the church, although tradition tells us that Thomas came to India with the Gospel as early as 52 A.D. India is a complex nation as far as people identity is concerned. Living within the same geographical area does not necessarily mean your culture is the same as your neighbor's. Two cultural factors in India are ethnic background and caste. Caste differences separate people from one another and often cause barriers to

> No doubt people are more open to someone speaking the same language and coming from the same cultural and caste background. If, however, we are sensitive to these factors, we, too, can present the Gospel to them.

communication. Although the government is trying to eradicate it, we find caste still playing a dominant role in the lives of the people. The caste system is embedded.

So, in presenting the Gospel in India, we always take notice of the language the audience speaks, their caste or community, and the kind of work they do. These three factors determine the way they will react to the Gospel. No doubt people are more open to someone speaking the same language and coming from the same cultural and caste background. If, however, we are sensitive to these factors, we, too, can present the Gospel to them.

I remember speaking at a mission in Bangalore, India. Although Bangalore is known as the Silicon Valley of India, yet I was told most of the folks living in the section where we were holding this mission were all potters; they made clay pots. I made my sermons very simple, using illustrations from the village life and concluded with the story of Jesus turning water into wine. I used the six water pots to denote the spiritual needs of our lives. That night, when I gave the invitation, we had a great number of commitments.

The Gospel Never Changes

The presentation of the Gospel must be biblical and orientated toward the personal needs of the people. But the Gospel never changes. Although we have seen that the point of contact is changed or adapted according to the types of audiences to whom it is presented, we notice that the core of the Gospel does not change.

"But those things which God foretold by the mouth of all His prophets, that the Christ would suffer, He has thus fulfilled. Repent therefore, and be converted, that your sins may be blotted out, so that times of refreshing may come from the presence of the Lord" (Acts 3:18–19, NKJV). "How that Christ died for our sins according to the scriptures; and that he was buried, and that he rose again the third day according to the scriptures" (1 Corinthians 15:3–4, KJV). This is the call of the Gospel. It is due to the fact that the soul of a man or a woman cries out to God. The desire for God is universal.

Sometimes we think people are not interested in God. But I want to tell you that deep down in every person there is a desire for God. The Gospel offers mankind the only solution. Jesus Christ says, "I am the way, the truth, and the life" (John 14:6, KJV). The Gospel of Jesus Christ never changes: Jesus shed His blood on the Cross for the sins of the world, He rose again on the third day, and we can claim the victory of the Cross by repenting and accepting Him by faith into our lives.

There are two important things we must remember as we present the Gospel to different audiences. Number one, the presentation of the Gospel is always dependent on the authority of the Word of God. Number two, we must focus on the Cross where Jesus died as mankind's substitute for sin. The Cross is foolishness to the ordinary man or woman, but unto them that are called it is the power of God and the wisdom of God (see 1 Corinthians 1:18). My dear friends, no matter which caste or creed or language or social status we preach to, the power of the simple Gospel always fills the deepest need of all human beings!

I conclude with a warning to myself and to all of us preachers of the Gospel. Preachers who are less sure of their message focus on techniques rather than on the audience. Paul had experienced the joy of being forgiven, the power of the Holy Spirit, and the presence of the Lord Jesus Christ in his life. He was confident of his message, he gave careful attention to the audience, and he was able to relate to them effectively. When they rejected his message, it was not because they did not understand Paul but because they were not ready to make the sacrifice that Christ demanded of them. "If any man will come after me, let him deny himself, and take up his cross, and follow me" (Matthew 16:24, KJV).

My dear friends, I say to myself and to all of us, no matter how well adapted, well prepared, well presented our message may be, if we do not spend time in prayer and dependence upon the Holy Spirit, we will fail to see men and women come to the saving knowledge of Jesus Christ. May the Holy Spirit help us.

Robert Cunville
Dr. Robert Cunville has been an Associate Evangelist with the Billy Graham Evangelistic Association since 1978, ministering in his native India and many other parts of the world. Dr. Cunville and his wife, Caroline, have two children and live in Shillong, Meghalaya, India.

The Evangelist and Spiritual Awakening

Dela Adadevoh

When we look at the theme of spiritual awakening, we need to ask ourselves, "If God brings revival and spiritual awakening in our time, are we ready?" Are we ready to partner with God? Spiritual awakening is a special work of the Holy Spirit among a people in creating an unusual awareness and openness to the Gospel of Jesus Christ. Spiritual awakening usually includes, or is preceded by, revival among God's people. The two are interlinked—revival and spiritual awakening—but they are not the same thing. Revival is primarily God's work in His church, while spiritual awakening is what God does in the church and in society, usually resulting in unprecedented harvest.

We would like to look at the kind of revival that will prepare us to receive a spiritual awakening as an opportunity from God to accelerate the fulfillment of the Great Commission.

Revival results in an exalted view of God, a renewed hunger for holiness, a deepened commitment to obeying God, and a deepened commitment to evangelism and the fulfillment of the Great Commission. It is the sovereign act of God. God is the one who initiates revival, and God is the one who brings extraordinary blessings during the time of revival. But it is our responsibility as God's people always to be ready for revival. Our part is to prepare ourselves for revival and spiritual awakening.

Preparation for Revival

What can we do in preparation for revival? I would like us to look at the example of Nehemiah, who gave leadership to what I believe was one of the greatest revivals recorded in the Old Testament. Nehemiah, we remember, helped in the rebuilding of the walls of Jerusalem. But remember, while there were three goings into exile, there were also three returns from exile, and there were three rebuildings. There was the rebuilding of the walls of Jerusalem. There was the rebuilding of the Temple, and then there was the rebuilding of the lives of the people of Israel.

Prayer played a key role in all of this. When Nehemiah was first confronted with the disgrace that God's people were in, he responded by committing himself spontaneously to prayer and fasting. I believe that when God is going to bring revival, one of the first blessings He brings is the spirit of prayer—the willingness on the part of His children to petition Him in prayer, to pour out their hearts before Him, and to expect His intervention. Fasting and prayer, I believe, play a very significant role in preparing for revival. The principle is that when we draw nigh to God, He will also draw nigh to us. Fasting is simply that discipline that will help us concentrate on God, focus on what would be the heartbeat of God, see God's perspective and cooperate with Him.

Something Extraordinary About United Prayer

God answers prayer. God answers the prayers of individuals. But I believe there is something extraordinary about united prayer. When God's people come together, putting aside denominational differences, theological differences, institutional differences, and unite in earnest praying, seeking God's intervention, His blessings, I believe such united prayer brings an unusual response from God.

And we see this very clearly in the example of the people of Israel. When they were praying, they prayed together as one. They united. They prayed in one accord.

A Reverence for the Word of God

A second element in preparing for revival is the Word of God. The people of Israel, after returning and gathering under the leadership of Nehemiah and Ezra, were going to listen to the reading of the law of God. They had not done this for a long time. As Ezra opened the book of the law, the people of Israel rose to their feet (see Nehemiah 8:5). That portrays a reverence for the Word of God that, I believe, is not common in contemporary Christianity.

An impression was made on me powerfully in Manila, 1989, during Lausanne II. I was sitting very close to Christian brothers and sisters from Russia. A speaker started his message by reading the Word of God. All of a sudden the Russian Christians stood up, and they remained on their feet until the speaker finished reading the Word of God. Then they sat down. They knew something about how precious the Word of God is.

But many of us are suffering from over-familiarity with the Word of God. We are so used to the Bible, the Word of God, that we face the danger of taking the Word of God for granted. When we are preparing for revival, we want to have reverential attitudes towards the Bible as the Word of God, because there is no book like the Bible and no voice like the Word of God.

In addition to having the right attitude, we also need to engage in proper interpretation, explanation and application of the Scriptures to our lives. When Ezra read the book of the law, there were people who explained the meaning and helped those who were there to understand how to apply it to their lives (see Nehemiah 8:8). As they understood the Word of God, they were very powerfully convicted. That is one of the ministries of the Word of God in our lives, through the grace of the Holy Spirit—conviction. They went into a state of mourning because they could see how far they had fallen short of God's standards.

A Time of Confession

Another ministry of God's Word in our lives is that when we are convicted, we go into a time of confession. Our confession is based on our understanding of the nature of God and how far we are from the will and ways of God. When they confessed their sins, they not only confessed their personal sins but they also confessed the sins of their land and they confessed the sins of their forefathers. I believe that we need to learn from this example—to be humble enough, when we come into the presence of God and are seeking revival from Him, to confess not only our personal sins but also the sins of our land, the sins of our people, the sins of our forefathers. If we do not acknowledge this, I believe that our repentance before God will not be deep enough or total enough.

We have a lot to learn from the East Africa revivals which started in 1929 in Uganda, Rwanda, and then across the rest of East Africa, and then influenced other parts of Africa. It started with two people who met in Kampala. They groaned over the state of the church in their time. The dryness of the church was their concern. They committed themselves to praying together and seeking God's intervention. They also confessed their sins one to the other. And they committed themselves to proclaiming the Gospel to people who were around them. Walking in the light, confessing known sins, became something that characterized the East Africa revivals.

If we want to see revival in our time, we need to acknowledge that the kind of repentance that begets revival is radical. It is repentance that does not compromise with sinful attitudes or actions.

I believe that if we want to see revival in our time, we need to acknowledge that the kind of repentance that begets revival is radical. It is repentance that does not compromise with sinful attitudes or actions. We must ask God for grace so that we are able to turn from all idols to Christ. We must renounce our allegiance to the idols of ancestral worship, the idols of materialism, and the idols of the human self. We must come to the point where Jesus Christ will be the only Lord of our lives. We must be willing not only to confess our sins, but also to enter into agreement with God that we are turning our backs to those things, and consecrating ourselves to the things that will please and honor God.

A Very Serious Commitment

That is the third ministry of the Word in our lives in relation to revival—covenanting before God. It's interesting that the people of Israel, when they established their covenant with God, had a written, binding agreement (see Nehemiah 9:38). In other words, it was very intentional and a very serious commitment. They established their covenant with God that they were: first, not going to be involved in intermarriages with other ethnic groups (see Nehemiah 10:30); second, they were going to honor the Sabbath (see verse 31); and third, that they would honor the Lord with the firstfruits of their labor (see verse 32). They not only confessed those sins, but they entered into a covenant with God not to go back to them.

Many times when God brings revival, our experience of revival is short-lived because we go back to the very things that we agreed with God we were not going to do. We need spiritual leaders who will encourage faithfulness on our part, as God's people, as we experience the outpouring of God's blessings amongst us. Nehemiah demonstrates to us the kind of leadership we need today. When he discovered that the people of Israel had gone back to the very same things they had confessed, his response was intense. He did not have any attitude of tolerance towards the ungodliness (see chapter 13). I'm not sure that we can follow his example of being physical in the situation, but we can follow his example of not compromising with sin, not compromising with disobedience to God.

I believe that we have lost this grace of not compromising with sin. In our times the word *sin* does not feature enough in our vocabularies. When we see sins of different kinds, we have more polished terminologies for them. When Africans are involved in syncretism—mixing idol worship, idolatry, with the Christian faith—we simply say they are making the effort to contextualize the Gospel and make the Gospel more African. When North Americans are involved in self-worship and ungodly sensuality, we say they are simply experiencing some of the negative byproducts of the great values of freedom and liberty. When Europeans are demonstrating apathy and coldness to the Gospel, we explain it by saying they are living in a post-Christian era; I would rather call it neo-paganism. We need to be careful about using words that are too polished for spiritual states that should be very disturbing to us. We need Nehemiahs who will tell us sin is deadly; it hurts God. God hates sin, and the people of God must hate sin.

Christ Above Everything Else

Our repentance and pursuit of revival must seek to place Jesus Christ above everything else. We must rediscover the sufficiency of Christ, and the sufficiency of God's Word for our salvation and for all things that pertain to life and godliness. We face the challenge in our time of having Jesus plus some other things, having the Word of God plus some other things. Brothers and sisters, the Christian life is not Jesus plus. It is Jesus period! Christ is sufficient for our salvation!

Revival is not simply a return to a past experience of God's blessings but the return to the person, the purpose and the power of Jesus Christ. Revival must not only be a desire to return to the times of Wesley, Müller and Whitefield. We must always seek a higher standard that is based on the nature and revealed will of Christ. The ways of Christ are always higher than our past experiences. "Forget the former things; do not dwell on the past. See, I am doing a new thing! Now it springs up; do you not perceive it?" (Isaiah 43:18–19, NIV). Let us ask God to open our eyes that we may be able to perceive what He is doing. He wants to do something that we have never heard of or seen before.

We all wish that we had that attitude and reverence for God, and that commitment to revival. But given our human nature, sometimes God has to take our idols from us in order to bring us to the point of depending on Him. That is what makes suffering an instrument for revival in the hands of God.

Results We Can Expect

When we are preparing for revival, what are some results that we can expect? First, we can expect repentance on the part of believers. Second, there will be renewal in the lives of believers. Third, we can expect reconciliation amongst believers. And fourth, we can expect reformation in society.

I'm reminded of the experience of one young man from Rwanda. He accepted the challenge of fasting and praying for 40 days. He went back to his country where Tutsi church leaders and Hutu church leaders decided, "We need God to intervene in our land. Our hatred for one another does not please God." So Hutu church leaders and Tutsi church leaders committed themselves to praying and fasting to ask God for forgiveness and reconciliation.

> When we experience personal revival, our spiritual eyes will be open so we can see what God is doing, and we will be partners with Him.

As they continued praying together, other people joined them from the two ethnic backgrounds. They came to that point where they were able to forgive one another, and these groups of people are continuing to pray, asking God for revival. Here is a situation where the church has experienced oneness, a reconciliation, and it has become an example for other people within the country.

When we have that kind of revival, it makes an impact on society. And when society experiences that impact, many times we see spiritual awakening. We have to be ready, as a prepared people, to make the most of the opportunities when there is openness to the Gospel.

Addressing the subject of evangelism and spiritual awakening, we need to keep in mind two things that are very important. First, we have to remember the words of the Lord Jesus Christ, "My Father is always at his work to this very day, and I, too, am working" (John 5:17, NIV). We cannot say that God is not at work. God is always at work!

Second, we need to be praying for more open doors for spiritual awakening.

Paul asks the church at Colosse to pray for him that doors would be open for him to proclaim the Gospel (see Colossians 4:3). So we are always aware of these two things—that God is at work right now, and we can make the most of the opportunities we have right now. Yet, at the same time, we are praying that God will open more doors, that God will visit us with spiritual awakening. God is at work!

We need to pray that God will open our spiritual eyes, that we will be able to discern what He is doing in our time, and that we'll also know what God wants to do through our lives. I believe many of us are not seeing what God is doing in our time because our spiritual eyes are not open. When we experience personal revival, our spiritual eyes will be open so we can see what God is doing, and we will be partners with Him.

Open Doors Have a Life Span

In partnering with God in evangelism within the context of spiritual awakening, it is so important that we remember that open doors do have a life span. Open doors are not forever. So when there is a great spiritual awakening, we need to make the most of the opportunities. Are we ready for a spiritual awakening? Are we ready to make the most of it?

What is the challenge that we have for making the most of a spiritual awakening? I believe it is that of asking God for boldness to step out in obedience, to maximize the opportunities we have. If we are honest, we will all agree that one of the reasons why it has taken us so long to finish the task of world evangelization is that the unevangelized regions of the world are not convenient mission fields. The places that we have to reach happen to be the difficult places, the 10/40 window for instance.

Are We Ready?

So we need to ask ourselves, are we really waiting for God to open doors to the Gospel, or are we waiting for the mission field to become more convenient and safe? There is a great difference between the two. If we are waiting for the mission field to become more convenient and safe, brothers and sisters, remember that the church was built on the blood of the martyrs. There is no reason why it will not continue to be built on the blood of the martyrs. I am not advocating that we initiate suffering and difficulty, but I am suggesting that to finish the unfinished task will require the same radical, sacrificial commitment that it took to bring the Gospel to many of the lands that did not have the Gospel in past centuries. Are we ready?

In 1910, when a group of mission leaders met in Scotland to review the state of Christianity in Africa, there were less than 10 million known believers on the continent of Africa. Towards the end of the 20th century, there were close to 400 million Africans who claimed to be Christians. God has done remarkable things. God is at work in our time!

To make the most of the opportunities we have now, even as we pray for a great worldwide spiritual awakening, we need to enter into partnership to work with one another, to maximize our resources as we reach the world with the Gospel. God has not called any one organization or institution or denomination to fulfill the Great Commission in the world. God has not given any one institution or denomination all the resources to reach the world. God's plan is not for us to work as independent entities. The love that we have for one another is part of our Gospel message.

We need all of God's people to use all of God's resources to reach all of God's world.

It is time for us to join our hands together, our hearts together, our resources together to bring the Good News of Christ to all people.

As we maximize the opportunities we have today, I believe the best is still to come. I believe that there will be a revival that will be worldwide, there will be a spiritual awakening that will be worldwide, and we will see a harvest that we have not seen before.

I want to challenge you: Let's make the most of the opportunities we have now. God is going to bless His people! Let us pray and trust God for a fresh anointing on His church, so that the revival and the spiritual awakening that we will experience in the 21st century will be like nothing we have ever seen before. We pray that God will do a new thing. Even so, come, Spirit, come. God bless you.

Dela Adadevoh

Reverend Dela Adadevoh serves as Vice President with Campus Crusade for Christ International. He is responsible for overseeing the ministry's work of evangelism and discipleship in Africa, as well as in other regions. Rev. Adadevoh also serves as International Director for Leadership Development for Campus Crusade for Christ International. A citizen of Ghana, West Africa, Rev. Adadevoh earned a B.S. at the University of Science and Technology in Kumasi, Ghana; a M.A. at Azusa Pacific University in Azusa, California, U.S.A.; and is currently a doctoral candidate at Leeds University in Leeds, England. Rev. Adadevoh and his wife, Elizabeth, have a son and two daughters. The family currently lives in Orlando, Florida, U.S.A.

The Heritage of Evangelism

Video

Throughout history God has called His people to the task of evangelism. Some He has called to the special ministry of preaching. Beginning with Peter, Paul, Philip and others, Christian evangelists proclaimed the Gospel in synagogues and marketplaces throughout the Roman Empire.

In the second and third centuries, evangelists took advantage of the political unity of the Roman Empire to spread the Gospel. Among them was Gregory Thaumaturgus who began to preach in Pontus when there was a handful of Christians in that city. At his death 30 years later, there were only a few dozen who did not believe.

In the third century, Barbarian tribes from Mongolia invaded vast areas, and Christian women were among the captives taken. Although forced into slavery, these women remained faithful and converted many of their captors to Christ. One descendant of slaves preached to the Goths and translated the Scriptures into their language. A native church arose, and Gothic preachers took the Gospel to other tribes in Europe.

The Barbarian invasions continued, and by the sixth century the Roman Empire had lost much of its territory and power. To the East, however, the Nestorians became a force for the extension of the Christian faith. In addition, the eloquent and persuasive preaching of John Chrysostom and others in the eastern part of the empire won countless people to Christ.

Europe entered the so-called Dark Ages, and Islam emerged as a powerful force, hindering the progress of Christian preaching in North Africa and slowing outreach in Asia. However, believers shared Christ across Central Asia, and Christianity continued to grow in India. In the West the Gospel continued to advance through evangelists like Columba, who was the first to bring the Gospel to the pagan tribes of Scotland. After establishing a Christian monastery on the small island of Iona, Columba converted many of the region's pagan clans to Christianity. Columba was just one example of how members of the monastic movement were a force for evangelism.

A century later King Oswald of Northumbria, who was introduced to the Gospel while living on Iona as a boy, invited several evangelists from the island to come and establish a monastery just a few miles from his castle in northern England. On what is now called Holy Island, devout men like Aidan and Cuthbert established a Christian learning center and traveled great distances throughout England and Scotland to deliver the Gospel message. Through the dedicated work of these men, many northern Europeans abandoned their pagan gods and turned to Christ.

In the Eastern Orthodox Church, the preaching and translation of the Scriptures by Cyril, Methodius and others led to the conversion of vast numbers of people in Russia and elsewhere. During the seventh century, Christians traveled east along China's Silk Road, witnessing for Christ as they went. Their work resulted in several thousand Asian converts and left an impact for decades. But when a new dynasty arose in China, their work was hindered and Christianity was reversed.

By the 11th century, Islam had spread from Spain to Indonesia. Between 1096 and 1272, the Church in the West responded to Muslim expansion with eight military crusades intended to purge the world of Islam. In contrast to these crusades, Francis of Assisi preached the Gospel of Christ's love and peace to the Muslims, attempting contact with them in North Africa and Spain.

Beginning in the 14th century, the Renaissance brought a renewed interest in art and learning. But the established Church failed to teach the Scriptures to the common people. God called John Wycliffe to preach to the English people and to translate the Scriptures into their language. The Gospel also spread to other parts of Europe. Jan Hus preached in Czechoslovakia, and in Italy, God called Jerome Savonarola to proclaim a message of repentance and faith. In response to Savonarola's preaching, churches were crowded. But his message troubled the established order, and Savonarola was hanged and burned in the city square of Florence.

At the beginning of the 16th century, the Western Church entered a time of unrest. A Reformation movement challenged the growing corruption and abuse of authority in the Church. Scholars like Erasmus, Martin Luther, John Calvin and others sought the essence of the Gospel message.

The dawn of the age of exploration provided new opportunities for the proclamation of the Gospel. Clergy committed to evangelism often accompanied explorers from France, Spain and Portugal. The much-feared pirates of the Caribbean produced some unlikely evangelists. After capture and imprisonment, some returned to their Christian roots and devoted their lives to preaching the Gospel to captors and to the people on the west coast of South America in Peru, Chile and Ecuador.

In Asia, Matteo Ricci, a scientist as well as a preacher, spent 20 years proclaiming Christ in China. Ricci took advantage of requests for scientific advice and preached as he worked. By 1650 his preaching had won a quarter million converts to Christ in China.

By the late 17th and 18th centuries, Europe had entered the age of reason. Great strides were made in science and medicine. Unfortunately for many, Christianity became a mere intellectual exercise and church attendance a formality. John Wesley, George Whitefield and others felt the call of God and began to preach with new enthusiasm. Wesley preached an average of 800 sermons a year to crowds as large as 20,000. A Great Awakening of faith swept the English-speaking world.

By the late 18th century, the North American population was expanding westward. To reach these scattered people on the frontier, the Methodists developed a network of circuit preachers. These men covered areas of 500 square miles or more on horseback. In 1800 camp meetings developed as another method of evangelizing the frontier. These events attracted people from miles around and sometimes lasted a week or more. The Spirit of God continued this renewal through evangelists like Charles Finney, Phoebe Palmer and former slave Amanda Smith.

Revival spread to other parts of the world as well. In Sierra Leone, hundreds of ex-slaves responded to Christian preaching. One of these, Samuel Crowther, preached Christ throughout Nigeria. The evangelists he trained were the first to bring the Gospel to many parts of West Africa.

Revival also spread across Europe. In Germany, evangelists joyfully proclaimed Christ in tent meetings and churches. In Latin America, an Italian emigrant, Francisco Penzotti, distributed Bibles and New Testaments all across the continent, which laid the foundation for thousands of converts.

In 1870, God called a shoe salesman named Dwight Moody to lead evangelistic meetings in America and England. Moody felt the urgency to reach large numbers and preached to nearly 100 million people during his lifetime. His systematic approach introduced the world to the modern age of mass evangelism.

In 1891, God called Billy Sunday to leave a successful career in professional baseball to become an evangelist. The American public loved his unique theatrical style of attacking sin and bias. Thousands were converted to Christ through Sunday's preaching.

Between 1914 and 1945, the world was ravaged by two major wars. But in Africa, Asia and Latin America, God spoke through His evangelists. In Japan, Paul Kanamori preached the message of salvation in mass rallies. Between 1916 and 1919, Kanamori recorded 43,000 decisions for Christ. In India, Sadhu Sundar Singh was converted following a vision of the Lord. Although ostracized by his family, he preached throughout India and Ceylon.

Following World War II, at the Christ for Greater Los Angeles Crusade in 1949, Billy Graham emerged as the leading figure of a new breed of evangelists. The use of radio, television and film multiplied the impact of his Crusades by reaching new and broader audiences. Mass evangelism now reached people who sat in the comfort of their own homes. Whether through electronic media or public meetings, the preaching of the Gospel continues today as gifted evangelists around the world are proclaiming Christ.

Since the first preaching of the apostles, God has called men and women to proclaim the Good News of salvation in Jesus Christ. There are many more wonderful stories about evangelists that could be told. This is the tradition in which we walk. These are our roots. This is our heritage and our high calling from God!

Waodani Testimony

Steve Saint with Tementa Nenguihui Huamoni
and Mincayi Enquedi Huahue

It is a high honor and an extreme pleasure to address you God followers from all over the world. I am here with two of my dearest friends in the whole world. Tementa is an elder in the Waodani church. His father was a stone-age warrior who had no friendly contact with the outside world until my father, Nate Saint, and four of his friends made an attempt to establish a friendly contact. Tementa's father, Nankiwi, was the only man in the tribe that people called Auca—although their proper name is Waodani—that my father ever met. When Nankiwi came to the beach where my father and his four friends had landed their small plane, he was fascinated with the airplane and showed by sign language that he wanted to ride in this airplane. Finally, he got into the airplane and my father didn't want to antagonize him, knowing that the tribe was famous for killing outsiders, so he decided to take him for a ride. My father took him for a little flight and then landed again. Nankiwi would not get out and made it obvious that he wanted to see his village from the air. So my dad flew him over the village. The door was off, and dad wrote in his journal that as they flew over the village, he realized that Nankiwi didn't want just to see the village from the air, he wanted the people in the village to see him in the air. To be sure that they would see him, Nankiwi tried to climb out of the open door onto the wing, and my dad said he didn't want him to fall so Dad reached over to grab him. But the Waodani didn't wear clothes except for a g-string, and Dad wasn't sure if Nankiwi might be offended if he grabbed that!

Three years ago the Waodani elders asked me to teach one of them to fly an airplane. They live in extremely rugged jungles in the eastern rain forests of Ecuador. They designated Tementa, Nankiwi's son, to be the first Waodani to learn how to fly. We've spent three years developing an airplane, and I thought you would want to know that last Saturday, Tementa flew an airplane by himself! I think it was an historic event, not only for Tementa, but also for his tribe and for the Gospel.

Now I would like to introduce to you Mama Mincayi, who will speak to you. "Mama" means grandfather, and I call him that because my children call him that. They love him dearly. Most of us know that God works in mysterious ways, don't we? It just happens that in God's economy, this man that my children call grandfather is the new grandfather who replaced their grandfather, a man who Mama Mincayi killed when I was a little boy.

Last week at this time, Mincayi's only blonde granddaughter, my daughter, Stephanie Rachel, was called home to heaven. When we rushed down to the hospital, Mincayi didn't know what was going on, and I didn't know what was going on. He was very concerned and asked if the doctors had done anything to hurt Stephanie. When I told him they hadn't done anything, he got excited, and he said, "Now I see this well, God is doing this." Then he said to all the people who were gathered there in the intensive care unit, "Memus-Star," as they call Stephanie in the tribe, "has gone to heaven. I am an old man and soon I'm going to heaven, too. There I'm going to wait with Young Star, and Old Star, who has already died (my aunt Rachel Saint), and Steve's father, and Gangita," and he named others in the tribe who have gone on to heaven. "When you come, living very well, we will be waiting for you in God's place," he concluded.

May I present to you one of my dearest friends and your brother in Christ, Mama Mincayi:

"I am a true person. My ancestors lived angry in hating each other. That's how they lived, they didn't know any other way. The older people, my ancestors, went over to the Coca River and they would spear people there. Whenever foreigners came into our land, living angry, we would just spear them. When we saw them we speared them; not only the foreigners but we also speared our people, that's how we lived."

Mincayi is wanting you to understand that they lived hating and killing one another. It was a bad way to live, but they didn't know any other trail.

"My ancestors didn't know God's carvings [Scriptures]. How could they walk God's trail if they didn't see God's carvings? I didn't know either until somebody came to teach me God's carvings, and then I began to understand. When I killed Steve's father, I didn't know any better. Nobody came to tell us, and we didn't know that his father was coming to teach us God's trail and that is why we speared him. Then Dayuma, a young girl who had run away from the killings in the tribe, she came back to us and she began to teach us God's carvings. But when we asked her questions, she said, 'I don't know any more. But if you see it well, I will invite my sister. She's a foreigner with white skin [Rachel Saint]! I will tell her to come here and she can teach us how to follow God's trail, seeing God's carvings!'

"My heart was black and sick in sin, but then I heard that God had sent His own Son, His blood dripping and dripping. He washed my heart clean; now I live well. Now you, God followers from all over the dirt [earth], now I see you well, because you are truly my brothers, God's blood having washed your hearts clean, too.

"Leaving in just a few days, I may never see you again here, but I will see you there. Speaking God's carvings all over the world, let's take lots of people following God's trail to live with us in heaven."

Today the Waodani are concerned for the next generation. Missions brought them the Gospel, but they see that the new generation is not listening to missionaries. And when my aunt Rachel died, they asked me to come, and I said, "What can I do for you that the other foreigners haven't done for you?" They said, "Babai, listen to us well. We don't say you do; we say you teach us, we ourselves will do. We will speak God's carvings to the new generation."

They realize that this is their commission. When they go home from this conference, Tementa and Mincayi can tell their people that this family that we're a part of covers the entire world.

There are things in this Western world that the Waodani don't understand. Mincayi doesn't understand why they cut so much grass to go and look for those little white things that you can't eat; he said maybe they should cook them more. I don't understand golf, so I couldn't help him. And then Tementa said, "How is it that eating so much grass and leaves, the foreigners are all so fat?"

They also don't understand that in God's economy, what they meant for evil so many years ago, God intended for good. I hope that I'm not imposing on you, but I have not been able to explain to them that God has used them, as well as my father and the four other missionaries, to spread His Gospel around this world. If what we call the "Auca" story has affected you in some way, would you stand so that Tementa and Mincayi can see that God worked good through what they meant for evil? [Thousands of people immediately stood!]

We see you God followers very well. God bless you.

Steve Saint

Tementa
Nenguihui
Huamoni

Mincayi Enquedi
Huahue

Steve Saint with Tementa Nenguihui Huamoni and Mincayi Enquedi Huahue

Steve Saint is the founder and director of I-TEC (Indigenous People's Technology & Education Center) in Dunnellon, Florida, U.S.A., which equips and trains indigenous believers from frontier areas, especially Ecuador.

The Gospel's Impact on a Province of Africa

Inonge Mbikusita Lewanika

It is my pleasure to share with you some brief testimonies on how the Gospel of Jesus Christ has impacted and changed lives in my part of the world. In the Bulozi province of Zambia, the missionaries were first welcomed, received and accommodated in 1884.

My grandfather, King Lewanika, was a friend of the missionaries. The first group of missionaries was led by a Frenchman, Francis Coillard, and it was comprised of Masuto (people from Lesotho) missionaries. The king's life was impacted and changed by the Gospel. In honor of the Gospel, the people of Bulozi composed a hymn of praise to God and thanks for their land, peace, tranquility and love: "Even our land and people now know the Word of the King of kings/Now we pray/The evil is diminishing/disappearing/Now we love each other."

King Lewanika's son Litia, my uncle, took over from him. He was crowned with the name of Yeta III. He was among the first converts and pupils in the missionary school. His wedding was the first Christian ceremony, and it was celebrated in the church. The impact of the Gospel on Yeta III was significant. He was the first Christian king of Bulozi. He abolished slavery and beer drinking. He detested wickedness and ignorance. Drunkards and adulterers were punished, both male and female, with the leaders receiving stiffer sentences. This caused fear and concern among some of the citizens, as some of their practices were contrary to the Gospel. Like his father, King Lewanika, Yeta III championed education, development, impartial application of the law and progress, and he freed all slaves throughout the country. From the reign of Yeta III, the major villages commenced each day with daily morning prayers.

The third testimony is of Akabiwa Mbikusita Lewanika, Lewanika II, the last surviving son of King Lewanika; he was my father. Lewanika II was king from 1969 to 1977. He was a missionary baby from his mother's womb. He attended local mission schools and later studied in South Africa, England and Wales. He worked for the Colonial Government in various parts of Northern Rhodesia (Zambia) and later as a social worker. He pioneered the Trade Union Movement in Zambia and was the first president of the Northern Rhodesia Africa National Congress, the first African political party. He translated the Bible into the Silozi language in the 1930s and met his wife at the mission station where the translation took place.

The Gospel had a profound impact on King Lewanika II. Studying the Bible thoroughly, visiting the Holy Land and translating the Bible affected his life deeply. He was full of love, laughter and joy. He was moved with compassion, and his house was always full of people and dependents. He was a great friend of young children. In his home the Bible was read frequently and openly. He was not ashamed to kneel before the King of kings and pray. He and his wife often shared testimonies of the early missionaries.

But today, Bulozi is among the poorest provinces in Zambia. It has among the highest numbers of HIV/AIDS orphans. Almost none of the young people go to universities. Like the children of Israel, there arose a generation that forgot their God. As a result, they suffer untold miseries. Beer drinking, which once was forbidden, now freely flows to the detriment of development. The church bells, which rang at sunrise to beckon people for early morning prayers, are no longer heard. Most mission schools and health services are closed. The people that walked in the light now walk in the dark.

Thank God for His remnant. The Lord has called a few local missionaries who stand in the gap and pray day and night for Bulozi. They see a revival coming and keep praying and praising while spreading the Gospel. They walk for miles and miles to share the Gospel. One of these young men grew up in town with all the urban facilities. The Lord called him nine years ago to Bulozi. For the first time, he and his family lived in a grass hut without electricity, running water and other conveniences. He and his team are turning the place right side up!

Some of these young people need training in Bible, theology, pastoral work and practical subjects, and they need material help. Let the Church of Jesus Christ rise and function as one Body, ensuring that each part fulfills the Commission of the King of kings. Let the Church of Jesus rise and walk together in unity and love. Let the Church of Jesus rise, share resources and redeem the time and lead the lost to the Kingdom of the light.

We are all evangelists and missionaries by order of the Master in His Commission. Often we can reach the frontline far away by our support. In the end, we shall together come rejoicing, bringing in the sheaves.

Inonge Mbikusita Lewanika
Dr. Inonge Mbikusita Lewanika is from Bulozi, Zambia. She is a member of the Zambian Parliament.

The Power of Christ's Gospel in Cultures Worldwide

Charles Colson

I appreciate every single evangelist around the world. What a blessed calling it is that you have, and what a wonderful job! It's a holy, sacred trust.

Augustine said there was never a message he preached that he was satisfied with. Moses didn't think he was adequate to speak, so God had to appoint someone to speak for him. Jeremiah couldn't speak until God touched his lips. Solomon was too young. Luther, who stood against the ecclesiastical and political powers of his time, said that every time he preached his knees knocked. Charles Haddon Spurgeon, perhaps the greatest preacher of the 19th century, said, "We tremble, lest we should mistake or misunderstand the Word."

To preach the whole truth is an awful charge. It is an awful charge that every single one of you have from wherever you come in the world today. It is a holy, sacred trust. Take it as a trust from God with great humility, but knowing that you can trust Him to do what you in your own power cannot do because He, our God, is sovereign.

Real Power Is in the Gospel

I was once in the office next to the President of the United States. I had what I thought was all the power in the world. Then along came Watergate, and I found myself in the midst of that terrible scandal. One night I visited a friend at his home. He had been converted at a Billy Graham Crusade in New York when he was one of the leading businessmen in America. That night he witnessed to me about Jesus Christ. And in a flood of tears in my friend's driveway, I surrendered my life to Christ. Nothing in these 27 years has ever been the same since; nothing can ever be the same again. I discovered real power. It isn't in the kingdoms of this world, which come and go. Real power is in the Gospel of Jesus Christ, which transforms the hardest human heart.

I want to expand on two themes—the sovereignty of God and the power of the Gospel—in the context of what I see to be the great battle going on in the world today between different understandings of reality, different worldviews, different ways to live our lives. One view says, "God is. He is not silent; He has spoken. He reigns, He rules. There is an order in life given to us by our Creator God." The other view says, "There is no God; He is dead. We can live without Him. We live our own lives." That's the conflict, and all across the world you're seeing the battle raging between these two fundamental worldviews.

The Christian Gospel Provides an Answer

Only the Christian worldview, the worldview that God gives us, can provide hope and meaning and an orderly way for us to structure our lives. No other worldview does that. People are hungry for this. They're desperate for it. They're searching.

What we have to understand is that the message we preach is more than John 3:16. The message we preach is that Christianity and biblical revelation form a worldview that helps us organize and structure our lives, our common lives together.

When you stop and think about the Christian Gospel, the Christian message, it answers all the fundamental questions that people have asked from the beginning of time:

> One view says, "God is. He is not silent; He has spoken. He reigns, He rules. There is an order in life given to us by our Creator God."

I was visiting a prison in Holland, and one man said, "I can't become a Christian because there's so much suffering in the world." But the Christian has an answer for that. God created us perfect in His image, then gave us a free will. Suffering comes when we ignore what God taught us. But the most glorious message of all is that standing alone among all points of view and understandings and philosophies and religions, the Christian Gospel provides an answer to that sin and suffering. Jesus Christ went to the Cross and died in our place, which is redemption. It also answers the question of how we can restore society, because when we live out the Christian faith we bring back those values and we restore the culture. God has given us a way to see all of life.

We Fulfill a Cultural Commission

Why is this so important? Well, one reason it's important is that we are evangelizing today in cultures that aren't familiar with the biblical message. So we have to go and show them what is wrong with their point of view, what they desperately need and how the Christian message provides an answer.

It's exactly what the apostle Paul did when he went to Mars' hill. The Scripture tells us that he went into the synagogue and he reasoned with the Jews. Then he preached that magnificent message to a meeting of the Areopagus in which he said, "You have put up an altar to an 'unknown god.' But your own poets tell you we are His offspring." He proceeded to critique their viewpoint and present the message of creation, and the message of the resurrection of Christ from the dead (see Acts 17:16–31). That's precisely what we must do.

The world today is like Athens. We have to show people why their values are false, and then present the truth of what we believe. Understanding the battle of worldviews is crucial to evangelists. Brothers and sisters, we fulfill not only the Great Commission of evangelism, seeing that people are brought into conformity with God's will; it's also crucial that we attempt to bring Christian truth into every area of life.

I love Psalm 8. How majestic is God's creation! All of it is God's! I love also what Abraham Kuyper, a great theologian, great pastor and also prime minister of Holland, said when he was dedicating the Free University in Amsterdam: "There is not one square inch in the whole domain of human existence as to which Christ, who is sovereign, does not cry out 'Mine!' And if Christ cries out 'Mine!' we as a church have to cry out 'His!' and we have to bring Christian truth to bear in every single walk of life."

Take Every Opportunity in Every Environment

Christianity profoundly influences politics. We give to Caesar what is Caesar's and to God what is God's. In the Reformation the doctrine came out that the king is not law, but the law is king. That's why Christians have been the great battlers for human rights. We see that government is not supreme; God is supreme, and God cares about every single human being. We see how Christian truth gives dignity to work. We see how Christian truth provides the basis for ethics, which no other worldview does. Christian truth gives a higher meaning to the arts and literature. Have no doubt about it, the Christian view of life enables us to live rationally, enables us to live intelligently.

> The other view says, "There is no God; He is dead. We can live without Him. We live our own lives."

We as evangelists have to present that message in our cultures and see to it that Christian truth influences how people live their lives. How do we do it? Well, we have to take every opportunity, in every environment that we're in, to present the truth. In every area of life you will see that the Christian Gospel provides the answer by which we can live our lives better. Culture is hungry today. If we present the truth, culture will listen to us.

We not only do it as apologists, but maybe the most powerful way we can do it is when we demonstrate the truth of the Gospel as we live it out in our own lives. A great hero for my life is William Wilberforce, the parliamentarian who rose up on the floor of the Parliament and denounced slavery. He had been converted to Christ, and for 20 years he campaigned against the slave trade. He finally succeeded. After 20 years the slave trade was abolished, and when he was on his deathbed, slavery itself was abolished. Wilberforce set upon the course of reforming the structures and life of Britain. Because of his courage not only was slavery ended, but also the values and morals of Britain were reformed. That's what happens when we live our Christian faith.

Does It Work?

I've seen this vividly firsthand in a prison in Texas. A few years ago we were invited to open the first Christian-run prison in America. It's an amazing place! I love to go there. It's like a spiritual retreat. The guys get up at 5:30 in the morning, they study their Bibles, they go to breakfast, then they go to classes, then they do their work, then they come back for more Bible study, then they have their evening meal, and then from 5 o'clock in the evening till 10 o'clock they are in devotions and Bible study. No television, no distractions, no waste of time. These men are serious about living as Christians inside this prison.

Does it work? We've had 45 men go through that prison. The prisoner recidivism rate, the repeat offender rate, in other prisons is around 70 or 80 percent. Forty-five men have gone through that prison for 18 months and then have been mentored on the outside for six months. Out of those 45 men, not a single man is back in custody. That's the power of God changing people's lives! It is a living demonstration of the glory of God's work in their lives. It's a living demonstration of how a culture is changed, because when that prison started there was just a handful of Christians. They banded together and they prayed, and then they began to witness. People came into the prison who were not Christians. I've been there now four times; there have been baptisms every time I've been there. People are coming to Christ! The culture is changing!

We Make the Invisible Kingdom Visible

What we need to understand, what Calvin taught so powerfully, is that we make the invisible Kingdom visible when we live out our faith. People around us are changed because the culture around us has changed. That's what we must teach. That's what we must work towards—not just presenting the Gospel, but presenting the whole biblical message so that life around us begins to be changed. Wherever we are, life around us has to begin to change as the evidence that we're really being witnesses to Christ in every single aspect of life.

Oh, how the world hungers for that! How desperately the world needs to hear that message. When we live that out in culture, people see that the biblical worldview makes sense. My brothers and sisters, the challenge for us is to be the church and to be faithful.

An Experience in Prison at Easter

I want to paint a picture and put it in your minds. This past Easter I was in prison, as I'm always in prison at Easter. Six hundred men wearing thin cotton white jumpers filled the center of that prison. They were pressing up against a chain-link fence. Our platform was on the other side. It was a brutally cold day, and those men were huddled against one another to keep warm. We had a great service and many men came to know Christ that day.

As we were getting ready to quit, I invited a man to pray who had never been in prison before. He didn't know the things you're not supposed to do in prison.

The first thing he did was to look out at the sea of 600 men, many of whom had come to Christ. It was brutally cold, everybody wanted to get back inside, and the service was almost over. He said, "I want all of you men up against the fence to back up." If you've preached in prisons, you know you don't order the men in prison around. He said, "Everybody back up 10, 12 feet." Slowly the men began to shuffle backwards. I held my breath. The guards all looked nervous.

Eventually, when they were where he wanted them to be, he said, "All right, stop. Now, I want all of you men who are Christians, who have given your lives to Christ, you're the church inside; I want you to all walk forward." You know what that's like in prison? There is terrible peer pressure against Christians, and particularly someone who walks forward in an event like that. Slowly men began to come out of the lines.

Two hundred men came forward. He said, "Now walk up to the fence." They all walked up to the fence. I was holding my breath, I was so nervous. And then he said, "Now turn around and face all the inmates." And 200 men turned and faced the inmate population. What courage! Then he said, "Now, I want you to look at those men. That's your mission field. I want you to pray for those men. You're going to evangelize them. Get on your knees!" Every one of those 200 Christian inmates got down on their knees. He said, "Put your hands on one another's shoulders."

I will never forget the sight, ever, as long as I live. I was looking out over the backs of 200 brothers down on their knees in one of the toughest prisons in America, with their hands on one another's shoulders while this man prayed that God would bring His power upon them so that they might go and evangelize the rest of that prison. Oh, what a sight! Tears were running down my cheeks. All I could think of was courage, humility, unity. They were holding one another's shoulders. They were one. The world wants to see us as one.

> I will never forget the sight, ever, as long as I live. I was looking out over the backs of 200 brothers down on their knees in one of the toughest prisons in America.

That's What the Church Needs to Look Like

Those men were together, bound together in that prison, on their knees before God. What a picture that was! It was a picture of the church. That's what the church needs to look like, boldly professing our faith, courageous to stand up for Christ, but humble enough to get on our knees and pray that God will use us and let the world see the way that Christians live.

Jesus prayed, "That all of them may be one, Father, just as you are in me and I am in you. May they also be in us so that the world may believe that you have sent me" (John 17:21, NIV).

Without unity there is no evangelism. We are different from the rest of the world. Let people see a biblical worldview lived out in our lives. Then we will see a great harvest and a great time of Christian renewal, because the world is despairing. The world is looking for something better, and they can see it in us.

You and I, the evangelists, are the ones to bring that message to the world.

Oh, Father, let Your Spirit fall. Let us be a people in whom the world sees something different.

God bless you.

Charles Colson

Mr. Charles Colson is a popular and widely known author, speaker and radio commentator. A former presidential aide to Richard Nixon, and founder of the international ministry Prison Fellowship, he has written several books that have shaped Christian thinking on a variety of subjects, including How Now Shall We Live? *In 1993, Colson was awarded the prestigious Templeton Prize for Progress in Religion, given for extraordinary leadership and originality in advancing humanity's understanding of God. Mr. Colson's wife, Patricia, is also involved in his ministry.*

Relying on
the Holy Spirit
Video

"The Holy Spirit has come upon you; and you shall be My witnesses both in Jerusalem, and in all Judea and Samaria, and even to the remotest part of the earth" (Acts 1:8, NASB).

In Charlotte, North Carolina, 1934, a high school student sat in a crusade meeting, listening to the Gospel. Little did he know the chain of events that led to this opportunity.

Many years earlier, 1855, Edward Kimball had been trying for months to reach a young shoe salesman who had been attending his Sunday school class. Eager to win Dwight Moody's heart to Christ, Kimball talked with him at his workplace. After a cold response, Kimball left the store. But unknown to this Sunday school teacher, the Holy Spirit was doing a work in Moody's heart. And that day Moody made the decision to become a new person in Christ.

Dwight Moody inherited the same hunger for souls that Kimball had. In June 1873, while in Liverpool, England, for a series of crusades, Moody encountered a scholarly Baptist pastor named F. B. Meyer, who at first had little time for the American's unsophisticated preaching style. But the Holy Spirit empowered Moody's words, and soon Meyer's heart was transformed by the message.

At Moody's invitation, Meyer toured America. At the Northfield Bible Conference he challenged the crowd saying, "If you are not willing to give up everything for Christ, are you willing to be made willing?" That remark changed the life of a struggling young minister named J. Wilbur Chapman. Within a few short years, Chapman proceeded to become a powerful traveling evangelist in the early 1900s, and he recruited a converted baseball player named Billy Sunday. Under Chapman's eye, Sunday became one of the most spectacular evangelists in American history.

Billy Sunday's crusade in Charlotte, North Carolina, produced a group of converts who continued praying for another such visitation of the Spirit. In 1934, they invited evangelist Mordecai Ham to conduct a citywide crusade. On October 8, Ham, searching for encouragement, wrote a prayer to God, "Lord, give us a Pentecost here. Pour out Thy Spirit tomorrow."

God answered Mordecai Ham's prayer beyond his dreams the next evening as he witnessed the scores of people who came forward to accept Christ. Among those who came that night stood a young Central High School student whose decision would later touch the lives of millions of people. This student's name: Billy Graham.

Kimball, Moody, Meyer, Chapman, Sunday, Ham, Graham. This movement of the Holy Spirit began with a humble Sunday school teacher. Even when we fail to see the results of our work as evangelists, the Holy Spirit opens the hearer's heart to receive Christ and makes the new believer a member of God's ongoing family.

The Evangelist Relies on the Holy Spirit

Paul Finkenbinder
("Hermano Pablo")

Who empowers the servant of God to be an evangelist? By whose authority does an evangelist present himself or herself to the world as God's emissary? For the answer, I submit the subject of this message: *"The Evangelist Relies on the Holy Spirit."*

It is by the sovereign authority and mandate of the Holy Spirit that we represent Christ to the world. Our reliance on the Holy Spirit touches every aspect of our ministry and life. From the moment we receive our commission—our divine call—in our private life, in our devotional life, in our public life, in our public speaking, in our spiritual quests, we as evangelists must learn to lean on the Holy Spirit, not on our own might and understanding.

Those who are just now obeying the call to full-time evangelism, as well as those who have had a lifetime in God's service, can be sure that our status as ministers of the Gospel of Christ is indisputable. May God's Holy Spirit give you the absolute assurance of His divine approval. The Lord said, "Surely I am with you always, to the very end of the age" (Matthew 28:20, NIV).

The Evangelist Is Specifically Called of God

First, the evangelist relies on the Holy Spirit in his commission. There can be no greater assurance of the evangelist's position in God's Kingdom than the fact that he is specifically called of God. And when I say "he," I obviously mean he or she. The reality of that call comes to us from the days of the apostles. I quote Acts 13:2, "While they were worshiping the Lord and fasting, the Holy Spirit said, 'Set apart for me Barnabas and Saul for the work to which I have called them'" (NIV).

We, my colleagues, were set apart by God Himself before we were born. From the earliest moment of our existence, God had appointed us to be ambassadors to the world. Nothing establishes more the sacredness of that divine call and the responsibility that that call involves than the fact that God, in His foreknowledge, chose us to be ministers of the Gospel of Christ, even before we were conceived. That, to me, is a miracle!

There are many scriptural examples of a person who is chosen by God from birth to serve Him. David said, "You brought me out of the womb; you made me trust in you even at my mother's breast. From birth I was cast upon you; from my mother's womb you have been my God" (Psalm 22:9–10, NIV).

Jeremiah said, "The word of the LORD came to me, saying, 'Before I formed you in the womb I knew you, before you were born I set you apart'" (Jeremiah 1:4–5, NIV). Scripture says of John the Baptist that an angel of the Lord appeared to Zechariah and said, "Your wife Elizabeth will bear you a son, and you are to give him the name John. . . . He will be filled with the Holy Spirit even from birth" (Luke 1:13, 15, NIV).

The apostle Paul said, "When God, who set me apart from birth and called me by his grace, was pleased to reveal his Son in me so that I might preach him among the Gentiles, I did not consult any man" (Galatians 1:15–16, NIV).

This is how we became evangelists. It was not of our own choosing, although we gave assent to it. God chose us and called us and sent us. We are evangelists because God, from before we were born, appointed us to be evangelists. In that lies the authority of our commission.

The Evangelist Relies on the Holy Spirit in Private Life

Second, the evangelist relies on the Holy Spirit in private life.

The year was 1960. That year television came to San Salvador. I saw in it a potential, especially to reach the more privileged classes. Driven by that call, I started a Sunday night, half-hour, dramatized TV program. In the spring of that year an evangelist came to El Salvador, and I was asked to interpret for him. His message was salvation and divine healing. Six-year-old Ellin, our youngest of five children, had a severely crossed right eye. She had worn corrective glasses for three years without help. The next step was surgery. One night she said, "Daddy, I want to go to the service. I know I will be healed if the evangelist prays for me."

We took her. And at a given moment the evangelist asked those who were sick to place their hands, if possible, over the part of their body that was sick. She placed her little hands over her eyes. The evangelist prayed. After prayer, she said, "Mommy, too bad we didn't bring the glasses case. I won't need the glasses anymore." Ellin was instantly healed of the pain that she suffered while not wearing the glasses. And within one month her eye, which without glasses was almost behind her nose, was completely straight. It was a beautiful testimony of God's grace and power.

But—and when I use the word *but*, it means there is another side to the story—the following Sunday evening, instead of going directly to the TV program, I went to the hotel to pick up the evangelist. When I walked into the lobby I glanced to my left and saw him sitting at the bar with his arm around a girl and with a glass of some drink in his hand. Needless to say, I was paralyzed. I knew he hadn't seen me, so I turned around quickly, left the hotel and went to the TV station. God somehow helped me through that program.

I then returned to the hotel. The evangelist was on the outside steps waiting for me, Bible in hand. He did his preaching and prayed for the sick. I half-heartedly interpreted the message. Though it's hard to believe, people were saved and healed.

On the way back to the hotel, with my wife in the car, I confronted the evangelist with what I had seen. He denied it vehemently. When I told him I would have to inform the leadership of his behavior, he broke down and began to cry. We spent a couple of hours in the car while he, crying out to God for forgiveness and asking us to forgive him, seemed to be genuinely repentant. Seeing his repentance and not wanting to disrupt the meeting that was ending in just a few days, I didn't say anything to anyone. However, not long after that he divorced his wife, gave himself over to drinking, and completely abandoned his loyalty to God.

Several questions come to mind. How could a man preach with sin in his life? And then how could his message have brought people to salvation and physical healing? On the latter question, all I can answer is that God, without doubt, honors His Word. He honored the faith of a little child named Ellin. On the first question, how could a man preach with sin in his heart? I can't understand it. Except to say that it is possible for a preacher to use his natural speaking abilities even after he has been divested of God's anointing on his life.

I wonder if some of us may have deluded ourselves into thinking that because we can preach a good sermon and because people respond to the call, those should be all the credentials we need to prove to the world that we are in a right standing with God.

The Lord never did say, "By their gifts you will recognize them." He said, "By their fruit you will recognize them" (Matthew 7:16, NIV). God does expect us to have a lifetime of uninterrupted fruitful ministry. But genuine and long-lasting success only comes as we depend solely on the Holy Spirit and His anointing upon our lives.

The apostle Paul's words are very clear: "Those who live according to the sinful nature have their minds set on what that nature desires; but those who live in accordance with the Spirit have their minds set on what the Spirit desires. The mind of sinful man is death, but the mind controlled by the Spirit is life and peace; the sinful mind is hostile to God. It does not submit to God's law, nor can it do so. Those controlled by the sinful nature cannot please God" (Romans 8:5–8, NIV).

Yes, the evangelist has gifts. These can be in operation with or without God's Holy Spirit anointing. But only as the evangelist's reliance is completely on the Holy Spirit and not upon his gifts will he or she enjoy a full lifetime of fruitful and lasting ministry. May God help us in that.

The Evangelist Relies on the Holy Spirit in the Devotional Life

Third, the evangelist relies on the Holy Spirit in the devotional life.

I had just finished my message in a church in the city of San Salvador, and people had responded. As I sat down, I was struck by a thought that terrified me. I heard my mind saying, "Paul, you don't believe what you've just preached." I went home that evening and could hardly sleep. I found myself doubting the miracles of the Bible. How could the Red Sea have parted by itself? How could Lazarus have come back to life, having been dead for four days? These and other similar questions were bouncing around in my head.

After about six weeks of this horrible turmoil that had me not only confused but frightened, I received a letter from Carolyn Lindblad, a Bible school friend of mine whom I had not seen in years. This was the gist of her letter: "Paul," she said, "I have dreamed that I saw you dressed in tattered beggar's clothes, totally destroyed and asking for alms." The dream so impressed her that she felt she had to tell me that God had not abandoned me and that I was in His heart and on His agenda. She wanted me to understand that whatever my situation was, God had not forsaken me.

> I was beginning to substitute human ways of becoming successful for the grace of our Lord Jesus Christ and the anointing of God's Holy Spirit in my life. For a short time I almost lost my confidence in God.

At that same time, I remember visiting an Indian village in one of the Central American countries where most of the inhabitants could neither read nor write. I saw them climb a hill in this mountainous village and approach a rock in which they had carved a face with eyes and nose and mouth. I saw them place flowers and fruit and light candles in front of this rock as they knelt before it. Though they knew very little of the outside world's civilization, they somehow knew about worship. It was, to be sure, elementary and misguided worship, but it was worship nonetheless.

I realized that from the time we are thrust into this world, we have an innate consciousness of God. A child does not have to be taught how to have faith. Yet as we become "mature" and—I use these words in quotes—"enlightened," "educated," somehow our higher learning can make us lose that which is a natural part of every human being: faith, especially faith in God.

What had happened to me? I had been studying books on self-awareness, on how to build myself up and take control of my own life. And though I understood that these things in themselves could be helpful, I was beginning to substitute human ways of becoming successful for the grace of our Lord Jesus Christ and the anointing of God's Holy Spirit in my life. For a short time I almost lost my confidence in God. I'm ashamed to say this, but it happened to me.

What was my solution? I needed to live every day of my life in disciplined consecration to our Lord Jesus Christ. I reinstated a practice that I had abandoned some time before—that of not allowing one single day to go by without reading God's Word. Though this happened almost 40 years ago, I have never again doubted God or the miracles in the Bible or His call upon my life.

My dear fellow evangelists, we cannot abandon our relationship with God and expect to maintain our confidence in Him. It is only as we realize our need of God and as we live consecrated to God by daily reading His Word, in meditation and prayer, and by relying on God's Holy Spirit that we can live victorious lives.

The apostle Paul's words to Timothy are absolutely vital for us today: "Watch your life and doctrine closely. Persevere in them, because if you do, you will save both yourself and your hearers" (1 Timothy 4:16, NIV). There is no way that we can live a holy life, maintaining an active ministry, without relying on God's Holy Spirit. God's Spirit instructs us, inspires us and anoints us.

Listen closely to the apostle Paul's words to the Corinthian church, "When I came to you, brothers, I did not come with eloquence or superior wisdom as I proclaimed to you the testimony about God. For I resolved to know nothing while I was with you except Jesus Christ and him crucified. I came to you in weakness and fear, and with much trembling. My message and my preaching were not with wise and persuasive words, but with a demonstration of the Spirit's power, so that your faith might not rest on men's wisdom, but on God's power" (1 Corinthians 2:1–5, NIV).

Unless we establish some disciplinary practice of daily spiritual activity, it will be impossible to maintain our closeness to God. Only as we read God's Holy Word every day in prayer and meditation will we live both conscious of God's holiness and aware of our own insufficiency.

I assume that most of us have discovered some Bible-reading program that will help us maintain daily fellowship with our Lord. I cannot overemphasize the importance of this. It does require rigid discipline, and yet I don't like to think of it as something done under duress. It is, to be sure, a daily discipline, but it should be fulfilling. I have read the Bible every day for many years, and I find enjoyment and strength and spiritual growth in the reading of God's Holy Word.

The Evangelist Relies on the Holy Spirit in the Public Life

Fourth, the evangelist relies on the Holy Spirit in the public life.

One of the dangers that we evangelists incur is that of getting into the spirit of competition. We look at the activity of other evangelists and try as best as we can to produce more, to promote more, to look better before the public than they.

There is an interesting story in the book of Numbers. It has to do with Moses dealing with what today is called "professional jealousy." God had ordered Moses to gather around him in the Tent of Meeting 70 elders who were known to be leaders among the people. Moses obeyed God's order, and the Lord took the Spirit that was on Moses and placed it on the 70 elders. They all began to prophesy.

Two men, Eldad and Medad, had remained in the camp. They were listed among the elders but had not gone to the tent. Yet the Spirit of God also rested on them and they also prophesied. A young man ran and told Moses, "Eldad and Medad are prophesying" (see Numbers 11:25–27).

At this, Joshua became upset. Here is how Numbers 11 describes the incident:

"Joshua son of Nun, who had been Moses' aide since youth, spoke up and said, 'Moses, my lord, stop them!' But Moses replied, 'Are you jealous for my sake? I wish that all the LORD's people were prophets and that the LORD would put his Spirit on them!'" (Numbers 11:28–29, NIV).

It is sad to admit, but the spirit of Joshua—at least the spirit that for that moment possessed him—prevails yet today. Why is there jealousy among us? Why do we have the tendency to compare ourselves with others? Why do we feel we must compete? Can we not accept the fact that every evangelist is unique, with his or her own capabilities and charisma and talents? Are we jealous because another seems to be getting all the open doors? Can we not conceive the fact that he is obeying the responsibilities that God has placed specifically on him?

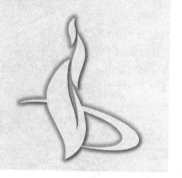

Why is there jealousy among us? Why do we have the tendency to compare ourselves with others?

Listen to the apostle Paul's words, "Just as each of us has one body with many members, and these members do not all have the same function, so in Christ we who are many form one body, and each member belongs to all the others" (Romans 12:4–5, NIV). No two of us are alike. For the complete needs of the Kingdom of God to be wholly fulfilled, it is necessary that each one of us do only that which he or she is called to do. If we try to copy someone else, we'll be rendering ourselves useless. Neither God nor His Kingdom needs two identical servants! All evangelists are an integral part of the "team." Since all of us are different, God's call is a very personal call; there is no competition.

If I were the only evangelist in the world and I was faithfully fulfilling my task, it would never occur to me to question my gifts or my acceptance or my success. Why? Because I would have no one else to compare myself to. Herein lies the problem. We, for some reason, feel we must compare and compete.

We don't have to compete. God needs us to be the people that we are. You are unique. There is not another person in the world like you; there never has been and there never will be. When God called you, He wanted and needed the "you" that you are! He needed your uniqueness to fill a place in God's Kingdom that only you can fill. To look upon a colleague and wish you were like him or that you had her gifts or that you were given his opportunities is to sacrifice the person that God needs and intends for you to be.

We don't need someone else's gifts. All we need is to be ourselves. Anointed with God's Holy Spirit, be the very best that you can be; then seek God every day of your life for the fullness of His divine Spirit. That will give you all the fulfillment that you can possibly contain.

The Evangelist Relies on the Holy Spirit in Public Speaking

Next, the evangelist relies on the Holy Spirit in public speaking.

Some 50 years ago, in the city of Santa Ana, El Salvador, Central America, I had been given the responsibility of delivering one of the main messages in the yearly conference of our denomination. It was the first time that I addressed this large group of several hundred leaders. And, frankly, I was scared.

I remember walking from my house to the church, a distance of some six or eight blocks, and trembling as I walked along. I was crossing the last street before arriving at the tabernacle when suddenly I sensed the Lord speaking to me. "Son, the reason you're so nervous is that you're afraid you'll fail. You know that you'll be speaking to many leaders, most of them more experienced than you, and you don't want to fail. Should you not fail, should you present My message with clarity and anointing, you will be a success. Should you, on the other hand, blunder through the message, losing your thoughts and your composure, you will still win. The fear of failure means your ego is very much alive and needs to be subdued. You are of no service to Me if you think you can be successful if you depend on your own abilities. So if you preach a good message, you'll be blessed. If not, you'll be humbled. In both cases, you'll succeed!"

That lesson has lasted me a lifetime. It made me realize that I was just a channel conveying God's message to the congregation. At the same time, it made me realize that my fear was caused by pride. I was afraid of becoming a fool in front of my peers and those leaders.

Colleagues, the message is not ours. We are only conveyors of it. Let's stand tall and deliver God's Word as Christ's messengers by the authority of God's Holy Spirit. Remember Paul's words to the Corinthians: "God . . . has committed to us the message of reconciliation. We are therefore Christ's ambassadors, as though God were making his appeal through us" (2 Corinthians 5:19–20, NIV).

Unlike a pastor who faces the same congregation Sunday after Sunday and therefore must prepare a new message for each service, the evangelist is before different people every time he conducts a new evangelistic crusade. This means he may feel free from time to time to repeat a message. There are only so many ways of expressing the salvation message. Man's sinful nature is the same in all areas of the world and throughout all generations. Likewise, there is no substitution for the redemption story. These are facts that cannot be altered. This is the message we will repeat over and over, and well we should.

I make mention of this because it could be easy for the evangelist to become mechanical, to deliver the message from memory without God's Holy Spirit anointing. If God's Spirit does not refresh the message in our hearts, the preaching of it can become only a performance. We may have the charisma to draw people forward, but unless the Spirit draws them, their deliverance will be as ineffective as our message. Jesus said it very clearly: "No one can come to me unless the Father who sent me draws him" (John 6:44, NIV).

I have adopted a practice which helps me keep alive the message that God has placed on my heart, even though I may have repeated it many times. I restudy the message, meditating again on the material and sometimes even rewriting the outline. It becomes new, as though it were the first time that I was preaching it. The message itself deserves this care. And even more than the message, the people to whom I am delivering it deserve this care. Let us, my fellow evangelists, however many times we may repeat a message, never go to the pulpit without asking God for a fresh anointing on that message. If it does not inspire us, it will not inspire our audience.

The Evangelist Relies on the Holy Spirit in the Spiritual Quest
Finally, the evangelist relies on the Holy Spirit in the spiritual quest.

Let us not forget that the message will never be more anointed than the messenger. It was because of this that Jesus demanded one specific thing of His disciples: "Do not leave Jerusalem, but wait for the gift my Father promised, which you have heard me speak about. For John baptized with water, but in a few days you will be baptized with the Holy Spirit" (Acts 1:4–5, NIV).

To the question, "Lord, are you at this time going to restore the kingdom to Israel?" the Lord answered, "It is not for you to know the times or dates the Father has set by his own authority. But you will receive power when the Holy Spirit comes on you; and you will be my witnesses in Jerusalem, and in all Judea and Samaria, and to the ends of the earth" (Acts 1:6–8, NIV).

God's Holy Spirit is what His disciples needed. Luke, in the book of Acts, relates the fulfillment of that promise. "When the day of Pentecost came, they were all together in one place. Suddenly a sound like the blowing of a violent wind came from heaven and filled the whole house where they were sitting. They saw what seemed to be tongues of fire that separated and came to rest on each of them. All of them were filled with the Holy Spirit and began to speak in other tongues as the Spirit enabled them" (Acts 2:1–4, NIV).

In his treatise *A Biblical Standard for Evangelists,* Dr. Graham writes the following, "The Holy Spirit is the great communicator. Without His supernatural work, there would be no such thing as conversion. Satan puts a veil over the truth, and this can be penetrated only by the power of the Holy Spirit. It is this third person of the Trinity who takes the message and communicates with power to the hearts and minds of men and women."

May I say in closing that though all of us that are here have submitted ourselves to the lordship of Jesus Christ, and though we all understand that there is only one church, the church of which Jesus said, "I will build my church, and the gates of Hades will not overcome it" (Matthew 16:18, NIV), and though also we all by the grace of Christ have been made part of that church, yet on certain—and I say this carefully—on certain biblical subjects, specifically the baptism with the Holy Spirit, we have varying convictions. This is especially so with regard to how the Holy Spirit baptism manifests itself in the individual lives. In view of this diversity, we must be very understanding and not think that everyone must experience God's blessing in the same manner.

I quote Dr. Graham again from his book *A Biblical Standard for Evangelists:* "When we are filled with the Holy Spirit," Dr. Graham says, "we renounce our dependency on ourselves and our own strength, and yield ourselves to His control. We commit our lives to the lordship of Jesus Christ each day that the Spirit of God might fill and empower us for the work He has for us to do."

What God really wants of us is the full and continuous commitment of our lives to the lordship of Jesus Christ. Let us not depend on a past experience to carry us through our whole life. We must seek the fullness of the Spirit every day. As bearers of the most important message that the world will ever hear, the message of eternal redemption, we have a responsibility unlike anyone else in the world. Let us be faithful to that responsibility. Along with seeking God for an anointed *message,* let us seek Him for an anointed *life.*

Let us pray, Father in heaven, we are here because we love You. And we're here because we've answered Your call. And we're here, Father, because we have surrendered our lives to You for the preaching of the Gospel of Jesus Christ. But we also recognize our need of the fullness of Your Holy Spirit in our lives. Please, God, every one of us who is here, fill us and not just at this moment, but every day, every day, every day, every day of our lives till the very last breath that we breathe. Fill us with your Holy Spirit, God. Without it, we have nothing. Without Him, we have nothing. Without the anointing of God's Holy Spirit, we have nothing and we are nothing. May we understand that, God, it is not our talents, it is not our gifts. It is not us, Father. It is the anointing of God's Holy Spirit that gives us the strength and the power and the might and the anointing and the words and the conviction to bring sinners to Christ. May we never lose sight of that. In Jesus' name. Amen.

Paul Finkenbinder
("Hermano Pablo")

Affectionately known by the Latin American community as "Hermano Pablo," Dr. Finkenbinder ministers in the Spanish-speaking world through media, pastors' seminars and crusades (in joint effort with the Billy Graham Evangelistic Association). Born in Puerto Rico, to missionary parents, his own missionary career began in New Mexico (U.S.A.), just after marrying his wife, Linda. They took up residency in El Salvador, where they lived and ministered for 21 years. Hermano Pablo Ministries is headquartered in Costa Mesa, California, U.S.A. The Finkenbinders have five children, eleven grandchildren and seven great-grandchildren.

The Evangelist and Prayer

Video: Billy Graham
Bruno Radzizewski, Argentina

Our Father which art in heaven, Hallowed be thy name. Thy kingdom come. Thy will be done in earth, as it is in heaven" (Matthew 6:9–10, KJV).

I think prayer is the most essential thing in evangelism. Prayer is the most essential thing in my own life. The men and women that God has used have been men and women of prayer. Sometimes we get so busy with all the planning and preparation necessary in being an evangelist that we neglect the importance of prayer.

Why do I believe prayer is important in evangelism?—because praying to Jesus makes me a faithful follower. Prayer opens the door for evangelism, and it gives me the power to do what I cannot do by myself. When we pray for others to know Jesus, the first thing that we receive is the love of lost souls. God opens our ears so that we can hear the cries for help of those who we pray for. The lost soul needs salvation, and since I am in contact with God, He allows me to feel the losts' need. He gives me faith in the Word and allows me to invite and bring those I pray for to the congregation.

Without prayer as a priority in our lives we are like a lamp with a bad connection: We have the potential of shining our light brightly into the darkness, but we are not receiving the full power of God.

Using the illustration of lost souls, we are the 99 and the lost are the 1. That one, that lost soul, is the one the Lord wants. He wants 100 percent, not 99 percent. The lost souls are far from God but close to us. We live, work and eat with them every day. When I pray for that lost soul, God gives me a special love because I am asking Him to save them. The Lord helps me find those who need Christ, because at one time I needed Jesus and someone else introduced me to salvation. That is why the best way for me to notice the lost is for me to pray to God so that He can open the doors—and He does open them.

Prayer is part of a well-rounded plan to reach others with the Gospel. One thing that we do in Latin America is playing the role of big brother. This action has five parts: First, ask that God be in charge of our prayers for others. Second, make a list of people who we know need salvation. Third, pray for them every day. Fourth, invite them to an evangelistic campaign, and fifth, prepare them to receive Jesus Christ. This is something we do every day. This is not only for an evangelistic campaign but for our local churches, too. Big brother looks out for little brother so that he can see Jesus. This is a great help for all of us.

God desires to have a complete relationship with us, and evangelists should not underestimate the importance of giving themselves to Him in daily prayer.

My prayer for the future is that the Lord does not let me forget this evangelistic vision of winning the world for Jesus Christ. God has given us the tools and He constantly gives us new ones. We want to win the world for Jesus. Every one of our congregations has discovered the vision of world evangelization.

Billy Graham and Bruno Radzizewski

Dr. Graham founded the Billy Graham Evangelistic Association in 1950, which headquarters in Minneapolis, Minnesota, U.S.A. Dr. Graham and his wife, Ruth, make their home in North Carolina, U.S.A. Rev. Bruno Radzizewski is a Nazarene pastor in Argentina.

Billy Graham   Bruno
                    Radzizewski

The Evangelist and Prayer

Bill Bright and Vonette Bright

WRB = Bill Bright
VZB = Vonette Bright

WRB: What a humbling and marvelous privilege for Vonette and me to be here to greet all of you, our fellow evangelists from around the world!

VZB: We are very excited about what God is going to do through this great historic occasion. And we believe that truly this is going to help to accelerate the fulfillment of the Great Commission and to send the Gospel all the more effectively to every person around the world.

WRB: The Scripture, Ephesians 5, admonishes the husband to love his wife as Christ loved the church (see v. 25). Since we're talking about prayer, I should mention that the apostle Peter had a special word of warning. He said, "You husbands must give honor to your wives. Treat her with understanding as you live together. . . . She is your equal partner in God's gift of new life. If you don't treat her as you should, your prayers will not be heard" (1 Peter 3:7, NLT).

If any of you are having problems in your ministry or if you are not getting answers to your prayers, I would exhort you to take a look into the mirror of God's holy, inspired Word. If you are truly loving God with all your heart, soul and mind, and your spouse as Christ loved the church, you will be blessed.

VZB: I have learned a new dimension to the aspect of submission and love as explained in Ephesians 5; that is, a wife should voluntarily submit to her husband, and the husband is to sacrificially love his wife as Christ loves the church (see vv. 22–25). Those two words, *voluntarily* and *sacrificially*, are not in the text but they are implied. I would like to add those two words for every couple to emphasize in order to assure a greater harmony, unity and love in their marriage. This will not only be pleasing to God but it will remove hindrances to prayer.

Prayer Is Communication

WRB: First, we know that all prayer is simply talking to God, if we are praying in the Spirit. It is a matter of communication with the great Creator God of the universe. He is our Savior, our Lord, our Master. He merely spoke and a hundred billion galaxies were flung into space. Having created all things, He became the God-man Jesus and died for us.

You and I as children of the living God have the incredible privilege of going right into the presence of the great Creator God and Savior of the universe. He is actually waiting for us. He delights in us. The Bible tells us that He has a great reservoir of blessing waiting for us. And marvel of marvels and miracle of miracles, having died on the Cross for our sins, He has been raised from the dead and now lives within each one of us. Our bodies are His temples. He is closer to us than our hands and feet and nearer than our breathing. We can literally talk with God more meaningfully and intimately than with our dearest loved ones and friends.

Developing an Intimate Relationship With God

VZB: This brings us to point two, that of developing an intimate relationship with God.

WRB: And that is what the Christian life is all about. Jesus said, "Love the Lord your God with all your heart and with all your soul and with all your mind" (Matthew 22:37, NIV). And the second part of the great commandment is, "Love your neighbor as yourself" (v. 39, NIV). The only way you can do this is by a balance of time in the Word and time in prayer.

VZB: Prayer is so rewarding. I must say, the more I pray, the more I wonder why I do not pray more. Reading God's Word and prayer are more satisfying to me than any other way that I could possibly be spending my time.

WRB: God has given me, I believe, a responsibility and calling to promote worldwide fasting and prayer. The responsibility and privilege of devoting a major part of the remaining years of my life to fasting and prayer for world revival consumes me. If I truly follow the model of the Lord Jesus, who at this very moment is interceding for us at the right hand of the Father, the greatest privilege I can have is to intercede for other members of the body of Christ, for the nations of the world, and for the fulfillment of the Great Commission.

VZB: I have just heard a very sobering report that the average Christian worker spends just enough time in prayer to sustain his ministry. Friends, if we are going to see God work in supernatural ways in our lives and in our ministries, we must spend more time than just a token amount reading God's Word, and just saying a brief prayer each day.

WRB: As we study the life of our Lord, we find that He was truly a person of prayer. The great apostle Paul was a man of prayer. Anyone who has ever been used of God in a significant way has been a person of prayer. God's Word makes it very clear that prayer is the key to personal revival, church revival, national revival. Nothing significant has ever been accomplished for the glory of God apart from prayer.

The Person of Prayer

VZB: And now we come to point three, the person of prayer. Actually, God calls all of us to a ministry of intercession—every believer. To intercede means to "stand in the gap for." He wants us to "stand in the gap for" whomever we are praying for and to stand between the person and the Lord—for circumstances, for needs, for situations, whatever they may be. We should intercede as passionately for the person or the event as if that answer to prayer depends totally upon us and as if we are personally responsible.

WRB: In other words, we should pray with such perseverance and such zeal, with the assumption that unless we pray that cause will fail or the salvation of that soul may be forever lost. God commands all of His children to pray and to "pray without ceasing" (1 Thessalonians 5:17, KJV), which means we should be in the spirit of prayer—worship, praising, interceding, always giving thanks—as a way of life. That is the greatest privilege we can know. And that's what makes prayer so exciting.

United in Prayer

VZB: This brings us to our fourth point, united in prayer. One day in my daily devotions I was impressed while reading in Acts 4 where Peter and John had just been released from prison. They went back to the disciples and reported to them all that the chief priests and elders had said to them. Then the believers united together in prayer to God. They prayed for Herod and the leaders of the day.

They were praying specifically, strategically, and they were praying with one heart and mind.

One translation puts it this way, "They won't stop at anything which you in your wise power will allow them to do. Now, Lord, consider their threats and enable your servants to speak your word with great boldness. Stretch out your hand to heal and perform miracles and signs and wonders through the name of the Lord Jesus Christ" (see Acts 4:24–30). And verse 32 records that all the believers were of one heart and mind. Notice that they prayed earnestly for boldness, for God's anointing. And they prayed specifically and strategically.

WRB: We want to emphasize particularly that they were united in prayer; they were praying for boldness, even if that boldness should result in further persecution. In their prayer they referred to the sovereignty of God. God rules in the affairs of men and nations. They knew this great truth about God, and they were excited about it.

VZB: What speaks to me in that passage is that they were united in prayer. They were praying specifically, strategically, and they were praying with one heart and mind. Think of what God would do through us as the Holy Spirit invites us to pray unitedly as believers around the world!

WRB: Think what God could do if we were united in a spirit of love and harmony as those disciples were. It's very important for us, as we talk about prayer, to remember that there are certain qualifications that are necessary before God will hear our prayers. I'd like to mention five of those.

First, the Bible says, "If I regard iniquity in my heart, the Lord will not hear me" (Psalm 66:18, KJV). So if we are going to be effective in our prayers, we must be sure there is no unconfessed sin in our lives. God promises, "If we confess our sins, he is faithful and just to forgive us our sins, and to cleanse us from all unrighteousness" (1 John 1:9, KJV).

Second, we must be sure to be filled with the Holy Spirit, not just when we speak but as a way of life. Everything about the Christian life, beginning with the new birth and the anointing and fullness for witnessing, depends upon the Holy Spirit.

Third, Scripture tells us that if we ask anything according to God's will, He hears and answers us (see 1 John 5:14–15). Let us always pray according to God's will.

Fourth, we must be sure that we are abiding in Christ, for Jesus said, "If ye abide in me, and my words abide in you, ye shall ask what ye will, and it shall be done unto you" (John 15:7, KJV). So it is very important that we be on praying ground. A lot of prayers are wasted words. God does not hear prayers offered by many believers because they are not praying according to biblical standards.

Fifth, as I have already mentioned, demonstrate your love for your spouse and your children. Be a model in your home of what you are preaching.

Praise in Prayer

VZB: The fifth point is that there are some very practical things that you can do to make prayer even more meaningful. I like to pray Scripture back to God. For example, good passages to pray back to God are Philippians 1:9–11, Colossians 1:9–12 and Ephesians 3:14–21.

WRB: I especially like that wonderful chapter, Psalm 145. I pray as I read and respond, "Father in heaven, I join with the writer of Psalm 145 to praise You for Your total power, Your wisdom and love and mercy, and all Your other magnificent attributes."

VZB: And the last five psalms are psalms of praise. It's wonderful to read a verse of Scripture and then pray that verse back to God, then read the second verse of Scripture and pray that back to God, and so on.

WRB: If you are not enjoying your prayer conversation with God, it may be that you don't fully understand the incredible, awesome privilege that is ours of talking to the great God—Creator, Savior. Always remember that prayer is just simply talking to Him, often using His holy, inspired Word to enrich that conversation.

VZB: I'd like to suggest that you even note in your Bible some verses of Scripture for a particular prayer request. For example, as you pray for nonbelievers, there are wonderful Scriptures to claim in praying for them. That surely is one of the most important prayers—for the souls of loved ones, neighbors and friends.

The Privilege of Prayer

WRB: Point six is the privilege of prayer. Let us encourage you, if you have non-believers in your family or among your friends, remember: "God so loved the world that He gave His only begotten Son, that whoever believes in Him should not perish but have everlasting life" (John 3:16, NKJV). Peter records that God is "not willing that any should perish" (2 Peter 3:9, KJV). He says further that the Lord has even delayed His return in order that more people may have a chance to hear the Good News of the Gospel.

I am often asked, "Will you pray for my loved one—my father, mother, wife or son?" to which I reply, "Do you believe it is God's will that they receive Christ?" They often say, "I've prayed for them for years and they've not responded." And then I explain, "God's Word declares that He is not willing that any should perish." Then I refer to 1 John 5:14–15 again, "If we ask anything according to his will, he hears us. And if we know that he hears us—whatever we ask—we know that we have what we asked of him" (NIV). So we know that when the Holy Spirit impresses us to pray for an individual—a loved one or neighbor or friend or a stranger—we are praying according to His will.

On the authority of Scripture, God honors faith. "Without faith it is impossible to please [God]" (Hebrews 11:6, KJV). "Whatsoever is not of faith is sin" (Romans 14:23, KJV). We can approach the needs of others in that spirit of faith.

So when you pray, "Lord, please save my husband, my wife, my parents, my children, neighbors or friends," you can be sure that you're always praying according to the will of God. Therefore, by faith you can thank Him for their salvation because we know that whatever we ask for according to God's will, He hears and answers. Now, if that sounds extreme, remember it's God's Word which says that if we ask anything according to His will. And we know it's His will that none should perish. You can trust God's Word!

Pray According to the Scripture

VZB: This brings us to point seven. Pray according to the Scripture. Look for Scriptures that apply to a particular subject and pray that subject. For example, choose Scriptures to pray for those who are ill, or choose other Scriptures for your children, your marriage or whatever the subject.

WRB: Always pray according to Scripture and obey the prompting of the Holy Spirit as you pray. Also, when praying in large groups, in many cultures it is appropriate for everyone to pray aloud for a particular person or a concern. In small groups it is sometimes helpful if various prayer requests are written down. Each participant prays only a few words for each request so that no one individual monopolizes the prayer time.

VZB: Pray in modern language. Pray just as if you're talking to your best friend, because you really are. This simple approach to prayer greatly encourages people to pray, especially new believers. There are people who are active church members who have never audibly said a prayer in a group or perhaps even alone.

A Five-Step Plan

Eighth, let me suggest a five-step plan that I have seen used effectively to help both the new believer and the mature person, even pastors, feel comfortable in praying together. Here's the five-step plan:

One: Thank God for anything.

Two: Thank God for something that has happened in the last 24 hours.

Three: A "please help" prayer—for yourself or someone else.

Four: Ask God for something you need or want.

Five: Thank God for answering your prayers.

WRB: Sometimes there are Christians who pray too long and too eloquently, and the people who hear them pray are often intimidated or get tired of hearing them. It is sometimes more inspiring when a new believer offers a brief prayer such as, "Lord, I love you." So we must not feel inferior if we are not gifted in our prayers. Everybody has to start somewhere.

Prayer and Fasting

Number nine, let's talk about what I believe is the most powerful Christian discipline available to every believer: fasting and prayer. For each of the past seven years we have fasted and prayed for 40 days for national and world revival and the fulfillment of the Great Commission.

VZB: I must say that it has been a wonderful time for us together.

> I encourage you to prayerfully consider spending a protracted time with God, seeking His face and fasting with prayer.

WRB: And our lives have been dramatically enriched. You know, when you are drawn closer to the Lord together, you are drawn closer to each other. Today millions of people are praying and fasting for revival. And we have every reason to believe that millions of people are now fasting and praying, many of them for 40 days, that God will do something supernatural, something absolutely unprecedented in history.

I would encourage you to prayerfully consider spending a protracted time with God, seeking His face and fasting with prayer. Don't enter into the fasting and prayer with the wrong motive. You are not to fast to find favor with God. You already have His favor, but you are to seek His face with a humble, trusting spirit. To me, fasting with prayer is the only Christian discipline that truly meets the conditions of 2 Chronicles 7:14. ["If my people, who are called by my name, will humble themselves and pray and seek my face and turn from their wicked ways, then will I hear from heaven and will forgive their sin and will heal their land" (NIV).] This also is the most powerful of all the biblical disciplines, and through fasting and prayer we destroy the strongholds of Satan.

That privilege is available to every believer, new and old alike.

VZB: I believe that we should dedicate our fast to a particular cause, something specific that we are praying for, and then use the time that we would ordinarily be preparing and eating food to pray. I believe that is the kind of dedication that God wants from us. There is a quote attributed to Andrew Murray: "Prayer grasps the power of heaven. Fasting loosens the hold on earthly pleasure." I have learned that fasting helps to focus our communication with God.

Prayer Changes the World

WRB: Number ten, prayer changes the world. Our dear brothers and sisters in Christ, you can literally help change the world starting in your own home, your community, your church, through fasting and prayer. God wants to bless His people. And whenever His children have united together in love, unity and harmony, and have sought the face of God, miracles have happened. As evangelists, you can be a part of a miracle wherever you are. Make prayer and fasting a vital part of your life.

There is no doubt that this is the greatest moment in the history of the Church. More people are hearing the Gospel, more people are receiving Christ, more people are being trained to serve the Lord than ever before in history.

VZB: And more people are praying unitedly, specifically and strategically than ever before. Truly, prayer is helping to change our world. The Great Commission is so near to being fulfilled. Let us give ourselves even more to the priority of prayer.

WRB: When ten thousand evangelists go back to their various countries filled with the Spirit, giving themselves to the discipline of fasting and prayer, we can indeed help change the course of history!

Bill Bright and Vonette Bright
Dr. William R. ("Bill") Bright is the founder and president of Campus Crusade for Christ International, and his wife, Dr. Vonette Bright, is the co-founder. Dr. Bill Bright did five years of graduate study at Princeton and Fuller Theological Seminaries. Dr. Vonette Bright received her bachelor's degree from Texas Women's University. Both Brights are recipients of numerous awards and are authors. Dr. Bill Bright has six honorary doctorates and was awarded the Templeton Prize. The Brights live in Orlando, Florida, U.S.A. They have two grown sons who are in Christian ministry.

The Evangelist's Heart of Compassion

Franklin Graham

I want to talk to you about a heart of compassion. We will look at God's Word together, and at how to win lost people to Jesus Christ.

In Samaritan's Purse we work in war areas and famine areas around the world. I believe when somebody is in the ditch along life's road and we stop to help, they are going to listen to what we have to say. You stop for people: Not only will they listen after you have helped them, but you have earned the right for their family to listen. The whole family is interested in why you stopped to help.

He Didn't Turn Anybody Away

When we go into a country, we look for opportunities to help the people who are in need. If you study the Lord's ministry, when He was here on earth He didn't turn away anybody who came to Him in need. Remember Bartimaeus on the side of the road in Jericho? He yelled, "Thou son of David, have mercy on me" (Mark 10:48, KJV). Jesus was passing through Jericho on His way to Jerusalem, to the Cross, and He stopped for blind Bartimaeus. We all know that story (see Mark 10:46–52).

Jesus turned no one away. Jesus had compassion for the sick, for the dying, for the hungry. Jesus did not come to this earth to give us a better life. He came to give eternal life. He came to die on a Cross for our sins. That's the purpose of Christ's coming. He had compassion.

I believe that as we evangelists go into the world to proclaim the Gospel message, we need to do it with love, and we need to be looking for ways we can help the people that we are talking to. In Samaritan's Purse we try to use both relief and evangelism. For more than 21 years we have had opportunity to work in some unusual areas.

We'll Wait for You to Come

During the war in Nicaragua, Central America, I got a call one afternoon from a general in the Contra army. This was a guerrilla army that was fighting against the Sandinista government. This man said that he was in the Contra military, and he wanted to know if we would send doctors to help sew up and bandage the soldiers. I didn't want to go. I didn't want to get involved in a war. It was very controversial, as you may remember.

I told the man that we were Christians, and I wasn't sure that he wanted Christian doctors. He said, "Oh, that would be fine. We would love to have Christian doctors." So I thought, "Well, I need to be a little stronger." I said,

"Our doctors are evangelical Christian doctors. They would want to preach and share their faith with your soldiers. I'm not sure you want that." "Oh," he said, "that would be wonderful. We would love to have these doctors preach and share their faith in our hospitals."

I thought, "Okay, that didn't work." I said, "Well, we don't send doctors to a hospital, especially in a war zone, unless I go see it first. It just wouldn't be right for me to send a doctor to a war area when I hadn't been there first, and I don't think I could be there for several months." He replied, "Well, we'll wait for you to come."

So I said, "Give me about three months and I will come." I thought he would forget about it, but about every two weeks he would call and tell me, "We're still waiting for you to come."

Then I realized that I was going to have to go. But one of the problems I had was that I needed somebody who could preach in Spanish. My prayer was, "Lord, if you want me to go, then you have to give me somebody who can preach in Spanish." When I arrived in Honduras and we were getting ready to go into the jungle, this general met me. Beside him was a man. I shook his hand. As we drove, this general told me all about the war and the problems, and for about two hours I talked to him. After this long car drive, we ran out of things to talk about. So I turned to the other man.

The whole time I had been praying, "God, please give me somebody who can preach in Spanish." I turned to this man and I asked, "What's your name?" He said, "My name is Ruben Guerrero." I thought he was a Honduran or maybe a Nicaraguan. I said, "Where are you from, Mr. Guerrero?" He said, "I'm from Dallas, Texas, in the United States." I asked, "What are you doing here?" He replied, "I'm an evangelist." I said, "An evangelist? Doing what?" "I'm preaching in the jungle to the soldiers." I just had to say, "Lord, thank you." So as our doctors went to the hospitals, he translated. He preached the Gospel, and we saw many of these soldiers put their faith and trust in Jesus Christ.

A few weeks later I got a call from this Contra general. He said, "Thank you very much for the doctors. I need your help again." I thought, "Uh oh, what does he want this time?" He said, "We would like to have chaplains. Our men are dying on the battlefield. We would like to have chaplains who can tell them about faith in God." I said, "Well, you know the chaplains that we would train for you would be evangelical Christians. Would that be a problem?" "Oh, no," he said, "We would love to have evangelical Christian chaplains."

So we went to the jungles and we trained 115 men. These men were soldiers, jungle fighters. The commander lined them up and pointing to different ones he said, "You be a chaplain. You be a chaplain." These were 115 men with machine guns and hand grenades, and I thought, "These are our chaplains? Oh, what a problem we have here!" These people knew how to fight; they knew how to kill. They knew nothing about God, knew nothing about His Son, Jesus Christ. So for the first three months, every time we had a meeting we presented the Gospel. And every time we gave the invitation, two or three or four of these chaplains would stand to their feet to trust Jesus Christ as their Lord and Savior. At the end of five months, all of those chaplains had put their faith and trust in Jesus Christ!

When the war was over those men went back to their country, and today most of those men are pastors of churches, and some of them are the largest churches in the country. Glory to His name!

We Can Give a Cup of Cold Water

We need to take the opportunities that God gives us to reach out to people in

time of need. I didn't realize when I got that first phone call asking for doctors that it would lead to training chaplains, who later would go back to their country as missionaries to their own people, serving some of the largest churches in that nation. I didn't know that was God's plan. I tried to get out of it. I didn't want to do it.

You say, "But, Franklin, we're not big like Samaritan's Purse. We don't have a big program." Jesus spoke of giving a cup of cold water. We can give a cup of cold water in time of need. The world is not only thirsty for water, but it is thirsty for the Word of God. It is our responsibility to take the Gospel.

When Jesus Christ died on the Cross for you and for me, while we were yet sinners, that was the greatest act of compassion in all of history.

The greatest act of compassion is when God sent His Son out of heaven down to this earth for sinful man. When Jesus Christ died on the Cross for you and for me, while we were yet sinners, that was the greatest act of compassion in all of history. No other act is greater than Christ dying on the Cross and shedding His blood for you and for me.

Now I want to look at what it takes to preach an evangelistic message. Watching my father, watching other evangelists, listening, preaching evangelistic messages myself, there are a few things I have learned. It doesn't mean you have to use them, but I want to share them with you.

Use a Text From the Bible

First, if we are going to preach an evangelistic message, we have got to be biblical. We must use a text from the Bible. Now you say, "Of course"—but, to be honest with you, I've heard people give messages that were not based in the Scriptures. They told stories, they gave wonderful examples of real-life experiences. They talked about God, they talked about Jesus, but they didn't use the Word of God. There is authority and power in the Word of God! We must preach God's Word, and we must be faithful to His Word.

Always emphasize "the Bible says." My father is known for saying over and over, "The Bible says," and he quotes the Scripture. There is authority in the Word of God.

Let me give an example. Here is a wonderful text to preach from: "Jesus went through the towns and villages, teaching as he made his way to Jerusalem. Someone asked him, 'Lord, are only a few people going to be saved?'" (Luke 13:22–23, NIV). What a great way to preach a message, because you can spin that around to your audience and you can say, "Maybe you want to know how you can be saved." I always ask questions of the audience. When I read a passage of Scripture, I ask, "How about you? Have you ever thought about that? Are you saved? Are you on your way to heaven? When you stand before almighty God, is He going to welcome you in?"

Then I ask another question, "Are you sure?" Then I'll talk like the audience would be talking back to me. I'll say, "Well, I think I'm going to heaven." "I'm not talking about thinking," I'll reply. "I'm talking about knowing. Do you know that you're going to heaven?" So you can use the passage and challenge them.

Give the Invitation Clearly and Early

When I read my text I give the invitation, right up front. I tell people, "Tonight I'm going to give you an opportunity to do something that maybe you've never done before in your life. In a few minutes I'm going to invite you to get up out of your seat and make your way to an aisle. And I want you to come stand in front of this platform. And if you don't know Jesus Christ as your Lord and Savior, if you've never experienced God's forgiveness, tonight I'm going to give you an opportunity to confess your sin to God and by faith receive Jesus Christ, God's Son, into your heart and life and make Him your Lord and your Master."

Why do I do that right at the beginning? I don't want there to be confusion. Lots of times there is confusion at the invitation, and people really aren't sure what to do. One evangelist, when he got to the invitation, said, "You want to come to Jesus? Come now." And the people sat there. He had preached a wonderful message, but when he got to the invitation he was afraid. He just blurted it out, and people were confused.

We don't want to confuse people at the invitation. Give the invitation clearly, early, up front, so that as people sit there the Holy Spirit of God can begin to work in their hearts and soften their hearts. This way they know what is expected of them and what is coming, and the Holy Spirit of God can prepare their hearts.

There Is Power in the Word of God

First, use the Scripture, a biblical text; second, give the invitation early, and then third, use Scripture throughout your message, because there is power in the Word of God.

Jesus said, "Make every effort to enter through the narrow door, because many, I tell you, will try to enter and will not be able to" (Luke 13:24, NIV). Jesus is talking about a narrow door. Many will want to go through it, but they won't be able to. You see, there is a barrier between a holy God and sinful people. This barrier is sin. There is only one door that goes through this barrier of sin, and that is the Cross. It is a narrow door.

The world is trying to open up a wide door, but that door doesn't get there. It's the door of religion, it's the door of good works, it's the door of this, and it's the door of that. But it's not the Cross, and there is only one way. Jesus said, "I am the way, the truth, and the life: no man cometh unto the Father, but by me" (John 14:6, KJV). We have a barrier of sin, and in our preaching we have to establish the fact that the person listening to you is a sinner; that's what the Bible says.

You have to establish the fact of sin. We have all sinned; we have come short of God's glory (see Romans 3:23). And the penalty of sin is death, "The wages of sin is death" (Romans 6:23, KJV). You have to make people understand that they are sinners.

People today, especially in Western society, don't even know what sin is. We have fallen morally. We have gone to such depths that many people in Western culture don't even understand sin. So I will explain sin. I'll take the Ten Commandments (see Exodus 20:1–17) or part of the Ten Commandments, and say, "Telling a lie is a sin, and some of you here tonight have lied. You're guilty. Sex outside of marriage, adultery, is a sin against God. And there are some of you who are guilty. But God loves you. God wants to forgive you."

Each time I'm very careful to say, "But if you're guilty of this, God loves you. God will forgive you. You can be set free tonight." Then I'll give the invitation, "In just a few minutes I'm going to ask you to do something—to get up out of your seat, come stand here and experience God's forgiveness." I give the invitation three or four times in my message because I want to be clear.

> **If you stand up there and try to have a ministry based on your power, your strength, you're going to fail. You're going to fall on your face. You've got to do it in His power, in His strength.**

God Is Calling You to Be an Evangelist

Years ago an evangelist from Canada by the name of John Wesley White said, "Franklin, I think God is calling you to be an evangelist." I answered, "What?" "Yes," he said, "I think God is calling you to be an evangelist." Well, God hadn't told me! But John said, "God has told me." I always love it when God tells somebody else but doesn't tell me. He said, "I think God is calling you to be an evangelist. I want you to come to Saskatoon, Saskatchewan. I'm having a meeting there. I want you to take one of the nights of my meeting and give the sermon. Preach the Gospel; give the invitation. And, Franklin, we'll be praying."

I said, "No, I'm not going to do that." He kept putting pressure on me, "I want you to." I said, "No." He kept putting on the pressure. I said, "No." Finally, just to make him be quiet I said, "Okay."

I went to Saskatoon. I was not prepared. Nobody had helped me. I took a passage of Scripture, I preached it and I did poorly. When I got to the invitation, I was scared. So I gave a poor invitation; it wasn't much of an invitation and nobody came. I walked off the platform and told John Wesley White, "I'm never going to preach again. Listen, my father has been called to evangelism; I've been called to the ditches of the world. I'm going to go and do the work that God has called me to. I am not going to be an evangelist—that's what my father does. No!"

Later he called me on the telephone and said, "Franklin, I'm so sorry. I'm going to have a meeting in Juneau, Alaska, next year. And I want you to come to Juneau, and you can preach." "I'll never preach again!" I said. "Franklin, you come. I want you to come." So finally I said, "Okay, I'll come to Juneau next year." I thought he would forget about it. But he did not forget about Juneau. He kept calling me, just like that Contra general. He said, "We're looking forward to having you in Juneau."

The time came. I went to Juneau. This time I did something I didn't do the last time. I bathed the message in prayer. If you want to be a successful evangelist, you have to bathe everything in prayer. I got down on my knees and prayed over that message. That night when I preached, five people came forward. Hallelujah! When those five people came forward I realized it wasn't because of anything I had said. It was the Holy Spirit of God touching their hearts. They responded to God's Word, not my word. It was His Word. It wasn't my invitation. It was God's invitation.

I think every one of us who are evangelists has been a little scared when we get to the invitation. We should be, because we're on holy ground at that moment. That is when the Holy Spirit of God is at work. But don't water down the Gospel. Don't give the invitation and say, "Now, for those of you who want me to pray for you, you come and let me pray for you." Listen, I have nothing against a prayer meeting. But we're calling sinners to repentance! We're calling sinners to put their faith in Jesus Christ. Don't water down the invitation.

Let's Make It Clear!

In our evangelistic preaching we establish the fact of sin. We give examples of sin. We want to be clear about what God has done for sinful people, that He has given His Son Jesus Christ. I use John 3:16—you can't find a better verse— "For God so loved the world, that he gave his only begotten Son, that whosoever believeth in him should not perish, but have everlasting life" (KJV). And I tell the person who is listening, "God loves you. You may have this wall of sin. You're looking for that narrow door. You haven't been able to find it. Jesus Christ is that door. You've got to come through Christ, because Jesus Christ is the only one in all of history to die for sin. No one in history came down to this earth to take your sin except the Lord Jesus Christ. And if you're willing to confess Him"—then I go into the invitation—"if you're willing to confess Him and make Him your Lord and ask Him to be your Savior, and if you're willing to repent and turn from your sins, you can leave here a changed man, a changed woman, forgiven, on your way to heaven."

You go verse by verse, but stop, come back, establish the fact of sin, establish the Cross, show that Jesus Christ died on that Cross for you and me, that He shed His blood. Don't be afraid to say *blood*. He shed *His blood* for you and for me. He went to the grave. He was buried. But on the third day God raised His Son from the grave, and now He is in heaven at the right hand of almighty God. And someday, friends, He's coming back!

Our Job, Our Calling, Our Mandate

God has called you and me; He has commissioned us to go into the world and to make disciples of all nations (see Matthew 28:19). That's our job. That's our mandate. That's our calling. But, friends, if we're going to do it, we've got to do it on our knees. We've got to do it in prayer; we've got to be biblical; we've got to use His Word. There is power in His Word. Give God's invitation. Call men and women to repentance and to put their faith in the Lord Jesus Christ.

I promise you, you will see success in your ministry, because it's not going to be by your power; it's going to be by His power. It's going to be His power through you. If you stand up there and try to have a ministry based on your power, your strength, you're going to fail. You're going to fall on your face. You've got to do it in His power, in His strength. Amen.

Franklin Graham

Reverend William Franklin Graham III is the eldest son of Billy Graham and Ruth Bell Graham. Raised near Asheville, North Carolina, U.S.A., Rev. Graham now lives in Boone, North Carolina, U.S.A. At age 22, Rev. Graham committed his life to Jesus Christ. Rev. Graham was elected to the Board of Samaritan's Purse in 1978, and one year later was elected President of the organization. In 1995, he was elected to serve as the First Vice Chairman of the BGEA, and in November 2000 he was elected to serve as Chief Executive Officer of the Billy Graham Evangelistic Association. Rev. Graham and his wife, Jane, have four children.

Principles of Mobilization for Evangelistic Activities

Edwin Martinez

Why are some crusades successful? Why are others not? Many times the evangelist is good and the facilities are good, but one or two ingredients are lacking. That is what we are going to look at. I have divided the material into two parts to make it easier to master: prerequisites for evangelistic efforts, and organizational structure—two different things.

What are those prerequisites for carrying out an evangelistic effort? How are those prerequisites identified? Many times as I travel around Latin America I jot things down; I make notes. Because I have made notes, some of the prerequisites come up and are the things that help determine if we should hold a crusade or not.

If any of these things are not there as ingredients before a crusade, I personally try not to have the crusade. I tell the people, "Let us pray, and maybe in one year or perhaps two, or even in three years' time we can have it. But this is not the right timing." I believe that holding a crusade in the right timing is of utmost importance, because the Lord will bless it when we find those prerequisites and affirm them.

Then comes the organizational structure. Regarding the organizational structure, we shall be dealing with things that could seem rather boring, but we will deal only with the basics that need to be there so that we can envision a successful crusade. Most of these principles can be applied to a small campaign in a small city or town, and are even applicable to a local church. They are principles derived from big, massive crusades, but we have used them also in smaller events.

Building the Lord's Church

The purpose of this presentation is to help us understand what is required at the local church level in order to carry out an evangelistic effort. Pastors and leaders are the key persons to teach the church. I have visited some evangelistic crusades where I had no participation in the coordination, and the people there have asked me this question: "Why do you think the pastors are not here? Why are the leaders not here?" Here lies one of the reasons why we do not obtain the expected success in a crusade. The Lord Jesus said, "I will build my church" (Matthew 16:18, KJV). Our ultimate goal should be to build the Lord's Church.

When we arrive at a place and our goal has been to see raised hands, to see people coming to the altar, we realize we have missed the mark. Not only will those people have no follow-up, we will not see them joining a local church. Jesus said He had come to build His Church. When we do evangelism, we are in the process of building the Lord's Church. So, dear evangelists, even though we may not be church planters, the pastors of the city in which we are to hold an evangelistic crusade will appreciate that we keep in mind the overall purpose of the churches. Not only do we need to focus on local church growth, but also on church planting, mainly in places where no churches exist. If you are not doing this in your country, I challenge you to think of this goal.

In order to make what we have said a reality, we need to make disciples of all nations, as stated in Matthew 28:18–20. Jesus also said, "Ye shall be witnesses unto me" (Acts 1:8, KJV), and He said it should be done everywhere. He wants us to proclaim the Gospel to all creation. In some parts of the world, evangelists do not get involved much in discipling or in church planting. They need to involve the church, the pastor and the leaders in order that they provide whatever is necessary for follow-up.

Lack of Unity, A Guarantee for Failure

Now, let us focus on the prerequisites for evangelistic efforts. The first element is unity. "By this shall all men know that ye are my disciples, if ye have love one to another" (John 13:35, KJV). I said before that when I go to other countries I take notes. One of the things I write down is the level of unity among the pastors. There are evangelical alliances, there are pastors' alliances and there are church alliances. But in spite of that, if there is no unity in the Lord's church we cannot carry out an evangelistic effort. Lack of unity is a guarantee for no success; it is our assurance of failure.

As I go to different places, I see the state of the church, how one minister speaks of another, and how they relate. Sometimes there is jealousy, and pastors do not speak kind words of other pastors. However, when you hear that one pastor commends another pastor, when you see them rejoicing over the growth of this or that church, when you hear one pastor say good things about another church or denomination and how the Lord is pouring out His blessing upon them, there you have unity! When you see unity among believers, that will bring success.

Unity does not mean standardization. We do not all need to do everything the same way. We need not think the same way. The important thing is that in the common domain of evangelism in which we are all involved, we do everything the best way we can, living out the unity that the Lord wants us to show.

A clear understanding of the goals will help to bring about unity. If it is clearly stated what we are going to do, and if it is understood that we are not setting the stage for a certain person, a church, a radio station, some organization or even a missionary agency, then more believers will be willing to join forces in the effort.

The task of evangelizing a whole nation brings together a wide range of denominations under a common objective. In the Dominican Republic, where Christians want to see one million new believers this year, there exists a tremendous unity, and believers are working and being creative in what they do to see their country come to the Lord. Set a national target, set a goal for your city, set a goal for your church. That will help you to instill a spirit of unity.

Ministry Is a Team Effort

Another important thing to bear in mind, my dear brothers, is that a spirit of unity is a spirit of forgiveness. Let us be forgiving towards those who are "cold" according to our own self-defined spiritual standards. Let there be a spirit of tolerance, of forgiveness. When we forgive others, the Lord makes us totally free. When He makes us free, we are able to embrace others in the Lord—something we would otherwise not be capable of doing, because they are in some way different from us and their doctrine is not the same as ours.

We need others. No evangelist can do it alone. No denomination can do it alone. No evangelistic team can do it alone. For that reason unity is important. We need to pray that the Lord will give us that spirit of unity. Each time someone sows the seed of dispute within an organizing body, he is weakening the evangelistic effort. We need to love that individual and help him. Most likely, in the process, the Lord will transform that person.

> **Do not go about things on your own. Let us not work individually. We need others. There are other people whom God wants to use besides us. We need to be interdependent.**

Make ministry a team effort. Do not go about things on your own. Let us not work individually. We need others. There are other people whom God wants to use besides us. We need to be interdependent. Scripture teaches this. Being interdependent means that I depend on others, that I need others, that the task will not be accomplished unless someone helps me, unless I work elbow to elbow with another.

I believe that on occasions our Latin American "machismo" [male pride] has been a hindrance to the success of crusades and campaigns. "Well, who needs Brother Jones? Who has any need for Brother Smith's ministry? Why, we don't need them. We can manage alone." Brothers, let us not be found acting this way. The Lord wants to see us practicing teamwork; that means each individual doing his or her part. This is one of my tasks—often encouraging those two or three lonesome laborers on a 10-, 15- or 20-member committee. Each one must do his or her part. If it is not done this way, we will never see success.

Let me give you an illustration. Think of migrating birds that fly in a formation. Surely you have seen them. Those who study bird behavior tell us there is a reason for this. They fly faster because the ones in front break the wind for those coming behind. Those in the lead get tired sooner, but the ones that follow can fly with less effort.

This principle is applied in cycling. The one in the lead cannot rush ahead alone and remain in that place. Why? Because he gets tired; he needs to be replaced. So another cyclist moves forward and takes the lead. This one works hard to keep the speed; and when after a while he gets tired, another moves forward, and so on. So we find this rotation. Going back to the bird formations, you may have noticed them chattering along. Bird watchers say this is a way of encouraging those that are in the lead so that they keep up the swiftness and don't slow down. Cyclists apply it; professionals apply it; you will hear it along the way—always encouraging the one in front. Then the one in the lead steps back and the one in second place takes the lead, and then the one in third place moves forward, and so on.

Now, there is something interesting that happens when one of those birds falls to the ground. Two of the strongest and healthiest birds fly down with it and keep it company until its full recovery. Once it is able to fly again, they catch up with the formation, which has reduced its speed for the benefit of those that had to stay behind. God teaches us a powerful lesson through nature. It is amazing to think that many times we who can talk, who can communicate, do not make this principle work.

Show Mutual Respect

Two important things are related to this. One is mutual respect. Mutual respect means to respect the fact that the most qualified person should be selected for the job. I will not appoint someone to a position just because he or she is my friend. I am not going to assign someone a task because that individual has been good to me in some way. I am going to have someone involved because he or she can get the job done. Brothers, one of our great mistakes is cliques. Cliques just kill us; they ruin us. That is another thing that guarantees lack of success in a crusade. Let us appoint the individual who is most qualified.

Mutual respect is made manifest in the way that we address another person. It is also expressed when we carry through what we have promised to do. One of the problems we have in our countries is that we say we will attend a meeting but we never turn up. Mutual respect needs to be lived out. "But let your yea be yea; and your nay, nay" (James 5:12, KJV). "Yes, I'll be at the meeting." "No, I won't be at the meeting." "I'll do this or that," and you do it! Or, "I'm not going to do that," and you stick to it!

I have attended meetings where 10 people were expected and only two or three came along. We canceled that meeting and scheduled another meeting for two or three days later. Everybody said yes they would be there. So that day we arrive for the new meeting, two or three of us, and we wait for one hour and nobody else comes. It is time to start developing an attitude of responsibility and accountability.

We Need Accountability and Communication

These things make a difference when we are organizing a campaign. These are the things that build up and make a big difference. Mutual respect is the first element, and then responsibility. The members of the team need to be accountable to one another—spiritually, financially and in terms of organization. The individual who submits to the team will grow and mature. When we pray together and are challenged by others, we grow. I have seen it happen.

The next is good communication. It is important that all people involved in the crusade receive the relevant information in a timely manner. This is one thing I have learned throughout the coordination of crusades. Communication: Let everyone know what is going on, what is being done. There should be no surprises for anybody.

If, when we get to a meeting, it is expected that everyone be informed about something, then make sure they are informed. If there is a person who is responsible for informing, make sure that person does it. How? Well, each one needs to do his or her best to contact the recipients. Phone them, meet them, drop them a note, or whatever. Just make sure that all people involved are informed.

> **Always speak showing forth Christ's love. Do not give Satan a victory by being irritated. . . . Discuss the issue, not the individual.**

One of the major problems I have come across in Latin America is that we do not communicate. For some unknown reason we hold things secret; we keep certain information to ourselves. I believe that one can see the effectiveness of coordination when everything is laid out on the table and all are informed and know where we are heading. People know what we are going to do, they know whom we are going to do it with, they know how we are going to do it, and they know when we are going to do it. If a meeting is scheduled, say where it will be, say what time it will start. Sometimes we get to a place and people say, "I didn't know about that; nobody told me anything."

It is important to let all those present at the meeting voice their opinion. I believe also that our "machismo" has brought us to a point in which we express our own opinion and do not leave room for others to voice their thoughts too. Sometimes there are fellow Christians who are of a quiet nature and do not say much unless you specifically ask them something. Many times these people have gems, real pearls that they want to share with us—and will, if only we would let them talk.

Let us avoid judging. Our mind-set is to point with our finger. But let us separate the message, what people are trying to communicate, from the way it is being said to us. Retain what is helpful, and let us forget that which could be easily criticized.

Always speak showing forth Christ's love. Do not give Satan a victory by being irritated. Some meetings need to address hard, difficult issues; some very significant decisions need to be made. Whenever possible, avoid confronting people. Confront the issue, not the person. Discuss the issue, not the individual. When you discuss a serious issue and you seem to be in opposition to a fellow Christian's point of view but you do not offend him, he will appreciate you for it. This brother will agree that we need to discuss the subject and that we need to give it a solution. If something is ultimately going to be decided which goes against what he thinks, he will come out unscathed. He will say, "I came out whole, even though my idea was not considered the best this time."

Let me mention the issue of humility. This is one of the most difficult topics. According to Matthew 20:28 the Lord Jesus Christ came not to be served but to serve. And this should be our prayer, that the Lord will help us to have servant hearts. I have seen evangelists who have tried to exalt themselves, and that is a sad thing because we are engaged in a strong battle. On the other hand, I have also seen evangelists whom the Lord has exalted. He does that when people humble themselves.

Organization: Honor Them by Including Them

Let us focus now on organizational structure, the organizing committee. Do not have an evangelistic campaign if the blessing of the church leadership is not upon you. Just don't do it! Do not force things. Get the church leadership in the city or town to bless the campaign. We will surely have some of those brothers in the organizing committee. Some will be members, others will be involved only on the advisory committee, but in this way we will honor them. We honor them by including them in the organization, in a role that perhaps does not demand a great deal of work from them. Some do not want to find themselves with a lot of work to do, but their blessing is very important.

The executive committee is a small group of leaders who will develop goals and plans and a budget for the crusade. You might say, "Well, my campaigns are only at the local church level. How can I put together an executive committee in my local church? It is not a big church; it is not a large crusade." Even if there are only two people, make sure that the committee will help you establish all the tasks that have to be done for the campaign.

One-on-One Evangelism on a Mass Scale

Friendship builds bridges. In the Billy Graham Evangelistic Association it has been stated that Billy Graham does not do mass evangelism. What he does is one-on-one evangelism on a massive scale. Fellow evangelists, if you hold campaigns and you want to ensure success—not regarding the number of people who attend or come forward, but success in terms of a greater number of people who stay in the church—then use a one-on-one program such as Operation Andrew, named after Andrew, who met Jesus and then immediately told his brother Simon and "brought him to Jesus" (John 1:42, KJV).

International Impact uses the 5 x 1 plan. Others use "the most sought-after man," "the most sought-after woman," or others; there are different methods and systems. Make a special card where you write down the names of relatives, friends, work colleagues and so on—people who do not know the Lord. You should expect these people to attend the campaign. You establish a natural and logical connection with people who come to the evangelistic meeting after you have invited them saying, "Come with me. There will be good music. You will hear about Jesus Christ. I would like you to come with me." Even if the seven on your card are not converted, even if the five are not converted, if just one person comes to Christ, that is one!

Suppose a small, 40-member church is involved in the event, and only one of those five or seven that each of us has been praying for is converted and comes into the church. We have had a commendable success. Our harvest will be 40 more people, or 100 percent in reference to those who were prayed for and invited. Challenge the whole congregation to pray for those five or seven people on their lists. When these people come, you will see them being saved. I can assure you, after 26 years of doing this, that the Lord will respond and you will see many new people joining the church.

Prayer, Finances, Publicity, Promotion and Handling Decisions

Billy Graham says, "The success of a Crusade depends on three things: The first is prayer, the second is prayer, and the third is prayer." So then if you want to put a star next to Operation Andrew, do that; then put a second star next to prayer. If you can do nothing else, you can still fill in a card and pray.

In regard to finances and fund-raising, some Christians do not have a collection at the campaign, and that is good. If you can raise the funds before the campaign, do so. Raising funds is important, and there are several ways to do it. You can do it through special activities such as fund-raising banquets; there are many ways to carry out fund-raising. However, if you need to have a time for an offering during the campaign, you can do it.

You are going to need ushers. Ushers need to be familiar with the venue. They are not only responsible for the collection, they need to know their way about the venue and be there for those who need information or orientation. Ushers in charge of the collection should also be organized to count and report. Please underscore report. Many times we do not report. We need to report how much we raised and how we spent the money.

Then there is publicity and promotion. Promotion has to do with the efforts within the church to let Christians know about the campaign. You never cease promoting. You should always be doing it. One of the best methods for promotion is Operation Andrew. The prayer card, if you use it well, will be a means of promotion. Determine the place of the campaign. Arrange the timetable. Decide who the preacher will be. Then you can start the promotion activities. Publicity is the effort to make the event known to non-Christians. Nonbelievers need to be informed regarding the event.

We come now to the decision card. The decision card is a part of counseling and follow-up. Counseling is one of the most important things in an evangelistic campaign. People come forward for different reasons. Some come for reconciliation, others to receive Christ for the first time, or they come for other reasons. If you are there to counsel a person who comes forward and you ask him or her, "Have you come here to receive Jesus as your personal Savior?" you are giving that person the opportunity to do so at that moment.

You have the decision card for the person who responded, you counsel that person, and you have follow-up to help that person come into the church. If you have those three things, you can have a better evangelistic crusade.

God bless you!

Edwin Martinez

Reverend Edwin Martinez is the director of pastoral ministries with the IMT (International Ministry Team) at O.C. International. His ministry involves the training of pastors and leaders in Latin America and other parts of the world in areas of church multiplication, missions and evangelism. Born and reared in Guatemala, Rev. Martinez is a graduate of SETECA, a seminary in Guatemala City. He also enjoys preaching in evangelistic crusades. Rev. Martinez and his wife, Evie, are the parents of two children, and they currently live in Miami, Florida (U.S.A.).

The Evangelist's Inner Life

Stephen F. Olford

I want to read those glorious building blocks of Christian character known as the Beatitudes: "Blessed are the poor in spirit, for theirs is the kingdom of heaven. Blessed are those who mourn, for they shall be comforted. Blessed are the meek, for they shall inherit the earth. Blessed are those who hunger and thirst for righteousness, for they shall be filled. Blessed are the merciful, for they shall obtain mercy. Blessed are the pure in heart, for they shall see God" (Matthew 5:3–8, NKJV).

I have been asked to address the subject of the inner life of the evangelist. This is an awesome task, and I've spent many hours examining my own heart in prayer and fasting. I have been studying God's Word, "Blessed are the pure in heart, for they shall see God" (Matthew 5:8, NKJV). I want to open it to you in a piece of teaching, a piece of exposition, applying it to our hearts with the support of many other Scriptures.

It is very solemn to realize that if we don't obey this wonderful injunction, we shall never serve Jesus faithfully here and we shall never hear His "well done" in heaven. "Oh, the blessedness of the pure in heart!" It's not just a statement, a proposition. It's an exclamation. "How blessed are the pure in heart, for they shall see God!"

The Consciousness of a Pure Heart

It is the consistent teaching of Holy Scripture that God is more interested in what we are than in what we do. If what we are doesn't please His holiness, then what we do is virtually worthless.

The prophet Isaiah says, "Be clean, you who bear the vessels of the LORD" (52:11, NKJV). That should drive us to our knees. For the writer here, and our Lord Jesus in particular, is reminding us that the consciousness of a pure heart is a personal awareness of a pure heart. It is the personal awareness of purity in our lives.

The heart stands for the control center of all our lives. Just as that physical heart of yours pumps blood to every part of your body and keeps you alive and keeps you clean, so in a similar way the heart—that inner person of yours—is the control point for all of your life. This is what Jesus is emphasizing here.

You ask, "Well, how can I keep my heart pure?" I want to give you three verses from the Word of God that amplify what we're talking about in this awareness of purity. They are disciplines I follow every day of my life. I call them the daily disciplines of devotion.

Dominated by the Word of God

We must be dominated by the Word of God. "Let the word of Christ dwell in you richly in all wisdom" (Colossians 3:16, KJV). Why *word* and *wisdom* in the one text? Well, the Word gives us God's revelation, God's knowledge, God's truth. But wisdom is the ability to apply that to every aspect of our lives. Every day we must say, "Lord, I'm reading your Word that it may dwell in me richly in all wisdom." This is not the legalism of a practice. It is loyalty to a person, the Lord Jesus Christ.

I want to ask, Did you have a quiet time today? Did you have a few minutes to open His Word? Did you say, "Lord, speak a word to me for today, just for me"? Did you engage in prayer? By faith did you pierce the heavens to see the face of your Savior?

"Let the word of Christ dwell in you richly in all wisdom" (Colossians 3:16, KJV). A quiet time is the most important thing in your life. It's the barometer of your Christian life. You'll never sense the anointing and power of the Spirit upon you unless you are being cleansed by His Word. "Let the word of Christ dwell in you richly in all wisdom" (Colossians 3:16, KJV).

Activated by the Spirit of God

We must be dominated by the Word of God. And we must be activated by the Spirit of God. "Be filled with the Spirit" (Ephesians 5:18, KJV). That is an imperative. It is the present tense—go on being filled with the Spirit. As that great and mighty preacher of another century, Charles Haddon Spurgeon, said, "That's not a promise to claim. That's a command to obey." If you are not filled with the Holy Spirit right now, you are blocking the way. There is sin in your life. "Be filled with the Spirit" (Ephesians 5:18, KJV). That is not something to think about or meditate upon. It is something to do, to yield your life to the person and power and presence of the Holy Spirit.

We talk about a higher life, we talk about a deeper life, we talk about a wider life, a broader life. But what we are talking about here is a normal Christian life, the Spirit-filled life.

Motivated by the Glory of God

Your will must be motivated by the glory of God; "Whether you eat or drink, or whatever you do, do all to the glory of God" (1 Corinthians 10:31, NKJV). The consuming passion of your life must be to do all to the glory of God. Man's chief end is to glorify God and to enjoy Him forever. If every day you are dominated by the Word of God, if you are activated by the Spirit of God, if you are motivated by the glory of God, you will sense an awareness of purity in your life.

The Practical Awareness of Purity

More than just a personal awareness, there is practical awareness. The pure in heart shall see God. Solomon says, "Keep your heart with all diligence, for out of it spring the issues of life" (Proverbs 4:23, NKJV). And again, "As [a man] thinks in his heart, so is he" (Proverbs 23:7, NKJV). That control center of your life, the heart, is the place where we have got to begin, for if that is not holy, then everything that issues from it is not holy.

And this calls for action. The writer to the Hebrews tells us that we are to "Pursue . . . holiness, without which no one will see the Lord" (Hebrews 12:14, NKJV). We are to pursue it. That word *pursue* is a picture of a hunter bearing down on the animal, on the prey. It's a picture of a young, zealous businessman following his calling, and he is not going to allow anything to stop him. Therefore, the awareness of purity comes through action, obedience to God's Word.

The Constancy of a Pure Heart

It is one thing to have a consciousness of purity because the Word of God is dwelling in us richly, because we are filled with the Spirit, because we are motivated for the glory of God alone. But how do we keep this constant? How are we to keep steadfast in the faith? We need the constancy of a pure heart.

Tied up in that word *pure* is the whole concept of constancy, steadfastness in purity. The very meaning of the word suggests that. It is a statement of constancy. I want to say two things about this: We must be daily cleansed, and we must be duly controlled.

The Heart Must Be Daily Cleansed

Look at the first: The heart must be daily cleansed. "Blessed are the pure in heart" (Matthew 5:8, NKJV). That word denotes cleansing by an agent outside of ourselves. We can't keep ourselves pure. Only He can do it. "The heart is deceitful above all things, and desperately wicked: who can know it? I the LORD search the heart" (Jeremiah 17:9–10, KJV).

So how can we keep our lives pure? I want to give you the four biblical means that God has given us to keep us pure. Number one is the application of the precious blood. "If we walk in the light, as he is in the light, we have fellowship one with another"—both vertically and horizontally—"and the blood of Jesus Christ his Son [goes on cleansing] us from all sin" (1 John 1:7, KJV). When Jesus died on Calvary's Cross, He not only conquered sin but provided for that inner cleansing day by day. There is the application of the precious blood of Jesus.

Number two is the ministration of the living Word. In that high priestly prayer of the Lord Jesus, He looked up to heaven and said, "Father, Father, sanctify My disciples by Your Word. Your Word is truth. Make them clean. Make them holy. Make them pure by Your Word" (see John 17:17). And that is how God cleanses us day by day. Not only by the precious blood of Jesus, but by the living ministration of the Word. Jesus said to His disciples, "Now ye are clean through the word which I have spoken unto you" (John 15:3, KJV). The great psalmist David says, "Wherewithal shall a young man cleanse his way?" Then comes the answer, "By taking heed thereto according to thy word" (Psalm 119:9, KJV).

Number three is the operation of the Holy Spirit. Paul is looking back at the life of some of those Corinthians before they were converted, and he says, "And such were some of you: but ye are washed, but ye are sanctified, but ye are justified in the name of the Lord Jesus [Christ], and by the Spirit of our God" (1 Corinthians 6:11, KJV). Our bodies are the very habitat, the very temple, the dwelling place of God the Holy Spirit. That is Paul's whole argument in Corinth. He says, "How is it that you are indwelt by the Holy Spirit and live unholy lives?" (see 1 Corinthians 6:19). That is a contradiction in terms.

> Our bodies are the very habitat, the very temple, the dwelling place of God.... The Holy Spirit dwells in a clean temple, a clean home, a clean house. Let us not grieve the Holy Spirit.

The Holy Spirit dwells in a clean temple, a clean home, a clean house. Let us not grieve the Holy Spirit. "Grieve not the holy Spirit of God" (Ephesians 4:30, KJV). "Quench not the [Holy] Spirit" (1 Thessalonians 5:19, KJV). We must allow the Holy Spirit to have unfettered, unhindered sway in our lives. Paul asks the question, "Do you not know that your body is the temple of the Holy Spirit who is in you, whom you have from God, and you are not your own?" (1 Corinthians 6:19, NKJV). Pause for a moment and reflect on the fact that, if you are a child of God, you are indwelt by God's Holy Spirit.

Number four is the inspiration of the blessed hope. Speaking of the coming again of our Lord and Savior Jesus Christ and our ultimate conformity to His likeness, John says this, "Everyone who has this hope in Him"— what?—"purifies himself, just as He is pure" (1 John 3:3, NKJV). How can we believe in the imminent return of our wonderful Lord and not live in the light of that coming? When John writes his epistle about the coming of the Lord, he is not stating a theological concept. He is issuing an ethical challenge. We are to look for the Lord Jesus Christ with anticipation and to live holy lives because He's coming back again. All of us are going to stand before that judgment seat of Christ to be judged for the deeds done in the body, whether they be good or bad. We shall all give an account of ourselves to God.

I am not talking about the great white throne. I am not talking about that awful day when great and small will be judged because they have rejected the Lord Jesus Christ and will be consigned to everlasting hell. I am talking about the judgment seat of Christ where we shall stand to receive rewards for a life lived to His glory. And we shall have a rebuke if we have failed to live as we should have done.

Our Lord Jesus Christ is coming again, and that hope should keep us living every day as if today were the last day. Peter had this in mind when he said,

"Sanctify [Christ as] Lord God in your hearts, and always be ready to give a defense to everyone who asks you a reason for the hope that is in you, with meekness and fear" (1 Peter 3:15, NKJV).

The Heart Must Be Duly Controlled

But it's not only that the heart must be daily cleansed. It is one thing to be cleansed, another thing to be controlled. In training young Timothy to be a pastor-evangelist, Paul said four very important things that need to be controlled in all our lives.

Number one is the area of unlawful sex. "Flee . . . youthful lusts" (2 Timothy 2:22, KJV). That is an imperative, and it is a present tense. Go on fleeing, go on fleeing, go on fleeing until Jesus comes. Our Christian world is littered with evangelists and Christian workers who have not heeded that powerful command of the apostle. Paul says, "Make [no] provision for the flesh, to fulfil the lusts thereof" (Romans 13:14, KJV). Don't put yourself into danger's ways. Don't pick up that pornographic literature in the airport or anywhere else. Don't look at a woman to lust after her. If you have done so, you have sinned already in your heart (see Matthew 5:28). Put on the Lord Jesus Christ. Clothe yourself with the protective garments of the Lord Jesus Christ against the lust of the eyes, the lust of the flesh.

Number two is the area of unbroken pride. Paul warns young men not to be "puffed up with pride" (1 Timothy 3:6, NKJV). There are two chapters in the Bible—Ezekiel 28 (see verses 11–19) and Isaiah 14 (see verses 12–15)—that warn us about this awful enemy, pride. The most beautiful, the most masterful of all of God's creation, Lucifer, daystar, son of the morning, fell because of pride and cursed an entire world ever since.

Are you puffed up with pride when you see crowds coming to hear you preach? Are you puffed up with pride when you see people responding to the Gospel? Are you puffed up with pride when you see your name in the newspapers and other media? If God is going to use you, beloved, you must walk the Calvary road of humility, brokenness and death to self. We can never live a life of blessing to the glory of God until we humble ourselves under the mighty hand of God.

Number three is a very subtle one, the area of unholy greed. When Paul says, "The love of money is the root of all evil" (1 Timothy 6:10, KJV), he is not writing to businessmen, he is not writing to the heads of corporations, he is not writing to CEOs; he is writing to a young pastor-evangelist, Timothy. He says, "The love of money is the root of all evil" (1 Timothy 6:10, KJV).

Nothing quite blinds like the glitter of gold. Paul warns of destruction and perdition to those who don't watch this very subtle enemy called filthy lucre. All of us can name evangelists who have crashed because of cash. Examine yourself right now about this matter. It's subtle; it creeps up on you and you begin to think of the materialistic aspect of your ministry. I don't believe that

Timothy was a wealthy man. But that didn't mean that he didn't need to be warned that the love of money is the root of every form of evil.

Number four, and one that is rarely named, is the area of unbalanced truth. Paul says to young Timothy, "Be a workman that needs not to be ashamed, rightly dividing the word of truth" (see 2 Timothy 2:15). In the context of that command he talks about two men, Hymenaeus and Philetus (see verse 17), who had become unbalanced in truth and then had pressed it to absolute error.

All across our land, either to the right or to the left, are extremes. Oh, for balanced, biblical preachers! I spend my life now training preachers to preach the Word of God faithfully and accurately. And when I say preach the Word, I mean to be expositors. Preach the Word. If you are under the anointing of the mighty Spirit of God, you will be kept balanced.

> I don't believe that Timothy was a wealthy man. But that didn't mean that he didn't need to be warned that the love of money is the root of every form of evil.

The Consequence of a Pure Heart

We can see the glory of Christ in the world around us. We read that "the heavens declare the glory of God; and the firmament showeth his handiwork" (Psalm 19:1, KJV). We must remember that "all things were made by him [the Lord Jesus Christ]; and without him was not any thing made that was made" (John 1:3, KJV). He is the center of creation. As we live we must not blind ourselves to all the glories of God's wonderful creation.

We can see the glory of Christ by God's work within us. "Christ in you, the hope of glory" (Colossians 1:27, KJV). Paul rejoiced in this. He rejoiced because he saw the unity of the church, Jew and Gentile come together. That's glory. I can add white and black, brown and yellow, oneness in Christ, the glory of God.

The glory of God is seen not only in the world around us, not only in God's work within us, but in God's Word before us. "We all, with open face beholding as in a glass the glory of the Lord" (2 Corinthians 3:18, KJV). As we see that glory and that Word, we are to go out and reflect it. Your only authority and opportunity for witnessing to Jesus Christ is that you have seen that glory, and that glory is now being reflected in you moment by moment and day by day.

Ask yourself, am I living a holy life? Am I consciously pure in my mind, my heart, my will? Do I flee youthful lusts? Do I focus on material things? Am I balanced in my doctrine, my teaching? Will I be ashamed at Christ's coming? Am I a holy man? Am I a holy woman?

A man who has challenged my life through his writings was a Scottish preacher who never reached the age of 30. Yet he transformed his church, his community, his city, his country. Robert Murray McCheyne had a prayer that hangs in my study, and I pray it every day. Here are the words: "O God, make me as holy as a saved sinner can be."

We have examined the consciousness, the constancy and the consequence of a pure life. Oh that we might be found following holiness as well as "perfecting holiness in the fear of God" (2 Corinthians 7:1, KJV) all the days of our lives.

Stephen F. Olford

Born in Africa, Dr. Stephen F. Olford currently serves as Founder and Senior Lecturer of the Stephen Olford Center for Biblical Preaching in Memphis, Tennessee, U.S.A. He has pastored large churches in London, England, and New York City, New York (U.S.A.), while maintaining an evangelistic ministry. Dr. Olford earned a Doctor of Theology degree from Luther Rice Seminary.

In 1970, while continuing to maintain the busy program of a pastor, Dr. Olford launched what is now known as Olford Ministries International, Incorporated, to fulfill the Great Commission through media, ministry and leadership training. Dr. Olford and his wife, Heather, live in Tennessee (U.S.A.), and have two sons and five grandchildren.

The Evangelist's Personal Life

Video: Cliff Barrows and Billy Graham

Cliff Barrows: "People have asked us, 'What's the secret of having been together all this length of time?' Well, there are several things, but one is that Mr. Graham has been a man of a single vision and a burden for evangelism. He's committed to that."

Billy Graham: "Many years ago, Cliff Barrows and one or two of us sat down and tried to list all the questions and criticisms of evangelists—financial integrity, moral purity, working with the church, and honesty in publicity. And we said, 'We're going to try to overcome this and set a new standard in our generation.' We decided that we would try to correct these things that evangelists are susceptible to, and I think the Lord has helped us because we turned it over to the Lord."

Cliff Barrows: "God has used those four major areas as guide points in our lives, and I thank and I praise Him for it. It has been God's divine mandate upon our lives. There is that wonderful challenging verse, 'Therefore, my beloved brethren, be ye steadfast, unmovable, always abounding in the work of the Lord, forasmuch as ye know that your labor is not in vain in the Lord' (1 Corinthians 15:58, KJV).

"It is very easy to become distracted, to lose focus. One of the greatest enemies is activity. That's something that I've had to wrestle with. We can get so busily involved or think we're so necessary to the project or to the ministry that we let the important areas slip. Paul said in Galatians, 'I am crucified with Christ: nevertheless I live; yet not I, but Christ liveth in me' (2:20, KJV). Each day we need to cultivate that personal relationship with the living Christ and the Holy Spirit within. That comes with our quiet time, our walk with the Lord, and in our meditation on His Word. I must be the first to confess that that can be infringed upon so quickly and so easily."

Billy Graham: "I think one has to have his own devotional life. My wife and I have a devotional life together. We never go to bed at night without a Bible reading and prayer together. This is a great strength to me. But also I have my own devotions in the morning."

Cliff Barrows: "We're never told to pray for humility. That's an interesting thing. We're told to humble ourselves in the sight of God (see James 4:10). I pray for grace to be humble. I need that. I need for God to show me, and He has ways of showing it. Oh, may He say, 'Well done, thou good and faithful servant' (Matthew 25:21, KJV). God gave us a good beginning. And we've traveled along this pathway. Our desire is to finish well. 'O God, keep us from stumbling, from dropping the baton.' The young ones are coming along behind us. We're not, at this age, trying to get a second wind and outpace them. We need to cheer the younger ones on and say with all of the creativity, all the ingenuity, all of the power and the anointing of the Spirit of God: 'Go forth and give your life to Him.'"

Billy Graham and Cliff Barrows
Dr. Graham founded the Billy Graham Evangelistic Association in 1950, which headquarters in Minneapolis, Minnesota, U.S.A. Dr. Graham and his wife, Ruth, make their home in North Carolina, U.S.A. The Reverend Cliff Barrows is the Music and Program Director for the Billy Graham Crusade Team.

The Evangelist's Family

Dennis Rainey

I believe family evangelism is one of the untapped resources for reaching a nation. I am going to focus my comments on equipping you to love your wife, to serve your wife, to be the shepherd of your family, and to live the Christian faith where it matters most—at home. Would God give us a wife and family and then call us to regularly and habitually abandon the needs of those sheep at home? I think not.

The question for you and me is, What kind of legacy will we leave? If you died right now, how would your children describe your legacy to their generation? The psalmist declares, "Praise the LORD! How blessed is the man who fears the LORD, who greatly delights in His commandments. His descendants will be mighty on earth"—did you hear that? "His descendants will be mighty on earth"—"The generation of the upright will be blessed. Wealth and riches are in his house, and his righteousness endures forever" (Psalm 112:1–3, NASB).

Your marriage, your family, are the headwaters of your legacy. Your legacy begins not in the public marketplace of ministry, but your legacy begins at home. What occurs downstream in your ministry will only be as deep as your own personal walk with Jesus Christ and how that has been lived out at home.

The Bible begins with a marriage in Genesis and concludes with a marriage in Revelation. Marriage and family were God's idea. The theme of family permeates all of Scripture. Marriage and family are central to God's work in your nation and in mine. They are central to what God is doing on planet Earth.

God designed the family to be the birthplace and the nursery of Christianity. It is the place where the fear of God and the love of God are taught and experienced. It is the place where humility is modeled, sacrificial love is demonstrated, and forgiveness is practiced and felt. The family is the place where character is planted, and then nourished and grown. It is the place where civility and respect for God and for others are learned. The family is the place where one generation passes on the Gospel to the next generation. My friend, if you and I do not begin by winning our own families and discipling them, then the phrase, "And there arose another generation after them, which knew not the LORD" (Judges 2:10, KJV), can be written over our families and our nations.

A Christian family is God's smallest battle formation for the soul of any nation. If the soul of your nation is to be redeemed, if it is to be restored, it must be done one home at a time. That is why the merger of your ministry with your marriage and family is so vitally important. If you do not begin at home, you will not have the message of the Gospel to preach in public. A German believer by the name of Dietrich Bonhoeffer once wrote, "The righteous man is the one who lives for the next generation."

I want to show you 12 ways that you can love and lead your wife and family. Having men here who are in leadership, most of my comments will be directed to the men, calling them to be sacrificial servant-lovers and leaders of their wives and families. I believe if men would give up their lives for their wives as Christ gave up His life for His bride, the church, many of the problems in our families would go away. Sacrificial love begins with the husband. I would encourage those of you who are single to write these principles down and save them, not only for your ministry and for passing them on to others but, you never know, God might still have marriage in mind for you in the future.

Leaving a Godly Legacy

First, you can leave a godly legacy by fulfilling your marriage covenant. In the last book of the Old Testament God said, "And this is another thing you do: you cover the altar of the LORD with tears, with weeping and with groaning, because He no longer regards the offering or accepts it with favor from your hand. Yet you say, 'For what reason?' Because the LORD has been a witness between you and the wife of your youth, against whom you have dealt treacherously, though she is your companion and your wife by covenant" (Malachi 2:13–14, NASB).

I am ashamed to say to you today that in my nation, the United States of America, marriages, even within the Christian community, are being shredded by divorce. God steps out of eternity and says three short words that slice through the fog and make it abundantly clear, "I hate divorce" (Malachi 2:16, NASB). He did not say He hated the one who is divorced. He said He hated the act of severing that which had become one. Why? If you read the context of Malachi chapter 2, it says that He was seeking a godly offspring. When a marriage covenant is ripped and torn asunder, it is not merely two people who get a divorce—it is a family. In my home nation, much to my grief, the church today has a higher divorce rate than the surrounding culture.

Will the church become salt and light? Will it become the protector, the preserver and guardian of the marriage covenant? It must! It is not the state's responsibility to encourage us to keep our marriage covenant. It is our spiritual responsibility. And so today, within the Christian community, we must speak boldly about the sin of divorce while still loving and embracing the friends and family members who have experienced divorce. The church is for broken people. We uphold the standard and love the people.

We have lost our cutting edge when it comes to speaking the truth about what divorce is doing. As a result, in the West today we suffer from a culture of divorce. We have a generation of young people filling our Christian colleges, our Christian organizations, the church and even our seminaries, who are coming from broken homes—and they, too, are broken. It is time for the Christian community to uphold the marriage covenant, and that begins with your marriage covenant.

Your Marriage Covenant

Your marriage covenant was more than just a promise to stay married. If you are a husband, you made a promise to be a sacrificial servant-leader. If you are a wife, you promised to respect him. You promised to love him, yes, to submit to him. That is your covenant.

How shall we live with one another as long as we both shall live? May I suggest three ways that I would apply this to your marriage and how you can be a marriage covenant keeper? Number one, never use the "D" word in your marriage. Never use divorce as a threat in your marriage. It is time to replace the "D" word with "C" words. Replace *divorce* with *covenant*. Replace *divorce* with *compassion*. Replace *divorce* with *commitment*. As a spiritual leader of your family do not ever threaten divorce. "There is no fear in love; but perfect love casts out [all] fear" (1 John 4:18, NASB). The threat of divorce puts fear into the soul of another person, and it certainly does in your children.

Fulfill your covenant by loving your wife as Christ loved the church. How did He do that? He put her needs before His needs. He sacrificed His life. If our Savior did that for us with a love so great, what kind of lovers of our wives ought we to be? You and I are commanded to put our spouses' needs before our own. Are you doing that in your marriage?

Write out your marriage covenant. Make it into a document, sign it, have your children witness it, frame it and hang it in your home. Proudly display that you are a covenant keeper. Your marriage, your family and, yes, your ministry will be no stronger than the marriage covenant that you have with your spouse. That marriage covenant is what sets you apart. Before God, you said to your spouse, "I choose you. And before God and these witnesses I choose and promise to love you." That is a covenant between a man, a woman and God for a lifetime.

> **Write out your marriage covenant. Make it into a document, sign it, have your children witness it, frame it and hang it in your home. Proudly display that you are a covenant keeper.**

Discipleship Begins as We Pray Together

The second way to leave a godly legacy is by praying daily with your spouse. Your wife is your number one disciple. Your children are your next disciples. Your ministry follows those disciples. I believe that discipleship begins as we pray together as husband and wife in the marriage relationship.

I am forever grateful to a wise man by the name of Dr. Carl Wilson whom I went to one day and asked, "Carl, what's the best advice you can give me as a newly married man?" Barbara and I had been married for about three months at the time. He said, "Oh, that's easy, Denny; pray every day with your wife."

So I began to pray every day with my wife. It was very easy at first. Then one night we went to bed, and my wife was facing one wall and I was facing the other wall. There was a little tap on my shoulder—and it was not Barbara. It was God. He was speaking to me in my conscience. He said, "Are you going to pray with her tonight?" "No. I don't like her tonight, Lord." God said, "I know; that's why you need to pray with her." And I began to argue with God and say, "You know, Lord, it's because of her. She's 90 percent wrong in this deal." Then the Lord said, "But it's your 10 percent that caused her to be 90 percent wrong." I struggled there with God.

I want to tell you, this discipline of praying together every day with Barbara has preserved our marriage covenant and, I believe, our ministry. Will I roll over and say to her, "Sweetheart, will you forgive me for being 10 percent wrong?" No! I did that one night and that night lasted for two days! I will roll over and ask, "Will you forgive me for being wrong?" And sometimes she says, "No." She wants to see if I am repentant, because I have hurt her deeply. That is the beginning of spiritual life in your marriage, your family and, yes, your ministry.

I want to challenge you to begin doing this. Perhaps you are saying, "That's so simple, we've been praying together for years." But there are many who do not pray every day with their spouse and do not care for their soul. Leave a godly legacy by praying daily with your spouse.

Embrace Suffering Together

Third, the way to leave a godly legacy is by embracing suffering together as a couple. There are hardships in ministry, in marriage, in family, that come with the spiritual mission that God has given us. Unless we as a couple embrace suffering together, we can fall apart as a couple. On more than four occasions my wife, Barbara, has developed an irregular heartbeat—a heart rate of over 300 beats a minute—and nearly died. We have been through the valley of the shadow of death. We have experienced heartache and hardship in our family. We are not raising perfect children because they have imperfect parents.

There has been discouragement and disappointment in ministry. It is important for a couple to share these valleys together and not go through them separately. We are commanded to "bear one another's burdens" (Galatians 6:2, NASB). We must stand together, looking to God to sustain us and guide us through these times.

Scripture tells us that "our struggle is not against flesh and blood, but against the rulers, against the powers, against the world forces of this darkness, against the spiritual forces of wickedness" (Ephesians 6:12, NASB). Your struggle is not against your mate. Your mate is not your enemy. You have a common mission, a common direction and a common enemy. It is important for you as a couple to establish that common direction and mission.

Keep Your Romance Alive

The fourth way of leaving a godly legacy is by keeping romance alive in your marriage.
Nowhere in marriage are the differences between men and women more evident
than when it comes to romance. Women spell romance "relationship, friendship,
communication, talking." Men spell it differently. Men spell romance "s-e-x," sex.
Where else could two people come together and miss one another so frequently?
She is in need of relationship; he is in need of coming together with his wife. Yet
God commands the man to love his wife and to meet her need for relationship.

It is important that you guard your marriage and keep romance alive. Husbands would do well to memorize the Scripture that says husbands should "live
with [their] wives in an understanding way" (1 Peter 3:7, NASB). Men, do you
understand what your wife needs when it comes to romance? What communicates love to your wife? Is it a love letter? Then write one. Is it a hug and a kiss
without expecting anything in return? Or is it helping at home with the children
and helping to do the dishes? What communicates love to your wife? I would
encourage you to find out, and then do it.

One of the things Barbara and I have done over the years to keep romance
alive in our marriage is a regular date night—one night a week when we seek to
catch up with one another, talk with one another, and have an extended period
of time where we can discuss her needs, my needs, the children's needs, our
family's needs, ministry needs, schedules, and so forth. Date night is an opportunity to share what is going on in our lives, family and ministry.

The Words in Your Marriage

Fifth, use words to edify your spouse. Did you know that words are like seeds? If
you want a harvest of weeds, then you plant weed seeds. If you want a harvest of
flowers and fruit, then you plant good seeds. Proverbs warns us, "Death and life
are in the power of the tongue" (Proverbs 18:21, NASB). The apostle James adds,
"No one can tame the tongue; it is a restless evil and full of deadly poison"
(James 3:8, NASB). Your tongue is the most powerful weapon in your control.
Do you use it to tear down your spouse, or to build up? Do you use it to criticize
and find fault? Or do you use it to bring mercy, compassion and care? What
kind of seeds do you plant in terms of words in your marriage?

I would challenge those who have been speaking disrespectfully, critically
and with an unforgiving spirit to their spouse, to repent. Turn from that and
begin to ask God, in the power of the Holy Spirit, to give you the strength to
deposit words of belief, value, affirmation, love and encouragement. It is at
home where we can be built up and strengthened. Your wife longs to hear
words of affirmation and love.

Know Your Spouse's Needs and Resolve Conflict

*Sixth, become a student of your wife's needs and make an action plan to meet those
needs.* If you are going to be successful at loving your wife as Christ loved the

church, you need to know how to meet those needs. This is important because we go through different seasons of life, and her needs change as the seasons change. Become a student of your wife's needs and establish a plan of action to meet them.

> If we allow issues to remain unresolved in our marriage, we give the enemy a chance to divide us. The words *I'm sorry, will you forgive me?* may be the most important words we ever utter in a marriage.

Seventh, leave a godly legacy by taking the initiative to resolve conflict. There is a reason why the Scripture admonishes us not to let the sun go down on our anger (see Ephesians 4:26). God knows that if we allow issues to remain unresolved in our marriage, we give the enemy a chance to divide us. The words *I'm sorry, will you forgive me?* may be the most important words we ever utter in a marriage relationship. Why? The glory of God is at stake in your marriage.

Jesus prayed that we would be one (see John 17:21). What happens when we allow little things to come between us, or big things? We are divided and isolated from our spouse. You and I cannot glorify God and be divided at home. It is not possible. Is there any unresolved conflict in your marriage right now? Are you harboring any bitterness toward your spouse? I plead with you to take the initiative to resolve those issues in a way that will honor Christ.

Do Not Stop Pursuing a Relationship With Your Children

The eighth way to leave a godly legacy is by pursuing a relationship with each of your children. Rules without relationship make people angry. They make children angry. That is why the apostle Paul admonishes fathers, "And, fathers, do not provoke your children to anger; but bring them up in the discipline and instruction of the Lord" (Ephesians 6:4, NASB).

If children are to receive the Gospel, if they are to receive our teaching and instruction in righteousness, then we need to pursue, build and maintain a relationship with them. Even when they do not want a relationship with you, you must not give up. No matter how much they may reject your Savior, your life or you as a person, you must pursue them with the same love that God pursued you with when you hated Him, when you were rebellious toward Him. He, as the hound of heaven, chased you and me down. It is never optional to stop loving and pursuing a relationship with your child.

One of the ways I have maintained a relationship with our children over the years is by taking them on a date, going out and getting an ice cream cone, going to a ball game, going hunting or fishing, regularly spending time with them. Let me encourage you to pursue a relationship with your children even as God pursues a relationship with you.

Be a Shepherd With Integrity

The ninth way to leave a godly legacy is to be a good shepherd to your flock. The psalmist declares, "So he shepherded them according to the integrity of his heart, and guided them with his skillful hands" (Psalm 78:72, NASB). The word in the Hebrew means he guided them with wisdom; he helped them become wise. The Scripture is telling us that if we are to be good shepherds, we need to have integrity of heart. Are you a man of integrity? Do you say what you are going to do, and then do you do it? Are you dependable? Are you the same person in private that you are in public?

I think one of the most deadly traps that captures men in ministry today is that of pornography. It is difficult today to travel to any city that does not have it—either on the newsstand or in the hotel room on the TV. Pornography can be a snare (see Proverbs 7:23). If you are to shepherd your flock at home with integrity—that word *integrity* means wholeness, holiness—that means you must repent and you must confess if you have a problem with pornography. Maybe for someone else the problem is anger. Maybe for another it is alcohol. Maybe for another it is abuse of a wife or child.

If you are to shepherd your family with integrity and righteousness, you have got to do three things. Number one, repent and turn from the sin. Second, ask God to fill you with the Holy Spirit. And third, tell both your wife and another Christian man, and become accountable for that sin. Come out of the closet, come clean and loose the bonds that the enemy is using to shame you. Will your life be the gate through which sin gains entrance to your family, or the gate through which righteousness gains entrance to your family? Which will it be?

Guard Your Family

The tenth way to leave a godly legacy is to protect your family from evil. A good shepherd guards his family from predators. Just as the Good Shepherd stands in the doorway to protect the sheep, so you and I must lay down our lives for our sheep. I will give you three practical ways you can do that. Number one, if you have children, and especially if you have daughters, guard your daughters from being taken advantage of by young men. It is time for us to no longer stick our heads in the sand. Sexual urges exist. Ask young men if their intentions with your daughter are honorable. Talk to them straight. Challenge them to abstain from sexual immorality. This culture has no boundaries! Where are we going to find boundaries if Christian families do not present them? This is primarily the responsibility of the shepherd of the family, beginning with Dad.

A second way you can protect your children from evil is to guard your sons from pornography. Ask them the hard questions that, hopefully, somebody asked you. Third, guard your children from negative influences of media, the Internet and peers. "Bad company corrupts good morals" (1 Corinthians 15:33, NASB). Do you know the friends that your children spend time with? This is especially important around the ages of 12, 13 and 14. Protect your family from evil.

Impart a Vision for the Great Commission

Eleventh, call your children to a spiritual mission. Help them to know what God wants to do with their lives. Our assignment as parents is not just to impart our knowledge of God but also to give them the experience of God's vision for the world. Pray for your children and give them a vision for the world by making them a part of your ministry, taking them with you as you go to proclaim the Gospel. Share stories at home around the dinner table of how God is at work in your life and in your ministry. If we do not impart a vision for the Great Commission to our children, who will? Dare we wait for someone else to challenge our children to the harvest? It is your responsibility and mine. You and I are a part of a generational relay race in which we must make a good hand-off to the next generation.

The Foundation of Your Ministry

Twelfth, leave a legacy by faithfully persevering. God has not called you to be successful; He has called you to be faithful. He has called you and me to do what is right, to faithfully love, faithfully serve, faithfully pass on truth to our children, faithfully lead our families, faithfully pray with our wives and children.

In summary, your marriage, your family, is the foundation of your ministry. Paul admonished Timothy that to find a leader in church they were first to look at how that person treated his own household (see 1 Timothy 3:12).

Your family members are not a hindrance to achieving all that God wants to achieve and accomplish through you. They are God's gift to you. They are anchors of reality. Husbands, your wife is your number one disciple. Fathers, your children are your disciples as well. God wants to be glorified in your marriage and your family.

Dennis Rainey
Mr. Dennis Rainey is the Executive Director for FamilyLife for Campus Crusade for Christ, having joined the ministry in 1970. In 1976, FamilyLife launched its first conference for engaged Campus Crusade staff members. From that beginning the ministry has gone on to found FamilyLife Marriage and Parenting conferences, which are attended by thousands each year. In addition to being heard on the daily FamilyLife Today radio program, Mr. Rainey is an author (along with his wife, Barbara). The Raineys have six children and live in Little Rock, Arkansas, U.S.A.

Personal Evangelism and Counselor Training

Roger Chilvers

We all come to Christ in different ways because God deals with us personally. We have different backgrounds, different understandings, different sensitivities and different aspects of our character.

About two years ago the United Bible Society did a research project related to thousands of Christians and churches. They asked questions about how people came to faith in Christ and also looked at churches that were effective in bringing people to Christ.

We don't have time to look at all of the results, but I'm going to pull out three statistics because they're quite important for our subject. The first question asked was, "How many people per 100 in the congregation came to faith in Christ in the previous year?"

These are the results: Churches of 201 or more in the congregation had 2.1 professions of faith in Christ during the previous year. When it came to churches of 100 to 200, the figure was 4.7 professions of faith per 100 during the previous year. In the third category, those churches with 51 to 100 in the congregation, the number was 6.2 professions of faith per 100 during the previous year. Those churches of 50 or fewer had 7.7 professions of faith per 100 during the previous year. Now, isn't that remarkable?

If I'd asked beforehand which would be the most effective churches, I guess most of us would have said, "Well, obviously the big churches." But the statistics show exactly the opposite, that the smaller the church, the more effective that church is in evangelism. The studies were done in the U.K. and Western Europe.

Influences That Bring People to Christ

Then they asked another question: "What was the most influential thing that brought you to faith in Christ? Was it an individual, a friend? Was it a spouse? Was it your children? Was it a church meeting?" Here are the results.

For women, the one thing above all others that brought them to faith in Christ was the influence of a Christian friend. As far as men were concerned, the most influential thing was their spouse. But, for both men and women, the relationship with a church leader was very important. The rest of the influences included the influence of parents over their children, personal Bible reading, some church activity or some evangelistic event. By far the most influential thing in both men and women was the relationship with somebody, whether it was their husband or wife or whether it was a Christian friend or a church leader.

They then asked a third question of people who had come to faith in Christ:

"How long did it take from the time you began to think seriously about becoming a Christian to the time when you said, 'Yes, I'm a committed Christian'?"

Six percent said about 11 years or more. Eight percent said six to ten years from the time they began to think seriously about what it meant to be a Christian to the time they could say, "Yes, I'm a committed Christian." Sixteen percent said three to five years. Eleven percent said two years. Ten percent said about a year. Twenty-one percent said it was less than a year. And 28 percent said, "Well, it's an ongoing process as far as I'm concerned."

Now if you average that out, the average it took from the time people began to think about what it means to be a Christian until the time they could say, "Yes, I'm a committed Christian"—the average time is four years. Yet most of our evangelism is crisis-orientated evangelism, isn't it? People come, we preach the Gospel to them, we invite them to respond, which is exactly what we should do, and we expect them to respond straightaway. We expect it to be done almost instantaneously. But, in fact, statistics show that there is a process going on from the time people first begin to think about it.

That's why Billy Graham has often said that his evangelism is most effective where people have had the Gospel shared with them, perhaps over a long period, and then he is able to come along and present the Gospel to them and call them to respond to what they have already known and understood. Many of those converted through Billy Graham's ministry have already had the foundation laid. But they've never been called upon to respond to the Gospel.

Evangelism Includes Relationship Building

Now, let's put those three statistics together. You can see why the smaller church is at no disadvantage from the big church because actually it isn't the church size that matters at all. It is building relationships with people that matters. That's why small churches are often more effective because it is easier to build relationships with people in a small group than it is in a large group. If you go to a massive church with 10,000 people, perhaps you know a handful of those people. But when you're in a small group, it's not like that. You act like a family. You act like a group of people who are related to one another.

Now that does not mean that large churches can't be effective, but it's likely that they will only be effective when the large group is broken down into smaller groups in one form or another so that relationships can be built. In fact, one other statistic that the United Bible Society researched is that 91 percent of churches that are growing rapidly have small groups. What does that teach us? It teaches us that small groups are very important to church growth, but they're not the complete answer. You can't just automatically assume that if you have small groups your church will grow. They are very important, though they may not be the complete answer. In fact, someone has written just recently that it is almost impossible to find a church that is growing rapidly today that does not have a small-group structure of some sort.

The Difference Between Evangelism and Counseling

I wanted to start with the difference between evangelism and counseling because this lays the foundation for the whole of what we want to say about personal evangelism and counselor training. Personal evangelism includes that relationship building we've been thinking about with someone over a period of time, maybe a long time or a short time. But counseling is usually a brief time after an evangelistic meeting.

Personal evangelism looks for an opportunity to share the Gospel with someone. But in counseling you're not there to share the Gospel with people; that's already been done by the evangelist. You're there to help them after the evangelist has done the work of presenting the Gospel.

Personal evangelism involves sharing the whole Gospel, what it's all about in becoming a Christian. Counseling, on the other hand, may just be the need to clarify one point here or there that has not been clear or has been misunderstood. Personal evangelism usually includes the invitation to act upon the Gospel, whereas in counseling, that invitation to accept Christ has already been given by the evangelist.

> Personal evangelism involves sharing the whole Gospel, what it's all about in becoming a Christian. Counseling, on the other hand, may just be the need to clarify one point here or there.

Explaining Who God Is

So there is a difference between personal evangelism and counselor training. In both personal evangelism and counselor training the inquirer needs to know certain things. Let me give you four points.

First, the person needs to know what God is like. Please do not assume that people understand what you mean when you use the word *God*. Most people have only a vague idea of what you're talking about. With the gods of the New Age and 1,001 other gods that are being promoted today, people may not have any idea what you mean when you speak about God. So to just say to somebody, "Do you know that God has a plan for your life?" is a very inadequate presentation because they may say, "What do you mean by God? What is God? Who is God? How does He actually act?" So you need to explain what God is like.

Some people have the idea of God as being a great ogre, a great giant, who's waiting to stomp on you if you do something wrong. Other people have a superstitious view about God. They've almost got to do certain things in a certain way at a certain time and a certain place, otherwise they'll have a long period of bad luck, or something like that.

We need to help people understand a scriptural view of God. This includes what the Bible talks about as the fear of the Lord. Now the fear of the Lord is not a cringing fear, but it means fear in a relationship. You see, I love my wife, but I'm not frightened of her. When I say I have a fear of my wife, it means I don't want to do anything that would harm her or our relationship. But I'm not frightened of my wife.

We need to explain that He is the Creator God who brought this whole world into being, who longed for the very best for us. One thing that needs to be emphasized in these days is that God is a God of love. "God so loved the world, that he gave his only begotten Son" (John 3:16, KJV). He longs for us to have life and have it to the full.

Of course, everybody has some understanding of God. Romans 1:18–21, tells us that everybody born has at least two things: They have conscience, and they have creation. Creation speaks of a God of order and power and control. And our conscience speaks to us of the difference between right and wrong. We may not always agree about what is right and wrong, but we know there is a difference.

Explaining Who We Are

Secondly, people need to know what they are like, what we are like, that I'm a needy person. Now when you use the word *sin,* that can have very negative vibrations in people's minds today. It's sometimes best not to start by using the word sin, not that we're ashamed of using it because it is a central part of Scripture. But I often talk about the fact that we are needy people. We have a felt need. I feel my weakness. I feel I don't have peace. I feel turmoil in my life. Whatever we call our needs, the Bible tells us that they are the result of being separated from God. Then we can use the word sin and explain what sin is. But if you start just by saying, "We're all sinners," people may misunderstand what you're saying. Scripture says, "Your iniquities [your sins] have separated . . . you and your God" (Isaiah 59:2, KJV). You need to explain that it doesn't matter whether you're better than him or he's better than she is. We're all needy people.

Explaining What God Did

Thirdly, what did God do? The important and central thing about the Gospel is this: that God did for us what we could not do for ourselves. The Gospel is not following Jesus—because that's something I do. The Gospel is that Jesus did something for me when I could not follow Him. That's good news! If we tell people that following Jesus is what it means to become a Christian, it's not good news because it puts the onus on us. But when we recognize that God has done something for us in Jesus that we could never do for ourselves, that's good news. He brought me back into a relationship with God. He died for me. He died on behalf of me. That is the central part of the Gospel. That's the key that we must get across, that when Jesus died it was on my behalf.

So what did God do? He sent His Son to be my substitute, to take my sin. He bore my sin in His body on the tree (see 1 Peter 2:24). And as Jesus hung on that Cross, God was putting onto the Lord Jesus your sin and mine. That's where the good news comes. It's not telling people, "You've got to follow Jesus."

Of course, when they realize what Jesus has done, they will want to follow Him. But He did something for me that I could never do for myself.

Explaining What We Must Do

The fourth thing is, what must I do? I must respond. Now at this point, in Europe in particular, if you stop and ask people on the street about those first three points, many people will say at an intellectual level, "Yes, I agree with you." But we must respond. I often use John 1:12. It speaks about those "who received him, . . . who believed in his name, he gave the right to become children of God" (NIV). I say to people, "There are two things you need to do to become a child of God. What are they?" And they stare at the verse and say, "Well, it says you've got to believe." And I say, "Yes, believe. You've got to believe. Do you believe?" "Yes, I believe." "But there's something else. What is it?" "Oh, it says you've got to receive." Those who received Him, who believed in His name, He gave the right to become children of God. So receiving as well as believing. It's not just a matter of an intellectual assent. There has to come a time where that is received.

So what is God like? What am I like? What did God do? What must I do? Those are the four main points of becoming a Christian. Now, when you share the Gospel with people, what's their reaction likely to be? Jesus told the story of the sower who went out to sow (see Luke 8:4–8).

Four Types of Hearers

There are four types of soil. One is the pathway, the hard rocky soil. This is the disinterested person. Some people will be disinterested, and the seed is snatched away. Then there is the rocky soil where there's shallow soil, but not much depth to it. This is the careless person. The seed seems to grow up quickly, but before very long it withers and fades. Then there's the soil that has a lot of weeds in it—Jesus said they are the cares and pleasures of this world—which choke the seed. And then there's the good soil into which some seed is sown that brings forth fruit.

Sometimes in our evangelistic work the press will say to us, "Your converts don't last, do they?" Well, Jesus said they won't all last. Even in that story He said that there would be some people who would receive the Word, as He puts it, with joy, and it springs up quickly. But it doesn't last. Even Jesus said that not all those who respond, continue.

Inquirers Need to Be Helped

When people do respond, that is not the end of the process. That's the start of the process. It is now time to start working with that person. There are three basic things that new believers need to know. First, new believers will feel that they don't know anything. Other Christians know so much and they know so little. Secondly, they will have a sense of insecurity. They don't feel very at home in Christian things. Third, they have a sense of inadequacy. Other Christians they meet can do so much; they can pray, they can read the Bible. But they don't even know there's a difference between the Old and the New Testament. They struggle. So aftercare is very important. New Christians need to be helped.

When you have an evangelistic event or a mission, it is very important to train those who will help new believers in counseling and follow-up. There are three main reasons. First, it extends the impact of the evangelistic work. Every individual who's trained becomes part of the mission. So put a lot of effort into training those who will share their faith in personal evangelism and in counseling. The impact of these folk will multiply the mission dramatically.

Second, when you train people it will ensure that all those who do respond to the Gospel will be adequately cared for. Third, training leaves a legacy behind of trained and equipped people in the churches. Ephesians 4 says that one of the purposes for Jesus giving evangelists to the church was for the evangelists to equip the saints for the work of ministry (see vv. 11–12).

We encourage as many people from as many churches as possible to come to the counselor training. Especially we emphasize that young people should come, because often the response at an evangelistic event has a large percentage of young people.

We usually arrange classes in several different places on several different nights so that if people can't make Wednesday, they can go to the class on Thursday. If they can't make Thursday, they can go to the Saturday morning class. We publicize the counseling courses and invite everybody to come, younger and older.

What Happens in Counselor Training?

Then we have the course itself. In the Billy Graham Evangelistic Association they have a course called the Christian Life and Witness Course, which is far more than just counselor training. It starts with four sessions. Those four sessions are there to help people learn witnessing as a way of life so that people can share their faith easily. Second, they are there so that they may be equipped for counseling at the mission meetings. Third, they are there so they may be renewed spiritually in their own lives.

The first two classes are about how Christians can walk with the Lord and share their faith with others. Here's how Peter puts it, "But in your hearts set apart Christ as Lord. Always be prepared to give an answer to everyone who asks you to give the reason for the hope that you have. But do this with gentleness and respect" (1 Peter 3:15, NIV).

The first key is "set apart Christ as Lord," and we talk about the lordship of Christ in a person's life. The second is "always [being] prepared to give an answer to everyone who asks you." People don't generally come up and ask you, "Excuse me, would you tell me the reason for the hope that you have?" But as people know you, they begin to see something in your life; and that should cause them to say, "Look, there's something different about you. What is it?" And on that occasion you should be ready to speak of your experience of the Lord, your testimony, how God is at work in your life.

Peter says, "Set apart Christ as Lord. Always be prepared to give an answer to everyone who asks you to give the reason for the hope that you have." Now, that word *reason* is the word *logos*, the logical presentation of our hope, the Word of hope. So he's speaking about more than just our testimony that causes people to say, "What's the reason for your hope?" He calls us to be ready to give to people the logic of our hope.

We also teach people to get a grip on God's Word as a means of being prepared. We teach people to memorize Scripture, to be able to share the Gospel with someone. "I have hidden your word in my heart that I might not sin against you" (Psalm 119:11, NIV). And meditate. We go over Scripture again and again and again, and we allow it to penetrate every area of our life in character and being.

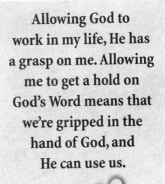

> Allowing God to work in my life, He has a grasp on me. Allowing me to get a hold on God's Word means that we're gripped in the hand of God, and He can use us.

Now you can see these two things: Allowing God to work in my life, He has a grasp on me. Allowing me to get a hold on God's Word means that we're gripped in the hand of God, and He can use us. Although this is how we start the counselor training, with two sessions on our Christian life, the last two sessions are specifically related to how we counsel.

Selecting Who Will Counsel

When we have trained people and gone through the Christian Life and Witness Classes, we then give people a counselor application form. The counselor application form asks details about them, their church, what experience they've had of counseling, if any. It asks them to give their personal testimony, and to give the answers to some basic questions about the Gospel: How do you become a Christian? What does it mean to become a Christian? So we have both their testimony, which tells us whether they're a true believer or not, and we have their answers to the questions about the Gospel, which will show us whether they've understood what the Gospel is all about and what needs to be communicated.

On the form, too, is a place that their minister or church leader needs to sign commending that person to be a counselor, so that even though we don't know all of them, they all come with the recommendation of their church leaders.

We give those forms out in the third week. The final week they come back with those forms, and each one who brings a form back has a brief interview with one of the team people, a brief discussion so that we know whether they can hold a conversation expressing the Gospel.

On the basis of that, the selection is made, inviting those who have applied to become counselors. Then they go on to a further session which has to do with procedure: where they go, what they do, where they get their literature, where they sit, how they respond at the time of the invitation. In that way we can ask everybody to attend the classes, but we actually end up with those who have what it takes to be a counselor in one of the meetings.

How Counseling Happens

Now, how do we actually pair inquirers and counselors at a big evangelistic meeting? We invite the counselors to come early, and we usually have a block of seats reserved for counselors. In those seats we put counselors for men, women and children.

Then the message is preached and people are invited to respond. When people respond, as an inquirer walks past the counselors, if it's a young man coming down, then a young male counselor will get up and walk down with him. If it's an older woman, an older female counselor will get up and walk down with her. Or if it's a child, a children's counselor will get up and walk down with him or her. They don't speak to the people at that time, they just walk down beside them. We make it a strict rule that it's men counseling men and women counseling women. And we seek to pair them up by age as well.

When the counseling starts we say to the inquirers, "Standing beside you is somebody wearing a badge." They look, and to their amazement there's another person about their age, the same sex as them, standing beside them. Then we ask, "Those who do not have a counselor standing beside you wearing a badge, put your hand up." And the counselors who've not been used will then slip in and find these people and be ready to counsel them at that point.

We also provide some specialist counselors dealing with problems—drug addiction, marriage problems, financial problems, homosexuality, and a whole variety of about 30 or 40 different specialized areas of counseling.

The counselors do nothing until the person on the platform tells them to. They don't start counseling straightaway. After a brief prayer by the evangelist, the counselor starts to work. Now at that point the counselor should not start preaching the Gospel all over again. The counselor is there to clarify points that are not clear and to pass on the Christian literature and then take the details so they can be followed up later.

So they begin to counsel the inquirers by asking, "Why did you come forward?" Now inquirers may have come forward for a number of reasons. About 60 percent come forward to accept Christ. About 12 percent come forward because they lack assurance. About 20 percent come forward as an act of rededication. Some people come forward for other reasons.

I've talked about this in the context of a large mission. But this is exactly the same process we follow if it's a one-church local mission, because in those situations, too, counselors are needed to help inquirers as they come forward. In personal evangelism or counseling we help people to share their faith.

Roger Chilvers
Mr. Roger Chilvers has worked in full-time ministry since 1970, mainly in the areas of evangelism and Bible teaching, with an emphasis on training. For nearly 10 years he has worked in Europe and many other countries with the Billy Graham Evangelistic Association (BGEA) leading the training, counseling and follow-up responsibilities in many of BGEA's national and international missions. Mr. Chilvers and his wife, Hazel, make their home in Gloucester, England. They have three grown children.

The Evangelist's Personal Life

Philemon Choi Yuen-Wan

Beloved brothers and sisters from 211 nations, I come before you with love, with fear and with trembling because of the topic that has been assigned to me, "The Evangelist's Personal Life."

As evangelists, we tend to pay more attention to our public lives—what we do, how we preach, the outcome, the results, the performance. Yet I know that God cares especially for our personal lives, our inner lives, where the streams of life flow, and where the Holy Spirit chooses to bear fruit inside.

Public life is about doing and achieving; our personal life is about being, the depth of our spirituality, the content of our thoughts, the quality of our relationship with God, and the quality of our relationships with those around us. So from that perspective, with fear and trembling, knowing that each one of us is vulnerable, I tried to draw lessons from the apostles and prophets.

We are so caught up with the prophets and apostles in action—Moses leading the Israelites through the Red Sea, Joshua in battle with the Amalekites, Elijah on the top of Mount Carmel fighting against the false prophets. Do not forget the other side of the apostles and prophets—Moses' personal encounter with God before the burning bush, Joshua alone waiting and praying for the empowering of God the Spirit, and Elijah alone in the cave listening to the still small voice of the Lord.

> **Public life is about doing and achieving; our personal life is about being.**

Creating Space for Intimacy With God

I tried to draw from the apostles and from the prophets and group them under three major themes. First, creating space for intimacy with God.

This is the age of speed. Key words for the 21st century would be *productivity, efficiency, profitability.* Everything moves with speed. Brothers and sisters, let us not forget that speed may symbolize this particular era, but at the same time there are things that invade our personal life—the mobile phone, the e-mail, the Internet. If we don't take care, all of this can interrupt our private life where God chooses to speak to us in silence, in solitude, when we are with Him alone.

C. S. Lewis once said, "Satan wanted to create the whole world into a big noise to drown out the voice of God, but God chooses to speak to us in silence, in solitude, when we are with Him alone."

The reason so often we tend to fill our schedules with business is that when we are alone in front of a holy God, not only will we catch a vision of God who is holy, holy, holy almighty, but in His light God will reveal who we really are. In His light we tremble. Woe unto me!

Isaiah as a young man encountered God. It is painful to be touched by burning coal. It can hurt when God deals with us in a very personal, deep way. Sometimes it is fearful to stand before a God who is fire. But let us humbly come before Him. The coal which touches the lips cleanses. Brothers and sisters, may I remind you that this cleansing is a continuous daily process. The blood of Jesus Christ cleanses our souls. Jesus Christ told the apostle Peter, "Unless I wash you, you have no part with me" (John 13:8, NIV). Lord Jesus, I want to have a part with You. Cleanse me. Bless me. Renew me.

We need time to be alone with God for worship, for confession. Not only that, but as we are in front of God, sometimes He digs deep into some of our past sins and wounds. Unless we get a personal healing from the Lord, those wounds and sins will catch up with us and show themselves in subsequent relationships with others.

I am reminded of Joseph (see Genesis 37–50). As an adolescent, in his arrogance actually, Joseph was a pain to his brothers—bragging about those dreams. Also, his father, out of love, almost killed his son with that beautiful, colorful, wonderful coat. His brothers got their revenge when he was thrown into the ditch. From the age of 17 until the age of 30, Joseph was living a life almost in total darkness—as slave, prisoner. Who, with that kind of wound, can emerge at the age of 30 and yet be gentle enough, be caring enough, to look into the eyes of his brothers who almost killed him and embrace them in tears?

What Joseph named his first son gives me a glimpse of how God dealt with his life. Joseph chose to name his first son Manasseh. That means "God, make me forget." That is divine-given forgetfulness. God, make me forget all my troubles.

Beware of Those Unhealed Wounds

Brothers and sisters, beware of those unhealed wounds which will haunt you deeply; they will come up subsequently in the form of anger, in the form of rage, in the form of resentment. One American psychologist has proclaimed that this 21st century will be the age of rage. By that he means there is rage in the office, attacks. Rage on the highways, reckless driving. Rage at home, family violence. Sometimes unknowingly we do things and we say things that hurt those who are closest to us. May I share with you one painful struggle that I had? It happened in my own family.

I am the eldest in the family of Chois. My father used to be a seaman. He started working on a ship when he was 14. But he really gave his heart to his family. I knew deep down that he loved me. Yet this man that I deeply loved and highly respected caused me a lot of pain.

I came to know Jesus Christ through one of my classmates in my high school, and for the first time I ran into direct conflict with my family because, as the eldest in my family I had the responsibility to burn incense every day to my ancestors and to the family gods. But then, convicted of sin and grasped by the love of Jesus Christ, I gave my life to Jesus. I went home that day, and for the first time in my life I dared to challenge the authority of my parents. And the roof came down.

Finally they became tolerant enough to allow me the freedom to attend church. Shortly after that I went to Canada for my medical training. When I came back, my father was so happy when I returned with my wife and my eldest son. Only later did he find out that the Lord had a special calling for me. I was called to serve the young people in Hong Kong. With fear I approached my parents. This time it wasn't the roof that came down; it was an earthquake.

For three hours my father gave me a lecture, and he asked my younger brother to be the witness. I knew how angry he was. As the eldest son in the family, I carried the honor, the expectations of generations of Chois. I was so deeply wounded. Even when I left Hong Kong for seminary study, I was weeping on the plane. My wife was sitting beside me. It was not just the pain that my father had inflicted upon me; unconsciously I harbored anger and resentment which showed itself in silence, in resistance, in fear, in avoidance. But God would not let me go.

One time two Christian brothers grabbed me and we prayed together. When they prayed, tears came. I couldn't control it. They were tears not just for my wound; they were tears for my own sins—for my sins of anger and resentment toward my father. I poured out my heart to God, "Cleanse me, O God. Forgive me. Take away that bitterness and anger." And then I felt liberated. I could go back to my home again and look into my father's eyes. Whether he was happy, upset, angry, joyful, I could look him in the eyes. And God was gracious. Let me tell you: If you are willing to submit yourself to the Lord Jesus Christ and receive His rebuke and cleansing and healing, miraculous things can happen.

One day I was invited to give an evangelistic sermon on the theme, "Jesus Heals the Wounds of the Family." In the stadium there were 10,000 people. When I gave the altar call, people came down, whole families.

There was someone waving at me, my younger sister. I said, "Cindy, what happened?" She said, "Daddy is here!" I almost fainted. It is against Chinese tradition for a son to preach to his father. So, I was glad that I didn't know he was there. I asked, "Where is he?" She said, "There, at the steps." I jumped off the platform. I approached my father. I said, "Daddy, do you want to accept Jesus Christ?" He nodded. I said, "You have to confess your sins." And there, accompanied by my sister and my family, he stepped on the platform; and for the first time in my life, I embraced him with the love of Jesus Christ. Jesus cleansed me.

He took away my anger. He took away my resentment. He healed my wound. God heals and forgives.

So I will not forget the words of Isaiah when he says, "In repentance and rest is your salvation, in quietness and trust is your strength" (Isaiah 30:15, NIV). Return, brothers and sisters. God is waiting. Repent, brothers and sisters. He wants to cleanse us. Rest in Him. So often we are lost in activities and we forget to rest in His love, in the grace of His forgiveness.

"In quietness and confidence." We are surrounded by noise—and we like some of the noise. And yet God chooses to speak to us in quietness. Confidence is God-given through our trust in Him. I will not forget these words, "In returning and rest is your salvation, in quietness and confidence is your strength" (see Isaiah 30:15).

> We are surrounded by noise—and we like some of the noise. And yet God chooses to speak to us in quietness.

A Space for Intimacy With God

The longer we serve the Lord, the more demands are put upon us. And we tend to respond. However, as we respond to all those invitations and demands upon our lives, we cannot forget our personal moments, to set aside time every day. Through one of my spiritual mentors the Lord has taught me, like Jesus Christ, to always retreat.

Do not forget that when Jesus Christ was surrounded by people, He touched them, He healed them, He preached the Gospel to them. But He always returned to His Father in the wilderness, in the quietness of the garden, in the quietness of the hills. Jesus, the Lord of action; Jesus, the Lord of silence. Jesus, the Lord who moved among people; Jesus, the Lord who withdrew to be alone with God. We need to learn from Him and create a space for intimacy with God.

Boundaries to Protect Our Souls

The second theme I would like to touch upon is about defining boundaries to protect our souls. People call this the age of moral deregulation. If you are a professional, you are supposed to be value-free. As I counsel young people, others challenge me, "How can you walk into that room with a Bible and impose your values on the counselee? Professionals are supposed to be value-free," they say.

And then we move and sail on the sea of information on the Internet, which is totally deregulated. There are a lot of good things on the Internet, but at the same time a lot of garbage. I have read survey after survey about how a lot of people are addicted to garbage. Addiction comes when there is a vacuum in the soul. People living in post-modernity admit to that vacuum. And yet they seek all kinds of experiential peaks for their lives. They turn to substances to fill that void. And those are pleasurable substances which tend to trap us into addiction.

The age of moral deregulation can be a trap for us if we do not draw a line. We need boundaries. Even adolescents, when they yell that they want freedom, actually at the same time are asking for boundaries. If we cannot draw a boundary for ourselves to protect our souls by God's grace, how are we going to declare that grace to this age where everything is value-free? Let us be aware that as evangelists we are supposed to be in touch with the world. We are going to be rubbing our shoulders with people in pain, with people in sin, as the Lord Jesus Christ did. Yet before we do that, we define our boundaries.

Jesus Christ reminded us that we are in the world and yet we are not of the world. Jesus told us to love the people in the world and yet love not the world, which is symbolized by lust of the flesh, lust of the eyes, and pride of life (see 1 John 2:15–16). Jesus Christ Himself drew the line. In His 40 days when He was led by the Holy Spirit into the wilderness, He encountered the temptations of Satan—lust of the eyes, lust of the flesh, and the pride of life. Yet Jesus Christ stood firm. By the Spirit, by the Word of God, He drew the line. He said, "Man shall not live by bread alone" (Matthew 4:4, KJV). Forget about the flesh. "Worship the Lord your God, and serve him only" (verse 10, NIV). Have nothing to do with shortcuts to glory. "Do not put the Lord your God to the test" (verse 7, NIV). By God's grace we have to draw the line against the world and Satan.

The apostle Paul, as an itinerant evangelist, traveled to different places. He was aware that God had given him the gift of being single. Yet he warned us to beware because you can be burned by your passions, by your lust (see 1 Corinthians 7:7–9). Draw a line.

Paul reminds us that our body is a temple of the Holy Spirit; do not defile it (see 1 Corinthians 6:18–20). Joseph, in his success, was tempted by none other than the wife of his master. Yet Joseph drew the line. He would not let lust defile his body (see Genesis 39:7–12). The prophet Daniel, as a young man, was thrown into the Babylonian palace. And yet, still a teenager, alone in front of God, he resolved not to defile himself (see Daniel 1:8). Brothers and sisters, if we are going to be effective evangelists, we have to enter the world and yet not be of the world.

May I share with you the testimony of a Chinese evangelist? When I was a young man, the story of this evangelist, Dr. John Song, captured my life. He was used by God mightily, traveling to different provinces of China bringing revival to many places. There was a biography which talked about his ministry. He was a strange man. He dressed funny; he had a very funny hairstyle. And he preached in an unusual way. When he preached on sin, he would bring a ball into the service and bounce it to demonstrate the rebelliousness of man. He would bring a coffin into the service to demonstrate the consequence of sin. He would bring a huge rock and carry it on his back to demonstrate the burden of sin. So I have a very colorful picture of what he did.

Only lately were his personal diary and journal discovered and published.

Do we have the courage to have our diaries and journals published? As I read those pages, I was deeply moved. He was not only a man who preached repentance and sin in public; he fought his own battles with Satan every day. He drew the line. No way would he allow Satan to touch his life. He prayed prostrate before the Lord. He asked the Lord's cleansing every day, dealing with his own personal sins in front of God. And he wrote that in his journal. How I wish this journal could be published into the 29 different languages of this conference so that you could read it. In our personal lives as evangelists, we draw the line, defining the boundaries to protect our souls by God's grace.

> Joseph, in his success, was tempted by none other than the wife of his master. Yet Joseph drew the line. He would not let lust defile his body.

A Generation With Disconnected Souls

We call this time the age of the individual, with all the blessings because of the respect for the individual, the respect for human rights. But, brothers and sisters, at the same time, the overemphasis on the individual causes us to be disconnected. One Christian counselor called this a generation with disconnected souls. By that he means the deepest part of who we are is attached to no one. We are profoundly unknown. Therefore, we experience neither the thrill of being believed in nor the joy of loving or of being loved. Unattached, unknown, unbelieved in, unloved—these are the signs, symptoms and disease of this generation.

As evangelists, sometimes we work alone, lonely souls facing the crowds. We can be trapped because we are accountable to no one, supported by no one. Brothers and sisters, let us practice accountability by living in community.

In a video we saw here in Amsterdam 2000, Cliff Barrows and Billy Graham shared the deepest part of their souls, 55 years of committing to one another, accountable to one another, loving one another, serving one another. We need that kind of community. Because of Jesus Christ, because of His presence in us, may we be accountable to our family and our immediate community. We need to be accountable to our spouse and also to brothers and sisters who know us, who care for us, and who will dare to confront us.

And so I leave you with those three words: Space—for intimacy with God. "In returning and rest is your salvation, in quietness and confidence is your strength" (see Isaiah 30:15).

Boundary—draw the line. May God help us by the Spirit, by the Word, to draw a line. Before you enter the world, make sure you are protected so that you will not be absorbed by the world.

And, finally, guard ourselves—we are not meant to live alone. It is a call to community—community with God, community with one another, and community with the saints.

I would like you to spend a moment in silence. Recommit yourself to God. Search your soul before the Lord. Ask God for cleansing, for healing. And may God reveal to us where we are most vulnerable and how we should draw the line. And pray for community, to be accountable to our family and to those who are closest to us.

O Father, have mercy on us. Cleanse us again with the Blood of Jesus Christ. Empower us with the Spirit and Your Word so that others may hear Jesus through our lips and see Jesus in our personal lives. To You be all the glory. In the name of Jesus we pray. Amen.

Philemon Choi Yuen-Wan

Dr. Philemon Choi Yuen-Wan, a medical doctor, is a highly respected evangelical leader and one of the best-selling authors in Hong Kong. Due to his deep concern for youth, Dr. Choi left his medical practice and furthered his studies at Trinity Evangelical Divinity School in Illinois (U.S.A.). As a co-founder of Breakthrough *magazine and general secretary of the Breakthrough ministry, his work extends throughout the Hong Kong community, reaching young people with the Gospel of Jesus Christ. Dr. Choi is also actively involved with other local Christian ministries, as well as within the social and educational sectors of Hong Kong. He and his wife, Ellen, have been married for 30 years, and they reside in Hong Kong. They have two grown sons.*

Working With the Local Church

Video: Kahlevi Lehtinen, Finland and Germany
Dennis White, Jamaica and Nigeria

As evangelists, we have a responsibility to work with the local churches as a part of our outreach. Long after we're gone, the local church will remain to carry out the work of evangelization. Two Christian leaders talked about this:

Kahlevi Lehtinen: "My most important contribution is not preaching as an evangelist, but the work which we do before the campaign where we build bridges between churches and build up the church members. There are more people who become Christians through personal evangelism by trained Christians than those who receive Christ through my preaching. So my whole purpose is to use the evangelistic campaign as a good reason to have as many Christians as possible equipped to reach the people. Then the process continues after I leave."

Dennis White: "I think it's important that we come together and fellowship with other churches in crusades and in ministry to their people. The unity of people of a common mind, and a common faith and bond, is a powerful witness to the Gospel of Jesus Christ."

For decades the Billy Graham crusades have relied heavily on the local church for the success of each crusade. Local churches provide outreach, training, follow-up and, ultimately, church planting. Church planting in many areas of the world is the most effective way to spread the Gospel. Communities see the symbol of the church and are drawn to the message of love and forgiveness. Our two leaders looked at that practice:

We have had classes on how to witness. We have had classes on how to do altar work. But the real preparation comes after the crusade is over. What do we do with these new disciples in Christ? We cannot forsake them. So we have classes on how to disciple people. That is the exciting thing. Long after the crusade is over, God is going to be doing a work in our community.

Kahlevi Lehtinen: "Love is irresistible. When we have genuine love, there will be credibility. It is hard work. It requires a lot of honesty and time. But it's worth it.

"We are not having private enterprises. We are building up the whole body of Christ in the world. Our accountability is not just toward the supporting church; we are accountable to the whole body of Jesus Christ in the world."

Kahlevi Lehtinen and Dennis White

Dr. Kahlevi Lehtinen is an evangelist in Europe for Campus Crusade for Christ. He is from Finland. Rev Dennis White is a missionary-evangelist from Jamaica who has planted large churches in Nigeria.

Working With
the Local Church

Video: Kahlevi Lehtinen, Finland and Germany
Dennis White, Jamaica and Nigeria

As evangelists, we have a responsibility to work with the local churches as a part of our outreach. Long after we're gone, the local church will remain to carry out the work of evangelization. Two Christian leaders talked about this:

Kahlevi Lehtinen: "My most important contribution is not preaching as an evangelist, but the work which we do before the campaign where we build bridges between churches and build up the church members. There are more people who become Christians through personal evangelism by trained Christians than those who receive Christ through my preaching. So my whole purpose is to use the evangelistic campaign as a good reason to have as many Christians as possible equipped to reach the people. Then the process continues after I leave."

Dennis White: "I think it's important that we come together and fellowship with other churches in crusades and in ministry to their people. The unity of people of a common mind, and a common faith and bond, is a powerful witness to the Gospel of Jesus Christ."

For decades the Billy Graham crusades have relied heavily on the local church for the success of each crusade. Local churches provide outreach, training, follow-up and, ultimately, church planting. Church planting in many areas of the world is the most effective way to spread the Gospel. Communities see the symbol of the church and are drawn to the message of love and forgiveness. Our two leaders looked at that practice:

We have had classes on how to witness. We have had classes on how to do altar work. But the real preparation comes after the crusade is over. What do we do with these new disciples in Christ? We cannot forsake them. So we have classes on how to disciple people. That is the exciting thing. Long after the crusade is over, God is going to be doing a work in our community.

Kahlevi Lehtinen: "Love is irresistible. When we have genuine love, there will be credibility. It is hard work. It requires a lot of honesty and time. But it's worth it.

"We are not having private enterprises. We are building up the whole body of Christ in the world. Our accountability is not just toward the supporting church; we are accountable to the whole body of Jesus Christ in the world."

Kahlevi Lehtinen and Dennis White
Dr. Kahlevi Lehtinen is an evangelist in Europe for Campus Crusade for Christ. He is from Finland. Rev Dennis White is a missionary-evangelist from Jamaica who has planted large churches in Nigeria.

The Evangelist Works With the Local Church

Paul Negrut

When Billy Graham visited Romania and preached in my church, it was a historic event in my life and in the lives of the Romanian believers. In spite of serious restrictions imposed by the authorities of that time, there were some **60,000** people in the auditorium, on the streets and on the rooftops of the surrounding buildings. All the loudspeakers of our church were placed on the trees and the surrounding buildings in order for the big crowd to hear the message. It was indeed a great day. Even today there are people who come to our church and ask to be baptized. They confess that they accepted Christ on that great day when Dr. Graham preached in our church.

After years of struggle and hesitation, they are still aware of the decision they made to follow Jesus. And they realize their need to join a local church. In their minds there is a clear association of the message of salvation with the local church.

My message centers on the relationship between the evangelist and the local church. I do believe that such a vital issue has both theological and practical implications for the contemporary Church and the evangelist. However, rather than taking a sociological, pragmatic or prescriptive approach to this issue, I will focus mainly on certain biblical and theological aspects concerning the church, evangelism and the relationship between them. It is my belief that clear, biblical theology generates clear practice. And it all must emerge from a clear understanding of the Bible. That is our source of truth.

We will approach the theme from a threefold perspective. We will look first at the nature of the Church, then the nature of evangelism, and finally how it all relates to evangelism.

The Nature of the Church

Some have accepted the idea that the Church is no more than a society which originates through free human action and can only continue to exist through such action. But biblically it can be argued that the Church is not simply an institution on the horizontal level, like a trade union, an association of fishermen or a local club. Under the power and leading of the Holy Spirit, the Church is far more than that. The being of the Church is dynamically related to the being of God. Using New Testament language, one can affirm that the Church is simultaneously a divine-human organism and a historical-eschatological community. Let us explore this idea further.

The Church Is Both a Divine and Human Organism

The divine dimension of the Church is given by Christ, who is the Head of the body, and by the Holy Spirit, who is the life of the body. Therefore, the apostle Paul could say to the Colossians, "And he [Christ] is the head of the body, the church; he is the beginning and the firstborn from among the dead, so that in everything he might have the supremacy" (Colossians 1:18, NIV). The human dimension is constituted of saved sinners who are baptized by the Holy Spirit into the body as members. The apostle Paul affirms, "Now you are the body of Christ, and each one of you is a part of it" (1 Corinthians 12:27, NIV), due to the fact that "we were all baptized by one Spirit into one body" (1 Corinthians 12:13, NIV).

> The Bible clearly declares that to belong to a local church is not an optional matter. It is not an optional issue because the metaphor of the body offers a clear, vertical dimension of the Church.

It is important to see that the body metaphor teaches the headship relation between Christ and believers in a clear, ecclesial, corporate setting and not as isolated believers or disjointed members. The source of everything in the body and every member of the body is Christ, the Head, and the life-giving Spirit. The glory and the strength of the Church reside in the Head and in the Spirit. The weakness and the failure of the Church reside in the body and its human members. However, there is a relationship between the body and the Head. The Head is not without a body and the body is not without a Head. Yet, it must be underlined that the Head and the body do not share the same attributes. The Head is divine, infallible and all-powerful, while the members of the body are human, fallible and weak.

Still, God the Father has designed the Church to exist in a dynamic union between the Head, Jesus Christ, and the body, the believers (both individually and corporately). Some are inclined, however, to believe that since the Church is the body of Christ then the Church shares the same attributes with the Head—that whatever is true about the Head is equally true about the body. The risk of such an approach is to develop a sort of triumphalistic, institutional ecclesiology. In other words, it is easy to think that one church has gotten everything right, so it no longer needs to give itself to constant reexamination. That can spell death.

The New Testament analogy of the body makes a clear distinction between the person of Christ and His body, the Church. Christ is declared to be the Savior of the body. The body receives its nurture and its unity from its Head. The body is to grow and mature in every respect in Him who is the Head.

Alternatively, there are others who believe that the Church is simply a voluntary, human organization with religious purposes on a horizontal level. This implies that the Church is not an essential part of the Christian life. However, the Bible clearly declares that to belong to a local church is not an optional matter. It is not an optional issue because the metaphor of the body offers a clear, vertical dimension of the Church. Believers are personally and corporately members of Christ Himself. The Church is related primarily to Jesus Christ. "God placed all things under his feet and appointed him to be head over everything for the church, which is his body, the fullness of him who fills everything in every way" (Ephesians 1:22–23, NIV).

Christ's Instrument in This World

Moreover, the Church is Christ's instrument in this world. Members serve the Head, and the Kingdom goes forward. This cannot be overlooked. The understanding of the Church as a simultaneous, human-divine organism offers a clear perspective on evangelism and provides its motivation. Thus, evangelism is not an additional work to the being of the Church, but its very mode of being. If that is true, the presence and the purpose of the New Testament church in this world must be evangelistic. The Church exists primarily to bring glory to God and lost sinners to Christ, in the power of the Holy Spirit.

When we speak about evangelism in the Church, we have in mind all the believers. All the believers are to be witnesses to Christ's power to save. In addition there are specially gifted believers in the ministry of evangelism. Evangelists are reapers. The evangelist is not and cannot be an isolated member of the body in his or her private relationship with Christ. The entire Church is to be involved in the task of evangelism.

The Church Is Simultaneously a Historical-Eschatological Community

Another analogy used by the apostle Paul to explain the mystery of the Church comes from the Old Testament idea of the people of God. Extreme individualism, as seen in much Western thought, is out. It is not biblical. As with the Hebrew predecessors, a corporate personality must characterize the new people of God, the community of those who trust in the risen Christ. Believers are one in Christ. As Paul says, "When one suffers, all suffer, and when one is exalted, all are exalted" (see 1 Corinthians 12:26). Behind the establishment of this new people of God is the reality of the risen Christ, "who gave himself for us to redeem us from all wickedness and to purify for himself a people that are his very own, eager to do what is good" (Titus 2:14, NIV).

It must be recognized and emphasized that although the Church as Christ's unified body lives in this world, it is not of this world. It is an eschatological community with its gaze fixed on the *Parousia*, the return of Christ. The people of God are simultaneously citizens of their lands *and* citizens of heaven. In other words, the Church is part of this age and the age to come.

The wedding of history and eschatology underlines the simultaneous nature of evangelism and worship. The historical mandate of the Church is, "Go into the whole world" (see Mark 16:15). The eschatological mandate of the Church is, "Come, you blessed of My Father" (see Matthew 25:34). When the Church fulfills its historical mandate, it scatters. It goes into the whole world. When it fulfills its eschatological mandate, the Church comes together in worship.

Yet, it must be emphasized that some people are more concerned with going than with coming. Some people are more aware of the historical mandate of the Church. They go and they keep going and keep going and never come with the other saints to worship Christ. Others are more aware of the Church's dimension in worship and they come and they come and they never go. Those who keep going and going collapse under the pressure. Those who come and never go transform the Church into a sort of eschatological ghetto. A biblical church keeps the two mandates in balance: Go and come.

In the teaching of the apostle Paul we see an extraordinary balance of history and eschatology. The historical and eschatological dimensions of the Church provide a theological frame of reference for the relation between evangelism and the local church. Evangelism is the way of life of the worshiping community. In other words, evangelism is the lifestyle of the believing community.

The Nature of Evangelism

The Bible uses a number of phrases to explain evangelism, such as proclamation of the Gospel, making disciples, bearing witness to Jesus Christ, fishing for men, and so forth. However, Christianity is far from having a universally accepted definition of evangelism. J. I. Packer has argued, "Some give the name of evangelism to any kind of meeting in which the leader works up an altar call of some sort, never mind what has or has not been affirmed before the calls come. Others will equate evangelism with any activity that expresses goodwill to persons outside the Church."

In spite of different definitions, there are some common trends—not all of which are helpful or biblical. First, the role of the local church in evangelism is being perceived by some almost exclusively as the place where the converts should be directed for fellowship and discipleship after evangelism. Second, evangelism is defined in either impersonal or individualistic terms and not in corporate terms. And finally, evangelism is defined in the context of the Kingdom of God and the lordship of Christ, with no clarification regarding the relationship between the Kingdom and the Church.

Due to the fact that some fail to understand the relation between the local church and the universal Church, some evangelists seem to have no clear church affiliation or accountability. And some churches have no commitment to evangelism.

Evangelism is at the same time both personal and corporate. Our triune God teaches us that the one and the many must work together. When Christ came to earth, He didn't come as an isolated, celestial being. He came as the Son of the Father, in the power and the fellowship of the Holy Spirit. When Christ sends us, He sends us as members of the body. We belong to a community because our God lives eternally in the communion of the Father, Son and Holy Spirit.

The Local Church and Evangelism

If the Church is simultaneously a divine-human organism and a historical-eschatological community, then evangelism is a central mode of being of the Church. The Church was not created to be an end in itself, but to perpetuate Christ's ministry to the world.

Millard Erickson argues that the function of the Church is fourfold: First, the Church exists to make disciples of all people. Second, it exists to edify believers through fellowship, teaching and the practice of the gifts of the Holy Spirit. Third is worship—praise and exaltation of the triune God. Fourth, the Church exists to demonstrate a social concern for believers and non-believers alike.

These functions are not additional activities to the being of the Church but the mode in which the Church exists. Consequently, all the aspects in which the Church expresses itself are simultaneously divine-human and historical-eschatological, all leading to the extension of the Kingdom of God. Believers are called to be a Kingdom of priests. In this Kingdom, the individual is not swallowed up by the crowd, and the community is not threatened by individual members. The ecclesial community is a historical mirror of the Trinity. The one and the many coexist in harmony.

> The Church was not created to be an end in itself, but to perpetuate Christ's ministry to the world.

Another aspect of concern is the balance between the priesthood of all believers and those with special callings according to the gifts of the Spirit. Some may be inclined to downplay the role of the many in the priesthood of believers in favor of the one who is specially gifted in evangelism, or to belittle the ministry of the gifted one in favor of the ministry of the many.

When such occurs, not only can there be tension in the Church, but the witness of the whole body is often affected in a negative way. In such cases, some gifted believers in the area of evangelism may consider taking an independent route as the best alternative—going it alone, leaving the Church behind. This can be a serious mistake. However attractive such a model appears to be, it must be realized that the apostles did not abandon the churches in time of crisis. To the contrary, they worked under the guidance of the Holy Spirit to correct the distorted theology that generated the crisis in order to heal the Church. Error must be corrected because the Church plays an essential role in evangelism.

Remember, Christ is the Head of the body. The Holy Spirit indwells the corporate body and imparts to it divine life. The Great Commission is given to the Church. Evangelists must, therefore, relate dynamically to the Church. Scripture demands it. Accountability to Christ can be found only in the local church. This may sound anachronistic, bearing in mind that the culture of post-modernity breeds individualism and relativistic ethics. Regardless of the pressure of the world, the Church must be held in a proper biblical position. The Church must constantly maintain the balance between history and eschatology, between this age and the age to come.

The evangelist must relate properly to the local church body of believers. As a pastor and an evangelist, I am aware that pastors, teachers, evangelists and missionaries, and local churches are not perfect yet. However, there is the great promise that Jesus gave Himself for the Church, "that he might present it to himself a glorious church, not having spot, or wrinkle, or any such thing; but that it should be holy and without blemish" (Ephesians 5:27, KJV). Such an eschatological perspective is calling us to commit ourselves afresh to our triune God, to His Church and to the Great Commission.

Therefore, the evangelist works with the local church. The evangelist is a special gift of Christ to His Church. The Church will pray for the evangelist and encourage the evangelist. The evangelist must belong to the Church and work with the Church and rejoice in whatever Christ is giving to the Church. May the church go forward and the Kingdom grow until that great day when the Kingdom will come. Let us say, "Even so, come, Lord Jesus. . . . Amen" (Revelation 22:20–21, KJV).

Paul Negrut

A native of Romania, Dr. Paul Negrut has been involved in proclaiming the message of Jesus Christ throughout Europe, North America, Asia, Australia and Africa. Dr. Negrut serves as president of Emmanuel Bible Institute in Oradea, Romania, and has pastored, since 1982, Oradea's 4,000-member Emmanuel Baptist Church. Dr. Negrut earned a B.A. from the University of Bucharest, Bucharest, Romania. In 1994, he earned a doctorate at Brunel University, London Bible College, in London, England. Dr. Negrut and his wife, Delia, have two daughters and reside in Romania.

Working With the Disabled

Joni Eareckson Tada

It's been a wonderful time here in Amsterdam 2000. Some of my favorite times have been in the hallways. In fact, an evangelist came up to me and said, "May I pray for your healing?" Well, who am I ever to deny prayer, right? But, as he began to pray for my healing, I thought to myself, "Lord Jesus, I wonder, if I were healed, would I be as close to You as I am now?"

This evangelist may not understand that when I wake up in the morning, I desperately need God. I look at my wheelchair in the corner of the bedroom, and I think to myself and I pray, "Lord Jesus, I just don't know that I can do this. Another year of quadriplegia, another day of use without hands. Show them that You are my life, Lord God; give me energy, give me strength." And then, miracle of miracles, He does!

I am so grateful for the grace that sustains me in my weakness. And I wonder if the really handicapped people aren't those who when they wake up in the morning, jump out of bed, take a quick shower, then rush out the door on automatic. I need God desperately. I am very much like my friends in Africa who said, "Welcome to our country where our God is bigger. He is bigger because we need Him more." This is why our weaker members may be indispensable in the body of Christ, because God's power shows up best in weakness. So when people crowd our churches in wheelchairs or walkers, or use white canes, or the blind or the deaf—it helps the rest of the body of Christ to look at them and think to themselves, "My goodness, how great that person's God must be to inspire such loyalty." If God's grace can sustain a woman in a wheelchair without use of her hands or use of her legs, then I can boast in my affliction. We all ought to be boasting in our infirmities and delighting in our weaknesses. For then we know God's power rests on us.

There are disabled people chained to the walls of institutions in Southeast Asia. There are disabled children being abandoned in Africa. There are elderly disabled people being euthanized in Europe and America. But the Lord Jesus tells us in Luke 14 to go out, find the disabled and bring them in so that we will be blessed, so that we will see that God's power can show up best in our weakness. The weaker members are indispensable. Jesus says, "Go out and find them, you will be blessed, so that the Father's house might be full" (see Luke 14:23).

Perhaps the best definition of church growth is to crowd the churches with people who are blind, deaf and disabled so that through their weaknesses the Lord's power will be made manifest. And we will end up boasting in our infirmities and delighting in our weaknesses. All too often though, we ignore the disabled, we neglect the blind, or we encounter someone in a wheelchair or a person with a disability and we feel that we must heal them. People with disabilities do not need physical healing so much as they need the Lord Jesus.

By the way, that evangelist prayed for my healing; he said, "Rise up and walk"—and I tried. But I'm still in this wheelchair. I thank the Lord Jesus that I'm still desperately needing His grace.

Joni Eareckson Tada
Joni Eareckson Tada directs the ministry of Joni and Friends, Agoura Hills, California, U.S.A.

Strategy for Harvest

Video: Henri Aoun, Lebanon
Luis Bush, Central America
Luciano Jaramillo, Colombia

When you fail to plan, you plan to fail. Time and resources must be used efficiently. Whether you're a seasoned evangelist or a recently called minister of the Lord, having a defined plan of action can make the difference between success and failure. What are the steps in developing a strategy for harvest? Three Christian leaders respond:

A harvest strategy calls for a harvest vision. Jesus said, "Open your eyes for the harvest" (see John 4:35). Second, He calls for harvest information. Jesus came to "seek . . . that which was lost" (Luke 19:10, KJV). Where are the lost? Who are the lost? Third, harvest strategy involves harvest prayer. Jesus said, "Pray to the Lord of the harvest for the harvest" (see Matthew 9:38). Fourth, harvest strategy is a harvest plan. For the 5,000 gathered, Jesus called His followers to divide them into groups of 50 and systematically distribute bread to those groups (see Mark 6:35–44).

Strategy needs harvest tools. We need to distribute Bibles widely. We need pamphlets on Gospel evangelism, Gospel recordings. We need to use the *Jesus* film. We need to use radio, television, satellite television, Internet. Get the tools into the hands of the laborers for the harvest.

Recognize an open door through prayer, seeking the plan of God, walking with the Lord. Then watch what opportunities are made available. What is being done that we can build on as the body of Christ? And what is not being done and why? What else can be done so we can work in partnership with the rest of the body?

Another key step in strategic planning is identifying the target. Many have focused their efforts on the 10/40 window, a region of the world located between the 10th and the 40th parallels.

More than 90 percent of the unevangelized people in the world live within the 10/40 window.

And, it is the most responsive region to the Gospel.

It's very important that we focus on where the greatest need is; that is, the countries of the 10/40 window.

As we move into the new millennium, the pressures on the evangelists are going to increase. It calls for personal integrity, as well as promoting Jesus and not self in the ministry.

God is not asking us to do impossible things. He asks us to do everything that is possible. Then, asking for the things that seem impossible, they will be possible.

Finally, for centuries evangelists have been developing techniques for sharing Christ. Efforts should be made to look for opportunities to take advantage of resources from others. We asked these leaders how to do this.

The thing that we have been talking about is a tremendous challenge that cannot be met by only one organization, one church.

Ministry and objectives need to be evaluated by partners in the ministry, people we're working with, especially outside our organizations.

God speaks to different people in different ways in different places. We must listen to one another and seek God together.

That means unity. We look for cooperation, for being one body in spite of our differences. God will bless that effort because God is with us.

We have to come out from Amsterdam with a conviction that God has given us a very clear ministry to preach the Gospel of Jesus Christ. That is the only hope of the world.

Henri Aoun, Luis Bush and Luciano Jaramillo
Rev. Henri Aoun is a Campus Crusade Director from Beirut, Lebanon. He lives in France.
Dr. Luis Bush is a former missionary pastor in Central America and was the director of AD 2000.
Dr. Luciano Jaramillo is from Colombia and is the Director of Hispanic Ministries and Director of Transactions for the Region of the Americas for the International Bible Society.

The Evangelist Has a Strategy for Harvest

Luis Palau

Brothers and sisters, there are more than six billion people live in this world. More than three billion of them have not heard the Gospel of Jesus Christ. What a fantastic challenge for preaching evangelists! What a calling and privilege for each one of us!

Now it's harvest time. The church is growing at incredible rates in countries that once seemed impossible to penetrate with the Gospel. God is doing a mighty work! And we need to be ready to help bring in the harvest. This calls for a clear strategy.

When we think of strategy we often think, of course, of grand schemes—big crusades, national missions. All of that is fabulous. But it's more than the logistics of big campaigns. What should an evangelist's strategy include? I see four major areas we must develop in order to harvest effectively: personal attitude, God-defined goals, flexible methods and biblical evaluation.

The Personal Attitude of the Evangelist

Look at 1 Corinthians 9 with me. Five elements should characterize our personal attitudes as evangelists. First, the apostle Paul tells us to maintain a sacrificial attitude—to "put up with anything rather than hinder the gospel of Christ" (1 Corinthians 9:12, NIV).

Second, an evangelist should be marked by an inner compulsion. Paul says, "I am compelled to preach. Woe to me if I do not preach the gospel!" (1 Corinthians 9:16, NIV). We evangelists are Good News vagabonds. We move; we go; we can't hold back. We must never allow ourselves to hold back.

Third, whenever we preach the Gospel, we are discharging our duty as evangelists. The apostle Paul says, "I am compelled to preach" (1 Corinthians 9:16, NIV). We're not doing evangelism because it's always a lot of fun. Oh, sometimes mass evangelism is the most wonderful thing in the world. Other times it's hard—when you're criticized or money's tight, and you feel like you're only there because the Commander in Chief says, "Do it!"

Fourth, we must walk in the Spirit. Galatians 2:20 says, "I have been crucified with Christ and I no longer live, but Christ lives in me. The life I live in the body, I live by faith in the Son of God, who loved me and gave himself for me" (NIV). We must always, always, rely on the power and anointing of the Holy Spirit. Are you preaching with clean hands and a pure heart? Do you have accountability? Are you living according to eternity's values? Ask God to keep you humble—completely dependent upon Him.

One final point on the personal attitude of the evangelist is this: to keep prayerfully and everlastingly at it. As Paul told Timothy, "Continue in what you have learned" (2 Timothy 3:14, NIV). "Be prepared in season and out of season" (2 Timothy 4:2, NIV). Don't give up! No matter what trials and suffering come your way, don't give up! Pray! Pray and persist. Persist until the Second Coming.

Have God-Defined Goals

As evangelists we need to move forward with a clear divine plan based on God-defined goals. That calls for three components: vision, clear goals and saturation.

Vision comes when you pray in the presence of God. John 4:35 says, "Open your eyes and look at the fields! They are ripe for harvest" (NIV). Forty years ago, an American missionary named Keith Bentson taught me to open my eyes and let God define my goals. One day he said to me, "Luis, every Wednesday afternoon I'd like to pray with you. Will you come to my office?"

> Every week the prayers and the vision grew and grew, until after a year and a half I found myself praying to be an evangelist to the whole world.

So I went. He had a map on the wall of the city where we lived, with a blue dot marking the church that my family and I attended. He memorized the names of my sisters, my little brother, my mom and the eight elders of our church. He prayed for them by name—and he didn't even go to our church. The next week he prayed for other churches like the one I attended. The following week we prayed for the churches of another denomination. Praying with Keith was like taking a drive through the city!

At that point my vision was the city of Córdoba. But the next Wednesday he came with a map of the province of Córdoba. And the following week he had a map of the whole country of Argentina. Then he had a map of the whole South American continent. Then Europe. Then Asia. Every week the prayers and the vision grew and grew, until after a year and a half I found myself praying to be an evangelist to the whole world.

When D. L. Moody went to England, he said he was going to win 10,000 souls for Jesus Christ. When I first read that I thought, "That sounds unspiritual." Well, he led 100,000 souls to Jesus Christ, and I'm sure he wasn't unhappy. But please note: Moody had a specific plan. Since I read that, I've asked the Lord for some pretty bold things—"Lord, before I die, help me to preach the Gospel in so many countries, let me minister to presidents, let me win so many thousands of souls . . ." and more.

Praying boldly and specifically has given me a great sense of direction, a great sense of purpose. If the apostle Paul did it and the Lord Jesus did it, you, as an evangelist in your village or your city or wherever you live, can have goals before God.

The fact that you plan doesn't mean you're resisting the Holy Spirit. In fact, not planning *is* planning—except your plan is sloppy. Therefore, plan before God, but be flexible to the Holy Spirit. In Acts 16:6-10, for example, we read that the apostle Paul wanted to go to Bithynia. But the Spirit led him to Macedonia instead. In the same way, let the Spirit adjust your direction as you go.

And when you go, saturate the city with the Gospel. Our team motto is, "Let all the city hear the voice of God!" Plan to touch every level of society—the poor, the rich, the young, the old. Plan to "win as many as possible" (1 Corinthians 9:19, NIV). God will make a way, even though you may not have all the contacts and cash you think you need to do it. Just say, "Lord, would you use me?" and take Jesus Christ to the city.

Use Flexible Methods

God's principles are rock solid and never change. But methods are to be adapted in every generation. An evangelist's ministry is never predictable. Approach your goals with a teachable spirit, open to new ideas. Let God's Holy Spirit creatively work through you. I've found three things to be highly effective in this: learning from the masters, using all available means to communicate, and using a team.

There's nothing like reading about God's great servants of the past. Read all you can about master evangelists such as Charles Finney, Dwight L. Moody, John Wesley, George Whitefield, John Sung and others. Read about the missionaries who came to your country. Observe their methods and how they adapted to different cultures and situations. What made them so useful to God in the harvesting of souls? What made them so effective?

Christians often consider the media a mortal enemy. My evangelistic team and I have found the media to be one of our greatest allies in communicating the Good News on a large scale. Building good relationships with local media can open doors you never thought would open for the Gospel. And you can shine the light of Jesus into the lives of media professionals as well. A young American reporter came to the Lord during one of our evangelistic festivals in Portland, Oregon. Now the Lord is using her testimony to save others because she is so well known. We've seen that happen again and again in cities all around the world.

Harness all available technologies for the harvest. Use the Internet, use television. And continue to proclaim the Gospel on radio, which is still the only technology available in some parts of the world.

Accomplishing great things for the Lord requires great teamwork. In turn, teamwork requires great flexibility and great patience. We need each other desperately. "The eye cannot say to the hand, 'I don't need you!' And the head cannot say to the feet, 'I don't need you!'" (1 Corinthians 12:21, NIV). We're fellow servants. An evangelist alone is a lonely person. Ask God to give you at least one, maybe three partners to travel with you and support you. Paul traveled with seven. Jesus selected 12. Pray over your team and ask the Holy Spirit to guide you.

Evangelists need other kinds of teams besides their immediate ministry team. We especially need to work with local churches. This is all part of the strategy for the harvest. An evangelistic event won't happen without the support and work and prayers of the local church. New believers need to be incorporated immediately and effectively into the Body of Christ. You'll need as many contacts as possible to do this.

Also—this may shock you—evangelists need other evangelists. We need each other all the time. Build partnerships. Invest in the lives of other evangelists. My team and I currently work with 10 partner evangelists. We offer training and resources to many other evangelists who are just getting started. Someone needs to carry on the work after you're gone. Show them how! It's the ultimate harvest strategy.

> We need each other all the time. Build partnerships. Invest in the lives of other evangelists.

Practice Biblical Evaluation

My last point deals with results. You can't look at results through worldly eyes or you'll lose your focus. But there are some things you need to look at as you go. This is a tricky balance and one that calls for prayer and sensitivity to the Holy Spirit.

First, evaluate the message you're preaching. My number one goal is to "preach the Word" (2 Timothy 4:2, NIV). Everything I preach must be clearly verified by Scripture. Every time I preach I must rely on the power of the Holy Spirit. Brothers and sisters, we are acting as the very mouth of God Himself (see Jeremiah 15:19–21). *Never* take that responsibility lightly. *Always* preach the same old message—the simple, biblical Gospel of Jesus Christ—and *always* pull the net. *Always* give listeners an opportunity to receive Jesus Christ as Lord and Savior. Harvest time is now!

Second, consider numbers. Numbers represent people. Did you reach as many people as you possibly could? If you think the numbers are a bit low, remember that God looks at the heart. We receive letters years and years later from people who committed their lives to Jesus Christ at evangelistic events. Many never raised their hand, never went forward or talked to anybody. And the blessings of radio, television and Internet ministry reach millions of people we may never hear from until heaven.

That's the bottom line. Only in heaven will we know the ultimate results of the harvest. In that we can rest secure, knowing that we have been faithful to our God and to our calling.

Years ago in Scotland a young evangelist preached his heart out repeatedly on a street corner in Edinburgh. But after several days of preaching, no one had publicly responded to his invitation to receive Christ.

Finally, one Sunday afternoon after he had preached with no response from his listeners, the young preacher turned dejectedly to a friend and said, "Well, that's it. I'm not cut out to be an evangelist—that was the last time I'm going to preach."

An elderly bystander overheard this comment, and taking the young preacher by the arm, he looked deep into the young man's eyes and said, "Laddie, God loves and blesses those who speak well of His Son. Don't stop preaching, and in His time God will give you the results you seek."

The young man pondered those words and decided to keep on preaching. Within a short time, he began seeing results, and he became an evangelist that God used powerfully across Scotland and in Central Africa.

So I urge you, fellow evangelists, continue to speak well of Jesus Christ to your dying day!

Luis Palau

Born in Argentina, Dr. Luis Palau gave his life to Christ at a Christian camp for children. During more than 30 years of mass evangelism, Luis Palau has spoken to hundreds of millions of people through radio, television broadcasts and face-to-face. While his ministry began in Latin America with evangelistic crusades and rallies across the continent, by the 1980s Luis Palau's ministry had made a worldwide impact and new doors were opening around the globe. Dr. Palau and his wife, Patricia, make their home in Oregon (U.S.A.). They have four married sons and eight grandchildren.

Principles and Methods of Follow-Up

Jim Chew

Please open your Bible to two passages of Scripture, from Lamentations 4:3–4 and Job 39:13–18. They are about ostriches and what they do. The ostrich is a very cruel bird, because ostriches do not look after their young. They can lose their young, because the young can be trampled upon. What did God say about His people? He said they are like the ostriches. Why? Because—and this is the simple lesson—because they don't do follow-up. The picture is a powerful one. Here are children begging for food, for bread, but no one among God's people feeds them.

For more than 40 years I have been involved in evangelism follow-up, the nurturing of new believers, seeing them grow into maturity. Our session is about nurturing believers and seeing them grow.

During a Billy Graham mission in Singapore, I served as the counseling and the follow-up director. A young businessman and his family came to the Lord at that time We followed up this person and his family personally in the context of nurture groups in our church. Today this young businessman is an elder of the church. He is influencing people right up to the president and the prime minister. He is also influencing people in business circles. When he gives seminars on business, he brings along New Testaments. He is such a natural evangelist, such a personal evangelist, that people cannot get angry with him. He is always smiling and gracious. And he is influencing people. We followed up on him; we nurtured him. Never think of evangelism apart from follow-up and seeing these people integrated into the church. It is essential!

I was in another Billy Graham Asian mission, also serving as follow-up director, and I remember following up a student. We got his name and we tried to follow him up, but we couldn't find him. We had to persist and persevere to try and track him down. Finally, we realized that he gave us another name. That was the problem. But we tracked him down and we nurtured him. We got him involved in Bible study; we got him memorizing Scripture, doing a daily quiet time. Today this young man is a businessman in East Asia, and he is witnessing to everybody from taxi drivers to businesspeople. He and his wife have led scores, hundreds of people to the Lord. He follows up on them because somebody did that for him.

Follow-Up Requires Persistence and Perseverance

You persist. You don't give up. It is essential. That was the passion of the apostle Paul when he said, "Warning every man, and teaching every man in all wisdom; that we may present every man"—what? . . . mature—"perfect in Christ Jesus" (Colossians 1:28, KJV). He said he labored with all his strength to do that. It requires persistence. It requires perseverance.

Look at the Great Commission. In Matthew 28:19–20, Jesus is speaking to 11 men. He says go—and what?—make disciples of all nations. He did not say you go around and you get decisions, important as that is, but you make disciples. That is the imperative of that commission, and we must take that command seriously. It is the most important part of the commission. Follow-up is essential in this process of disciple-making because Jesus wants people to follow Him. That is the mission statement of the church I attend—making people total followers of Jesus Christ.

When the disciples were given that commission, they knew what it meant. Jesus had spent three years with them. They watched His life, they heard His teaching, they watched Him pray, and they wanted to learn to pray. Jesus discipled them. He trained them. And now He was giving them this final commission. And because they faithfully obeyed that commission, you and I are disciples. Do you realize that?

Encouragement to Remain True

Paul and his team had a passion for follow-up. It was a deep conviction with him and his team. We read in Acts 14:21–23 that in his first mission he and his team returned to Lystra, Iconium and Antioch, cities they had gone to earlier. They returned—why? To strengthen those who had believed. Those young disciples were facing hardships. What if Paul and his team had become ostriches and just left them alone in their hardships? Well, they did not. These young disciples received encouragement, instruction to remain true to the faith in spite of persecution.

We see this in Paul's second mission in Acts 15:36 when he said his aim was to strengthen the new churches that had emerged. "Let us go back," he says, "let us visit the towns where we preached the Word and see how they're doing." And what about his third mission? We read in Acts 18:23 that he set out from his home base, Antioch, and traveled throughout the region of Galatia and Phrygia. What did he do? He strengthened all the disciples. He had a deep burden for follow-up. We need to have that too.

Follow-Up Is Personal

What was Paul's follow-up strategy? First of all, Paul followed up personally. *Follow-up is not just giving materials; follow-up is personal.* He and his team had already preached the Gospel. We read in 1 Thessalonians 1:5–6 how Paul and his team went to Thessalonica. He said, "We lived among them." He identified with the Thessalonians. He wanted to be sure that the message that he was communicating was such that, later on, because he had gained rapport with the people, they would listen. His Gospel message came in power because they wanted to hear what he had to say. He understood them and they understood him. Because of that, he says, the Gospel was received with deep conviction and with the Holy Spirit's power.

Paul's personal ministry was absolutely awesome. It says that they turned from idols to serve the living God. And then they began to spread the message. They became an example to all the believers around (see 1 Thessalonians 1:7–9).

When we go on to 1 Thessalonians 2:6–8, we read those amazing words. Paul says in verse 6 onwards, "We could have been a burden to you, but we were gentle"—underline that word *gentle*—"among you" (NIV). A gentle evangelist is powerful—gentle in character, gentle as a mother caring for her little children.

Then he goes on to say, "We loved you so much that we were delighted to share with you not only the gospel . . . but our lives as well" (NIV). For Paul it was the Gospel *and* his life. Why? He says, "Because you had become so dear to us" (NIV). He and his team developed this personal caring relationship with these individuals. And if you go on reading—and I like the New English Bible—it says, "We dealt with you one by one" (verse 11).

> Follow-up is the process of giving continued attention to new believers until they are at home in the local church, discover how they can serve, develop their full potential for Jesus Christ, and help to build His church.

Then we read that Paul had to leave these Thessalonians early because of opposition. But what did he do? He followed up through other persons. He sent Timothy back, we read in 1 Thessalonians 3 (see verses 1–2). The reason we have this letter is because Timothy came back to Paul and gave a good report, and so he wrote this letter. Paul was really encouraged. So if you cannot do it for some reason, send another person or other persons to see that the follow-up is being done.

Transformation Is a Process

Paul wrote many letters. When we study the epistles, we see that they are rich and have to do with the development of Christian conduct, character and with doctrinal issues. We have these letters because Paul knew that transformation was a process. We think young converts will grow overnight. They don't. They have to be nurtured.

Sure, Paul says, if anyone is in Christ, he is a new person (see 2 Corinthians 5:17). We know that. But read about the church in Corinth; were they new persons? They were new in the sense that the seed of the new birth was there, but growth and transformation is a process. So you have got to treat evangelism as a process, too, not just some big event and it's over. Paul taught them so that they could grow. Sometimes he remained a long time to teach them in order that the church could be strengthened.

Follow-up is the process of giving continued attention to new believers until they are at home in the local church, discover how they can serve, develop their full potential for Jesus Christ, and help to build His Church. That is a comprehensive definition—until they are at home in the church.

Nurture the New Believers

Very often these new believers come from Buddhist, Shinto, Hindu or other backgrounds, and they don't feel at home. Some have had no religious background. They need a safe place. This is why we have nurture groups so that they can get used to being a part of God's family, be nurtured and share their lives with one another. We need to see that they are part of a little home group, a fellowship group, where they can be nurtured and be given attention.

Let's talk now of some goals in follow-up. *The primary goal is to see the maturity of these believers, their growth in Christlikeness* (see Colossians 1:28). That is a process of God's transforming work as we nurture these believers in the context of the church. So first of all, new believers need to be strengthened in their faith. We want to see that. Second, we want new believers to know what true fellowship with Christ is all about, what it is to abide in Him, to know what it is to pray, what it is to enjoy the Bible. Third, we want to see that these new believers will function as partners within local bodies of believers. Romans 12:5 talks about the body having many parts. We want them to grow in that context so that they can be useful members of the church.

And finally, we want to see that these believers' testimonies and their witness will spread to others (see 1 Thessalonians 1:8). To do this we have got to ensure that they have spiritual nurture. We have seen that the one essential in the Great Commission is to make disciples, and discipleship is a process of growth from being new believers to being mature.

Laying Solid Foundations of Faith

Remember that some of these people come from backgrounds where they know nothing about the Bible and very little or nothing about Jesus. I have nurtured such people who had zero knowledge of Jesus Christ. Just in the last couple of years, my wife and I have been nurturing three couples. The first couple we met, the husband had a Ph.D., but he knew nothing about Jesus. We had to start, as they say, from square one. You see, they are on a spiritual journey, a new one. When a person believes in Christ, whatever his physical age or his professional age, spiritually he is a newborn baby. Don't forget that. A baby needs lots of care! A baby needs feeding, protecting, training.

When I received Christ, the first verse I was asked to memorize was, "As newborn babes, desire the sincere milk of the word" (1 Peter 2:2, KJV). And I am thankful that my father got me started in reading the Bible when I received the Lord at a young age. I never missed reading the Bible every day because it was my milk, and later it became meat. When you feed babies, you don't give them meat. They will get indigestion. Seek the milk of the Word so that you may grow, it says in 1 Peter 2:2.

You have the privilege of laying sound foundations of faith. These foundations will help new believers to understand what the Gospel is. I work across cultures, and this is the important question to me: What is the Gospel? You say, "Oh, the evangelist has preached it." Yes, he has. But these people need to understand the depths of the meaning of the Gospel of grace. Help them to understand it. They need Scripture in order to grasp it.

They need Scripture in order to resist Satan. One of the best ways to do that is to help them memorize a verse of Scripture about assurance of salvation. People need to be sure that they really are saved, and they can only be sure when the Spirit of God takes the Word of God and gives them that conviction based on the promises of the Word of God. Get them to memorize Scripture.

You Are the Teachers and the Trainers

Paul said, "But I am afraid that just as Eve was deceived by the serpent's cunning, your minds may somehow be led astray from your sincere and pure devotion to Christ" (2 Corinthians 11:3, NIV). They need protecting and they need training. They need practical training in the basics of Christian living. You and your team are the teachers and the trainers.

Help them to learn the Bible until the time when they learn to feed themselves. There are so many people in our churches who just listen to sermons, but they have not been taught to feed themselves. They are still babes, although they may have been in your church for 10 years. Scripture says, "So then, just as you received Christ Jesus as Lord, continue to live in him, rooted and built up in him, strengthened in the faith as you were taught, and overflowing with thankfulness" (Colossians

> Who is responsible for follow-up? You are, as an evangelist, and your team that works with you.

2:6–7, NIV). The Colossian believers were taught; they were trained to be rooted and to be built up in Christ. They were taught how to live in the midst of a worldly society that tried to shake their convictions about Jesus Christ. They were rooted in the Scriptures.

Who is responsible for follow-up? You are, as an evangelist, and your team that works with you. Paul says you can have 10,000 instructors in Christ but you don't have many fathers (see 1 Corinthians 4:15). You are an evangelist, a pastor, a teacher, for the building up of the body of Christ. You are responsible for that. Take on that responsibility! Paul took it on. You are to equip these people so that they can function in the context of the church.

Have a Follow-Up Plan

What are your responsibilities? First, you want your young believers to know and understand the Gospel. Second, they need to be part of the church in order to contribute to its witness. To ensure that they are at home in the church, their emotional and spiritual needs have to be met so that they are truly part of the fellowship. This takes time. This requires relationship building and caring.

You need to ensure that you have a follow-up plan where you train personal workers. This is why I believe God has blessed people such as Billy Graham and others who see that they arrive before the Crusade and train personal workers. These inquirers or new converts are going to be channeled into the churches. Train them.

Train nurture-group leaders. A nurture-group leader learns how to patiently nurture young believers so that they slowly learn how to have their own devotional life, how to grow in the Christian life. What happens if there are no churches? You need to take responsibility, when there are no churches, to stay long enough—following the example of the apostle Paul—and then plan to return.

I have gone to the villages of different countries in Asia where I have seen a nucleus of believers. I have seen a family coming to Christ, brothers and sisters coming to Christ. That is the nucleus of a church. They don't even have to build a building. Sometimes they just meet in the home, as they did in the first century. That's church!

In many places where I go, in places hostile to the Gospel, it is lovely to see a nucleus of these few believers. They are worshiping in ways that are beyond your imagination or mine. The Spirit of God starts to nurture them, and it's thrilling to see that. I saw that in Indonesia this year, and I couldn't help weeping to see what God was doing in this nucleus of believers.

Use Suitable Helps

So stay for a period and plan to return. And use suitable helps. Make your own materials. If you have your Bible, that's a good start. It is all you need. Be creative when there are no churches. In areas where people are illiterate, you can use visual aids. I have been to those areas, and I have watched evangelists who show pictures and placards. Use the kind of aids that can help you. One good way is just through storytelling from the Bible. Follow the example of Jesus; it is a powerful way. Where there is literacy and when there are churches, try to see that these people get portions of the Bible so that they can have the Scriptures in their own hands to learn to read the Bible and, in time to come, to study it.

Assurance Based on the Word of God

Now there are certain basics, certain essentials in the Christian faith. You have already explained the Gospel—who Jesus is, what He did, that He is the only Savior, He is the Lord, He is God. You have explained the meaning of the Cross, the resurrection. I love to help a convert go through the Gospel of John. Some people don't have a strong Christian background, like the couples that I have been helping. We went through the whole Gospel of John before they even trusted the Lord. Go through slowly so that they have a grasp of the Gospel. Help them to have salvation and assurance. They need assurance based on the Word of God—verses like John 1:12. That was the first assurance verse I memorized. John 3:16—what a terrific assurance verse!—or John 5:24; 1 John 5:11–12. You may want to get some cards and write out these verses so that they can review them.

I go to some places where they don't write these verses on small cards; they write them on big cards in small print so that they can get as many verses as possible on a card. In one place I visited in China, they memorize a verse a day. They review the Scriptures and pray. Teach them to have time alone with God. The best way I know to teach a person to have a quiet time is to do it with that person. Read with that person a portion of the Bible and then pray very simply.

Teach them that Jesus is Lord and that He wants every area of their lives to be under His control. Teach them what it is to obey Christ and to obey Him joyfully. Jesus said, "If you love Me, keep My commandments" (John 14:15, NKJV; also see verse 21).

Teach about the Holy Spirit. Teach them that they have this wonderful person living in them, One just like Jesus, who wants to fill their lives with Himself and with His fruits. Teach them about fellowship. Teach them about the Church. The Church is people who believe in Jesus Christ. They love one another, they encourage one another and they serve one another. Then teach them how to share their story very simply. Like the blind man, "I was blind, now I see" (John 9:25, KJV).

The Most Important Habits for a Young Believer

Don't attempt to rush through these topics. Sometimes going through this can take a couple of years. Especially important is to get the convert to develop the habit of daily fellowship with Christ. If you were to ask me the most important habits that you can encourage in a young believer, I would say it is first a daily quiet time when they read the Bible and pray. I have my four "Rs." Teach them to read; teach them to record, write down just one thought; teach them to reflect, to think over; and then teach them to respond, to pray it back. To read, record, reflect and to respond. That is what a quiet time is all about. Tell the person why that habit is important.

The second habit is Scripture memory. Why is that important? I have not seen anyone backslide who has memorized Scripture consistently. Consistently apply the Word of God, memorizing it. Show the person how to do it. I am very grateful that a person in Youth for Christ helped me with these habits when I was a young student. He was very strict, especially on Scripture memory. I had to memorize two verses a week and, finally, 108 verses in the topical memory system. And I had to recite them word perfect! He would listen to me, check up on me. I had to say the reference before and after, and I couldn't even breathe between the reference and the verse; I just had to recite.

People give excuses why they can't memorize Scripture. I like to tell the story of an 86-year-old woman who came to Christ in Vietnam. She sat down in front of us, recited the whole 108 verses of the topical memory system, references before and after, at one sitting. She was a new believer. So if an 86-year-old woman can do it, well, you young people better do something!

Get people started by doing it with them, and then help them to pass it on. This is where you find believers not only established and equipped, but soon they start to reproduce in their ministry.

An Assignment for Where You Work

I want to give you a little assignment. Describe your audience, the people you are evangelizing. How literate are they? What are their needs? What do they need to hear? Are there churches where you work? What can you do to prepare for follow-up? What can you use to train follow-up workers?

Then I want you to draw up a follow-up plan to ensure that you can preserve the fruit of evangelism. Ask yourself what is the first specific step you need to take as soon as possible. What other help or resources will you need to ensure effective follow-up? For example, what do you need for the training of small group leaders? What materials should you use to adapt to your situation? Take time to do this.

Jim Chew

Mr. Jim Chew has been with The Navigators since 1963, currently serving as Asia Missions Facilitator and New Zealand Missions Director. Mr. Chew grew up in Singapore and graduated from the University of Malaya, Singapore, with a Bachelor of Arts degree. Mr. Chew and his wife, Selene, were the first Asians to be appointed as Navigator representatives. They initiated the work in Malaysia and have directed ministries in various parts of Asia. They are now based in New Zealand.

The Pastor and the Communist Politician

Uwe Holmer

Trying to survive as Christians in East Germany, a nation guided by "confrontational atheism" was very difficult for Lutheran pastor Rev. Uwe Holmer and his family. They had suffered much. But then, the head of the East German state was deposed. Rev. Holmer described what happened when Erich Honecker and his wife, with no place to go, asked for asylum in the pastor's home. The Holmer family struggled with issues of forgiveness and acceptance of this man who had hurt them so much—and they began witnessing to the former dictator about their faith in Jesus.

Erich Honecker and his wife had lived in Wandlitz near Berlin, which was a home to the famous and guarded by the military. On February 1, 1990, they lost all of their privileges, and even their house. After hospital treatment, Honecker had no home to return to. The state authorities refused to accept him, or they offered him accommodation that was so poorly protected that he feared an attack by angry citizens.

He therefore asked the Protestant State Church of Berlin-Brandenburg (Landeskirche) whether they were willing to grant him asylum. The church leadership reached a majority consensus that his request should not be rejected. But this was a problem. Even though they wanted to grant Honecker accommodation, it was not clear where this could be successfully done. Here, again, there was reason to fear that the accommodation would be attacked.

At the time I was leader of a Christian village, the social ministry complex at Lobetal, near Berlin, which was home to about 500 old people suffering from epilepsy or mental illness. There were also 270 staff and family members in our village.

The church leadership therefore thought that if Honecker could live with us in a Christian environment, this might shield him some from attacks that could be expected.

To explain what this request from Erich Honecker meant for me, I must describe an experience which lay a long time before that, but which shows the intellectual and spiritual climate in which we had lived for 40 years. Even we theology students had to study Marxism-Leninism in our first few semesters. So we sat in a large lecture theater together with many new students from other faculties. The lecturer explained to us the "epoch-making" social transformation that had taken place in the German Democratic Republic (GDR). He said that exploitation of man by man had finally been overcome because all of the means of production now belonged to the people. Now socialism was being built up, and it offered all of us unexpected economic and social prospects. And when socialism had fully matured and developed, it would lead to a radical leap to the next higher stage, the final stage of social development: communism. Then, there would no longer be any difference in wages. Everybody would then get what he needed. Nobody would want to have more than anybody else, and a wonderful peace would reign among mankind.

The lecturer paused for a moment and then shouted, "And then we will build heaven on earth!" He paused again and continued, "And then the church will die a natural death, because if people experience heaven here on earth, they will not seek any other heaven."

Our little band of theology students sat there in the middle of the great lecture theater, and we felt distinctly that everyone was looking at us and thinking, "You poor theologians, these are pitiful prospects that they are giving you! Is it really worth going into the church ministry at a time like this?" I remember even today how I sat there quietly and prayed, "Lord, I believe in spite of it all that You have the victory and that the gates of hell will not overcome Your Church."

This experience, and others like it, created an atmosphere of intellectual battle in our society. I never knew whether the communist party would perhaps one day resort to violent means to accelerate the demise of the Church, but I still often thanked God that I was able to be a messenger of peace in the middle of a country of confrontational atheism.

And now the highest man among those who had predicted the end of the Church came and asked this very Church for asylum! My wife and I were not filled with a feeling of triumph, we simply sympathized with this married couple who were experiencing failure. We could not simply reject it!

However, for Lobetal and its staff this caused a problem. A social ministry which gives shelter to sick and sensitive people needs peace and order. But if Erich Honecker and his wife came to us, it would bring disquiet and excitement, or worse. The first reaction in our staff meeting was that they would not fit into our setting and that we should refuse the request. But in the course of our discussion we noticed that it was a challenge to our faith. Could we continue to pray with sincerity, "Forgive us our sins as we forgive those who have sinned against us," if we refused to grant Honecker forgiveness and help?

After long discussions and deep inner struggles, a large majority of our staff came to the conviction that we should do it, and in doing so create a symbol of reconciliation and peace for our country. We did in fact have protests from the outside. Many people came to our village and expressed their anger. We even received bomb threats. In the 10 weeks from the end of January to the beginning of April 1990, we received about 3,000 letters. Half of them expressed rejection, the others encouragement.

Because the homes in the Lobetal institution did not have any free space, we as a family decided to put the Honeckers up with us in the vicarage. So now we had in our house the man and woman who had been responsible for the fact that our children were not accepted into the senior school. We had also experienced other kinds of oppression, even the threat of prison. And now we needed to offer them protection and safety, and even love. You can't do that if your spirit is full of enmity. Thus, my wish was that this 10-week period with Erich Honecker as a guest would not only help him, but that it would also be a symbol for all political opponents, and that this symbol would be taken up by many people in our nation.

The question of forgiveness was no longer very relevant for me when the Honeckers came to us. It had been relevant 17 years previously when my oldest children, in spite of their very good performance in school, had been excluded from senior high school education because they had not joined in the atheistic youth ceremony of the "Jugendweihe," were not willing to sing the ungodly verses of the "Internationale," and did not take part in the pre-military shooting practice.

At the time, I wrote to all the highest school, party and government authorities, and my objections were rejected. In the end, I gave up the struggle and left the matter with God. I said to myself, "You expected that this could happen to your family when you consciously decided to stay in the GDR when your parents, brothers and sisters fled to the West. You stayed here for the sake of the Gospel. What is now happening to you is nothing out of the ordinary, nothing 'strange,' as the apostle Peter says. This is just a small part of the suffering for Christ's sake which every Christian must suffer in some way." Later I was thankful that I did not carry a grudge around with me for 17 years, that I had been able to give it up. Otherwise, our family would have carried a very heavy inner burden!

In the last resort, the fact that we were able to take in Erich Honecker without extreme inner battles resulted from the fact that my wife and I were both converted at the age of 19 and experienced God's forgiveness for all of our sins. A person who lives from God's forgiveness day by day can also forgive others.

But I don't want to be misunderstood here. Forgiveness is not an easy thing. In those days I experienced how difficult it was for some of our contemporaries to forgive political opponents such as Erich Honecker, and his wife, who had been the People's Minister of Education and was therefore responsible for the discrimination against Christians in the schools. I can understand them. Some of them really had a terrible time. If a person has not personally experienced forgiveness for his own sins, it is difficult, or almost impossible, for him to forgive those who have done him so much wrong.

Thus, I was now also free to speak with Erich Honecker and his wife. We ate our meals together, and of course we gave thanks beforehand. The Honeckers respected that. Later, Mrs. Honecker cooked for her husband because he needed a light diet and my wife was always involved in conversations with people. In the evening, the Honeckers and I then walked through the village or around the lake under the cover of darkness. He didn't do this by day because he feared the many journalists and their sensationalism. We spoke about our families or about the 10 years that he had spent in prison under Hitler. We almost never spoke about political issues. I sensed that he had great hurts in this area and was not yet ready to talk about them. I had to respect that.

Of course, spiritual questions were more important for me. Here he was usually silent, but he did not noticeably disagree. For example, I was able to tell him that I did not regard the reunification of Germany as a chance event or the result of mere political forces. The two German states were founded in 1949. Reunification came in 1989. So our country was divided for exactly 40 years. In the history of God's dealings with mankind, 40 years is an important period, a time of humiliation and purification such as Israel had to bear in the wilderness. And God had evidently decided to follow this pattern with our nation after all of the horrible crimes under Hitler.

Honecker listened carefully, but did not express any real opinions. His reactions were similar when I suggested that socialism, like humanism and idealism, had fallen into an error by believing that man is good by nature. That if we could abolish the exploitation of man by man, we could banish all evil from the world and create good people. I said that the whole development of socialism and its collapse had been yet another proof of this error. I said that man is not good, that he is a sinner and needs redemption. I said that this is the reason why God begins His Kingdom by changing people. Mr. Honecker was probably too much of a Marxist to agree with me. But he was not able to contradict me. Probably he had simply not yet found his own answer to these questions.

What makes me glad is that fact that our relationship on the personal and human level was, in fact, rather friendly. Even though violence and crimes were committed under Honecker's rule, as a person with us he was rather easygoing. He was a convinced, almost fanatical communist. That made him dangerous. But he was also a friendly person. That alleviated the dangers of his rule slightly. Many terrible things could have happened to our nation if there had been a brutal man in his place. In the end, our relationship with the Honeckers even became one of friendship. It is not possible to live together under one roof for 10 weeks without developing a personal concern for the other person. At least it is something that we Christians can't do, because we have done away with all that stood between us and our fellow humans and now we are free to relate to them, especially if they are in need. That was our experience with the Honeckers, too.

When they eventually left us for accommodation and medical treatment in the Soviet military hospital at Beelitz, a human friendship remained between us. After he was expelled from Russia, we visited Honecker in prison in Berlin. In the course of our conversation he spoke of his serious illness and said, "And soon the time will come when I must leave this earth." I referred to those words later and told him that was not the end, that life continues and that it can continue in peace with God if we accept the forgiveness of Jesus. We still correspond with his wife even today.

In this experience, I realized that forgiveness is not crucial when small things happen and it is easy to forgive. Forgiveness is particularly crucial when serious guilt is involved. That brought me back to the importance of Jesus' words which He spoke for all of us, not just with a view to our political opponents: "If you do not forgive others, my Father in heaven will not forgive you, either" (see Matthew 6:15).

In our family, our church, our nation, and in the crisis areas of this world, there will be no real peace without forgiveness. The message for forgiveness through the Cross of Christ, of peace with God and peace with others, has never been more relevant than it is now. That is why the word of Scripture also applies to us: "How beautiful . . . are the feet of those who bring good news, who proclaim peace, who bring good tidings, who proclaim salvation, who say to Zion, 'Your God reigns!'" (Isaiah 52:7, NIV).

Uwe Holmer
Rev. Uwe Holmer is a pastor in the German Lutheran Church.

The Evangelist Preaches and Lives the Cross

Antoine Rutayisire

I come with a certain feeling of inadequacy. The subject, "The Evangelist Preaches and Lives the Cross," is too big for me. I don't think there is any person who has ever contemplated the Cross who has done so without feeling inadequate. When you are going to talk about the Cross, you are obliged to leave a lot of things aside because it is too big for us. You see, the Cross is the whole message of the Bible.

From the time Adam and Eve committed sin, everything in the Bible pointed to the Cross. The Law, the sacrifices, the prophets, all point to the Cross. In the New Testament, Christ always spoke about the Cross. His life was focused on the Cross. The apostles—Paul, Peter and the others—always preached Christ and Christ crucified.

"You are worthy," sang the angels and the redeemed, "to take the scroll and to open its seals, because you were slain, and with your blood you purchased men for God from every tribe and language and people and nation. You have made them to be a kingdom and priests to serve our God, and they will reign on the earth" (Revelation 5:9–10, NIV). That is the song we are going to sing when we get to heaven, and it is a reminder that everything that we are and everything that we have we owe to Christ and His Cross. That is why I feel quite inadequate to speak about the Cross.

But I have picked out four things to talk about. I will start by giving a short personal testimony about my encounter with the Cross. Then, second, we are going to look at the Cross and lost humanity. Third, we are going to look at the Cross and wounded humanity. And, fourth, we are going to look at the Cross and the modern crisis of identity.

My Encounter With the Cross

First, here is how I came to know the Cross. The first significant encounter I had with the Cross came when I was 12 years old. I went to study in a Roman Catholic junior seminary. During the period of Lent, the 40 days leading up to Easter, they had what was called the service of the stations of the Cross. In my mind I could see all the people around Jesus—the fickle, gregarious, angry mob; the plotting, jealous, religious leaders; the cruel soldiers. And I saw Jesus—alone, abandoned by all, but calm. Every time they got to the place where they read, "And when they got to the place called The Skull, there they crucified Him" (see Matthew 27:33–35), I always wept. At the end of the service, I went home feeling that I should do something. But no one ever explained to me what I had to do.

I spent seven years in the junior seminary, and then I went to the university. Six years of university life—wasted years, a shameful life, immorality and drinking. But, I praise the Lord, that feeling about the Cross remained with me. I was seeking for something. I was looking for commitment to the Lord.

Then one day, when I was going through a very rough time, a friend sent me a Bible and I started reading it. When I got into the middle of the New Testament, with the writings of Paul, my life changed. Because when you read the letters of Paul, you find that the presence of Christ is overwhelming. Paul speaks so well of Christ. He says that for him living is Christ. He says that even dying for Christ would be a gain. He says that no matter what happens to him, as long as Christ is preached, he is very happy.

I started questioning my Christianity because, you see, I was a very religious young man—very sinful but also very religious. I went to church every Sunday, but all the other days I went my own way. But then I started wondering, "Where is Christ in my life?" I went on reading and, finally, I took the decision to read the whole Bible because I wanted to find out what it is all about and I wanted to make a commitment.

I want to ask, "Do you have room for Christ in your life?" Because very often we may have a lot of religion; we may even have room for God. But do you have room for Christ in your life? Is Christ at the center of your life? That was the question that really changed my life. I started reading the Bible, reading about Christ, and those passages about the Cross came back again and I wept. I wept looking at Christ dying for me on the Cross, and that time I made a commitment. I remember the first sentence I wrote in my Bible. I wrote, "From this day on I'm going to live for Jesus, and the objective of my life will be to glorify the name of Jesus." And every day I pray, "Lord, help me to glorify Your name. Help me to be focused on Jesus—to live for Jesus, to work for Jesus, to glorify Jesus."

Preaching the Cross

From my experience I have drawn two lessons about preaching the Cross. First, if we are going to preach the Cross, we need to show what Jesus has done for us so that people will understand what it is. We need to present the reality of the Cross in such a way that people will understand how much Jesus has paid to redeem them. Make them see what you are talking about.

Second, preaching the Cross of Jesus Christ should always be related to the daily lives of our audience. People respond to our appeal when they can identify with what we are talking about. Very often people ask, "What is the relevance, what is the pertinence, of believing in something that happened 2,000 years ago?" We need to preach the Gospel and relate it to people's lives. I have heard people debating about the Cross. I have heard people preaching sermons that are philosophical debates. But we need to preach the Cross of Jesus Christ clearly so that people will understand, and we need to make an appeal. All the prophets of the Old Testament made an appeal. Jesus Christ Himself, when He preached, made an appeal. Peter and Paul and the others, when they preached, called for people to make commitments for Christ. Why are we afraid of calling people to make commitments? Why are we afraid of making an appeal?

I go to some places where they say, "Don't preach as you preach in Africa. Don't make an appeal." But we need to make an appeal because, I'm sure, when I was 12 years old in the junior seminary, after the stations of the Cross, if the priest had made an appeal, he would have spared me years of wasted life. We need to make the preaching of the Cross clear and make an appeal for people to make a commitment to Jesus Christ.

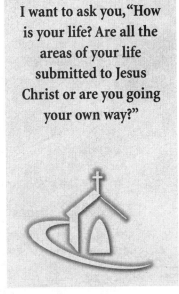

> I want to ask you, "How is your life? Are all the areas of your life submitted to Jesus Christ or are you going your own way?"

The Cross and Lost Humanity

As my second emphasis, the Cross is our message to lost humanity. One day I was traveling on a bus. I had a small badge on my jacket that said, "Jesus Christ is Lord." A woman looked at me and said, "I don't like your badge." I asked, "Why?" She said, "I don't like your Jesus, I don't like His Cross and I don't like His lordship." I was very much amazed because I was praying in my heart to see how I could introduce Jesus Christ to this woman. Then, I started explaining to her what Jesus meant in my life. I explained what He could mean in her life. Finally, she said, "Well, you know, I think you are right. But I don't want to take your Jesus because I'm already serving another master and he doesn't like your Jesus." She confessed to me that she was a member of a satanic sect. But at least she had that opportunity to make a choice for Jesus—for or against. That's our mission.

Let's preach the Cross with clarity and passion and conviction. Let the world make a choice. But if we are going to preach the Cross with conviction, we ourselves need to live the Cross. Paul said that if we don't live the Cross, if we don't live the message, we are going to be disqualified after having preached to others. We need to live the Cross by obedience and in holiness—total obedience, total surrender to the authority of Christ.

Obedience is the issue. In the Garden of Eden obedience was the issue because Adam and Eve had to make a choice. In the Garden of Gethsemane the issue of obedience was again at stake because Jesus had to make a choice. His prayer was, "My Father, if it is possible, may this cup be taken from me. Yet not as I will, but as you will" (Matthew 26:39, NIV). His final prayer was, "May your will be done" (Matthew 26:42, NIV). That is obedience. In the Garden of Eden, Adam and Eve chose to go their own way. In the Garden of Gethsemane, Jesus chose to go His Father's way.

Today we need to make a choice. In a society of self-indulgence, in a society of self-assertiveness, the evangelist is called to live a life of total surrender, a life of humility and of total obedience to God. I want to ask you, "How is your life? Are all the areas of your life submitted to Jesus Christ or are you going your own way?" Because the Bible says, "For the grace of God that brings salvation has appeared to all men. It teaches us to say 'No' to ungodliness and worldly passions, and to live self-controlled, upright and godly lives in this present age, while we wait for the blessed hope—the glorious appearing of our great God and Savior, Jesus Christ, who gave himself for us to redeem us from all wickedness and to purify for himself a people that are his very own, eager to do what is good" (Titus 2:11–14, NIV).

The Bible says, "You are not your own; you were bought at a price. Therefore honor God with your body" (1 Corinthians 6:19–20, NIV). Paul wrote to the Galatians, "May I never boast except in the cross of our Lord Jesus Christ, through which the world has been crucified to me, and I to the world" (Galatians 6:14, NIV). So if we are going to be convincing in this modern world, we need to surrender everything—talents, possessions, time. Let us put everything on the Lord's altar. Let us be living sacrifices, holy and pleasing to our God. Because what God needs most is not our abilities but our obedience and availability.

The Cross and Wounded Humanity

The third point that I want to make is about the Cross of Jesus and the woundedness of modern man. We live in a wounded, bruised, broken world. We live in a time of ethnic wars and clashes. We live in a world of ruthless competition between nations and companies and individuals. This is a time when many people are faced with family breakdowns; many people are wounded, crushed, brokenhearted. This is a consequence of sin, because sin divides and sin alienates.

The first time sin came into the world, it brought division—division between man and God, division between a man and his wife, and division inside the heart of man. Adam looked at himself and said, "I'm naked" (see Genesis 3:10). He was alienated from himself, alienated from his wife, alienated from God, and alienated from his environment. All the problems we are faced with today are on one or another level of alienation brought by sin. And the Cross of Jesus is the answer.

Very often we speak of Jesus Christ, our Sin-Bearer—the One who took our sins. But the Bible speaks also of Jesus Christ, our pain bearer—the One who suffered for our wounded world. The Bible says, "Surely he took up our infirmities and carried our sorrows. . . . He was pierced for our transgressions, he was crushed for our iniquities; the punishment that brought us peace was upon him, and by his wounds we are healed" (Isaiah 53:4–5, NIV).

I come from Rwanda. Rwanda is one of the most wounded nations of the world today because of four decades of ethnic tensions and massacres and class struggles that have culminated in a genocide that took more than one million people in less than 100 days. Today when you go to Rwanda, everything looks normal outside, but inside our hearts are broken and bleeding. I myself came to the Lord at a time when I was so wounded because I was born in a Tutsi family and my father was killed when I was five years old by Hutus among our neighbors. When I was 15 years old, we had another wave of massacres against Tutsis. I saw many of my friends killed. I survived, but with a wounded heart.

When I came to the Lord it was very easy to give away my sins, but it was so difficult to give away my anger. I felt that I had the right to hate the people who killed the members of my family, who killed my friends. I felt I had the right to hate them—until the day I came to the Cross. One day I was reading about Jesus. He was hanging on the Cross with a crown of thorns on His head, with nails in His hands, with nails in His feet. He looked at those wicked people and He said, "Father, forgive them" (Luke 23:34, KJV).

That is the sentence that changed my life. I was sitting there and I thought, "How can He forgive these people? When they were sick, He healed them. When they were hungry, He fed them. When their children were dead, He resurrected them. All of them are turning against Him and saying, 'Crucify Him' [Luke 23:21, KJV], but He repays them good for evil, and He says, 'Father, forgive them' [Luke 23:34, KJV]." As I sat there I heard the words of the Lord saying, "This is the path you have to walk. You have to forgive those people."

I tell you, it was the most difficult day of my life because I sat there and I said, "Lord, do you mean to tell me I can forgive those people who came to our home and killed my father and looted our property?" But the voice of the Lord said, "You know, when Jesus was hanging on the Cross with nails in His hands, with a crown of thorns on His head, that's when He prayed, 'Father, forgive them.' That's the path you have to walk."

That day I made a long list of people I hated with cause. I could say, "Lord, I hate this one because he did this. I hate this one because. . . ." Finally I took the long list and said, "Father, I give you all my reasons for hating these people. Give me Your grace to love them." But the most difficult was still to come because the Lord said, "Now, pray for them. Pray a blessing on these people." I started praying, "Lord, bless. . . . Lord, bless. . . . Lord. . . ."—the names of these people didn't want to come out of my mouth because I still hated them, despite the prayer I had made. Deep inside the wound was still there.

Finally, I broke down and wept. I wept, I tell you. I wept and I wept, praying for those people. I prayed for the second one, the third one, the fourth one. Finally, I finished my list, and I was tired and I went to sleep. When I woke up, I said, "Lord, every time I remember these people, I will pray for them." Because, you see, when you hate someone, he is the first person you remember. When you wake up in the morning, he is still there, big as a mountain. You go to sleep in the evening, he's sitting on your mind as big as an elephant. I said, "Every time I remember these people, I'm going to pray for them. I'm going to bless them, bless their families, bless their homes, bless their businesses." The Cross of Jesus Christ is so powerful. I forgave those people.

But then came the genocide. During the genocide it was so difficult. It was so difficult seeing people dying around me. Finally I heard the voice of the Lord saying, "Keep the grace I have given you. Keep loving these people, despite what they're doing. Pray for them." And I did. When the war ended and the genocide was over, most of the people who took part in the genocide were put in jail. Many people were rejoicing. They said, "At last they are going to suffer." And in our prisons they do suffer because they are so congested.

The Lord told me, "I want you to preach in the prisons and tell those people that I love them." The first day I went there, I was trembling inside. I preached about the Cross of Jesus Christ and the Blood of Jesus Christ that washes away all sins. One man became fidgety. When I made a call, he stood up and said, "I want to confess, but first I want to ask a question. Does the Blood of Jesus wash us of all sins?" I said, "Yes." He said, "Now, let me confess to God and to people what I have done." And he confessed of the people he killed—the children, women and men. Then another person stood and then another one and then another one and then another one. I said, "Lord, thank You because Your grace has made me see things I couldn't see if I had kept my anger." I tell you, it is a great privilege to stand here telling you that Jesus is the answer, even for woundedness.

> **Then another person stood and then another one and then another one and then another one. I said, "Lord, thank You because Your grace has made me see things I couldn't see if I had kept my anger."**

I usually give my testimony when I preach. I tell people, "Look, I know what we have suffered. You widows, I know that you have suffered because my mother was a widow when she was 25. I know your pain. You orphans, I know what you are suffering because I too lost my father." And I've seen many widows and orphans who are now following Jesus, who have found hope, despite all the things they have gone through. That is the power of the Cross in a wounded environment.

I think no one is exempt from woundedness. When I travel on ministry tours, I meet children of broken homes who are suffering like the orphan children of Rwanda. I meet women who are widows although they have husbands because they have been abandoned. Deep inside, the wound is the same. I tell people, if you have a wound from a piece of glass and I have a wound from a piece of metal, it's still the same—we bleed. All over the world we are living with wounded people.

But the answer is in Jesus. The Bible says, "We do not have a high priest who is unable to sympathize with our weaknesses, but we have one who has been tempted in every way, just as we are—yet was without sin. Let us then approach the throne of grace with confidence, so that we may receive mercy and find grace to help us in our time of need" (Hebrews 4:15–16, NIV).

Maybe today you are feeling angry, beaten, wounded, disappointed, discouraged. Turn to Jesus, because He knows everything. He was hated for nothing. He was betrayed. He was rejected. He was beaten. He was put in jail. He was crucified. Everything we suffer, He suffered. He can understand. That is why the Cross of Jesus Christ is so powerful today, even in a wounded situation.

I call upon you to "make every effort to live in peace with all men and to be holy," because the Bible says, "without holiness no one will see the Lord. See to it that no one misses the grace of God and that no bitter root grows up to cause trouble and defile many" (Hebrews 12:14–15, NIV).

The Cross and the Crisis of Identity

My last point is the Cross of Jesus Christ and the crisis of identity. People are wondering, "Who am I?" It's a problem of identity. Because of urban explosion and the fast changes in science and technology, we live in a more impersonal, stone-cold, lonely world. We live in socially disconnected, individualistic environments, feeding on self-gratification and self-centeredness. Many have lost their sense of belonging and community. Knowing who you are in Jesus Christ is a great thing because in a genocide, the first thing which is denied to you is your value as a human being. And during those days the voice of the Lord kept telling me, "Remember, you are not a Tutsi. That's not your identity. You are a child of God." And I tell you, that is who we are. We need to preach the Cross of Jesus Christ to give value to the world.

The Bible says, "It was not with perishable things such as silver or gold that you were redeemed . . . but with the precious blood of Christ, a lamb without blemish or defect" (1 Peter 1:18–19, NIV). That is the value God has given us. Usually a thing is valuable according to the price you pay to get it. God paid for us with the blood of His own Son. That is your value in the eyes of God. The Bible says, "The Spirit himself testifies with our spirit that we are God's children. Now if we are children, then we are heirs—heirs of God and co-heirs with Christ, if indeed we share in his sufferings in order that we may also share in his glory" (Romans 8:16–17, NIV). And, "How great is the love the Father has lavished on us, that we should be called children of God! And that is what we are!" (1 John 3:1, NIV). That is what we are. We are God's children. That is the value that He has given to us.

Not only God's children—that is our identity—but we are also God's community. The Bible says, "You are a chosen people, a royal priesthood, a holy nation, a people belonging to God, that you may declare the praises of him who called you out of darkness into his wonderful light" (1 Peter 2:9, NIV). Again the Bible says, "Jesus Christ . . . gave himself for us to redeem us from all wickedness and to purify for himself a people that are his very own, eager to do what is good" (Titus 2:13–14, NIV). That is our identity in Christ. That is our community in Christ.

The Bible says that when you are in Christ, "There is no Greek or Jew, circumcised or uncircumcised, barbarian, Scythian, slave or free, but Christ is all, and is in all" (Colossians 3:11, NIV). We are one family in Christ. We need to work hard at rebuilding the fellowship of the holy nation of God. The closer we get to Christ, the closer we get to each other. And that is how we build our community. Get nearer to Christ; you will get nearer and closer to your neighbor and your friend.

Christ is the answer in a broken world. In a wounded world we need to preach Christ and Him crucified. And we need to be people of Christ—loving Christ, living for Christ, proclaiming Christ until He comes. Let us preach Christ with more passion. May the Lord bless you.

Antoine Rutayisire

In 1994, Mr. Antoine Rutayisire began his work with the African Evangelistic Enterprise. He is currently the team leader in Rwanda. A native of Rwanda, Mr. Rutayisire earned a M.A. at the National University of Rwanda in Butare, and a M.A. at the University College of North Wales in Bangor, Wales. He and his wife, Penina, have four children, and they live in Kigali, Rwanda. The couple also adopted four of their relatives' children who were orphaned during the recent period of genocide in Rwanda.

The Evangelist Is a Servant-Leader

Viktor Hamm

Recently a secular observer asked a profound question: "Why are so many evangelists in the year 2000 so ineffective in what they do?" It is, I believe, because we have taken this world to be a model for our evangelistic ministry, both in leadership and service. And God is not pleased. He says to us, as He said to Joshua years ago, "There are things under the ban in your midst. . . . You cannot stand before your enemies until you have removed the things under the ban from your midst" (Joshua 7:13, NASB). My friends, the contemporary model for the evangelist is not this world, but the Word.

Now, what does it mean to be a servant-leader evangelist from the biblical point of view? The evangelist is not just a leader. Neither is he or she just a servant. The evangelist is a servant-leader, servant being first. Paul the apostle says of himself, "Paul, a servant of Jesus Christ, . . . set apart for the gospel of God." (Romans 1:1, RSV). The implication is that if a person claiming to have the gift of the evangelist is not a servant-leader, he or she is not a messenger of the eternal Gospel. Oh, yes, that person can have the word *evangelist* printed in gold on a business card. That person can even have an evangelistic association bearing his name. But true servant-leadership has its roots in the Bible, not in our sinful, secular world.

The Biblical Characteristics of a Servant

What are the biblical characteristics of a servant? The New Testament uses a variety of terms to describe a servant. However, in all of these terms the core meaning is the same. *It is service.* A servant *belongs* to the master. A servant *lives* by principles and rules set by the master. A servant is *totally dependent* on the master. And *everything* a servant has *comes from* the master, from above.

A servant comes under the rule of the master voluntarily. A servant has only one duty, and that is to serve the master. A servant never negotiates his pay. A servant is obedient. The will of the master is his command, whether he understands it or not. A servant is rightly motivated. And a servant is not ashamed to be identified as a servant of his master. Paul the apostle said, "I am not ashamed, because I know whom I have believed" (2 Timothy 1:12, NKJV).

To be a servant is the highest honor possible because God reserves this title only for those whom He finds absolutely faithful. Servitude for the evangelist is a yoked privilege, since Christ also considers him or her a friend. Jesus said, "You are My friends" (John 15:14, NKJV). Brothers and sisters, are you sure God would call you "My servant," using the highest honor possible?

The Biblical Characteristics of a Leader

What are the biblical characteristics of a leader? A leader *sees the goal* clearly. He knows exactly where to go. A leader *realizes the responsibility* entrusted to him—to lead and to develop others in their calling. A leader is *willing to pay the price:* to be lonely, to be blamed for the mistakes of others. A leader *is willing to take risks* for the sake of the Gospel. A leader *is not ashamed to ask for forgiveness.* A biblical leader *does not play politics.* There is so much politicking going on among contemporary Christian leaders it makes even the devil uneasy.

A leader does not use his positional power. A leader motivates and encourages people by example. Humbly, yet with confidence, a leader has courage to say, "I urge you to imitate me" (1 Corinthians 4:16, NIV). A leader is willing to stand alone against the enemy. A leader has a vision. He sees the fields that are ripe for harvest, both at home and far beyond. A leader considers every individual as someone created in the image of God. A leader knows that he is a follower himself, since there is an ultimate leader to whom he is accountable, the Lord of lords. My friends, it is no small matter to be a leader. It would be hopelessly impossible to lead if it weren't for the Holy Spirit's empowering.

> The evangelist is a hybrid of a servant and a leader. Only by divine intervention can these two seemingly opposite characteristics be united in one body, one heart and one mind.

Fusion of Leader and Servant

The qualities of a servant and a leader are the extreme opposites, and they almost seem to contradict each other. But many things are beyond human understanding. It is well to remember what Saint Augustine said years ago: "If you can understand it, it is not God." The evangelist is a hybrid of a servant and a leader. Only by divine intervention can these two seemingly opposite characteristics be united in one body, one heart and one mind.

I used to work in a factory with metals. As you know, pure aluminum is a very soft metal. You can mold it with your bare hands. Pure titanium is a very hard metal. If you melt them together, the soft and the hard, the alloy—that is, the result—becomes three times as hard as titanium. Do you want to be strong in your character and your ministry? Allow God to break you, melt you, remold you into a new entity. You will come out stronger morally, mentally and spiritually.

Why is the fusion of the qualities of a leader and a servant so important in the life and work of the evangelist? Because it brings glory to God; that is the only thing that matters. It is what evangelists were like in biblical times. It is the only kind of an evangelist that will not dishonor the Gospel he or she preaches. It is the only combination that brings lasting results for the Kingdom, not just statistics for prayer letters and news releases. It is the only combination that receives a respectful hearing from our cynical, pragmatic, post-modern contemporaries.

Portrait of a Servant-Leader Evangelist: John the Baptist

Look with me at the portrait of a servant-leader evangelist. Of course, the ultimate model is the Lord Jesus Christ. Yet the Bible gives us another model—a mortal man, a sinner, like all of us, saved by the same faith in the Lamb of God. His name is John the Baptist.

John the Baptist bridged two Testaments. He bridged two millennia. He bridged two centuries. And he is a noble example for all of us. In the desert of Palestine the Holy Spirit fused these great qualities of a servant and a leader into a new entity: a servant-leader.

John the Baptist Served and Led by Being Sure of His Calling

First of all, John the Baptist served and led by being sure of his calling. Brothers and sisters, are you sure of your calling? Has God really called you to evangelism? John the Baptist was called by God to evangelize. Even though he was born into a priestly family, he was called to a call.

John the Baptist was a prophet-evangelist, though in the Bible he is never explicitly called an evangelist. Yet he is our fellow evangelist because he preached the Good News. You do not have to have your own organization, have the latest technical equipment, a musical team with great musicians. If you are faithfully preaching the Gospel, if you are committed to the cause, you are an evangelist. And God will prove His anointing on you by giving real results.

John the Baptist was passionate about his call. People in opposition who challenged his every move did not sidetrack him. He said, "I am the voice" (John 1:23, KJV). Jesus was the Word, and John was the voice. What a voice he was!

Hudson Taylor, a hero for Christ in China with a vision of preaching where Christ was not named, was equally passionate about his call. He said on one occasion, "Perishing China so filled my heart and mind that there was no rest by day and little sleep by night." His close friend, Lord Radstock, prayed for ten years for an open door in Russia. Then God opened the door, and he took the Gospel to the nobles of Russia, starting a revival there. Both China and Russia are indebted to those who have responded to the call of God.

John the Baptist had the heart of an evangelist. His heart could find rest only in the knowledge that the Gospel was widely preached. When John languished in prison, Jesus reported to him on the progress of evangelism, saying, "The good news is preached to the poor" (Matthew 11:5, NIV). That assurance gave John courage to face the sword. Jesus knows how to encourage His evangelists—with a single report of souls being saved.

John the Baptist Served and Led by Character

Second, John the Baptist served and led by character. He was morally pure. Albert Camus, the great French writer, describing his contemporaries wrote, "A single sentence will suffice for modern man: he fornicated and read the papers" (*The Fall*).

Immorality raises its ugly head today. And no evangelist is free from committing the worst of sins. Paul the apostle tells us, "Keep yourself pure" (1 Timothy 5:22, NKJV).

John the Baptist was humble. John could not stand pride, no matter how piously people covered it up. A truly humble man or woman of God has a God-given capacity to detect any form of pride. Everything John wore, ate and did radiated humility. Paul says, "Do not think of yourself more highly than you ought, but rather think of yourself with sober judgment" (Romans 12:3, NIV). John the Baptist led people by humility, not position. His modus operandi was, "He," that is Jesus, "must become greater and I must become less and less and less, until I'm not seen anymore" (see John 3:30).

A true evangelist never parades himself as "the evangelist." He understands that he is only a tool in the hand of God. Isaiah the prophet wrote, "Is the saw to exalt itself over the one who wields it?" (Isaiah 10:15, NASB). My friends, we should never forget that in the New Testament it was always others who gave testimony to an evangelistic calling, never the evangelist himself.

John the Baptist preached, lived and acted so much like the awaited Messiah that people said, "This is the Messiah." Evangelists of the world, has anyone ever said, "There comes the resemblance of the Messiah?" Does your life resemble Christ's?

John the Baptist was not concerned about creating a positive image. He had no image makers on his team. John the Baptist was honest in every way possible. He did not take credit when it was clearly not his. John the Baptist ministered with joy. It was very hard for him to be a preacher in those early days. And yet he said, "That joy is mine" (John 3:29, NIV).

Because of his moral purity, his humility, his honesty and convictions, John the Baptist was believable. In Matthew 21 (see verse 32) we read that tax collectors and sinners believed. They put their trust in Jesus because the messenger was credible and believable.

The character of John the Baptist was formed in a desert, not in ivory towers. A desert is not for cowards. It is a place inhabited by scorpions, leveled by sandstorms, scorched by the sun, and lacking marked roads. The desert experience is the best experience for the evangelist. Every true evangelist has gone through the desert school of theology.

John the Baptist Served and Led by Preaching

Third, John the Baptist served and led by preaching. We see John the Baptist standing against the blue sky, long hair floating in the wind and the words of the Gospel echoing through the valley. His preaching was evangelistic to the core. It was theologically sound. He addressed the sinful nature of a human heart. He called sin "sin."

Sin is still sin. It separates people from God and it sends them to a camp of loneliness. The Gospel addresses the reality of sin in a redemptive way. John preached repentance. He said, "Repent, for the kingdom of heaven is near" (Matthew 3:2, NIV). The closer we come to the end of the age, the clearer our call for repentance must be.

John the Baptist also preached grace. He said, "Grace and truth came through Jesus Christ" (John 1:17, NIV). Salvation is by grace from beginning to end.

The message of John the Baptist was scriptural. He knew Scriptures well and he quoted Scriptures often. Scriptures were his final authority. Fellow evangelists, be people of the Book. Preach the Word!

John the Baptist had a balanced view of the Holy Spirit. His preaching was Spirit-filled. His preaching was Christ-centered, atonement-based. John pointed to Jesus, "Behold the Lamb of God" (John 1:29, KJV).

John preached for a verdict. "Whoever believes in the Son has eternal life, but whoever rejects the Son will not see life" (John 3:36, NIV). When people heard him they asked, "What should we do?" When people listen to us, what do they say? "Thank you, Reverend, it was lovely." Or do they say, "God, what should we do?" That is the ultimate goal in evangelistic preaching. Everything else is secondary.

John's preaching was sensational, very much so, but not due to miracles performed. We see no record of miracles whatsoever in John's ministry. His message did not change over the years. It was the same at the end of his ministry as it was in the beginning.

> The message of John the Baptist was scriptural. He knew Scriptures well and he quoted Scriptures often. Scriptures were his final authority. Fellow evangelists, be people of the Book. Preach the Word!

Billy Graham's message has not changed. Just as Billy Graham preached on the Cross of Jesus back in 1938, so Dr. Graham still preaches on the Cross of Christ. For him, "the Bible still says." John the Baptist's message was uncompromising because he knew that God was in his audience. The evangelist always has God in his audience.

John the Baptist Served and Led by Serving

Fourth, John the Baptist served and led by serving. The *London Sunday Express* had a quote: "Most people wish to serve God, but in advisory capacity only." John laid his life on the line for God. John served people. He did not wait for people to come to him. Scripture says, "He went into all the country" (Luke 3:3, NIV). And people responded to his genuine preaching.

John the Baptist served the church. Today, 20 centuries later, we are still benefiting from his humble service. He was thinking about the future, preparing others who would do what he did. John the Baptist mentored the first apostles of Jesus Christ. He taught Andrew how to bring people to the Lord. He taught John how to love. He most likely instilled in Peter the love for preaching. He understood the power of mentoring.

Some church leaders today are suggesting that we are approaching an era of an evangelistic lull when both the world and the church will be waiting for some kind of a prophetic word. Whose voice will it be? I challenge every leader from every country represented here to start asking God to raise up from among your own people a national evangelist who will be recognized by your nation as a God-fearing evangelist. We need that today more than anything else.

Training a new generation of church leaders is imperative. How do you train evangelists? Tell them your own story. Give them your best sermon notes and let them preach your sermons. Pray for them daily. Keep them accountable. Then release them to God. You have done your part. That is what happened in the life of John the Baptist.

God Honored John the Baptist

Finally, God honored John the Baptist for his servant-leader evangelistic ministry. God allowed him to see results, tremendous results. In the last 12 years in the former Soviet Union we have seen God moving and doing tremendous works. The enemies of Christ are becoming messengers of God's grace. One of the leading architects of Soviet atheism, Dr. Boris Galperin, came to the Lord, and now he preaches the Gospel faithfully.

John the Baptist left an evangelistic legacy. His ministry lived on, even after his voice fell silent. He had a great influence on this world. The heads of states came to him and asked for advice. The military came to him. They saw him as a great man. The Jewish historian Josephus says of John the Baptist, "[People] seemed ready to do anything he should advise." John understood the power and the influence he had on society, but he never abused his influence. Never.

God honored John the Baptist by allowing him to suffer for His name. Many Christians have a wrong perception of afflictions. When afflictions strike they think of them as a deficiency in God's sovereignty. The future of evangelism is not rosy. We need to get ready for the real tests of faith. Many of our fellow believers throughout the world are suffering behind bars.

Having listened to a young preacher, the wife of the late G. Campbell Morgan said, "He is a good preacher, isn't he?" To which the illustrious Bible teacher replied, "Yes, and he will be a better preacher when he has suffered some."

This Royal Calling

The evangelist is a servant-leader, servant being first. There's no better description of this royal calling. But is it realistic to expect that the evangelist of today will resemble the great servant-leader John the Baptist? Yes, a thousand times, yes! You might be called Reverend So-and-So or Doctor So-and-So. But the real question is, are you a servant-leader? That's what counts.

You can say, "John the Baptist certainly is a great inspiration," and leave it at that. You can even recommend the model of John the Baptist to other people.

Or you can be so hardened in your heart from all the secret sins, disappointments and hardships that you are not even warmed by the truth.

Whatever state you are in, if it is not the state of a servant-leader, servant being first, it needs to change. How to change is something you know so well. You tell others how to change every time you preach. Let me tell you how to change *evangelist to servant-leader evangelist.* You need to come to God and say, "God, I've sinned. Forgive me! I've been a hypocrite. Forgive me!"

Allow God's Spirit to touch your heart and to revive your heart. Follow the Lord Jesus faithfully, all the way, without reservation, in the fellowship of a local church. Are you willing? Are you ready?

John Wesley kept a diary, and this is what he wrote at the end of a meaningful day: "I could truly say when I lay down at night, now I have lived a day."

Brothers and sisters, do that which God requires of you. Be a servant-leader evangelist, and then you will be able to say, "Now I have lived a day." And may this day be that day.

Viktor Hamm
Regional Director for the Commonwealth of Independent States (CIS) and the Baltic States with the Billy Graham Evangelistic Association, Rev. Viktor Hamm oversees the BGEA projects and conducts crusades in that region. Rev. Hamm received a B.R.S. in Theology; a B.A. in Religion from the University of Winnipeg; and a M.A. in Communications from Wheaton College Graduate School, Wheaton, Illinois, U.S.A. Born in Vorkuta, Russia, Rev. Hamm resides in Winnipeg, Canada, with his wife, Margarete, and their three children.

John Harper *Titanic* Story

Video

It was April 15, 1912, when the HMS *Titanic* sank beneath the icy waters of the North Atlantic, taking with it 1,517 lives. The largest and most luxurious ship at the time was gone, reminding the world of our frailty as human beings. But there is more to the sinking of the *Titanic* than a historical tragedy. There is a story of courageous heroism and unshakable faith.

John Harper was aboard the *Titanic* when she set sail from Southampton, England, on her maiden voyage. An evangelist originally from Glasgow, Scotland, he was well known throughout the United Kingdom as a charismatic, passionate speaker who led many to Christ through his gift of preaching. In 1912, Reverend Harper received an invitation to speak at the Moody Church in Chicago, U.S.A. On April 11, 1912, John Harper boarded the *Titanic*.

Some of the wealthiest people in the world were aboard. While many passengers spoke of business deals, acquisitions and material desires, John Harper was diligently sharing the love of Christ with others. In the days leading up to the tragedy, survivors reported seeing Harper living like a man of faith, speaking kind words and sharing the love of Christ.

On the evening of April 14, as passengers danced in the ballroom and tried their luck at the card tables, John Harper put his daughter to bed and read his devotions as he did every night. At 11:40 p.m., the *Titanic* struck an iceberg. The "unsinkable" ship was doomed. Either in disbelief or unaware at the time, passengers continued about their pleasures. It wasn't until the ship's crew sent up a series of distress flares that passengers realized the seriousness of their situation. Then chaos ensued.

It all happened so fast. But John Harper's response left an historic example of courage and faith. Harper awakened his daughter, picked her up and wrapped her in a blanket before carrying her up to the deck. There he kissed her good-bye and handed her to a crewman who put her into lifeboat number 11. Harper knew he would never see his daughter again. His daughter would be left an orphan at six years of age.

Harper then gave his life jacket to a fellow passenger, ending any chance of his own survival. From a survivor we learn that he was calling out, "Women and children and unsaved people into the lifeboats." So he understood that there was a more important thing than surviving that terrible disaster. He understood that there were those who were unprepared to face eternity.

As the sounds of terror and mayhem continued, Harper focused on his God-given purpose. Survivors reported seeing him on the upper deck on his knees, surrounded by terrified passengers, praying for their salvation.

At 2:40 a.m., the *Titanic* disappeared beneath the North Atlantic, leaving a mushroom-like cloud of smoke and steam above her grave and, tragically, over 1,000 people, including Harper, fighting for their lives in the icy water. He managed to find a piece of floating wreckage to hold onto. Quickly he swam to every person he could find, urging those about him to put their faith in Jesus Christ. While death forced others to face the folly of their life's pursuits, John Harper's goal of winning people to Jesus Christ became more vital.

In the water, John Harper was moving around as best he could, speaking to as many people as possible. His question was, "Are you saved?" And if they weren't saved and if they didn't understand that terminology, then as rapidly as he could he explained the Christian Gospel.

Soon John Harper succumbed to the icy sea. But even in his last moment, this tireless man of undying faith continued his life pursuit of winning lost souls.

One person remembered, "I am a survivor of the *Titanic*. I was one of only six people out of 1,517 to be pulled from the icy waters on that dreadful night. Like the hundreds around me, I found myself struggling in the cold, dark waters of the North Atlantic. The wail of the perishing was ringing in my ears when there floated by me a man who called to me, 'Is your soul saved?' Then I heard him call out to others as he and everyone around me sank beneath the waters. There, alone in the night with two miles of water under me, I cried to Christ to save me. I am John Harper's last convert."

The Evangelist Is Faithful in a Hostile World

Sami Dagher

I am very happy to be here with you. I was invited to Amsterdam in 1971 to attend a conference like this. At that time I was working in the hotel business, but after hearing Dr. Graham preaching and presenting the needs of Europe and the Middle East, I accepted the challenge and promised the Lord that when I got back to Lebanon I would serve Him.

In 1973, I resigned from my work and started church planting. At that time we were only three people: my wife and I, and another person whom I had led to the Lord. Now, by the grace of God, we have six churches. We have four in the Arabic language for the Lebanese, one for the Sri Lankans, one for the Sudanese. Also, we have a Bible school. We are training people from the Middle East to send to all the Arab world because we know a day is coming when all the countries in the world—and especially in the Middle East—may be closed to foreign missionaries. We are preparing men and women to go from Lebanon to preach the Gospel of Christ in the Arab world.

We have sent a missionary to the Ivory Coast to work among the 60,000 Lebanese there. We have sent short-term missionaries to Iraq. And all of that is a result of a conference like this in Amsterdam.

He Would Not Change One Word

The subject given to me is, "The Evangelist Is Faithful in a Hostile World." I have a wish in my heart that the Lord Jesus Himself would stand here, in the flesh, and teach us this morning. Wouldn't that be wonderful? Brothers and sisters, if Jesus would come again, He would not come as a preacher but in great glory to judge the living and the dead. But I assure you that if Jesus were standing here today to teach us about this subject, He would not change one word of what He said before. It is written about Him in Malachi, "For I am the LORD, I change not" (3:6, KJV). And because He is the Lord and He changes not, His Word will not change.

Hostility Is to Be Expected

I have a few thoughts that I want to share with you. The first is that hostility is to be expected whenever we take a stand for Jesus. In John 17:14 our Lord prayed to the Father saying, "I have given them Your word; and the world has hated them because they are not of the world, just as I am not of the world" (NKJV). And Paul wrote to Timothy in 2 Timothy 3:12, "All who desire to live godly in Christ Jesus will suffer persecution" (NKJV).

So according to the teaching of our Lord and according to the inspiration of the Holy Spirit, there is no escape from persecution. Why? Because we are hated by the world. Jesus made it so clear. He said, "I have given them Your word; and the world has hated them" (John 17:14, NKJV). Every one of us here who lives godly in Christ Jesus may face persecution. But what is our responsibility? Brothers and sisters, our responsibility is to prepare ourselves to endure persecution, and to prepare others to endure persecution. Jesus said, "'A servant is not greater than his master.' If they persecuted Me, they will also persecute you" (John 15:20, NKJV).

Our problem today when we present Christ to the people is that we present peace, stability, joy and prosperity. Then when a new believer faces persecution, he or she is shocked and falls back. Of course in Christ we have peace. Of course in Christ we have joy. Of course in Christ we have prosperity. But we have to explain to people what kind of peace, what kind of joy, and what kind of prosperity. Jesus said, "These things I have spoken to you, that in Me you may have peace. In the world you will have tribulation; but be of good cheer, I have overcome the world" (John 16:33, NKJV).

Our peace is in Christ. Our victory is in Christ. Our riches are in Christ. Brothers and sisters, I pray you, in Jesus' name, don't present Christ far away from the Cross, because a Christ far away from the Cross does not save. And don't accept people coming to Christ without the Cross, because Jesus said, "If anyone wants to follow Me, he has to carry his Cross and follow Me" (see Matthew 16:24). Carrying the Cross means denying self; it means dying to self; it means persecution and pain. Paul said, "I have been crucified with Christ, nevertheless I live; yet not I, but Christ lives in me" (see Galatians 2:20). So don't present to the people a cheap Christ. The Christ that we present to the people is God. He is the Lord of lords and King of kings! He is the Creator and Maker of heaven and earth!

We Are Not in the Business of Selling Tomatoes

You know, in my country we have people who sell tomatoes at the roadside. And when the tomatoes are red and starting to rot, they start begging people, "Come and buy. Come and buy." They give them a very cheap price. We are not in the business of selling tomatoes. We are in the business of presenting Christ, the Lord of glory, to all people.

Don't beg people to accept Christ. Lift Him up as you are preaching. Lift Him up in your life because He said, "When you lift Me up, I will draw all men to Myself" (see John 12:32). There is no other way that God will draw people to Himself—only when we evangelists lift Jesus up in our lives, in our teaching and in our words.

Many times we evangelists shy away from the Word of God because we want popularity from the world. Many times when people come to our churches, we try new programs and we try to shorten the message and have some more entertainment. We are not in the business of entertainment. We are in the business of presenting Christ, the Lord of glory.

We are in business to save souls from hellfire. Do you believe that without Christ there is no salvation? Do you believe that He is the only way, and the truth and the life, and no one comes to the Father but through Him? Do you believe that without the Word of God there is no salvation? There is no repentance? There is no revival? The Gospel is the power of God unto salvation to everyone who believes, to the Jew first and also to the Greek (see Romans 1:16). So without the Word of God there would be no repentance, there would be no salvation and there would be no revival.

We are hated by the world because we are not of the world. If we were of the world, the world would love its own. But we are not. We are in the world, but we are not of the world. Our goals are different. Our nature is different. We are partakers of the divine nature.

> After a while, when they discovered that we have no goals except to show them the love of Christ, that we have no hidden agenda, they gave us their trust.

What Does a Stranger Expect in a Strange Country?

We are strangers and pilgrims in this world. What does a stranger expect in a strange country? I am sure a stranger in a foreign country expects suffering, pain and persecution. The prophets of the Old Testament and the saints of the New Testament confessed that they were strangers and pilgrims in the world. They suffered persecution. They were stoned. They were killed with the sword. And it is written that the world did not deserve them. But they stayed faithful to the Word of God right to the end.

That brings me to my second point. The upright life of the evangelist gives him respect in a hostile world. Again, I beseech you in the name of Jesus, if we want to escape some of the suffering in a hostile world, we have to live a godly life. We have to live an honest life. Paul said in Romans 13:3, "Rulers are not a terror to good works, but to evil" (NKJV). If you don't want to be afraid of their power, do good and you will receive their praise.

We have been working in one of the Arab countries for nearly 10 years. The people of that country look to the Western world as if it were Christian, and they accuse Westerners of killing their children, destroying their homes and destroying their futures. In the beginning we faced a lot of difficulties because every step we made was watched. But after a while, when they discovered that we have no goals except to show them the love of Christ, that we have no hidden agenda, they gave us their trust. And they gave us permission to give out New Testaments in the streets of their cities. We have given tens of thousands of New Testaments in that country. And to my surprise, the president of that country gave the order that the film *Jesus* be shown on national television. Twenty million people saw that film.

The difficulty of preaching the Gospel in the Middle East is not only due to the fanaticism of religion there, but also due to the lives of the people who confess to be Christians. Instead of being a blessing, they are a curse. I encourage you in the name of Jesus that you walk worthy of your calling. In Ephesians 4:1–2, Paul said to the church, "I . . . beseech you to have a walk worthy of the calling with which you were called, with all lowliness and gentleness, with longsuffering" (NKJV).

Daniel lived in a country that was hostile to his faith and his religion. There were so many enemies just looking to find a fault in him. But because his life was honest, because he was a godly man, they couldn't find one fault. In the end they trapped him and put him in the lions' den. What was the result? God sent His angel and closed the mouth of the lions and saved Daniel. Not only that, but the king gave a decree that no god should be worshiped but the God of Daniel (see Daniel 6). Daniel stayed faithful right to the end. I pray you, in Jesus' name, to be like Daniel.

We Have a Great Responsibility

Brothers and sisters, we are strangers and we are pilgrims, and we are hated by the world. But we have a great responsibility to the world. Jesus said, "You are the light of the world" (Matthew 5:14, NKJV). You know, when we see the world stumbling in darkness, it is time to stand and examine ourselves. When we see the world stumbling in darkness, that doesn't mean that our light is not shining brightly. Our responsibility is to live godly in front of the world. Our responsibility is to pray for the world. Our responsibility is to pray for them that persecute us. In the Old Testament, there is a command from God almighty to His people. In Jeremiah 29:7, it is written, "And seek the peace of the city where I have caused you to be carried away captive, and pray to the LORD for it; for in its peace you will have peace" (NKJV).

Can you imagine being taken captive to another city, being a refugee in another country, and here you are kneeling down and praying for that country, for your enemies, that they will have peace? Yes, because in their peace you shall have peace. It is a command from God. We have to pray for our people. We have to pray that the light of Christ will go through to their hearts and minds and they will accept Christ. Then we will live in a peaceful world. Paul gives the same command in 1 Timothy 2:2: "[Pray] for kings and all who are in authority, that we may lead a quiet and peaceable life in all godliness and reverence" (NKJV). Brothers and sisters, can you imagine if we all lived by this standard? We would make a difference in our society; we would make a difference in the world.

I invited a preacher to speak in a church of Sidon. The city of Sidon is 99 percent another religion, and 80 percent of the people present in that meeting were from another religious background. The preacher was preaching about the Christian life—the real Christian life—and after he finished preaching, a lawyer said to him, "You know, if the Christians will live at this standard of Christianity, there will be no other religion in the Middle East."

Our Need Today Is to Live the Real Christian Life

I pray you, in Jesus' name, walk worthy of your calling. We have a high calling and we have to walk worthy of our calling. Our need today is not to talk about the Christian life; our need today is to live the real Christian life. You might say to me, "We have prayed and we have lived a godly life, but they still persecute us. What can we do?"

That brings me to my third point. We should know that faithfulness is a divine request in spite of hostility. Jesus said to the angel of the church of Smyrna, "Do not fear any of those things which you are about to suffer. Indeed, the devil is about to throw some of you into prison, that you may be tested, and you will have tribulation ten days. Be faithful until death, and I will give you the crown of life" (Revelation 2:10, NKJV). Does that surprise you? God almighty, who can do everything, who can fight for us, knows that we are going to be put in prison. He knows that we are going to suffer persecution, but He does not move to save us. Instead, He asks us to be faithful unto death that we might have the crown of life.

You know, brothers and sisters, the secret of this chapter is in one word: testing. He is going to test you. He is going to test your faith. He is going to test your character. And when we pass the test, He will give us the crown of life. I don't want to frighten you, but I want to prepare you. A day is coming when if they kill one of us, they will think that they are doing a great service to the Lord. "Be faithful until death" (Revelation 2:10, NKJV).

Keep up Your Courage

You might say to me, "I am afraid. Is there a way that I can keep up my courage?" Yes, there is. The only way to keep up your courage is to remember that "All authority has been given to Me in heaven and on earth" (Matthew 28:18, NKJV). Brothers and sisters, we serve the Lord of glory, the almighty God, the Creator and Maker of heaven and earth.

We have to remember that He has the power in heaven and on earth. We have to remember that He wrote with His hand on the wall of the palace of the king, and He terminated his kingdom (see Daniel 5). We have to remember that He sent His angel to a lions' den and closed the mouths of the lions. We have to remember that He walked in the furnace fire, and He saved the three Hebrew children (see Daniel 3). We have to remember that He gave an order to the water of the River Jordan, and it stood like a wall (see Joshua 3). We have to remember that He stood at Lazarus's tomb and said to Lazarus, "Come forth!" (John 11:43, NKJV). We have to remember that He ordered the sea and the storm to cease (see Mark 4:35–41). We have to remember that He is God.

Doesn't He deserve for us to trust Him? Doesn't He deserve that we should die for Him? Why are we afraid of death? Death is not an enemy for us anymore. Death is the way that will lead us to our eternal home. Death is the way by which, when we go through it, we see Jesus because it is written that as long as we are in this body we are absent from Christ (see 2 Corinthians 5:6).

He Had a Pistol and He Said, "Stop!"

One day I was going to a Bible study in a small village up in the mountains. To be able to reach that village, I had to go through another town which was controlled by the militia. When I was driving in the streets of that town, two men riding a motorbike came right next to me, and the one behind showed me his side. He had a pistol and he said, "Stop!" So I stopped. Then he came and sat next to me and, putting the pistol into my side, said, "Drive!" So I was driving, and when we got away from the main road, I was afraid. They took me to a house far away from the village and took me into a room. They took everything from me—the car keys, my money, everything. They only left the New Testament. When they closed the door and left, I was afraid. I prayed, "Lord, help me. I am afraid." I took my New Testament. I wanted to read, but I was shaking like a leaf. I couldn't really read. I couldn't see anything. Then I prayed again. I fell before Him on the floor and said, "Lord, I pray you help me. I am afraid." Do you know what verse He gave me? He gave me, "To be absent from the body is to be present with Christ" (see 2 Corinthians 5:8). I thought, "I'm going to die!" And I started meditating, "To be absent from the body is to be present with Christ."

> They started questioning me. I said, "I am telling you I only know about my church, and all that you can do to me is to kill me. And when you kill me, I'll see Jesus."

After a while they came back and took me to another room. There were about six or seven people there, and they started questioning me. I said, "I am telling you I only know about my church, and all that you can do to me is to kill me. And when you kill me, I'll see Jesus." After a while, a handsome man came in. He was tall, very well dressed, and they all saluted him. He gave an order that I was to go to the other room. After half an hour, one man came back and said, "Here are the keys, and I am bringing you a cup of coffee. We are sorry we stopped you." I said, "Don't worry. Don't bring coffee; I don't have time. I have to go to the Bible study." Then I promised him that the next week I would come and have a coffee with him. The next week I went with a Bible and a letter to explain the way of salvation. And I had that coffee with them. "Be faithful until death, and I will give you the crown of life" (Revelation 2:10, NKJV).

Paul said, "I desire to go and be with Christ, which is far better" (see Philippians

1:23). Brothers and sisters, I pray you in Jesus' name, don't be afraid of them that kill the body. They cannot do anything to the soul. But be afraid of Him who has authority to kill soul and body in hellfire (see Matthew 10:28). That's the one we have to be afraid of, and when you are afraid of God, you are afraid of no one else.

An Evangelist Needs Wisdom From Heaven Above

Lastly, an evangelist needs wisdom from heaven above. We need wisdom to know when to be silent and when to speak. In Ecclesiastes 3:1, it is written, "To everything there is a season, a time for every purpose under heaven" (NKJV). There is a time to keep silent and a time to speak. If we speak when it is the time to be silent, it is dangerous. And if we are silent when it is time to speak, it is dangerous also. James said, "If any of you lacks wisdom, let him ask of God, who gives to all liberally and without reproach, and it will be given to him" (James 1:5, NKJV). Pray for wisdom. Ask the Lord for wisdom, and I am sure He will give it to you.

But do you know what our problem is? Our problem is that we do not pray as we ought to pray. I say it with a broken heart: We have substituted the prayer power of God, which is given to us, for programs. We thought that with new methods and new programs we would have a successful ministry. Do you want the secret of successful ministry? In Joshua 1:8, it is written, "This Book of the Law shall not depart from your mouth, but you shall meditate in it day and night, that you may observe to do according to all that is [might learn all of what's] written in it. For then you will make your way prosperous, and then you will have good success" (NKJV). And the Bible says also, "Pray without ceasing" (1 Thessalonians 5:17, NKJV). All the prophets of the Old Testament and the saints of the New Testament got victory over the world by prayer.

Elijah prayed, and for three years and six months it did not rain. And then he prayed for rain and the Lord sent the rain (see 1 Kings 17–18). Joshua prayed that the sun would stop so that he could finish the battle with his enemies (see Joshua 10:1–15). For God to answer that prayer, He had to change the solar system. Listen to what is written, "And there has been no day like that, before it or after it, that the LORD heeded the voice of a man; for the LORD fought for Israel" (Joshua 10:14, NKJV). Has the God of Joshua changed? Has the God of Elijah died? No. But let me ask a question, where are the Elijahs of today? I pray you in Jesus' name, listen to what the Spirit is saying to the churches.

In 2 Chronicles 7:14, it says, "If My people who are called by My name will humble themselves, and pray and seek My face, and turn from their wicked ways, then I will hear from heaven, and will forgive their sin and heal their land" (NKJV). We have four responsibilities: We have to humble ourselves, we have to pray, we have to seek the face of our Lord, and we have to turn from our wicked ways. Then His responsibility will start. He said, "I will answer your prayer. I will forgive your sins, and I will heal your land."

Let Us Go Back Remembering

Our land in Lebanon needs healing. Your land needs healing. Your churches need healing. Your ministry needs healing. Your personality needs healing. God has promised to heal our land. God has promised to forgive our sins. God has promised to hear our prayers.

Brothers and sisters, let us go back from this conference remembering that we are pilgrims and strangers on the earth, that we are hated by the world. Let us go back from this conference remembering that an upright life will give us respect and reverence from the world. Let us go back from this conference remembering that Jesus has all authority in heaven and on earth. Let us go back from this conference knowing that the power of the Holy Spirit is ours when we glorify Jesus and lift Him up. Let us go back from this conference armed with the power of prayer.

Let us go back from this conference knowing that the suffering of the present time does not compare with the glory which is going to be revealed in us (see Romans 8:18). Let us go back from this conference knowing that a day is coming when the kingdom of the earth is going to be the Kingdom of our Christ (see Revelation 11:15). Let us go back from this conference remembering that every knee shall bow and every tongue shall confess that Jesus Christ is Lord, to the glory of God (see Philippians 2:10–11)!

May the Lord bless you and bring glory to His name.

Sami Dagher

Reverend Sami Dagher is president of the National Evangelical Christian and Missionary Alliance Church in Beirut, Lebanon. He is also pastor of the Karantina Church in Beirut, one of the many churches that he has founded. As well as churches, he has founded the Christian Alliance Institute of Theology (Bible Training School), and he serves as director for relief and development work in Lebanon and nearby areas. Rev. Dagher and his wife, Joy, have two grown children and six grandchildren. They make their home in Beirut, Lebanon.

How to Conduct a National Conference for Evangelists

Don Osman

Our topic concerns how we conduct in our nations and regions a seminar, a congress or a conference for training evangelists. I believe that it is incumbent on us to think about what we are going to do to have an impact with the Gospel of Jesus Christ on our nations. I believe that God has called us not only to evangelize, but He has called us to make disciples.

The New Testament is replete with injunctions to that effect. In Matthew 28, in what we call the Great Commission, the mandate is to make disciples (see vv. 19–20). In Ephesians 4:11 and following, where Paul describes the ministry gifts, he specifically says that God has given these gifts so that they will be used in the development of people to bring them to maturity in Christ. And in 2 Timothy 2:2, Paul says that we should develop others. We should mentor, disciple others, so that they in turn will produce leaders.

In any consideration of putting together a national conference for evangelists, we have to look at the Scriptures and get our motivation from the Scripture. As you look at Scripture, you need to ask yourself, "What are these Scriptures saying to me?" I ask you to define the five ministry gifts that are mentioned in Ephesians 4:11–12.

A Multiplication Ministry

Where are we as individuals, as a church, as a community, in the whole mentoring and discipleship process? I once gave the illustration to somebody that if I were a big-time evangelist and every year I led 30,000 people to Christ, over a 22-year period I would have led 660,000 people to Christ.

But if I decided as a strategic evangelist to reach one unsaved person and disciple that one person so that this one person then reached another person and discipled that person so that he or she would reach another person, over a 22-year period, through a multiplication process, I would have reached about 1.04 million people. Do you see the difference? In the first ministry I was doing addition—every year 30,000. But in a discipleship model where I was specifically training trainers, I was doing a multiplication type of a ministry. The multiplication ministry in which disciples are being made has a far greater impact.

So first of all, where are you and I in that mentoring and training process? Is it possible that you and I live in situations where there are people who might have a heart for evangelism, but they are lacking basic ministry skills that will make them effective in discipling others and thereby fulfilling the Great Commission?

Then, second, any effort or activity has to be bathed in prayer. Our Lord Jesus Christ, before He selected the disciples, spent a whole night in prayer. Before He started His earthly ministry, He went into the wilderness and fasted for 40 days and 40 nights. Before He was to face Golgotha, He spent a night praying in the Garden of Gethsemane. In the life of Jesus, prayer was the bedrock of His ministry. Any effort that is done in the name of the Lord to reach others has to be bathed in prayer. Because the ministry is a spiritual ministry, prayer has to play a very important role.

Third, we need to be very clear as to what we want to do. For that to be possible, we have to set for ourselves certain objectives that we want to shoot for. We should ask God for guidance as to what He desires us to do. What are the needs that evangelists in your nation, in your region, have? You have to come up with a mechanism to do a needs assessment, to see in what areas they are lacking, what it is that they need to be trained in so that we don't have too many people wanting to do only what they please.

We have to identify the reasons for holding a conference. What do we want to accomplish? At the end of the day, what are the expected outcomes? I have always said to people, "If you are doing discipleship you have to ask the question, 'What will a disciple look like? What will a participant who has gone through your training program look like?'" You need to be able to specifically identify that. Then you can write out in a paragraph or in bullet form what the expected accomplishments or outcome should be.

We Need to Communicate the Vision

The next area I want to address as we move on is how to sell this vision to the rest of the Christian community. It is one thing to have a vision, to have a passion about something; it is another thing to be able to communicate that effectively and to bring others in, to take ownership of that vision. How do we do that?

First, it is important that you organize a time to meet one-on-one with various church, denominational or Christian ministry leaders to share with them your vision. Work to bring them along to support the idea that you have. I have found in my own experience in Africa, because we are a people who are relational by nature, that it is not enough to write a letter to a bishop or to a church leader and say, "Sir, we have this thing coming up, and we are asking for your support." Because we all know that unless there is that personal touch, nothing gets done.

In my experience I have found that when I go to church leaders I first try to sell the idea to them and get them excited about the idea; then when I am leaving, having gotten some feedback from them, I leave them with the letter that I have written officially. There needs to be that personal touch. In most instances, you have to go to the same leader maybe two or three or four times to get him or her to come on board.

Second, you need to develop an organizing committee of leaders who are sold on the idea and agree with the objectives. There has to be that core group to work with you, because that core group becomes significant in your planning of the event. Many times church leaders and heads of denominations get so bogged down with the routines and demands of ministry that they cannot add another meeting to attend. But if they act as an advisory group where you give them information and get input from them, then they can better serve you in that way. Your organizing committee is there to provide counsel to the working committee, hopefully through the person that you appoint as your Conference Coordinator.

The reason you need the organizing committee, even though the working committee will ensure that implementation takes place, is that your organizing committee are the people who will be praying for you, giving you feedback as to how you are doing, and they will be the ones who will be your greatest public relations people. By getting them involved at that level to advise, to give counsel, you will be able to benefit from their wisdom.

> **There has to be a group that always keeps the big picture in view, because once you start to get your various committees functioning, they tend to have only a limited vision as to what they are doing.**

Make sure that the group you select reflects geographically, organizationally and denominationally the Christian community in which you live. If your group is made up primarily of parachurch organizations such as Youth for Christ, Campus Crusade and Scripture Union, then many times there is a bit of suspicion. But if your group has the Baptist, Methodist, Anglican and Pentecostal leaders, then it gives a much better impression of the constituency that you are working with.

You need to define your target audience. Who are you trying to reach? Who are the people whose ministry needs match the objectives? We're to identify who these people are. Who should be invited to attend this conference? Obviously you cannot invite everybody. How many can you invite? What mechanism will you use for inviting people to attend the conference?

Choosing the Conference Leaders

The next area is how you develop the working committee. Let's assume that you have sold the idea. You have the Christian community—not everyone, but a large part of the community—with you. What do we do next? How do we get ourselves organized? How do we put in place the infrastructure, the machinery to help us facilitate this whole process?

You start with what I call a primary authority or final decision-making body for the conference. It is what I call a working committee. The working committee will be the office bearers for the conference. It is like having a board. There has to be a group that always keeps the big picture in view, because once you start to get your various committees functioning, they tend to have only a limited vision as to what they are doing. They are doing just one part; they don't see the full picture. But at any given time this working committee should have the ability to see the big picture, to see how things are developing and to see where the problem areas are, and then problem-solve to move forward.

The next step is to have a Conference Coordinator. Somebody has to be in charge, to be responsible for everything that happens. The coordinator of the conference will be appointed by the working committee and will serve as the Chief Executive Officer. All committees report to that person directly.

The next area is financial concerns. The working committee will appoint a Treasurer, or Financial Committee Chairperson. This person is in control of everything that happens dealing with finance. It is that person's duty to see that the proposed expenditures are within budget and that sufficient cash is available to meet the expenditures.

Now the actual work of planning and implementing the various aspects of the conference will be spread across various committees. The Chairperson of each committee will sit on the working committee. It is imperative that we work in committees because then we get a lot more involvement. When people get involved in various ways, it gives a strong sense of ownership.

The Program Committee

The first committee I want to identify is what I call the program committee. The primary responsibility of the program committee is to develop the topics and themes that deal with the issues and needs of the target audience. The areas of responsibility for the program committee are program design, which means the design of the program to accomplish the objectives for the conference as set by the working committee. This will include the cooperation of ministry partners who may be involved in various aspects of the program itself. The second area would be to find qualified resource people who are capable of speaking to the issues on topics addressing the needs of the target audience.

The next area is staging. Somebody has to think of a concept that will reflect that culture or that locality, and make this the motif that they will use for staging. That is the work of the arrangements committee. That is where you need people who can create graphics, who are visual types of people, who can crystallize what you are discussing into images and pictures that you can use to create the staging.

Then there is the whole issue of sound. When you are having something that big, you need a good sound system for the chosen venue. Also, get adequate lighting for the chosen venue. It would be foolish to plan a conference and not make sure that we have backup power to meet our needs.

The arrangements committee will also be responsible for security at the venue. Now this can be something that they arrange with the police force, if there is a police force. In many missions there is a Christian ministry among the police. The police help us maintain order and ensure that there is adequate security.

The next committee to be organized is the hospitality committee. We have to make sure that there is adequate water for our needs, that the venue either has water or that they will make arrangements for water to be made available for the period that you will be there. Many venues do not provide catering. So you have to make arrangements for catering, either through a professional caterer or get people organized to handle the catering aspect of the conference. Arrangements have to be made for sleeping, for adequate toilet facilities, and to make allowance for rubbish collection. This committee will also arrange for medical facilities. Often there are Christian doctors and nurses who will volunteer their services to provide the necessary assistance.

This committee will also handle such things as product sales. They will arrange for booths and tables for the sale of T-shirts (if you have printed T-shirts), books or other things that you want to sell, or if you have exhibitors. They also will be the ones to make arrangements for the transportation of delegates to the place where the conference will take place.

Committees for Venue and Funding

The arrangements committee will determine and reserve the location or venue. Their responsibility is to acquire a venue or get approval for the use of the venue from whoever owns the facility. Once they have been able to acquire the venue, then the Conference Coordinator and the Arrangements Chairperson will enter into an agreement with the proprietors of the facility.

The fund-raising/finance committee is primarily responsible for fund-raising and to develop a budget for the conference based on input received from various committees and also from the working committee. They will then not only create a budget, but they will have a funding plan. The budget shows you what your anticipated expenditures will be. In each line item of the funding plan there is a step-by-step way in which you're going to raise money for the conference. This committee will work in cooperation with the Conference Coordinator to ensure that expenses for the conference stay within budget and that there is sufficient cash to cover approved expenses.

Committees for Publicity and Volunteers

We also have the publicity and public relations committee. The primary responsibility for this committee is to generate awareness of the conference so that it will lead people to attend. They will be responsible for print, radio and television media. They will develop a strategy to present the conference to churches and denominations. They will be responsible for the production of printed materials such as posters, ads, banners, handbills, etc. And, if you can afford it, they will be responsible for television and radio production as well.

There are ways to advertise that do not cost you anything. Many times our newspapers are looking for news or feature items. If you know a Christian who works for a newspaper, there is nothing wrong with his interviewing you and writing an article. That is free publicity. Or go to the broadcasters to get somebody there to interview you about the conference. Many of them have slots for religious programming, and they are looking for creative things to put there.

The volunteers committee will help in recruiting and managing volunteers and their efforts in various aspects of conference activity. Each committee should help the volunteer committee by giving specific job descriptions of what they are looking for in volunteers for their areas. It is crucial that volunteers know what you expect from them and what they should expect from you. This committee will develop a system that allows the various committees to have the volunteers they need at the time they need them, and to ensure that the volunteers' time is well spent.

When the time has come, and you have done what you can do, leave the rest to the Lord.

We have to define what we mean by a volunteer. Let me tell you why. At one conference people came to us and said they were volunteers. At the end of the conference, they brought us bills saying, "You owe us this much for helping." We replied, "But you said you were volunteers." "No, no, no, we meant that we are not on your payroll as staff. When we come and volunteer, it means that you should pay us for the time we volunteer." Now that was different from what we meant and it created, as you can imagine, all sorts of problems for us. So we have to be clear that when we ask for volunteers we define what we mean by a volunteer.

Committees for Prayer and Follow-Up

Next is the prayer committee. Prayer should be the bedrock on which the conference is based because it is a spiritual ministry. The committee's responsibility is to develop a prayer strategy for the conference. This should be the first committee that you put in place. They are bathing the whole conference in prayer and developing a strategy to ensure that the entire Christian community is praying for the conference. They will be involved in putting together things such as prayer rallies, prayer chains, prayer triplets, etc. You can have bulletins sent to churches with prayer needs so that at church services, Sunday school classes, Bible studies or cell group meetings, people are praying specifically for the conference. They will also develop the materials that give information for people to pray intelligently for the conference.

Last, we have the follow-up committee. Part of their objective is to define what they expect to happen at the end of the conference. We spend time planning the event, but we should spend twice as much time planning what happens after the event, because follow-up is crucial. The job of the follow-up committee is to develop and implement plans that will take advantage of the momentum gained at the conference to enhance ongoing ministry evangelism across that nation or region and beyond. This follow-up group will help them determine how they can maximize what they have learned, help them in training trainers, in reaching the unreached, and in benefiting from the exposure and energy created by the conference.

They will also follow through with participants so that those who attend the conference will be encouraged to be active in sharing their faith and to get connected with one of the ministry partners for support and accountability. Many times we talk about accountability when it comes to finances, but do you know that we need to be accountable in our training?

Participants should not only give a report of what happened at the conference they attended, they should be given time to write down in specific terms that are measurable how they are going to implement what they have learned. We should hold them accountable for that plan. The follow-up committee can assist various missions, Christian groups and churches in doing just that.

In conclusion, when the time has come, and you have done what you can do, leave the rest to the Lord. Pray your heart out, and keep on praying!

Don Osman

The Reverend Don Osman is Area Director of Youth For Christ International (YFCI)/Africa Region. Born in Sierra Leone, at age 20 Rev. Osman accepted Jesus Christ as his Savior. He went on to study at Sierra Leone Bible College before transferring to Colorado Christian University (Denver, Colorado, U.S.A.), where he earned a Bachelor of Biblical Education degree; in 1986, he earned a Master of Arts degree from Denver Seminary (Denver, Colorado, U.S.A.). He and his wife, Nadaline, have four children, and they live in Nairobi, Kenya.

Closing Ceremony— Communion Service

Richard Bewes

Please look with me at Ephesians 4:20–21, "Surely you heard . . . him" (NIV)—is how it should read. You can cross out that word *of* if you've got a modern version. Most of the modern versions have got it wrong. The Greek has not got that word *of*. "Surely you heard . . . him."

But, Paul, you're writing to those people in Ephesus. They've never seen Jesus. They're only seeing you, Silas, Timothy and Luke. "No," Paul says, "but you heard Him. We spoke—Timothy spoke or Barnabas spoke—it was Christ you heard." And that is the wonder of God's message when it is preached by people. Preachers, let's take this to heart. Let's be encouraged about it! "You heard . . . him."

My grandpa, aged 14, Tommy Bewes on Tuesday night, 26th of September, 1882, went along as the youngest of 12 to hear D. L. Moody, the famed evangelist in Plymouth. Young Tommy was one of 100,000 people that Mr. Moody pointed to Christ in England. He heard one sentence from the Bible: "[Adam,] where are you?" (Genesis 3:9, NIV). That arrested my grandpa, and that started the whole Bible line in our family—missionaries, clergy, ministers. One sermon pitched several generations into the Kingdom of God!

So you never know what comes out of your preaching. You may be a brand-new preacher, never done anything before. Your very first time, expect that they will hear Jesus. That is what we expect. "You heard . . . him."

Let's come on then to our communion service as we now encourage each other in the Lord Jesus Christ together. We meet together now, drawn by the magnetic power of the Cross of Calvary. We're going to share in powerful remembrance of the central event of all time, the saving death of Jesus for the sins of the world. And, surely, we're never going to forget these next few minutes as we participate in what is the most internationally representative Christian service of all time. We can't believe it, but it's true.

In this, we're anticipating the vision of John the evangelist, who in Revelation 7 saw heaven opened and wrote, "I looked and there before me was a great multitude that no one could count, from every nation, tribe, people and language, standing before the throne and in front of the Lamb" (v. 9, NIV).

We shouldn't imagine for a moment that this is *our* service to which we are inviting Jesus Christ. It's His service and this is His table to which *He* is summoning us. So in obedience we come, just as in the upper room of old with those 12 disciples, to partake of the broken bread and the poured-out cup that symbolize His body and blood given in violent death that we might live forever.

Almighty God, to whom all hearts are open, all desires known, and from whom no secrets are hidden, cleanse the thoughts of our hearts by the inspiration of Your Holy Spirit that we may perfectly love You and worthily magnify Your holy name through Christ our Lord. Amen.

We're right there at Calvary. We're right there at the foot of the Cross together. And it's you and Jesus. And among us all here, the ground is level. We come to Him quietly in repentance for the things we know need to be put right and for His forgiving, reinstating power. We're just quiet at the Cross.

"If [anyone sins], we have an advocate with the Father, Jesus Christ the righteous: And he is the propitiation for our sins" (1 John 2:1–2, KJV).

"Simon, son of John, do you truly love me?" (John 21:15, NIV). See, we could put our own name right in there at this moment as we answer the question of Jesus, "Do you truly love me?"

Then let's stand for a moment. There's another thing. Are we at peace with each other? Are we at peace with our fellow evangelists and preachers in the Gospel? How do we deal with these strange things that attack preachers, like jealousy? I think we know the answer. You write to the person who is doing better than you; you write to them and congratulate them, and you tell them you wish that one day you would be as good as they are. Then you praise them. You praise them publicly. And as we know, a miracle of grace takes place. That ugly, cold, stabbing thrust of jealousy melts away like the morning mist, and the warm, reassuring presence of the Holy Spirit fills our hearts and our lives. We know that.

Do you need to put something right, even at this moment? Or to make a resolve to reinforce those resolves we have made in our Amsterdam Covenant? Some may want to just sit in prayer for a moment and be quiet. Others may want to give a brotherly hug to somebody nearby or a warm handshake, a Christian greeting. Let's spend a moment in a bit of international greeting and love.

Loving helpers have prepared for each of us the cup and the bread. So when the time comes to receive the bread, I will invite you to hold that piece of bread in your hand until we can all partake together at the same time as I read a verse of Scripture.

And then the cup: When I say a sentence from Scripture, we can all drink simultaneously in remembrance of the death of Jesus.

A question quickly—and you've got to get this right—what does it mean to eat the flesh, to drink the blood of our Lord Jesus Christ? It sounds strange to modern ears. Let's remind ourselves that the phrases come right out of the Old Testament, out of Jewish background.

Think of David the psalmist, Psalm 27:2—"When . . . mine enemies . . . came upon me to eat up my flesh, they stumbled and fell" (KJV). He meant that his enemies were coming upon him to take advantage of his downfall.

Or we think of 2 Samuel 23:15–17. David's men had brought cold water from the well of Bethlehem at great risk. But he couldn't drink it; he poured it out on the ground. And he said, "God forbid that I should drink the blood of these who have risked their lives" (see v. 17). He meant he didn't want to take advantage of their possible death for him.

To eat the flesh, to drink the blood of Jesus in this symbolical way, is to take advantage of His death for you. It is to be assured all over again what it is to be forgiven, to be assured all over again what it is to be in the international family of Christ and to be on the road to the new heaven and the new earth that awaits His people. The bread and the cup are powerful Gospel visual aids reminding us. So, beloved friends, let's share together in the communion of the Lord, remembering His death until He comes. Let's pray now.

Almighty God, our heavenly Father—who of Your tender mercy gave Your only Son Jesus Christ to suffer death upon the Cross for our redemption; who made there by His one oblation of Himself once offered a full, perfect and sufficient sacrifice, oblation and satisfaction for the sins of the whole world; and who instituted and in His holy Gospel commanded us to continue a perpetual memory of His precious death until His coming again—hear us, merciful Father, that as we receive these visible gifts of bread and wine, we may be partakers by faith of Christ's blessed body and blood.

"[Who] on the night [that] he was betrayed, took bread, and when he had given thanks, he broke it." He gave it to His disciples saying, "'This is my body, [given] for you; do this in remembrance of me.' In the same way, after supper he took the cup, saying, 'This cup is the new covenant in my blood; do this, whenever you drink it, in remembrance of me.' For whenever you eat this bread and drink this cup, you proclaim the Lord's death until he comes" (1 Corinthians 11:23–26, NIV). Amen.

So we partake of the bread now. Because there is one loaf, we who are many are one body, for we all partake of the one loaf. Amen.

Where two or three are together in the name of Christ, He's among them (see Matthew 18:20). It's wonderful to delight to be in His presence!

And now, in deep fellowship, we receive from the cup together until He comes.

"You heard . . . him" (Ephesians 4:21, NIV). Come back to that little verse. Come back to the day of your own conversion. Some of you may be coming to Christ right now through the wonder of this service, right now putting your trust in Him for the very first time. Can you remember when you did it?

There's an interpreter here called Oleg, who is interpreting into Russian right now. I met him some years ago just before the Billy Graham Crusade in Moscow.

I said to Oleg, "I suppose you've been a Christian for a long time." "Oh, no," he said. "Until recently I was an atheist, a young intellectual teacher in a school, an ardent member of the Youth Communist League." And he said, "In my school my headmaster sent for me and said, 'There's a little girl there, and she's misbehaving. She's calling herself a Christian. Go and shut her up.'"

And Oleg went. To his amazement she was only seven. And then she startled him with her first question, "How sure are you that there's no God?" He didn't know what to say. He said he wasn't 100 percent sure. She opened up his defenses, and that little girl of seven led the young Russian intellectual to faith in Jesus Christ that very day!

So God bless you, Oleg. And thousands others of us, we know that it continues to happen in evangelism this way—"Surely you heard . . . him." Now let us pray.

Dear Lord Jesus, we thank You for this time of communion and fellowship with You. It is a delight to be in Your presence. In affection and mutual trust we now commend to You one another who all too soon must return to the place of our calling and contend for the faith once for all delivered to the saints.

We pay humble tribute to the noble army of martyrs, many of whom were to have been with us in this hall but are now in glory, beloved saints who were known to many of us, slain because of the Word of God and the testimony they had borne, and who must wait a little longer with us for the avenging of their blood.

And we share at the end of this communion service in the vision that captivated Your evangelist John and that has inspired Your church on earth across the high roads of time: "Then I saw heaven opened, and behold, a white horse! He who sat [on] it is called Faithful and True, and in righteousness he judges and makes war. His eyes are like a flame of fire, . . . on his head are many diadems; and he has a name inscribed which no one knows but himself. He [has] a robe dipped in blood; and the name by which he is called is The Word of God. And the armies of heaven, arrayed in fine linen, white and pure, followed him on white horses. From his mouth issues a sharp sword with which to smite the nations, and he will rule them with a rod of iron; he will tread the wine press of the fury of the wrath of God the Almighty. On his robe and on his thigh he has a name inscribed, King of kings and Lord of lords" (Revelation 19:11–16, RSV).

So now we are being sent out from this place once again, over these next few hours, Lord Jesus, fanning out from Amsterdam 2000 to light a fire on six continents. We know that we will never meet again quite like this. And we know that although Your mission is now crisscrossing in every direction across the world and many of us will see one another at different times, although e-mails and letters will maintain our mutual contact, although the bonds of our mutual intercession and prayer will hold us together, in spite of all that, many of us will never meet again until that day when the stars shall fall from heaven, the sun turns black as night, the sky recedes and vanishes, and we see You, the Son of Man, in Your irradiated glory coming at the sound of the trumpet. We can hardly wait!

Keep and sustain us, then, in between now and then as we return to the places of our appointments. Here we are, dear Lord, thousands of us, Your faithful, loving helpers and friends. We are gazing in anticipation at what lies ahead of each of us, and we cry to You afresh in the prayer of Caleb of old as we look at the task in front of us, "Give me this mountain" (Joshua 14:12, KJV). We commend one another to You now in mutual affection and trust.

May the God of peace who through the blood of the eternal covenant brought back from the dead our Lord Jesus, that great shepherd of the sheep, equip us with everything good for doing His will. And may He work in us what is pleasing to Him through Jesus Christ to whom be glory forever and ever. Amen.

Richard Bewes

The Reverend Richard Bewes leads the work of All Souls Church, Langham Place, London, England, where he became Rector in 1983. He is also a Prebendary of St. Paul's Cathedral. Born and reared in Kenya as the son of missionaries, Rev. Bewes serves as the United Kingdom chairman of African Enterprise, which specializes in evangelism, relief work and reconciliation across Africa. A preacher, broadcaster and writer, he has had 17 books published. He also hosts the newly produced Open Home, Open Bible *international video teaching program. He chaired Billy Graham's "Mission '89" in London. He and his wife, Elisabeth, have three children and two grandchildren.*

Challenge: Commitment to Christ and the Gospel

Billy Graham
Delivered via satellite for Amsterdam 2000
From Rochester, Minnesota, to Amsterdam, The Netherlands

Greetings in the name of the Lord Jesus Christ.

I have been with you every day by satellite and have been convicted, challenged and blessed with what my ears have heard and my eyes have seen and my heart has felt. I thank God for the great spiritual blessings He has poured upon you during your days in Amsterdam. Many people around the world have been praying for this event, and I rejoice that their prayers have been more than answered. Already many stories have been passed on to me that indicate God has clearly been at work in your midst, and we give Him all the praise and the glory.

Thank you for your letters which I have received. Many of you have said that you are praying for my health. I am getting stronger every day, and I have confidence that I will be in good strength to proclaim the Gospel by the time of our next scheduled evangelistic campaign in early November. I would appreciate your continued prayers.

Only eternity will reveal the full results of what has been accomplished at Amsterdam 2000. But I know that many of you have already made important decisions that will change your lives and your ministries.

It has been my privilege to travel through much of the world proclaiming this Gospel. As I have traveled, I have constantly been reminded of a story that I heard in India about Mahatma Gandhi, who is alleged to have said, "I would become a Christian if I could see one." How we live as evangelists and ministers is just as important as what we say.

As you leave this conference, you are going not only with the thrill of being in the city of Amsterdam, but also with the excitement of these meetings in the RAI and the thrill of smaller meetings in Jaarbeurs or other places where you have gathered. You also have made the joy of new friendships and a new networking across national, linguistic, and racial barriers. None of you will ever be the same.

As I have been in my room here at the Mayo Clinic in Rochester, Minnesota, I have had tears in my eyes and the joy of the Lord in my heart at what I have seen and felt through the satellite relay. I wish I could have been with you in person, but in my heart I have been there with you and feel that I am one of you. My love is extended to each one of you there.

I want to be among those who represent a generation of evangelists that hands the torch to a new generation of God's servants. I believe that the fire of God the Holy Spirit has fallen on this conference and that we have rededicated our lives in a new way to reflect the light of the glory of God. We are concluding this Amsterdam conference with a new fire burning in our hearts to touch a lost world.

The story is told of two Christian martyrs in the 16th century who were burned at the stake. As the fire was being lit, one of them said to the other, "Be of good cheer. We shall this day light a fire that by God's grace shall never be put out." Their bodies were consumed, but their message of Christ's saving grace lives on to this day.

I do not believe that we should spend our time cursing the darkness. I do not believe we should spend our time in useless controversy, trying to root out the tares while harming the wheat. I do not believe that we should give in to the forces of evil and violence and indifference. Instead, let us light a fire.

Let us light a fire that will banish moral and spiritual blight wherever we go.

Let us light a fire that will guide men and women into tomorrow and eternity.

Let us light a fire that will roll back the poisons of racism, poverty and injustice.

Let us light a fire of renewed faith in the Scriptures as the Word of God, and in worship and evangelism as the priority of the Church.

Let us light a fire of commitment to proclaim the Gospel of Jesus Christ in the power of the Holy Spirit to the ends of the earth, using every resource at our command and with every ounce of our strength.

Let's light a fire in this generation that, by God's grace, will never be put out.

A number of years ago the Christopher Society held a meeting in one of the great stadiums of America. On the closing night each person was given a candle. At the conclusion of the service they were told to light their candles as an act of dedication. Then they lifted their candles high, and the light from those candles sent forth a glow that could be seen all over the city.

I am asking you to take the light from here in Amsterdam that you found during these days; hold that light high as you return to your home. And with the light of the thousands of other participants from around the world we can make a fire that will shine brightly and will never be put out. I say to you tonight as you leave this conference, light a fire. Let the light of Jesus Christ, the Light of the World, shine throughout the whole earth until He comes again!

May God bless you and use you, my beloved brothers and sisters in Christ, and keep you close to Himself forever.

And as you go home, I want all of you to know that I love you—individually and collectively—with all my heart. You've come from over two hundred countries. I've been in many of your countries; some I have not been to. But please know that I will be praying for each one of you and love you with all my heart. Give my love to your family, your churches, and your people. God bless you forever.

Billy Graham
Dr. Graham founded the Billy Graham Evangelistic Association in 1950, which headquarters in Minneapolis, Minnesota, U.S.A. Dr. Graham and his wife, Ruth, make their home in North Carolina, U.S.A.

Amsterdam 2000
Workshops

Reaching Counter-Culture Youth

Roy Crowne

The largest people group in the world is the youth culture. Some Christians are down on the culture. Others look at the culture prophetically and hear what the culture is saying. They use it to communicate the Gospel. As we connect with this culture, what are the trends?

One trend is consumerism. The media says your needs will be met by the products you buy. If you don't have those things, then your value and significance as a person is not good. Image is everything. This influences the presentation of the Gospel message because there's a massive paradigm shift whereby they're seeing Christianity as a resource that you buy into. You pick and mix that resource.

A second trend is the changing family impact on young people. In some families the children see one parent during the week and another parent on the weekend. What impact does that have on worship? We may have to do church on Thursday or Friday night because they can't be there on Sunday.

A third trend is technology. Teenagers have not known life without a VCR or a CD-ROM or Internet access. This is their world. Discipleship may not be with a friend next door but with a person on the other side of the world through the Internet. Because the third most popular sites visited on the Internet are the spirituality sites, technology in youth ministry is an essential access point.

The world is becoming smaller, and rock stars, MTV, sports, films and television all work together to create a global youth culture. This contributes to a global world of fashion, music, media and ideologies, and gives young people more in common with other young people in the world than with the adults in their same culture. At the same time, tribalism is on the increase. In this world where their families are not together, where they feel they don't fit, the tribe (the people like them) becomes critical to their identity. To live in this world without being part of a tribe is very scary. When the church connects with these tribes, we will see a transformation occur in lives.

A fourth trend is the erosion of moral values. They want to know why you believe the Bible. Youth workers who model a relational approach will score with this generation. "What I want is an adult that I can relate to, someone who is going to enter my world, understand where I'm coming from and model a Christian life and teaching that I respect." Love kids and mix with them; then they will ask what you believe. Build a relationship and you will start to see change in their lives.

Sometimes when we go relational we back off on the Gospel. If we just go relational without the truth of Jesus Christ, we're not doing justice to young people. What Jesus taught was central to who He was as a person. In exactly the same way, we build relationships but also hold central the truth that causes us to be the people of God.

This is a spiritual generation. Young people are saying, "I want an experience with God." They're looking for an intimate encounter with the risen Christ. Give them a spiritual experience that comes out of mission, a taste of ministry. We tell young people, "You've got to pray and read the Bible." But they don't do it. Get them involved in mission and they'll read the Bible and they'll pray. Ministry and mission will transform them more than teaching and entertaining. There they'll see the supernatural and they'll see revival. Then challenge them about what they believe. Keep the biblical base but have new models of ministry.

Roy Crowne
Roy Crowne is National Director of British Youth for Christ.

Mobilizing Student Leaders for Outreach

Tom Harriger

Half of the people who have lived in history will be alive within our lifetime, and half of those people will be under the age of 20! By reaching youth we have an opportunity to present the message of salvation to a fourth of the people who have ever lived. God's heart is that He's "not willing that any should perish, but that all should come to repentance" (2 Peter 3:9, KJV).

It takes a broken generation to heal a broken world. The things that make this generation so needy also make them prime candidates for God to use because they are searching, they are empty. Now is the time for teenagers to become spiritual leaders in evangelism and discipleship. Teens are hungry for something that works, and they want relationships. Because some of them have broken families and broken homes, discipleship creates a community where they feel needed. This generation wants a purpose. They want something bigger than themselves.

How can we create an environment to build spiritual leadership among young people? First, we create a "come and see" program. This is an evangelistic outreach, anything that you might do to gather non-Christians to see more about God and to come to faith. You want to be relevant. Work with the Christian students to decide what would be most effective, because they know better than we do what's going to attract the non-Christian students.

Second, have interactive Bible studies. These are small-group Bible studies where you say, "We want to teach you to grow in your faith and to walk by faith day by day." Third, have training events, retreats or training conferences, where you're asking them to "come and do." We equip them by asking, "How can you reach your campus for Christ? How can you share your faith? How can you follow up somebody? How can you lead a Bible study?" Teach them; train them. Once they're equipped they'll know what to do.

Fourth, take them "out there" where they can catch a vision for how God can use them. Youth trained and on fire are going to be the catalysts in the churches for revival. Fifth, enable them to lead their own discipleship groups. We want to see them multiply their faith. So we instruct them to instruct others with everything they've learned.

There are certain characteristics to look for in student leaders. Who is the young man or woman on whom God will put His hand to use? God is not looking for the superstar, but for the Spirit-filled servant. Look for young men and women who are full of faith and the Holy Spirit. Show them that they can make a difference with their lives for Jesus Christ.

What are some of the ingredients of multiplication? First, correct spiritual priorities. Our objective is that student leaders become multipliers. Always be praying, depending on the ministry of the Holy Spirit. The second emphasis is relationships. Teenagers want adults who accept them and will help them develop the adult side of their lives. Your ministry will be as effective as the relationships that you develop. Be an adult mentor. The third emphasis is the programs and activities that need to be in place so that we can continually be growing.

The environment you create is going to help you evaluate where your students are and how to lead them in their next steps, through the process of discipleship, to help them become spiritual multipliers.

Tom Harriger
Tom Harriger is Director of Student Venture International, a ministry of Campus Crusade for Christ. He lives in Minnesota, U.S.A.

How to Communicate With Young People

Ron Hutchcraft

Many times when we speak to young people, we are talking but they're not getting it. Explain the Gospel in a way that a teenager can understand. Young people force us to communicate clearly. This is our mandate: "We will tell the next generation" (Psalm 78:4, NIV).

We show Christ with our love and our life, but we don't just show them. Young people could watch us for 50 years, but they're never going to say, "You know, Joe is such a nice guy. I'll bet Jesus died on the Cross for my sins." They're not going to figure that out just by watching us. We have to tell them. There are three factors in a persuasive presentation of the Gospel of Jesus Christ. Number one is power for the message. Here are five sources of power in presenting the Gospel to young people.

The first source of power is the heart. A powerful lesson starts with the person's heart, then goes to the mind, and at the end returns to the heart. Some speakers are all head. They have a lot of impressive information. We walk out knowing a lot, but we don't feel much. Other speakers are all heart. They stir us, but if someone asked afterwards what they talked about, we wouldn't know. There wasn't much content. Don't start with our facts; start with their feelings, something young people care about. But give their minds information, too. Then, with an illustration or a Scripture, come back and touch their hearts at the end. It's the heart that has to believe. Heart, mind, heart—that's powerful communication.

A second source of power is language. It may not be Christ they reject, it may be our religious vocabulary. Find nonreligious ways to say it so that they will understand. A third source of power is personality. We don't have to be someone else to communicate to young people. Let the truth come through your personality. A fourth source of power is takeover. It is a prayer that says, "Lord, get me out of the way." A fifth source of power is passion. Young people can tell if you love them and desperately want them to understand. That will capture their hearts more than humor, jokes, style or image. Passion in your heart will ignite passion in theirs.

A second factor in a powerful and persuasive message is preparation. A message that is attractive, clear, relevant and complete takes preparation. Here are six ingredients in preparing to speak to young people about the Good News of Jesus Christ.

First, have a key verse. When we give young people lots of Bible verses, we lose them. One verse will get to their hearts. The centerpiece of your message is the Word of God. Nothing else has supernatural power. Second, have a relevant starting point. Talk about something they care about. A powerful message is a road from where they are to where God wants them to be. Imagine that the young people are holding up a sign that says, "Why should I care about this?" Answer their question; start where they are.

Third, summarize what you want to say in one sentence. Think, "The one thing that I really want them to remember is this," and then just keep hammering that home. Fourth, build a clear case. Use simple logic that gets their head nodding yes. Start with their need—whether it's emptiness, loneliness, lack of peace, fear of death, depression, anger, whatever. Go from the symptom of the disease that keeps them away from God to the cure of the Cross.

Fifth, young people need stories. Use personal stories, life experiences, object lessons, metaphors, kids' comments, the media—the movies, television—because that's the common culture. Sixth, preach for a verdict. Know what you're going to ask them to do. Give them reasons to respond and lead them in a nonreligious language commitment to Jesus Christ.

Ron Hutchcraft

Ron Hutchcraft is an evangelist, author and the president of Ron Hutchcraft Ministries. He lives in Arkansas, U.S.A.

Reaching the Global Youth Culture

Ron Hutchcraft

Nearly 50 percent of the world is under age 25: three billion, the largest generation of young people ever. Three-quarters of those who come to Christ do so by age 18. If they leave their early years without Christ, they will probably live without Christ, die without Christ, and spend eternity without Christ. We can't ignore half the world!

This youth culture is worldwide. Kids are watching the same movies, the same videos, listening to the same music, wearing the same clothes, making the same mistakes and desperately needing the same Savior. Young people are tormented by loneliness, saturated by sex, fascinated with the dark side of the supernatural, and susceptible to suicide. We cannot abandon them.

Ten points define this generation. First: Loneliness runs deep. They are home alone, raised by their music, by television, by video games. They will do anything to get a loving feeling, even if only for a night. A lot of what's going on sexually isn't about biology. It's about intimacy, feeling close to someone for a few minutes.

Second: Boundaries don't matter. Absolutes have been challenged, relativism rules. Young people are like athletes trying to play sports on a field that has no boundaries. It is chaos. Third: Worth is a struggle: "I'm junk." They are throwing themselves away, socially, chemically, by suicide. Fourth: Escape is a solution. The problem isn't just the drugs, the alcohol and the sex. The problem is the pain that's driving them to those things. They look for pain relievers, but these just give them more problems and more pain.

Fifth: Anger is rising. Pain causes anger. In some countries it's leading to street violence and street mobs. Sixth: Music is their language. "When I'm hurting I turn on my music. It understands me." Adults say, "You call that music? That's just noise. Listen to that man screaming. He's angry, profane." But they listen to music that expresses what's in their souls.

Seventh: Life is pointless. It has no meaning. Why? Because they don't know the reason they were created. Eighth: Now is what matters. If all we talk to them about is a Christ who offers heaven, they won't hear us. They want to know, "What can Jesus do for me today?"

Ninth: Hardness comes sooner. Sin and darkness is available at such early ages. We need to be reaching them when they are younger. Tenth: They are ready for Jesus. What has made them lost has made them ready.

How do we reach young people? Number one: Leave the walls. No lost sheep comes wandering home to the shepherd. The shepherd goes after it. If we stay inside the walls of the church, most young people will go on dying. Leave the walls or you're going to leave them lost.

Second: Focus on Jesus. Young people are not interested in Christianity or the church. But Jesus interests them. Give them Christ and give them the Cross. Third: Start with their need. They can't see the disease, but they can see the symptoms. Start with the symptoms, move to the disease, and offer the cure.

Fourth: Say it plainly. We talk about accept Christ, sin, believe, repent, born again, save. They have no idea what we're talking about. They're not rejecting our Savior; they're rejecting our vocabulary. Think like a missionary. Express the Christian message in the language of the person you're trying to reach.

Fifth: Present a relationship as opposed to a religion. "There's a relationship you're created to have, you don't have, you can have and you must choose." Sixth: Package it attractively. Satan offers guilt, disappointment, regrets and death. Why would anybody buy Satan's product? Because he's got the brightest packages. Why do young people walk right past the Gospel of Jesus Christ that offers what they're looking for? Could it be that we have boring packages? They're not rejecting the product. They're rejecting the package.

Seventh: Build a team. Nehemiah rebuilt his city by getting everybody on his team with him. And lastly: Pray it done. Prayer must be your primary method of getting this job done. This is a spiritual battle. It will only be won on our knees.

Ron Hutchcraft
Ron Hutchcraft is an evangelist, author and the president of Ron Hutchcraft Ministries. He lives in Arkansas, U.S.A.

Evangelizing Contemporary Youth

Rick Marshall

There is a way that the Spirit of God can reach the next generation. But it's a moving target. They are a generation hostile, not to Jesus Christ, but to the church. They are a generation that is wired, worldly and wounded.

Life for them is spiritually empty; it is dissatisfying; and it is dangerous. Life in this technologically intoxicated zone favors the quick fix. This generation blurs the distinction between real and fake. Stimulation always has to increase. They love technology as a toy.

Yet these are the very things that make this generation ready to receive Jesus Christ. I believe that we are on the verge of a revival, but we're going to have to—like the priests of old—put our feet in the water and take some risks.

We need to evaluate and understand their world. Loneliness is inevitable without Christ. Relationships matter. Self-worth is a constant struggle. They lack boundaries and they want authority, despite what they say. Now matters more than the future. Commitment is risky. We need to keep current by spending time with youth, reading, listening and watching. The church has been in lecture mode for far too long. It's time to change that.

Now, let's think about evangelism. For a strategic event that could occur in your community, meet with the local leadership. Avoid the egotistical swat team strategy that says, "God told us to come," but they didn't invite you. It's not biblical, and it's not even good manners. Give an opportunity for the church to embrace this outreach. Then pray. We need a strategy of prayer. We need to set ministry objectives and get students on their knees.

Book a neutral setting and develop an aggressive advertising campaign. Radio is without a doubt the most effective electronic medium; it's also the cheapest. But advertising can't do anything unless there's a relationship. Eighty percent of the kids who come to evangelistic events are prayed for by name, related to in friendship, invited and brought by a friend.

Music is a huge component. You don't have to find famous musicians. You need music, testimony and video. And you need the Word of God, straight talk from a caring adult.

You will make mistakes. There's misunderstanding, the music is too loud, older people can't understand the words. But it's all about the audience that you're trying to reach.

There's aggression in this kind of evangelism. There's a great chasm, the church over here and the next generation over there. That chasm is getting wider and deeper. To get the attention of the other side, somebody is going to have to go to the edge. When they know that we understand their world, they'll know that our motives are right, and they will listen.

This generation longs for an encounter with God. We must creatively reach this generation with a fresh, vibrant, relevant message of faith that is understood by the hearers. I don't believe that using the cultural form is unbiblical. Beware of the danger of judgment and its cousin, dogmatism. When the heart gets hard, then the mind closes.

Jesus did not call us to hug the safe harbors. We are on a rescue mission. As partners together for Jesus Christ, it's time to head out for the deep. And deep the waters are.

Rick Marshall

Rick Marshall is Director of Billy Graham Crusades for the Billy Graham Evangelistic Association.

Reaching International Students

Tom Phillips

The potential of an international student ministry is expansive. In the United States we have over 600,000 international students from approximately 200 countries. Around the world there are about 1.5 million international students. Often they are the best and the brightest of their country. We have an incredible opportunity to reach nations by reaching those who are studying in our nations.

We do not have to learn another language or another culture, though it is wise to understand the culture of the international students with whom we are partnering. They've come to us. They are away from peer pressure, family pressure and religious pressure. They're lonely; they want a friend and they're seeking. What a great opportunity to help them to know Christ and to disciple them. We can all do this on our campuses, in our cities and through our churches.

When we meet international students, we tell them, "There are five things we can do for you." Number one, "If you want to know God personally, we can help you." Tell them right up front that the most important thing in your life is your faith in God through Jesus Christ. Tell them, "You're going to be in our country two to four years. During that time, if you decide you want to know more about God, you want to know Him personally, we're here to help you."

Second, we offer an international student a friend while they are in our country. We do evangelism through friendship, pointing them to the greatest friend of all. We train "friendship partners" how to utilize simple evangelistic Bible studies and how to be cross-culturally sensitive.

Third, we offer an international Christian fellowship. We have a meal that's usually provided by a church, a worship time, and then we break into a Bible study or even a course on how to buy a used automobile or do laundry or use the telephone or get help with immigration questions. International students don't know many of these things.

The fourth thing that we offer is English as a second language—ESL. We can partner them with a friend who will meet with them and just talk, helping with colloquial English, the idioms of the country. Most international students' English is exceptionally good, but it's formal, and they need to know the colloquial or the idiomatic expressions.

The fifth thing that we offer international students is "other," which can be anything from getting furniture for their apartments to clothing or medical help. This is how we exalt Jesus Christ.

This mission field can touch the lives of billions because it is strategic reproductive evangelistic discipleship that, in turn, has an impact on the world through these emerging leaders. These young men and women will soon lead their nations and have concentric circles of influence. We want to see them go home as indigenous missionaries at the highest level of government or industry and change their world. We want to establish churches all over the world through these students. Students are change agents. Find them, love them, be their friend, point them to Jesus!

Tom Phillips
Tom Phillips is Vice President of Training, BGEA, Asheville, North Carolina, U.S.A.

"Let's Meet Jesus"—Leading Children to Christ

Vernie Schorr

Our mission is to win children to Christ, and to develop their conscience and character toward God. Eighty-five percent of the people who make a decision for Christ do so before the age of 14.

Often when we speak about God as Father, we want to communicate that God loves us, forgives us and never leaves us. But a child's thinking is limited by perspective. When we teach children whose natural fathers are abusive or are not in the home, their perspective of a father is different from what we want them to know about God. Their perspective will be stronger than our words.

We want to be concrete with children, yet most of what we teach in God's book, the Bible, is abstract. Many concepts cannot be touched—you can't use the five senses to understand, for instance, hope. We need to look at things that children can touch or feel or see, and help them with their perspective of God.

Here are three topics to think about: First, children tend to focus their attention on limited or nonessential aspects of a situation. As you are teaching, children will often interrupt with ideas that aren't part of the story. Give them the opportunity to blurt out their ideas, to be accepted, which is what Jesus does with us. Building relationships with children in many ways is more important than telling the story.

Second, children may give correct answers that are, in fact, meaningless to them. We must be careful, because when children repeat things back to us, we may think they understand when in reality they don't. Third, many times a child merely repeats. Children can memorize whole chapters of Scripture and not understand what those Scripture verses mean. When we want a child to experience an abstract concept such as kindness, we need to create a firsthand experience to demonstrate it. Abstract ideas must be recast into physical terms.

How do we help children make a decision about Jesus? First, avoid symbolism. Second, explain words to children. In explaining words we need to use the principles about children's perspective—the fact that they need to have firsthand experiences, and that they need physical activities.

Third, work with children individually or in small groups. We need to be able to interact with children when we're helping them make a voluntary decision for Jesus. That word *voluntary* leads to the fourth point, which is to allow for free choice and avoid pressure. If children are starved for the affection of a significant adult and you say to them, "I want you all to raise your hand and pray to receive Christ," they'll do it for you.

Finally, help children to tell others about Jesus. If we don't train children to tell others about Jesus, we're going to lose a whole bunch of children. They are champions for their friends.

Get people praying for you. The battlefield is for our children. There is so much evil influencing our children. Arm yourselves with the armor of God and pray for one another.

Vernie Schorr

Vernie Schorr is Children's Consultant for The JESUS Film Project, San Clemente, California, U.S.A.

Discipling Young People Into the Church

Barry St. Clair

Our vision is to influence teenagers to become followers of Jesus. Young people need to receive Jesus as their Savior and Lord, and grow in their faith so that the choices they make are godly choices. Then they will become life-changers, having an effective ministry with their friends.

If we're going to disciple students, then several things have to take place. Number one: We have to have a Jesus-focused ministry. Many times Jesus is in the background. Some young people grow up in the Church but don't really know Him. If I'm the youth leader and Jesus is filling my life and His character is coming through me, then I am reproducing with my young people the life of Jesus. Number two: We have to have an environment of prayer. We're not going to see effective evangelism until young people are praying for their friends. Number three: We have to train leaders for evangelism and discipling. Youth leaders can disciple a few. But who's going to disciple the many? We need trained adults ready to disciple those students.

There are six principles that help us. First is the principle of receiving or the principle of grace. It's an environment of grace as opposed to an environment of legalism. Following Jesus is better than keeping a bunch of rules. Grace is God's Holy Spirit working in us. Why do young people wander away from youth ministry? The reason is they have external motivation, the values of their parents and the church, but they have never internalized those. How much better if, in the context of discipleship, we say to them, "What do you believe God wants you to do about . . . ?" When they struggle with that, God's Holy Spirit working in them, their character is stronger. They are internally motivated rather than externally motivated.

Second, we want to have a discipling ministry centered in relationships. When I know what's going on in your life and you know what's going on in my life, discipleship becomes more effective. We cannot disciple young people without having personal relationships. Third, we help young people reflect the character of Christ. We teach them the Bible, train them in the disciplines of the Christian life and show them how to have a quiet time and how to witness and worship. The Holy Spirit works in them causing them to be stronger and stronger. Then when they're with their friends they become the light and salt of Jesus.

Fourth is the principle of reality. Discipleship takes place in real-life situations. We're going to fail. We need to be honest enough to say, "This is what I'm struggling with." Be vulnerable and transparent. When we open our hearts and lives up to young people, then they will open up their hearts and lives to us.

Fifth is the principle of recruiting. "The things which you have heard from me in the presence of many witnesses, these entrust to faithful men" (2 Timothy 2:2, NASB). We're recruiting young men and women who are faithful, available, teachable, sold out to Jesus. When you say to them, "I want you to become a man of God; I want you to become a woman of God; would you meet with me to learn how to do that?" and they say, "Yes," then take them right where they are and begin to invest in them.

Sixth is the principle of reproduction. Paul says, "These entrust to faithful men, who will be able to teach others also" (2 Timothy 2:2, NASB). As we invest in the lives of young people, and they in turn invest in other young people, it's amazing what God will do. Invest your life in close, personal, grace-oriented, relationship-centered discipleship ministry with young people. God will multiply what you do!

Barry St. Clair
Barry St. Clair is President of Reachout Youth Solutions, Norcross, Georgia, U.S.A.

Training Church-Planting Evangelists

Mike Evans

As evangelists we are accountable to the church and should always carry out our ministry with a view to building up the local church. Any evangelism that is not aimed at building up the church, whether in terms of planting new churches or sustaining the growth of existing ones, is defective evangelism. We must constantly examine our ministries in order to check if our work directly contributes to the building up of the Church of Jesus Christ.

There is no incompatibility between theoretical training and training for the practice of the ministry. There must be a combination of the two in training church-planting evangelists.

First, we need a theological philosophy about life, the world and the ministry. Even though we may start off out of zeal and a devotion to evangelism, at some stage we need to get a biblical or theological foundation to sustain our practice of the ministry. Do we convey this foundation for the practice of the ministry? Or is it rather abstract knowledge? A survey carried out among Christian ministers three years after they completed their studies found that more than half of them could not see the connection between their studies and the ministry, between the classroom and reality in the field. There must be a connection between knowledge and the practice of the ministry.

Second, we need competence or skill. Church planting cannot be learned in a classroom. It is necessary to learn by doing. It is the concept of an apprenticeship. Here are three principles concerning the role of a trainer. First, the trainer chooses the trainee with whom he wants to work. It is not the trainee who offers his services. He is not the volunteer. If the trainee is imposed on the trainer by a church union or a mission, very often things do not go off smoothly. I do not want to share two years of my life with a trainee with whom I do not get on well or whose understanding of the ministry is totally different from mine. So it is for the trainer to exercise this prerogative of choice.

The second principle is personal investment. The trainee is not an assistant to whom you can leave all the work you do not want to do yourself. To be a trainer, you must release yourself of your current responsibilities in order to have enough time to invest in your trainee. The time investment is enormous. The third principle has to do with the content of the training for church planting. Once you have made your choice and agree to give your time, then you can concentrate on the content.

There are three stages in training for church planting. The first stage is observation. I tell trainees, "Don't say anything; don't do anything. Just go around with me and observe what goes on." They go with me everywhere. It was the same for the disciples; they observed Jesus at work.

The second stage is supervision, when the trainer lets the trainee take over in door-to-door evangelism, in visits with a newly converted Christian, in Bible study with a new convert, in preaching or in leading prayer meetings. The trainer supervises, assesses, to enable the trainee to make progress and improve. The trainee must be humble enough to accept being assessed. Criticism is not there to destroy but to enable improvement.

The third stage is autonomy. The trainer entrusts the trainee with responsibilities without himself being present. This enables the trainee to get used to working on his own in the ministry. If you are involved in church planting, become trainers so you can initiate others into this wonderful ministry.

Mike Evans
Mike Evans serves with Institute Biblique de Geneve, Cologny, Switzerland.

Mobilizing the Church for Area-Wide Evangelism

Greg Laurie and John Collins

A strong area-wide crusade needs agreement among the churches, crossing denominational lines. Be sure that there's a strong prayer base. People must have a sense that they need God's touch on their community. As evangelists we are there to serve the churches. Here are three keys to ensure an effective area-wide crusade: praying, equipping and discipling.

First, mobilize people to pray. Prayer should start even before the invitation comes to hold the crusade, and continue throughout the entire process. It's God's work that leads a person into the Kingdom. "The harvest is plentiful but the workers are few. Ask the Lord of the harvest, therefore, to send out workers into his harvest field" (Matthew 9:37–38, NIV). Prayer prepares the hearts of the workers, and it prepares the soil for evangelism.

Second, equip the saints for the work of the ministry: "For the perfecting of the saints, for the work of the ministry, for the edifying of the body of Christ" (Ephesians 4:12, KJV). We're involved in the work of evangelism, so we need to equip people accordingly. The heart and soul of every successful crusade event is this: Christians, praying specifically for individuals and then bringing them to that event. Most people come to an area-wide event because they are invited.

Third, prepare people to disciple others. A long time before the crusade begins, teach people how to follow up the new believers and disciple them. The church needs instruction because it must be ready for new believers.

The hardest thing about doing area-wide evangelism is getting pastors to trust you and become involved. You need to show pastors that the crusade is going to motivate their people, and that their church will grow in direct proportion to how involved their people are.

Mobilize the community; be organized; set goals. Even though you might have a broad coalition of churches coming together, a lot of the preparation can be done independently. In other words, denominations can have their distinctives yet agree on the need for evangelism. So just because we're focusing on evangelism together, we can still do a lot of our preparation within denominational lines. Churches can be fully involved with the crusade and never even visit another church, if that's a problem for them. They can do it all within the context of their own churches and still get the full benefit of a crusade.

As evangelists we want to check our motives and make sure that what we want is for the glory of God. Our goal is not to see how we can expand our ministries, but to do what we are called to do as faithfully as possible.

When we see men and women, boys and girls making commitments to Christ, then we will be able to say, "It's worth it."

Greg Laurie and John Collins

Greg Laurie is Senior Pastor of Harvest Christian Fellowship in California and speaker at Harvest Crusades. John Collins is Director of Harvest Crusades at Harvest Christian Fellowship.

Greg Laurie

Coaching Church Planters in Evangelism

Paul Johnson

If it is your mission to start churches, I challenge you to support church planters. Your mission should be to equip the planters, not start the churches. You'll have more healthy starts and more success.

Evangelism and church planting go hand in hand. Give church planters tools for evangelism and pre-evangelism, and help them start churches. As a coach, come alongside to guide, counsel, encourage and hold accountable. Coaching is important, because in my country six out of ten new churches close within five years. But with coaching, 80 percent of our new churches are thriving after five years, and most have started a daughter church.

There are strategies for supporting church planters. The first is spiritual dynamics. That simply means that rather than trying to find the latest techniques we go back to the Bible and back to prayer. Second, we recruit planters. We ask people to consider starting churches.

Third, we assess them to see if they have the gifts and skills and calling to do church planting. We have a four-day assessment that looks at 18 different behavioral characteristics to see if candidates will be good church planters. Fourth, we do training events. Fifth is coaching. Coaching guards doctrine and keeps people committed to the church-planting movement. Sixth is funding. Seventh is resourcing, where planters share ideas with one another.

Here's the first commitment we ask for in coaching. Agree with 1 Timothy 4:12, that you will not despise young leaders. We need to look for young leaders and equip them. In my church we start looking at junior high students, people who are 10, 11 and 12, to give them ministry experiences to see if God is calling them into ministry or church planting. Young leaders have new ideas, they want to do things in new ways, and they're going to make mistakes. But young leaders can make mistakes and recover a lot easier than older leaders.

A second commitment for coaches is to be available. Once a month, coaches must have a personal contact with the church planter. When coaches make that commitment, the number of church plants that succeed goes way up.

Form a coaching team and meet with that team monthly to learn, to encourage and for accountability. Then ask the team to dream about what God wants them to do in terms of seeing other churches start. In the process someone will say, "I think we should start a church here," or, "Here is a young leader. Let's work with this person for the next two years and then send him to the next village or to this other part of the urban center that we're involved in." That team will coach, help with funding and support that church plant.

I've started five churches and have a passion to start another. But I have learned that if I create coaching communities, teams that look at a given region and empower planters, many more churches get started. In that process church planting mushrooms and multiplies.

Paul Johnson

Paul Johnson is a pastor and the National Director of Church Planting for the Baptist General Conference, U.S.A.

Cooperative Evangelism

Kevin Palau

In an evangelistic event, look at the value of churches working together. First, cooperating in evangelism reaches more people than a local church can on its own. Second, an event creates a God-consciousness in the community. When the whole body of Christ is working together and the media picks up on that it's easier for Christians to share their faith.

Third is unity in the body of Christ. The best way to express unity is to work together in presenting the Gospel. Fourth, believers are equipped in personal evangelism. For many pastors, equipping their people in evangelism is the number one reason that they'll get involved. Finally, people will respond to the Gospel. There are people who have been prayed for over many years and who are ready to make a commitment to Christ.

In a cooperative event, local ownership is important. If there are 1,000 churches in the community and only 10 are inviting you, it's going to be difficult to touch a city. Meet with local pastors, and with bishops and superintendents as well. The larger the church, the more personal attention you need to give to answering its questions. Next, form an interdenominational group of pastors to promote the vision in the community. Recruit the Christian media from the beginning. When they feel involved, they're more likely to have ownership and be willing to help. Find out what venues are available. It's better to be in a slightly smaller place than you need. Empty seats are discouraging. So picking a location is important.

A large pastors' meeting gives opportunity for them to gain confidence from seeing their fellow pastors involved. A group dynamic happens. Have Christian business people involved for the doors they can open and the influence they have in the community.

It's important for pastors to understand that an evangelistic event is a four-phase process. The first step is prayer. Don't go to a place unless people have been praying to see God work in their area. Encourage people to pray specifically for their friends and family members.

Second is the preparation itself. Once you've got dates and a location, help each church present the event to their people. Ask every local church to give 10 or 15 minutes on a Sunday morning for a crusade presentation. We have a five-minute video that shows the sights and sounds of an event to give people a sense of what's coming up. Have a launching rally challenging believers to get involved in evangelism. The majority of people don't have a burning passion for reaching out with the Gospel. We have to give them that passion. Train believers in personal evangelism and discipleship.

Third is proclamation. The more an event is culturally sensitive, one that people will want to bring their friends to, the better.

Fourth is preservation. Emphasize the discipleship of new believers. Since 80 percent of the people who make a commitment were brought by a friend, we take down information not just about a new believer but also about that friend who got them to the meeting in the first place. That relationship can be included in the discipleship process. Have material to give new believers—a Scripture portion, Bible study materials. Unless you have a follow-up plan, it's going to be difficult for local pastors to give enthusiastic support.

Kevin Palau

Kevin Palau is Executive Vice-President of the Luis Palau Evangelistic Association, Portland, Oregon, U.S.A.

Ways to Stimulate Evangelism in Denominations

Robert Reccord and John Yarbrough

How can denominations facilitate evangelism? The denomination has to be a servant. The denomination asks the churches, "What is your greatest need, and what can we do to meet that need?" It's in evangelism that the denomination will likely meet the greatest need of the church. If we're going to help churches, we must have a strategy that is uncompromisingly biblical and culturally knowledgeable. It must be contextually adapted, simply transferable and congregationally applicable.

First, we must be uncompromisingly biblical. People don't care about church programs. But they are desperate to hear about a life-changing person whose name is Jesus Christ. In Acts 2, it says the early Church adhered to the apostles' doctrine. They stuck to it like glue. Their message was nothing more, nothing less, than the Word of God. That message brought people to Jesus Christ. We have to get back to a biblical message centered on the absolute exclusivity of Jesus Christ as the one and only Savior.

Five biblical points have to be in the Gospel. First, the message must include the nature, the incarnation and the mission of Jesus Christ. Second, the sinfulness of the individual must be clearly pointed out. There is a sinful nature that separates us from God. Third is the death and the resurrection of Jesus Christ. Fourth is repentance and faith. The call of the Gospel is a call to repentance, a call to change. Fifth is eternal destiny. Salvation gives a person a relationship with Jesus Christ in the present and also leads to eternal life. Rejection or passive indifference to Christ's offer of salvation will lead to eternal separation from God.

Next, we must be culturally knowledgeable. The denomination must understand church culture and secular culture. George Barna's studies show that churches are filled with people who are customizing their own faith. Culture is affecting the church more than the church is affecting the culture. Faith has been repositioned as a commodity to consume.

In addition, it is important that we understand the changes demographically that are happening in the culture. In the West, the future is in multicultural ministries. We must understand the philosophical issues of the culture as well. The church serves in a world that says there are no absolutes. Rather, the world says that all truth is relative and determined experientially. It says that there is no divine and ultimate purpose in living. The focus is on the present, not on preparing for the future. There is no omnipotent, omniscient God. Each of us is our own god. Also, we're told that every religious worldview and value system is equally valid.

That's the sociological, cultural world that the church must face. Culture is the container. We put the message in whatever container the culture gives us. We help the church in evangelizing and reaching its community in its context, whatever that context may be.

Next, it is simply transferable. The days of complicated processes and involved procedures are over. Don't make the Gospel more complicated than God does. People are not impressed with our great theological discourses. Keep it simple.

Finally, it is congregationally applicable and church-driven. Evangelism must be tied to the local church.

Robert Reccord and John Yarbrough
Robert Reccord is president of the North American Mission Board of Southern Baptist Life. John Yarbrough is vice-president of evangelism of the Southern Baptist Convention, Atlanta, Georgia, U.S.A.

Robert Reccord

Developing a Heart for Lost People in an Apathetic Church

David Schmidt

What is apathy? When I think of the word apathy, I think of words like unconcerned, not caring, hard-hearted. It is seeing people with our eyes but not with our hearts. It's not caring about lost people. As God's people, we are to be living invitations for lost people to come to Christ.

Matthew 9:36 says, "And seeing the multitudes, He felt compassion for them, because they were distressed and downcast like sheep without a shepherd" (NASB). Today Jesus sees the world exactly the same way. The question we must wrestle with is, how do we see as God wants us to see, not with just our eyes but with our hearts?

Why don't believers have compassion for lost people as Jesus did? In many of our churches we have made it normal to be a Christian follower and not be salt and light in a needy world. People say, "I don't have nonbelieving friends." Or we let sin exist in the lives and hearts of believers without challenging it. When I let sin exist in my life, then my heart gets cold to the voice of God. Or we do not provide consistent training to believers on how to share their faith.

In many of our churches we don't give Christians permission to be in relationships with unbelievers. We send this message: "Be pure and sanctified. Separate yourself from the world." But we need to be with lost people. Jesus spent time with lost people. Keep yourself pure from their ways and their habits, but go be with them. Evangelism is a love-driven process. People hurt; they're in pain. We need to go love them.

Another reason is that often we don't release our grip on old methodologies and ways of doing evangelism. When the same words and phrases are used over and over again, people's ears slowly close. They don't hear anymore. Ask yourself, what is the communication method most used in my culture to get the message across?

Believing that people are lost is not enough. We must value lost people. I must have something that guides me from my belief system to my behavior. Here are seven strategic steps to turn apathetic hearts into hearts that care for lost people.

The first step is to ask the Lord for wisdom. James 1:5 says, "If any of you lacks wisdom, he should ask God"—for wisdom—"who gives generously to all" (NIV).

The second step is to teach the truth about evangelism in new ways. It is in new voices and in new ways that God speaks. Stop the old pattern. If it's not working, stop.

Step three is to help people's hearts to soften toward lost people. Expose them to the testimonies of once-lost people who have come to Christ; tell how lives have been changed by Christ.

Step four is to be proactively training people in evangelism.

Step five, give people opportunity to practice caring for lost people. Create an environment where we can bring lost friends to church with us to hear the Gospel. Christians are crying out to their churches saying, "Help me. I cannot do this alone."

Step six, give people opportunities to be with lost people. Give them the time to do it, and create special events. Make caring about lost people a priority.

Step seven is always to keep the needs of lost people in front of believers.

In applying these seven principles, we can do as Jesus did. Seeing the multitudes, He felt compassion for them. Now it's up to us.

David Schmidt

David Schmidt is President of David Schmidt and Associates, Wheaton, Illinois, U.S.A.

Principles of the Seeker-Sensitive Church

David Schmidt

What makes seeker-sensitive churches different? How do these churches function? What are the biblical, internationally applicable principles that make these churches work?

Seeker-sensitive churches are known for their evangelistic impact. Lost people are the primary focal point of the ministries of that church. It is about taking any person who does not know Jesus Christ and watching God bring that person into full devotion to Christ. Partnership is the key because believers build the bridges to lost people.

In many places people are saying, "My church is not friendly to my unchurched friends. Not because people will not speak to them but because they say, 'I don't understand your language. It's too religious. It's too different. Your church service moves right by me; I do not understand it.'" In a postmodern world, people need the Gospel presented through music and drama, and then hear a message presented plainly to them in terms they can relate to. In the seeker-sensitive model, the local church comes alongside the believer and says, "We'll help you do evangelism by providing you with ministries to people with addictions, troubled marriages, whatever is a relevant ministry."

Once they come to Christ, how do they transition into worship? The worship is not traditional or liturgical. It's contemporary worship. But now the focal point is not the lost person. It is helping the believer give worship to God.

Here are nine principles that God works through in seeker-sensitive churches. First, seeker-sensitive churches place ministry to lost people at the top of their priority list. Second, seeker-sensitive churches work hard to be biblically sound and culturally relevant. Third, in seeker-sensitive churches there is a very clear path from being lost to being found and to growing in Christ. It's not haphazard. It is a well-thought-out strategy.

Fourth, a seeker-sensitive church says it's important to have friends who are lost and then gives an opportunity to bring those friends to church where they hear the Gospel.

Fifth, seeker-sensitive churches value lost people. That's expressed in evangelism training, not just once in a while but regularly. Sixth, seeker-sensitive churches deploy the spiritual gifts that God has given His Church. When God releases all of the gifts in a church, that church comes to life. When seekers come into the church, they sense the work of the Holy Spirit expressed in many different ways.

Seventh, seeker-sensitive churches pursue excellence because it honors God and reflects His character. To be excellent is to represent Jesus Christ in all of His glory and grace. Eighth, seeker-sensitive churches organize for the results they seek. The goal is making the Gospel biblically and culturally relevant to lost people. Beginning with that goal, we work back from there asking, "How do we do that?" We organize for the results we seek. Ninth, seeker-sensitive churches realize that to authentically care for a crowd of lost people, we must begin by caring for one. In our family, God opened our eyes to the family next door to us. Then God opened our eyes to others.

Seeker-sensitive churches are willing to give up the old solutions and grasp new ways of doing church, new ways of doing evangelism.

David Schmidt
David Schmidt is President of David Schmidt and Associates and lives in Wheaton, Illinois, U.S.A.

The Church Engaging the World

Gerry Seale

We use the word *church* in various ways. I'm using it in terms of the covenant community, the people of God. In church history, the evangelical church was very involved in the fight against slavery and child labor and in the development of hospitals. But somewhere along the line, we seem to have backed off and reversed. Yet the church does not operate in a vacuum. The church operates in the world.

One key area of involvement in society is preservation. Jesus said, "[You] are the salt of the earth" (Matthew 5:13, KJV). To preserve the world, the salt must come into contact with the world.

What institutions preserve life? One is the family. The church has a vested interest in the preservation of the family. Another institution that preserves life is the government. If we withdraw from government and ungodly men and women take over the government, do we have a right to complain? Shouldn't some of our people be taking an interest in the governments of our countries?

Another key area is the institution of work. We should have an interest in the preservation of the society in which we work, whether human resources, financial resources or technological resources. We should bring a Christian perspective to workers' unions and the social agencies.

Another area is the ecology. All things were made by Him, for Him, through Him, and in Him all things consist (see Colossians 1:17). Surely we have a vested interest in the preservation of God's creation. Another area is freedom. If we take away somebody's freedom today, one of these days somebody's going to take away our freedom to proclaim what we believe.

When we evangelize and change individuals, we are changing the society in which we operate. To engage society redemptively, we have to participate in the society. As the Gospel penetrates society and individuals are transformed, we should see a reduction in poverty. There should be social peace. When I'm the first person in my family to make a commitment to Christ, I'm the first peacemaker in my family. There should be justice. As a nation is discipled, we should have growing national righteousness.

Are we engaging the society in which we live? Let us be the ones to start; then, others will follow.

Gerry Seale
Gerry Seale is general secretary of the Evangelical Association of the Caribbean, Bridgetown, Barbados.

Church-Based Servant Evangelism

Steve Sjogren

Servant evangelism is a simple idea of using acts of generosity and kindness to bring people toward Christ. There are many ways of showing love to people, from free car washes to putting money in expired parking meters to serving cool drinks on hot days to cleaning toilets. It can be anything from cleaning up trash on the side of the road to giving away flower seeds to collecting food door-to-door from the rich and giving it to the poor. In one of the small churches in Kenya, they're giving away "Bananas for Jesus." In another church they have a bicycle clinic. They fix bicycles, and people want to hear about Christ. It is whatever makes people ask, "Why are you doing this?"

Servant evangelism is something that the average Christian can do. Small things done with great love will change the world. Here are four simple principles of servant evangelism:

First, any of us can do these things. Some people say, "But isn't what you're talking about just being nice to people?" No, not really. We're talking about being nice by the power of the Holy Spirit. There's a big difference. By the power of the Holy Spirit, we are moved to show the kindness of Christ so that people will come to faith in Christ.

Second, getting to know God happens through a process. It isn't so much "right-on-the-spot" leading people to Christ. We're nudging people, escorting them along the way toward Christ. We're helping them go from where they are toward being receptive to Christ. Deeds of love shown, plus answering people's questions, plus an adequate amount of time bring people along to faith in Christ. It's sowing and watering.

Third, people will change as we love them profoundly. As we go out and do these things, there is an implied invitation to come into our group, whether it's a small group or our church. Are people allowed to come into our meetings and be a part of our community, at the edge at least, and not yet believe? Are not-yet believers allowed to come in and explore the possibility of coming to Christ? We go out and invite people to come to church by loving them in thousands of ways. When we do these things, the numbers begin to add up pretty quickly.

We love them into change. It's like the prodigal son story. The son began to realize, "You know, I think my father will forgive and accept me if I go back and throw myself at his mercy" (see Luke 15:11–32).

Fourth, the best time to show God's kindness is now. Everything mentioned in Matthew 25 can be done if we decide right here, right now, "Let's just do it."

There is always the danger of too much serving and not enough evangelism.

But also, there can be too much evangelism and not enough serving. We go from the heart to the head. In a post-modern world, we've got to go to people at a heart-to-heart level. Once we've gained entrance into their lives, we have the credibility to convey the Gospel at a head-to-head level. It's not a complicated thing.

Steve Sjogren

Steve Sjogren is Senior Pastor of Vineyard Community Church, Cincinnati, Ohio, U.S.A.

Evangelism, Follow-Up and Training in the Local Church

Donald Tabb

We proclaim Christ. We teach everyone we can all that we know about Him so that we may bring every person to maturity in Christ. I want to impress you with the process of winning a hearing, presenting the facts, giving the invitation, leading in prayer, and confirming the commitment using the Word of God—bringing people into a relationship with Jesus Christ and then discipling them, training them and ejecting them into their world. Unless you have a personal commitment to evangelism, you will never establish an evangelistic and discipling ministry in your church. We use A, B, C, D and E. "A" is for aggressive evangelism. "B" is Bible teaching. "C" is conserving the fruits of evangelism. "D" is discipling, and "E" is ejecting disciples.

First is aggressive evangelism. Does that mean that I wham you over the head and drag you senseless to the feet of Jesus? No, it's not that kind of aggressive. It's not being aggressive toward others but rather being aggressive with myself. Before we can have aggressive evangelism and discipleship in our churches, we must develop a spirit of aggressive evangelism in our own hearts.

Second, be committed to Bible teaching. Don't teach about the Bible; teach the Bible. To teach the Word, you have to have the Word. There are five ways to get the Word. You hear it, you read it, you study it, you memorize it and you meditate upon it. Then when God brings you to the right person at the right time, you have the right words to say.

Third, conserve the fruits of evangelism. We do that in three ways. One is classes. Find one or two who can teach the Bible and let them teach others. Second, develop small groups. The early church was a series of small groups that met from house to house. In every small group in our church, there must be Bible intake, prayer and fellowship. And we encourage people to bring one new person or new couple every time if possible. In other words, we're thinking evangelism. A warm, friendly, accepting atmosphere is much easier to come into than a large church service that might intimidate at first.

Number four, discipling. An important part of conserving the fruit of evangelism is to look out for those who meet with you one-on-one. The apostle Paul talked about sitting at the feet of Gamaliel, one-on-one training. Jesus "ordained twelve, that they should be with him, and that he might send them forth to preach" (Mark 3:14, KJV). The key phrase is "with him." Find three or four who will meet with you, where you can teach them the principles of Bible study, memorizing God's Word, how to share their faith, how to pray, how to evangelize. Hands-on training. Then they, in turn, do the same. This is infectious.

Fifth, you eject. Send them out. Don't worry about building a kingdom. Encourage them to go. If you look at the New Testament, that's the predominant word—*go*. "As my Father hath sent me, even so send I you" (John 20:21, KJV). "Go into all the world" (Mark 16:15, KJV). Don't hang on to control. Send them; start other churches.

You must decide that you're going to be an aggressive evangelist, a Bible teacher, that you're going to conserve the fruit of evangelism, you are going to disciple the core group, and you are going to eject them; you're going to move them out.

Donald Tabb
Donald Tabb is Senior Pastor of the Chapel on the Campus, Baton Rouge, Louisiana, U.S.A.

Helping Build Purpose-Driven Churches

Rick Warren

We often ask the wrong question: What will make my church grow? That's the wrong question. The right question is, what is keeping us from growing?

All living things grow. If something isn't growing, it's dying. The Church is a living organism. The Church is a body, not a business. It is an organism, not an organization. So it is natural for the Church to grow.

This is not about being a big church. There is no correlation between the size and strength of a church. A church can be big and strong, or it can be big and flabby. A church can be small and strong, or it can be small and wimpy. Big is not necessarily better. Small is not necessarily better. The issue is church health, not church growth. When churches are healthy, they reproduce.

To be a purpose-driven church, you first have to define your purpose: A common purpose builds morale and reduces conflict. The Bible says, "Where there is no vision, the people perish" (Proverbs 29:18, KJV).

Second, having a purpose reduces frustration. You reduce a lot of problems when you know where you're going. The Bible says, "A man of that kind . . . is double-minded, and never can keep a steady course" (James 1:7–8, NEB).

Third, clear purpose keeps priorities straight. In our church we focus on five priorities: worship, evangelism, fellowship, discipleship and ministry.

Fourth is cooperation. People want to join the church that knows where it's going. The people told Ezra, "Tell us how to proceed in setting things straight, and we will fully cooperate" (Ezra 10:4, TLB).

Fifth, purpose assists evaluation. "Examine yourselves to see whether you are in the faith; test yourselves" (2 Corinthians 13:5, NIV). You know your ministry is on track by identifying the purposes of God for your church.

Lead your members in a study of the biblical passages about the Church. Study Christ's ministry. Whatever Jesus did in the flesh, He wants continued in the Church today. The Church is called a body, a bride, an army, a flock of sheep and a community. There are implications for every one of these that help us know the purposes. Study the New Testament churches. The church at Jerusalem was very different from the church at Antioch. The church in Antioch was different from the church at Corinth, but they had the same purposes. Study the commands of Christ. What did Jesus command us to do? As you study, ask two questions: What are we to be? What are we to do?

Here are characteristics of a good purpose statement: Is it biblical? Is it specific? Is it transferable? It is memorable? The shorter the better. Is it measurable?

There are five biblical purposes for the Church—love God with all your heart, love your neighbor as yourself, make disciples, baptize them, teach them. The first church practiced these five purposes.

The Church exists to celebrate God's presence, to communicate God's Word, to incorporate God's family, to educate God's people, to demonstrate God's love. So we bring people in, we build them up, we train them for ministry, and we send them out. Here's the purpose statement of Saddleback Valley Community Church: "A great commitment to the Great Commandment and the Great Commission will grow a great church."

Rick Warren

Rick Warren is Senior Pastor of Saddleback Valley Community Church, Lake Forest, California, U.S.A.

Evangelism and Church Planting

Avery Willis and David Garrison

God is doing something amazing in the world today. It's called the church-planting movement. One church becomes two, and two churches become four, and they multiply across a people group.

There are five basic principles or foundational beliefs about church planting. First, God loves all people and wants them to be saved. Second, wherever Jesus Christ is lifted up and proclaimed in a bold, positive, culturally relevant witness, people will be saved. Third, where people are being saved, born again by the Holy Spirit, they will be drawn together into a fellowship, a New Testament church. Fourth, God will provide the leaders needed to minister within that body. Fifth, it is the very nature of a church, as any living organism, to grow and multiply. If it does not grow and multiply, we've got to ask ourselves, "Is it a living organism?"

We can't fulfill the Great Commission by just starting a church here and there. The world population is exploding. In many countries churches are not multiplying as rapidly as the population. A church-planting movement is a rapid and exponential increase of indigenous churches planting churches within a given people group or population segment. Incremental increase says, "We've got five churches; we'll add one church this year." Exponential says, "We've got two churches; they need to multiply and form four churches. Four churches need to become sixteen churches." That's exponential increase, not incremental increase.

What kind of churches? Indigenous churches. These churches are able to reproduce themselves, reaching out to an entire people group or population segment. If a church is depending on foreign resources, it cannot multiply. A church may have had help at first, but if it feels that it must have that same help to start another church, it'll never have multiplication. This movement must generate its own pastors and teachers. Training can't wait for leaders to finish years of theological training. Leadership training is on the job. There will be a time when they need seminary-trained leaders to make sure they have their theology correct, but not in this beginning stage.

One obstacle to church planting is imposing extra-biblical requirements for churches, such as needing a building or a seminary-trained pastor or so many members. These are all good things, but not prerequisites to being a church. A second obstacle is a loss of cultural identity. If people must change their cultural identity in order to become believers, there won't be a church-planting movement among that people.

Another obstacle is poor examples of Christianity where people in churches do not really believe the Word of God or do not have good ethical lives. If the local church doesn't love the lost or there's a sin problem in the church, it's very difficult to work through that church to launch a church-planting movement. Another obstacle is subsidies that create dependence. Outside money has to support a missionary coming in cross-culturally. But if that support continues, the church never becomes indigenous. The key is creating dependence on God, not on others.

Avery Willis   David Garrison

Avery Willis and David Garrison
Avery Willis is Senior Vice-President for Overseas Operations for the Southern Baptist International Mission Board. David Garrison is Associate Vice-President for Strategy Coordination for Southern Baptist Missionaries, Southern Baptist Convention, Richmond, Virginia, U.S.A.

The Training and Development of Evangelists

Werner Burklin

An evangelist has to exemplify the virtues of Christ and then, with passion, proclaim the life-changing Gospel. But even though someone may have the calling and the gift to be an evangelist, he or she needs to develop this gift. What are some basic issues that need to be addressed in training or *developing the gifts* of an evangelist?

First is doctrinal fidelity (see 2 Timothy 2:15–17). The world is inundated with false doctrines. Even evangelical churches are not spared. Therefore, we evangelists must discipline ourselves to fill our minds and mouths with biblical theology. Only then will we stay true to the basic doctrines of the Bible. Second is financial integrity (see Acts 5:1–11). The Christian leader, whether pastor or evangelist, must set the example for honesty. Ananias and Sapphira, filled with greed, set a disastrous example. Financial integrity in our personal lives sets the tone for financial integrity in our evangelistic outreaches. Nothing can turn off people faster than the mishandling of funds.

Third is sexual morality (see 1 Corinthians 5:1–5). Throughout the centuries this God-given drive has been misused. The evangelist needs to be vigilant to keep sexually pure. God has given the power of the Holy Spirit to help us overcome every kind of sin. As evangelists live an exemplary life, they can challenge their listeners to do the same.

Fourth is spiritual humility (see Philippians 2:1–8). Christ is the greatest example of true humility. To conquer the world with its sin, He became a servant. The evangelists are working in the name of Jesus. Therefore, they have to adopt His Spirit. Humility is the virtue that all can learn by serving people. Fifth is biblical loyalty. The evangelists have to be loyal to their team or co-workers and to the churches that call them to evangelize. But foremost, they have to be loyal to their calling, and thus be loyal to their Lord.

What are some of the *responsibilities* of an evangelist? First is the privilege of proclaiming. Some preachers are eloquent, some are profound, and some are dazzling. They are not the ones who touch lives. The ones who walk with Jesus do. Does the evangelist live out what he or she proclaims? Charles Haddon Spurgeon said, "Most of us Christians are experts, but not examples."

Second is vigilance. The word *vigilance* makes us think of prayer. Jesus taught us to pray at all times. Hudson Taylor said, "When you work, you work; but when you pray, God works." An evangelist has to learn the art of praying and develop the desire to pray. Third is the secret of spiritual power. The person who wielded more power than anyone else in history was Jesus. As He suffered in love, He demonstrated power. As the evangelist proclaims the Good News with godly power, listeners will sense his or her walk with God and will respond to God's message.

Learning is a lifelong endeavor. To enhance preaching skills, evangelists should learn from each other, seek out opportunities to attend workshops or seminars on evangelism, read biographies of evangelists, listen to evangelistic messages on radio or audiotape and read evangelistic sermons in books and magazines.

Werner Burklin

Werner Burklin is founder and president of China Partner, Inc. He lives in Boca Raton, Florida, U.S.A.

Partnerships in Evangelism

Phill Butler and Brian O'Connell

Partnership can be extremely relevant to your ministry. There are many different kinds of partnerships. It may be a church in Australia linked with a church in Papua New Guinea. It may be a local church that connects with some mission agency. It may be mission agencies working together. Partnerships respond to world conditions, provide increased effectiveness, reflect community and bring hope.

There is a part of the world where there's an established church and a part of the world where there's an emerging church. But there is a segment of the world, nearly 35 to 38 percent, about two billion people, who have never had a chance to say yes to Christ.

How do we mobilize partnership resources out of the first two segments into the third segment? Increasingly our funding partners, who are giving us the prayer, financial and technical resources to do our work, are requiring that we avoid duplication and increase effectiveness. People are tired of seeing Kingdom money wasted because of private agendas. When we do not cooperate, the work of Christ does not move forward in an effective way.

One reason we have seen such little progress in Islamic, Hindu and Buddhist areas of the world is that those cultures are community-based cultures. Historically, the missionary movement has been a highly individualistic approach, which is totally foreign to the local culture. When God's people work together in community, in partnership, the credibility or believability of the message goes up.

Hope is another reason why partnerships are so relevant. Imagine what it's like for evangelists and others who have worked alone to interact, to plan and pray with other people who are committed to the same vision. It brings them hope!

The old way was good people doing good things, trying to establish the church but with no mechanism or forum for them to meet, talk, pray, plan and work together. Strategic evangelism partnerships look at the whole picture and incorporate the body of Christ. It is not just traditional church planters or preaching evangelists. It includes people who are working in environmental issues or leadership development or setting up businesses to support the emerging national church. So it's strategic in its view and in its participation. It is evangelism, because the focus is on evangelism and the establishment of the church. And it is partnership, because that's the methodology.

In strategic evangelism partnerships, the ministries retain their own identities. They do not become part of some new super organization. They operate by consensus rather than by constitution. It's a structure that's open, and it's a process. First, they explore relationships to see whether a partnership can occur. Second is the launch phase, when a partnership actually gets formed. Third, there's the operation stages, where a partnership accomplishes something together.

Partnerships have never just spontaneously ignited. There has to be a facilitator who has the twin vision of purpose and process. An evangelist is a key catalyst for partnership because evangelists need other ministries in order to be effective. But the objective must be clear to all the partners. It is not some private agenda. It is something that God wants done that is impossible to do individually or separately. Every participating ministry must see the value of that objective to its own ministry. Everyone must have ownership of the vision.

Phill Butler   **Brian O'Connell**

Phill Butler and Brian O'Connell
Phill Butler and Brian O'Connell serve with Interdev, Seattle, Washington, U.S.A.

How to Begin an Effective Evangelistic Preaching Ministry

James Davis

Evangelism is a command for every believer to be involved in soul winning. But the evangelist is God's unique gift to the Church.

There are five steps to beginning a full-time evangelistic ministry. Step number one is to study the conditions. Here are three principles for the study of conditions. Principle number one: The potential is in the soil, the person's heart. Number two: God gives the results. You don't cause the seed to grow. God causes the seed to grow. Number three: The power is in the Gospel. Sow the Gospel seed knowing that there could be a 30-, 60- or 100-fold harvest.

Step number two is to secure your call. Nail it down. Sometimes the rain is going to fall and sometimes the sun is going to shine. If you don't secure your call, there may come a day when you've got more bills than you have money, when seemingly your prayers are not getting higher than the light bulbs, when the automobile will break down, or there will not be enough food to take care of the family. Know that God has called you to be an evangelist.

An evangelistic calling is providential. Moses was called to lead the Israelites out of Egyptian bondage. Joshua was called to lead the people into Canaan. Paul was called to preach the Gospel to the Gentiles. God has a divine purpose for your life. When God calls you to a task, He gives you the gifts for that task. A gift is so natural that sometimes we overlook it. The evangelistic calling is powerful. There is a sense of creativity and excitement when people know that they are fulfilling what God wants them to do. The evangelistic call is perplexing. Sometimes it takes years for us to become comfortable with who we are and what God has called us to do. Keep on keeping on. Lean on God's grace in times of difficulty.

Step number three is to serve the church. To serve the church we need trust, transparency and time. People will give us only as much rope as they can trust us with. The higher the trust the more doors will open. It takes time for this to become a reality. Be transparent. There is a difference between integrity and image. Image is public; integrity is private. If a person doesn't take care of the integrity, eventually the image will erode as well.

It takes time to build an effective ministry. Imagine a farmer procrastinating throughout the spring and summer, then cramming the seed into the ground in early fall and expecting there to be a harvest. Imagine an evangelist wasting time, week after week, and expecting to have bountiful results. Work, dig and sow and water and there will come a harvest.

Step number four is to select your commitments. No one else can write our priorities for us. There are at least five general priorities: One is our faith in God. Two is our family. Three is our fitness; strive to stay healthy. Four is finances. Five is the future. Know where you're going. Write down the word *goals*. G-O-A-L-S. G stands for gather the facts. O, organize a plan. A, act on the plan. L, look back and review. S, select new commitments.

Step number five: Always strive to communicate. When we preach the Word of God, people want to know how that relates to today. People are asking, "So what? How does that get me through Monday?" If we're not answering these questions, they'll be long gone.

There's a difference between substance and style. Some people have substance but no style, and some people have style with no substance. Some people hit the head but not the heart. Other people hit the heart but not the head. God wants to hit the head *and* the heart.

James Davis

Dr. James Davis is National Evangelists' Representative for the Assemblies of God, Springfield, Missouri, U.S.A.

Leadership Development for Evangelists

Leighton Ford

In times like these, what kind of leadership do we need? Traditional leadership says, "Here's where we're going. You follow me. Help me to work. Here's what we've always done." We need transforming leadership that says, "We must do this together. What new things is God doing in our world that we need to be part of? Let me help you to do the work that God has called you to." Transforming leaders get attention through vision, bring meaning through communication, earn trust because people know where they're headed and share leadership through empowering others.

Think of Jesus as the transforming leader. Learn to lead as Jesus did. What are the leadership marks of Jesus? First, transforming leadership grows from a relationship with the Father as He had it—"My beloved Son" (Matthew 3:17, KJV). How strongly do you know that you are a beloved son or daughter of God?

Second, the transforming leader sees in fresh, new ways. What does it mean to be a visionary leader? The focus of Jesus' vision was the eternal in the everyday. Looking into the hearts of people, He saw their potential for the Kingdom of God. What is your vision? What do you see? What is God's call as far as you know it? Look at the world prayerfully until you are attracted to something. Then say, "Maybe that's what God wants me to do." You might see somebody else ministering and say, "I think maybe that's what God wants." Pray about it. Observe, reflect and act. Begin doing something in ministry and see if God confirms your vision. May God help us to see and raise up others who can see.

Third is the leader as storyteller. Transforming leadership is passed on through transforming stories. Jesus was a storyteller. He taught many things by parables. If we follow Jesus, we're going to need to be storytellers. In a world that has lost its story, this is so very important. Storytelling is powerful in evangelism. When you're trying to win someone to Christ, listen to that person's story. See where God is working in that person's life. Then tell your story of meeting Jesus, particularly if there's some point that meets his or her life. Then point from that to His story, the story of Jesus. Storytelling is important to help developing leaders remember the past, see the present and envision the future.

Jesus chose Peter, saying, "God wants you to serve Him. I'm enlisting you to be close to Me and to send you out to do what I have shown you." Peter was close to Jesus. He could watch Him and see when He was hungry or tired, when He prayed and when He struggled with people. Jesus rebuked Peter, but also motivated him to keep going even after he'd failed. Who has done that for you?

Who was the first person to call you to serve Christ, saying, "I think God could use you?" Are you seeing and calling people, entrusting people, letting them get close to you? Whom do you motivate to keep going?

If you want to make an impact on the world, invest in people. May God make us leaders like Jesus. And may He help us, as leaders, to lead people to Jesus.

Leighton Ford
Leighton Ford is President of Leighton Ford Ministries, Charlotte, North Carolina, U.S.A.

Effective Evangelistic Campaigns

John Guest

Let's define a successful evangelistic campaign. By "successful," we're talking about a number of things. First, we're talking about working with a gathering of the Christian community who want to preach the Gospel. Second, we have unbelievers present. It's not enough just to get the church crowd in and have a great praise gathering. Third, a successful campaign includes reaching young people. To have a successful campaign, you've got to have people praying, the Gospel preached, decisions called for publicly, and local follow-up. Those are givens in any successful campaign.

Let me mention two huge things: leadership and money. You will never have a successful evangelistic campaign without local leadership, gifted leadership that will take the responsibility to put it together. Nothing moves without leadership. Second, you've got to have money. Nothing moves without financial resources.

When Jesus began His ministry, He built a team. You must build a team. Don't just think, "What can I do by myself?" Think, "Whom can I get to do this with me?" We are serving the local church. It will be the church that will nourish and follow up those who've made commitments to Christ.

First, you need a team to prepare the way, working a year or two ahead of time. Second, you need a team to manage the campaign itself while you are there. Third, you need to team-tackle a community and bring other people in with you, not just your own organization. Involve other ministries in a community with you. You alone can't be to that community all that it needs evangelistically. Fourth, you need an office/support team. This is a group of people with whom you can pray, share your heart, who will hold you accountable and will work with you.

In an evangelistic campaign there is the home setting. I've gone into people's homes, they've invited in their friends, and I've presented the Gospel. There is individual church evangelism, a campaign for one church. But the essentials of a campaign are still the same. You can get denominations together by region for evangelism. That is, you can have Baptists or Pentecostals or Presbyterians or Lutherans working together to have a region-wide campaign. You can have a city-wide campaign. City-wide campaigns are very difficult because many pastors, sad to say, are skeptical of evangelists; it's tough to mobilize a city.

To be an authentic evangelist you need to be doing evangelism all the time. You have to be authentic with individuals if you're going to be authentic in front of a crowd. See yourself doing the work of an evangelist all the time, on foot, wherever you go.

John Guest

Rev. John Guest is an evangelist and the Senior Pastor of Christ Church at Grove Farm in Sewickley, Pennsylvania, U.S.A.

Raising Funds for Evangelism in Your Own Regions

Panel of Ministry Leaders

Here are some principles about trusting God for support. First, "Will God bless if I ask?" "Jabez cried out to . . . God . . . , 'Oh, that you would bless me and enlarge my territory!' . . . And God granted his request" (1 Chronicles 4:10, NIV). Pull up the tent pegs, stretch out the tent; ask God to bless and enlarge your ministry.

Second, "Is God looking for someone to bless?" 2 Chronicles 16:9 makes this statement, "The eyes of the LORD range throughout the earth." He wants "to strengthen those whose hearts are fully committed to him" (NIV). God is looking for people who are fully trusting Him.

Third, "Does the Lord have a plan for me?" Jeremiah 29:11 says, "'I know the plans I have for you,' declares the LORD, 'plans to prosper you and not to harm you, plans to give you hope and a future'" (NIV). God has a plan for you. And not just "a" plan; the word is plural, it's "plans." God is working them out in your life to do them in His time and in His place.

Fourth, "Where is the place of my blessing?" 1 Kings 17 (see verses 1–4) relates this story. Elijah, prophesying in Ahab's day, realizes he's going to be killed. He runs away, but he has no place to go. God has a plan and a place for you just as He did for Elijah. We have to find out where "there" is. It's where God has told you to go. You may not be comfortable there. It may not be the place you want to be. But it's where God will meet your need.

Fifth, "Is my need going to be met?" Isaiah 65:24 says, "Before they call I will answer" (NIV). God wants to meet every need. Maybe not in the amount that you thought, or in the place you thought, or in the way you thought. But He has what you need.

Sixth, "Can I really trust God?" Hebrews 11:1 says, "Faith is being sure of what we hope for and certain of what we do not see" (NIV). There is one resource only. It is not a North American church or a rich friend. It is God who meets your need. If you look in any other direction, your support will dwindle away. Philippians 4:19 says, "My God will meet all your needs according to his glorious riches in Christ Jesus" (NIV). Every gift comes from God who is with us in the place He has sent us.

Here are some ways to trust God for your needs. Number one, your ministry is the overflow of your life with God. Pay attention to your heart. If you do not have a relationship with God, you will have activity, but not ministry. Number two is to determine God's will for you. There are people in ministry who are doing what they want to do, but it's not what God is asking them to do. Pray and search the Scriptures until you are sure you clearly understand what God is directing you to do.

Number three is to determine prayerfully what is needed. Form a budget. How many people will this take, what kind of materials and equipment? Will you need a building? Consider a dream budget. If you could do everything you believe necessary for this ministry, what would you include? Put on paper what it would cost. Then ask God, "Do you want to do all of this?"

Number four is to ask God, "What is my part in meeting this need?" And be willing to do what God says. Number five is to pray, "Lord, what's *your* part in meeting this need?" God will lead each of us differently. He will ask some of you to present your vision to people and ask them to give money. There is enough money in every country to evangelize that country if we reach the right people. God will ask others to pray without telling anybody about their needs. Let God decide what our part is to be and what His part is to be.

Organizing a Local Prison Ministry

David Stillman

During his student days at Oxford University, John Wesley always made time to minister to those who were incarcerated in prison. As a result of the evangelical awakening in Britain in the 1730s, there was both a return to biblical preaching and a new awareness of social responsibility toward people in need. As a result, John Howard committed himself to visiting prisons. He was instrumental in getting through the British parliament two penal reform acts that improved the sanitary conditions and health care of people in prison.

A whole variety of evangelistic activities makes it easy to have contact with inmates in prison: discussions, chapel services, films, materials they can read, teaching videos, literacy classes. From these initial contacts there will be those who show interest in the Gospel or come to faith. So there is a second level of activities, such as providing Bible study courses, Christian books and Bibles in a translation or modern paraphrase that they can understand. Make sure that the material is basic for people who know nothing about the Bible.

A lot of activities are sowing activities. They're very broad. But eventually many of the people who come to the Lord do so through personal correspondence, counseling, one-on-one ministry and discussion. You don't get to this point if you don't first make the contact. Prisoners may not take the Gospel from us the first time, but they need to know that we're for real and that we love them. It's not enough to simply talk about the love of God to people in prison. We have got to *be* the love of God for them.

Another level of activity is meeting practical needs, things such as food parcels, clothing, toiletries, writing paper and postage stamps. In many countries if you're going to build relationships in prison and have any credibility as a minister of the Gospel, you need to meet some of these important practical needs.

Family members may also have needs. If the husband is the only source of income for the family and he is incarcerated, the family will have no means of support. That's an area where we can mobilize other members of the church. Not everybody in the church can go into the prisons, but they can minister to inmates' families outside the prison.

When somebody in prison comes to faith in Christ, our responsibility has only just started. A lot of support is needed to help that person grow in the Christian faith. In our ministry we seek to ensure that a person who becomes a Christian in prison is linked to another Christian on the outside. We want these Christian inmates to know a local church in the communities where they're going to be released, churches that will care for them and love them and do all they can to make it possible for them to develop in the Christian life.

An effective ministry to prisoners takes time. Be prepared to give a lot of time to an individual without necessarily seeing progress in the short term, in order to be effective in the long term.

David Stillman
David Stillman is Founder of David Stillman Evangelistic Association, Reading, England.

Developing Your Ministry's Strategic Plan

Dick Wynn

In a planning process one of our key roles is to find God's plan for our ministry. Each of us has creative ideas. We have a lot of things that we would really like to do. But what is key to this whole process is finding the mind of God, determining what His plans are for our lives, our mission and our ministry. He tells us He does have a hope-filled plan (see Jeremiah 29:11). Strategic planning is more than a leadership exercise. It is a spiritual exercise. Devote much time to prayer, seeking God and asking Him to give you His direction and His wisdom (see James 3:17).

I want to highlight four types of planning: conceptual planning, strategic planning, long-term planning and annual operational planning.

Conceptual planning is when one person dreams a little bit. It has no limits. In conceptual planning you ask, "Why? Why would we do this? Why should we do this? Why is it important that we focus in this area?"

Strategic planning happens with a few people, your basic leadership team. In strategic planning you move from conceptual dreaming to articulating a vision. Often, the concept comes to you as you are in a time of extended prayer. A vision is what you see (a mission is what you do).

Vision is very important. When you have the vision, you can begin to deal with the approach to ministry. What are you going to do? Good strategic planning starts not where you are but with where you want to be. You plan backwards from where you want to be rather than starting from where you are and planning forward. Why do you do that? If you plan forward from where you are, you take a lot of baggage with you—every problem that you currently have in your ministry.

In long-term planning you begin to move into ideas. "What can we do to accomplish the vision that's before us? Let's test these ideas. What kind of results do we want to produce? How are we going to get it done? What methodology are we going to incorporate?" Run out your long-term planning about three years. Revisit your statement of faith. Don't ever violate your belief system.

Finally in the planning cycle is the annual operational plan. How many people are involved in conceptual planning? One. How many people are involved in strategic planning? A few. How many people are involved in long-term planning? A few. Now, how many people are involved in your next year's plan? Everybody. You need to have everybody feel a part of it. With the annual operational plan, everybody's involved. Then you begin to deal with your objectives, your goals.

It's very important that you not only determine what you're going to do, but that you put a timetable on it.

A strategic plan defines purpose, a sense of direction, and gives motivation. It provides an outline for the future. It evaluates your current program and creates new ideas. Don't be afraid to change methodology. Strategic planning allows you to be open to change. It helps you establish an evaluation process. We need to know what we will look like if we succeed. In the planning process, refocus and keep looking at your biblical foundation, your Bible-based motivation. And always make sure you are Christ-centered.

Some people feel that strategic planning will cause division. It will not cause division; it will bring unity, and it will lead you to a "preferred future," the future to which God is calling you. Strategic planning can and should be simple, effective and powerful.

Finally, to implement your strategic plan you need to make critical decisions regarding the following: your vision, a shared mission statement, your core values and your objectives or key result areas, and you need to keep your belief system (statement of faith) in focus and practice servant-leadership.

Dick Wynn

Dick Wynn is President of Emerging Young Leaders, Englewood, Colorado, U.S.A.

Managing Your Personal Finances

Jerry Bell

God has made it very clear that He is owner of all things. Psalm 24:1—"The earth is the LORD's, and everything in it, the world, and all who live in it [and on it]" (NIV). He did not make any exceptions; everything belongs to God. Genesis 37–50 is the story of Joseph, God's steward. Joseph never owned anything, but he managed an entire country.

A steward manages what belongs to another. We are stewards and managers, not owners, over what belongs to God. To administer the affairs of an organization, a ministry, a household or a business is to have a defined goal or an objective that you move toward achieving. Jesus said, "No servant can serve two masters. Either he will hate the one and love the other. . . . You cannot serve both God and Money" (Luke 16:13, NIV). You can't abide in God's economic system unless you bring your money under His lordship and His principles. Because God knew we would struggle with money matters, He put more than a thousand verses in the Bible about money. We need not feel that we're out in a desert with no help.

As a steward or manager, don't worry about what He hasn't given you; manage what He has given you. Proverbs 27:23, "Be sure you know the condition of your flocks, give careful attention to your herds" (NIV). Determine how you are spending what God is giving you. Have a system that will let you know how you are doing as the month progresses. As you do this, you will begin to feel freedom and peace in this particular area of your life.

Get down on paper all of the expenses that you have for 30 days, what you're spending right now. On the income side, put down what you earn. This is the money you've got to work with. If you're spending more than you've got, then spend less, earn more, or a combination of those two: spend a little less, earn a little more. Sometimes that means a temporary second job.

Write down your debts so you know what you're talking about, not guessing. As you write them down, possibilities begin coming. "Here's a small debt; we'll work on that one first." It's the first part of having a plan. If you are in ministry on a fixed salary, lay these income/expenditure figures before your board. They'll look with an entirely different view when you come to them with this budget explanation and say, "I need more money."

If you are married, pray together, husband and wife. God sees you as one in money matters, the same as in everything else. Don't hide financial difficulties from a mate. If you have children, they will learn Bible truths about money from you. Remember, you don't have money; God has money. What you have belongs to the Father. You're His steward, not an owner.

Jerry Bell
Jerry Bell is a Christian Financial Counselor with Scope Ministries, Oklahoma City, Oklahoma, U.S.A.

Keeping Your Evangelistic Vision

Werner Burklin

When Jesus left this earth, He admonished His disciples to go into all the world and preach the Gospel to every creature. To be an evangelist is the highest calling of all. First, we need to be focused on our calling. Satan will try everything in his power to sideline us from what God intended us to do. Once the Lord has called us to be evangelists, we have to constantly remind ourselves that this is what God wants us to do.

Second, we need to be focused on the power of the Holy Spirit. No evangelist will be effective unless he or she is totally dependent upon the power of the Holy Spirit. The evangelist is the communicator, but the Holy Spirit changes lives. The evangelist has been sent to proclaim, but the Holy Spirit is the sender. The evangelist is the channel God uses, but the Holy Spirit flows through that channel to receiving hearts.

Third, we need to be focused on the infallibility of the Bible. No evangelist will be spiritually successful unless he or she believes without hesitation in the infallibility of the Word of God. Billy Graham is an example of this. Only after settling in his mind about whether the Bible is infallible or not was he able to declare with authority the evangelistic message. Fourth, we need to be focused on the presentation of God's message. The evangelist has to be a student of the Bible, for in it the true Gospel is found. This includes the basic need of mankind. The root cause of the world's ills is sin, and with it, separation from God. This has to be fully understood in order to treat it correctly.

Fifth, we need to be focused on the unreached. It is easy to lose the evangelistic vision. The evangelist needs to have a clear vision of the world that is filled with people who have no idea who Jesus Christ is. The evangelist's message must be geared to those people. Sixth, we need to be focused on the miracle of changed lives. Nothing is more exhilarating than to see men and women, boys and girls, come to know Christ through the preaching of God's Word.

Seventh, we need to be focused on the climax of our message. Once the message has been presented about who Jesus is, what He did for lost mankind, and how to accept Him as Savior and Lord, the evangelist has to "draw in the net," to invite the seeker to make a decision to follow Christ. After that commitment is made, the follow-up of each seeker is of tremendous importance. Eighth, we need to be focused on our own integrity. We evangelists must live what we preach. We have to lead lives so holy that believers and unbelievers will see us as role models. We must live lives of integrity.

The evangelistic vision can get blurred very easily. Many evangelists who started out well lost their passion for the lost; they stopped focusing on what God wanted them to do. Let us be evangelists who never lose the vision of reaching out to a lost world.

Werner Burklin

Werner Burklin is President of China Partner, Inc. He lives in Boca Raton, Florida, U.S.A.

Resolving Conflicts in the Ministry Team

Jim Chew

Some Christians have had unresolved conflicts for years. Think of the blessings they have missed because they have not seen these conflicts resolved. Conflict takes place when a difference in opinion or purpose leads to the frustration of somebody else's desires or goals.

When handled correctly, differences can be opportunities for growth and maturity. Christian unity is not necessarily uniformity. However, conflicts can cause severe damage. James 4:1–2 talks about quarrels. When conflict is the result of selfish desires, we need to deal with it, and the Bible tells us how to do it. For example, Matthew 18:15 says, "If your brother sins against you, go and show him his fault, just between the two of you" (NIV). That's a very important guideline.

On the positive side, a conflict provides an opportunity for you to glorify God. We read that in 1 Corinthians 10:31–33 and 1 Peter 2:12. It's an opportunity to build others up and to grow in Christ's likeness. James talks of trials and pressures developing in us the quality of perseverance and maturity. There are three objectives: First, commit to the process of reconciliation and conflict resolution. Second, understand and apply God's pattern for reconciliation and conflict resolution. Third, know how to offer and receive forgiveness.

First is commitment. Go and be reconciled to your brother. Then come and offer your gift (see Matthew 5:23–24). Settle it first before worship. Take the first step to mend it. Second, conflict resolution brings glory to God. "Whatever you do, do it all for the glory of God" (1 Corinthians 10:31, NIV). John 13:34–35 says that when Christians love one another, then people will take note that we are disciples of Jesus. They're watching us. Third, I must deal with my own faults before I deal with the faults of others (see Matthew 7:5).

There are a couple of issues here. You may be oversensitive or you may have contributed to the conflict yourself. "A man's wisdom gives him patience; it is to his glory to overlook an offense" (Proverbs 19:11, NIV). Some things are not worth fighting over; they're too small. Second, 1 Corinthians 13:5 tells us that love does not keep a record of all these little faults and problems people have.

Does exercising my rights please God? Does exercising my rights build other people up? Will it advance the Gospel? Have my own sins affected the relationship? Admit your attitudes and actions. Avoid words like, "Oh, if I've offended you." Don't try to justify your actions. Ask for forgiveness. Then alter your behavior and ask God for grace to act differently.

When should you take action? You may choose to overlook an offense if it's a little thing. You need discernment here. If it's not an offense to be overlooked, you have to go to your brother. Then, "If he will not listen, take one or two others along" (Matthew 18:16, NIV). If the person still won't listen, get the leadership of the church involved. The goal is still restoration and reconciliation.

Forgiveness is the key to the healing of relationships. To be unforgiving is to be unmerciful. If you don't forgive, you remain spiritually imprisoned yourself. When you forgive, there's freedom. Major on reconciliation, not on proving who is right. Speak to the issue and do not attack the person. You're seeking the good of the other person.

Jim Chew

Jim Chew is Asia Missions Facilitator and New Zealand Missions Director for The Navigators.

Maintaining a Strong Family While the Spouse Travels

Ruth Conard, with an international panel

We divide this discussion on the family into three sections: first, being a spouse; second, parenting; and third, our environment, how we build up our own selves as the spouse of a leader.

First, one of the greatest challenges is to adapt to changes in the life of your spouse and to grow with your spouse in the ministries God has called you to. Accept the call of God in your life; know that this is God's will. Embrace that calling and vision, and grow together.

God has called you to be a team. If God opens the door for the spouse to expand in the ministry, be enthusiastic, be that number-one supporter. A spouse needs to know that there is at least one genuine person who is a friend, a supporter who tells the truth in love. Communication is basic for a good relationship. Always talk and plan things together.

Second, parenting children. Our relationship with God must be strong for two reasons. First, Satan is out to attack the Christian family and especially one in full-time ministry. Second, we must have a strong relationship with God because then we will be happy and excited about what the spouse is doing. If we are not happy, the children are going to sense it. Then they will become angry with their parents and, ultimately, angry with God.

Spouses need to agree on disciplining the children as well as on how the home should function and the lifestyle. Then, whether or not the spouse is at home, carry out the agreement on discipline, on values, on the functioning of the home. Sometimes a spouse is busy and insensitive to feelings. At that time we should talk, saying, "I'm finding it difficult. I feel that I'm being neglected. I feel that the children are being neglected."

Practice acceptance, an attitude of appreciation, an atmosphere of thanksgiving in the home, and lots of affirmation towards the spouse and the children. If you want your children to obey you, build a relationship. Relationship precedes rules. We have to live what we believe. If the children find us losing our tempers over the slightest thing, if they find us gossiping, if they find that we cannot get along with our neighbors, we are not practicing our Christianity at home.

We must try to lead our children early to Christ. As they grow up, encourage them to become involved in Christian activities, to join youth group meetings in the church, and to attend camps and seminars. They need Christian friends who think and act like them. Ask them to introduce their friends and bring them home, so that you may know them. Play with the children. Arrange a time to go out with them, sit together with them, talk to them, read the Bible with them, pray together. Be there for them, go through their homework, and give them a sense of security. Seek God's guidance so that you may help your children, or else you may lose them. The Word of God says that the Lord is my fortress, a refuge in times of trouble. That's what we should be for our children.

Third, our own environment and what we do to keep growing. Find friends, others you can trust who will give you strength. Develop the gifts that God gives you. Live with a goal. Be grounded in the Word of God. Be truthful with your spouse. You won't grow unless you can be honest. Find a place where you can study God's Word in a systematic way. Find fulfillment in being a disciple. As you learn that, God will fill the spaces in your life with deep satisfaction.

Ruth Conard

Mrs. Ruth Conard is a Bible teacher and former missionary who lives in Minneapolis, Minnesota, U.S.A. The international panel included Mrs. Norma Ortiz, Dr. Giaw Foon Foon (Patrina), Mrs. Nelun Fernando, Mrs. Eodie Havyarimana and Mrs. Angeline Kopwe.

The Power of Personal Worship

Jim Craddock

Worship is the foundation of a vital Christian walk and the spiritual gauge of a Christian's faith. Worship not only gives to God what is rightfully His, but it brings us into the very presence of our sovereign Lord. Worship is the highest spiritual experience a Christian can have. It allows us to know the intimacy of God and to experience the power of God.

Worship suffers when the love of God grows cold. As one's sense of love for God wanes, the first casualty is worship and with it the sense of His majesty and the exercise of spiritual power. This is not surprising, for worship and majesty and a vital Christian walk go hand in hand. Without one you cannot have the other. Majesty is discovered in worship. Spiritual power is unleashed through personal worship.

Worship belongs uniquely to God. It is giving to God those things that are rightfully His, the magnifying of God in our hearts and rejoicing in Him. Is this kind of worship possible? Of course it is.

First, you must go to Jesus. As you go, ask God to reveal Himself to you. As you ask, also ask the Holy Spirit to reveal to you anything in your life that hinders your worship. Perhaps there are things or family or money. Perhaps it's a ministry. Whatever He points out in your life that is wrong, deal with it immediately.

Second, you must see God. If you want to know God, study the attributes of God, see who He is, look to His names. Then search the gospels to see the Father revealed in the Son. Read the Psalms. God will reveal Himself to you; He always does.

Third, you're to submit. This is probably the most difficult area of worship. Paul wrote: "I beseech you, I beg of you, I plead with you to present your bodies a living and holy sacrifice" (see Romans 12:1). This is the very heart of worship. Either God will rule our lives or someone or something else will.

Fourth, we must listen to God. The psalmist wrote in Psalm 46:10: "Be still, and know that I am God" (NIV). Choose a quiet place where you can talk with God. Listen to God as you read and meditate on His Word, but listen.

Fifth, we must practice worship. Worship is not only essential to our Christian life, it is the highest privilege any human being can have.

Worship honors God and transforms us. It's a two-edged sword, one edge toward God and the other toward us. Because of its impact upon us, right worship becomes imperative.

Jim Craddock
Jim Craddock is the President of Scope Ministries in Oklahoma City, Oklahoma, U.S.A.

A Woman's Call to Evangelism

Pamela Hiscock

The four Gospels record the scenes surrounding the resurrection of Jesus. Women went to tell the disciples that the tomb was empty and that angels had told them that Jesus had risen. But on the way, fear took hold. They knew no one would believe them. In their culture women's testimonies did not count. But Mary did speak up, and the response was, "You women are talking nonsense. You're hysterical. You've got to be wrong." "But they did not believe the women, because their words seemed to them like nonsense" (Luke 24:11, NIV).

Peter and John then run to the tomb, find it empty and go home. Mary, however, stays. Jesus appears to her and commands, "Go and tell my brothers." And Mary goes back with the news, "I have seen the Lord!" The form of the word *go* that Jesus used to commission Mary is the present imperative, a command that involves continuous or repeated action. Jesus is saying, "Mary, go and tell and keep going and keep telling." Jesus isn't telling Mary to go and tell once. He is giving her a call and a mission.

Why were women the first ones called by the angels and by Jesus to be preaching evangelists after the resurrection? Why not Peter or John? Why not Andrew, who seemed to have a gift for evangelism? Jesus knew the prophecy of Joel, "And afterward, I will pour out my Spirit on all people. Your sons and daughters will prophesy, your old men will dream dreams, your young men will see visions. Even on my servants, both men and women, I will pour out my Spirit in those days" (Joel 2:28–29, NIV).

Jesus knew that in order for the Holy Spirit to be poured out, both men and women had to be prepared, because both men and women would be called to prophesy, to speak out the Word of God. Jesus knew that women needed to be specifically affirmed and commissioned if they were to be open to the Spirit of God and the job that He had for them.

Before Jesus' crucifixion, He ensured that women were included in His ministry. Jesus taught women and accepted their financial support. But Jesus also knew His culture. Jesus knew that within days the women would have been pushed aside, seen as their culture saw them—women who could not be trusted to know or communicate the truth, women who couldn't be legal witnesses, who were of little value. For the Church to be prepared for the Spirit to be poured out, something had to change. Jesus was communicating loudly and clearly: Women are to be included in the work of the ministry in order for the Spirit to be poured out.

Today people say, "We need more of God's Spirit to be poured out." Could it be that women, who have been called by Jesus Christ Himself to go and tell, to be preaching evangelists, are to prepare the Church for the Spirit to be more fully poured out? Women must be faithful to that call because much is at stake.

Some face challenges, persecution, being discredited. How hard to stay faithful to a call under those circumstances. But remember, it was because of the women's faithfulness and their report that the disciples gathered together and heard Jesus give the Great Commission. If it will take women being faithful to the evangelistic call and commission of Jesus for the Holy Spirit to be more fully poured out on this world, then women must obey Jesus' call. We must go and tell, and keep going and keep telling, and keep going and keep telling.

Pamela Hiscock

Pamela Hiscock is pastor of Cedarcrest Free Methodist Church, Bloomington, Minnesota, U.S.A.

The Evangelist and Listening to God's Voice

Anne Graham Lotz

In 1 Samuel 3, we learn that Samuel had to be taught how to hear the voice of God speaking to him. And sometimes we, too, need instructions on how to listen to the voice of God. Listening to His voice and speaking to Him in prayer are part of our communication with God.

Sometimes God is trying to say something to us and we don't understand. We get frustrated, disappointed. He's speaking to us, but we just don't know how to listen. I want to give you some simple tools that will enable you to listen to the voice of God when you read your Bible. The Scripture is a supernatural book; we always approach it with prayer and ask God to speak to us through His Word. There's a depth to it that you don't get if you don't pray. So ask the Holy Spirit to speak to you as you read His Word.

There are three questions to ask yourself as you read a passage of Scripture: (1) What does the passage say? (2) What does the passage mean? (3) What does it mean to me?

Read a passage and list the facts from that passage. What does it say? Go verse by verse. Don't paraphrase. Pull the facts right from the passage. We want to know exactly what God has said in His Word before we start interpreting it and finding the lessons from it.

In considering what the passage means, for every fact listed earlier find at least one lesson. It may be about accountability, authority, the resources that God has given you or how God can work even in impossible situations.

To answer "What does the passage mean to me?" take the lessons you learned from the previous question, and ask yourself personal questions. Is there something that God wants to say to you through the passage you studied? As you do that, listen for the Lord to speak to your heart. You don't have to do every verse; go to the verses that seemed to strike you the most or the lessons that were the most meaningful to you, and put them in the form of questions to ask yourself—about your attitude, your words, your relationship with God and with others, etc.

People often ask me where to start. I suggest that you go to your favorite passage of Scripture—if it's Psalm 23, the Good Shepherd; or John 17, our Lord's prayer; or Romans 8, that we're never separated from God; or whatever your favorite passage is—and start there.

Sometimes we think we've got to get through the Gospel of John so we can get to Acts, and get through Acts so we can get to Romans. But the idea of this plan is to read so that we can hear God speaking to us. Take a few verses at a time. List the facts in the passage, and then find the lessons from the facts. Ask yourself what those lessons mean to you. When you do this, I believe God will speak to you.

These are simple instructions: (1) What does it say? (2) What does it mean? (3) What does it mean to me? But I believe you're going to hear the Spirit of God speaking to your heart. It will transform not only your devotional life, but it will also transform your relationship with God. It's one of the best ways I know to put God's Word into your heart.

Anne Graham Lotz

Mrs. Anne Graham Lotz is an international Bible teacher, an award-winning author and the founder of AnGel ministries.

Foundations for Leadership in Evangelism

Mpundu Mutala

Am I a leader? Have I been called into leadership? We need to be sure of the pattern that God uses in calling men and women to leadership. Here are some ways in which we can identify the call of God upon a leader.

First is family influence. The mother of Moses kept her son from being killed (see Exodus 1:8–2:10). Moses never misunderstood who he was or where he belonged. This challenged him to think of ways in which God could use him to bring freedom to his people. Look at the prophet Samuel. Hannah didn't have children, but she prayed to God and God answered her prayer. She said, "If God answers my prayer, I am going to give this son of mine back to God," which she did. She never forgot (see 1 Samuel 1:1–28). Samuel had a family influence.

Second is divine contact or affirmation. Paul made a deliberate effort to invite Timothy to come on his team. Probably Timothy was living in Ephesus without many ideas of what he could do for God. Through the influence of Paul, Timothy increased his vision. Divine contact, small beginnings, lead to something greater and bigger. God may be laying it on our hearts to be a divine contact for others, used of Him to choose the leaders who will carry the mandate forward. It's a tremendous challenge. We need the grace and the help of God to do it.

There may be people who say, "I am this; I am that." It might be a reliable rule of thumb that the person who is ambitious to lead is disqualified as a leader. Leaders will desire that Christ may be seen through them, through their compassion, and will live and speak in such a way that they draw others to God. Without spiritual leadership, God's purposes cannot be fulfilled. People may appoint someone to a position, but that doesn't give them spiritual leadership. It is not based upon natural talent. No matter how skilled or talented or intelligent we are, we may not qualify. Spiritual leadership comes from God. It is His choice.

Five things sum up the basic characteristics of a leader. First, leadership is a sovereign act of God. He doesn't consult anybody. Second is the anointing. The presence of God comes upon us so that we may do the work of leadership. He not only calls by His own sovereign choice but He also gives the power. Third, the work of God is spiritual. It is not commercial. God's true leaders are spiritual men and women.

Fourth, faithfulness, promptness and humility characterize leadership. A true leader does not have to be asked to do menial jobs but sees a need and lends a hand. Service is a spirit, not an outward obligation. We can do very little with leaders who don't see that they are to set an example in everything. By promptness we mean obedience in responding to the work of God, a readiness to pursue the plan of God, to meet needs as they appear. Fifth is vision. God unveils His mind to us about what He has purposed to complete in Christ. Leaders will be vision carriers, responsible to see the vision implemented by empowering and inspiring others.

Mpundu Mutala
Mpundu Mutala is General Secretary of the Bible Society of Zambia.

Temptations Faced by the Evangelist

Bill Newman

Charisma without character leads to catastrophe. Our lives must match what we're saying. There are temptations that we face as evangelists and others involved in Christian work.

Number one is the opposite sex. Here are a few pointers on how to affair-proof your marriage. First, learn to face the fact that adultery can happen to anyone. Second, discuss everything in your marriage with your spouse. If you have pressures, share them openly with your spouse. Third, spend a lot of good time together. Fourth, manage your environment. On the road I'm listening to praise music that lifts my spirit. I've always got good books and things that I enjoy. Fifth, fill your time with positive work. Keep busy. Don't let your mind wander and stray. Sixth, work at having good sex at home. God invented sex. It's a precious gift that He's given. Seventh, keep close to the Lord Jesus Christ.

L-O-V-E: L—listen to each other. Let your spouse talk. O—overlook faults. We've all got faults. If I look for faults in you, I'll find them. If you look for faults in me, you'll find them. V—value your marriage. Your partner is the greatest treasure that you will have in life. E—encourage one another. It's easy to nit-pick, pull down. Don't be hung by the tongue. The biggest need in marriage is encouragement.

Three "R's" for a rich marriage: Respect. If you lose respect, the marriage is going down the tube. Romance. Keep romance in your marriage. Repentance. Forgive one another. We all make mistakes; ask for forgiveness.

Number two is purity in your private world. Guard yourself from hidden lusts. If you are having difficulties, get with a friend. Be accountable. Pray together and encourage one another.

Number three is the problem of money or the lack of it. You have to address the money problem if you are serving the Lord. Number four is laziness. The people who support us in the ministry are up early, working hard, and we must be doing the same. Number five is pride. Pride is a stench in the nostrils of God. We are called to walk humbly with God. Number six is jealousy of others. There's no room in the body of Christ for competition. Let us rejoice when others are being magnified and mightily used of God. Number seven is professionalism. It is all too easy to traffic in unfelt truths. Preaching is not a profession, it's a passion.

Number eight is intellectual snobbery. Preachers have the privilege of perhaps a little more education than some. God says, "Feed my sheep," not "Feed my giraffes." Bring the teaching down to where people are. Number nine is self-pity. There's loneliness in leadership. We need to be constantly looking away from ourselves to the needy souls around us. Number ten is the peril of pettiness. Don't be caught up in pettiness. You're doing a great work for God.

Number eleven is being sorry for our sacrifices. We see what others have and we feel sorry for ourselves. Number twelve is neglecting our devotions. Your ministry will sink or swim in relation to the time you spend alone with God. Number thirteen is cynicism. Don't get cynical in the ministry. Number fourteen is boasting. Give God the glory; great things He has done in your ministry. Number fifteen is your speech. Don't put others down. Don't gossip about others' problems. Leave that with the Lord.

Finally, there is the temptation to give up. Perseverance, staying power, is the thing that sets leaders apart. Keep going on for the Lord Jesus Christ!

Bill Newman
Bill Newman is President of Bill Newman International, Queensland, Australia.

Managing Your Time and Energy

Don Osman

Two management areas to deal with are managing your desk and delegation. First, how do you manage your desk? About 60 percent of the papers on your desk no longer have any value or meaning. They've piled up because instead of deciding what should be done with them, you just put them on a pile. A disorganized office creates a disorganized desk, which creates a disorganized "to do" list, and eventually creates disorganized thinking, which develops into disorganized ministry.

How do we create order out of disorder? To make this change will require as much time as is needed to clean up the mess and get organized. Here are five steps for developing an organized, clean desk. One, look at each piece of paper on your desk and make an immediate decision to either keep it or throw it out. Two, create a master list. Your master list will become an inventory of all your unfinished work and ongoing projects. Three, prioritize your list. Place the number one against all the critical items that must be completed first. Place the number 2 on all of the next important items and the number three on all of the remaining items on your list.

Four, develop a simple filing system. The first files are tickler files. Get 45 file folders. Number the first 31 to represent the days of the month. The next 12 files represent the months of the year. The two files left are for this year and next year. The first thing each morning I go through my mail. I open every letter and glance through to get the gist of what it is saying. If it is something that requires my attention, I place it in my tickler file. That will be the first correspondence I will do. I then deal with the correspondence I have set aside for that day.

Seldom will I reply to a letter I receive the same day. Even when I get e-mail, I print it out and it goes into the tickler file.

The next file is a project or event file. If you are responsible for a project or a ministry event, you have to develop a filing system for that event. The next one is a read file. The read file has reports, or a magazine or a newsletter—any reading—so that when I am traveling I can use my time productively. Next is a staff file. Have a file for each staff person who is directly responsible to you. Last, keep a board file, if you have a board that you are working under. An organized desk will release you. You will be able to stay on top of your unfinished work, locate your papers and files within seconds, and become more productive.

Second is delegation. Nobody has the gift of delegation; it is a skill that has to be learned. Delegation means "to entrust or to commit to another person with confidence." Sometimes we say, "I'll do it myself." But that does not develop people. Management is the development of people. When we delegate, we help people experience six things. First, they experience a sense of achievement. Second, they feel they have value. Third, they have ownership. Fourth, they experience an increased sense of responsibility. Fifth, they experience growth and maturity. Sixth, delegation gives them enjoyment and fulfillment.

If you want people to stay long in ministry, then create a climate that will produce these six basic things that people are looking for. They will feel affirmed, recognized and appreciated. Delegation implemented with the proper attitude moves the program forward. People will be motivated to do even greater things.

Don Osman
Don Osman directs Youth for Christ in Africa. He lives in Nairobi, Kenya.

Post-Modernism and Evangelism

Paul Blackham

Today the mission of the Church takes place in a world that has changed significantly compared to 100 years ago. The move is away from established, institutional religion to ad hoc individual spirituality or else politicized fundamentalism. This new world offers both challenges and opportunities for the Gospel.

The apostle Paul was greatly distressed to see that Athens was full of idols. So he reasoned with Jews and God-fearing Greeks in the synagogue, as well as in the marketplace (see Acts 17:16–17), where hundreds of other philosophical and religious products were on sale. The 21st century is very much like the first century. Increasingly the world we're living in is pagan, with people who know nothing about the Gospel.

The word *modernism* was first used in 1127 by the builder of the basilica of Saint Denis in Paris to refer to a new style of architecture. He said, "It's modern." It belonged to the present and not to the past. The word *progress* is at the very heart of modernism.

The 20th century ended the belief in progress, particularly after the world wars. The modern age believed that it was possible to discover truth if we just worked at it. Science was the holy temple of truth, and scientists were its priests. But the post-modernist sees science in a more negative way. Science can produce medicine and flush toilets; it can also produce weapons of mass destruction, global pollution, dehumanized lifestyles, unjust economic systems, dysfunctional families and disintegrated societies. Post-modernists say, "Other ways of looking at the world are just as good, just as true, just as valid, and more useful."

Post-modernism is aware that each person sees the world differently. Attempts to force everybody to see the same way are considered to be not about truth but about power. "Why can't you just let everybody see it the way they want to see it?"

Truth is relative, dependent on each person. Image and feeling, form rather than content, are more important than truth-telling. MTV on television is one of the purist forms of post-modernism—total image and feeling, zero content. Pop culture has replaced objective truth.

Where does this put evangelism? Christianity refuses to acknowledge the sacrosanct right of a post-modern world, "I can think and live exactly as I want." The Gospel is based on the authority of God, who controls everything and everybody—a radically unpopular message. Yet there are some real advantages of sharing the Gospel in a post-modern world. It's a much more mysterious world in which the miraculous happens all the time.

In the days of modernism, religion wasn't spoken of in polite company. It was seen as primitive, belonging to a pre-scientific world, something for superstitious and weak people. Talking about religion is much easier today. In the post-modern world the fashionable people are the most religious, although most of their beliefs are a form of New Age spirituality revolving around the idea that reality is found through looking within and discovering that I am God.

God has spoken truth. But what matters more than the quality of our argument is the quality of our lives. When Christians show love and integrity, their words gain weight. Most important is our understanding of the work of the Holy Spirit to convince people. Otherwise the Gospel we present will just seem like one of many options in the marketplace.

Paul Blackham
Paul Blackham is Associate Minister (Theology) at All Souls Church, London, England.

Global Forces Changing Today's Ministries

Art Deyo

I've always been interested in culture trends, the global forces that affect ministries, especially youth ministries.

Today, virtually every area of our lives is being twisted and turned by forces beyond our control. Demographic, technological, economic and political changes are unraveling the very fabric of the family and society. Just as we have changed our strategies in the past, any ministry, to stay alive in such a world, needs to develop an understanding of the forces reshaping the globe as well as the implications of those forces for that ministry. Like the ocean tides, change drivers cannot be controlled nor can they be ignored, but they can be used. Effective ministries are the ones, like the "men of Issachar" (1 Chronicles 12:32), that recognize these forces and position themselves so that the change drivers push the ministry forward.

One of the factors driving change is demographics. In October 1999, the world's population passed the six billion mark. By 2050 the population will be nine billion. Ninety-nine percent of that increase will occur in Africa, Asia and Latin America. Also, over the course of the next 25 years the number of people over 65 will more than double while the world's youth population will grow by only six percent. Yet in many countries of the world half the population is under 20 years old. As population doubles, the urban population triples. Today fewer than half of the world's people are urban dwellers, but by 2025 that proportion is likely to exceed 60 percent. And the HIV-AIDS tragedy is dramatically changing all the parameters, especially in Africa, but also in other continents.

Another change driver is technology. The world is being wired up. The number of Internet users is doubling every six months. Young people, even small children, feel very at home using computers, video games and interactive TV. Distance learning is becoming increasingly popular.

Some technology has had a negative social influence by changing values, behavior and lifestyles. Pluralism encourages the view that "anything goes," bringing together forces that are having an unprecedented attack on the family. Society is presuming to reengineer the family itself. Movies, television, the Internet have a profound effect on young people. The media brings sex, pornography, violence and deviant behavior into the homes of hundreds of millions of kids. There are now more than 40,000 pornography sites on the Web and hundreds more are being added every day.

Another change driver is economics. The total amount of goods and services produced in the 20th century is estimated to have exceeded the total cumulative output over all of human history up until 1900. Yet the gap between the rich and the poor has widened enormously.

Politics is another change driver. With the end of the Cold War, global peace was forecast. But there has been no peace. In some countries political instability has degenerated into open armed conflict. Millions of people fleeing in search of safety bear witness to the persecution and violence around the world. Christians are among the most persecuted.

Still, the Church continues to grow in the midst of this chaos. Christians are maintaining strong prayer vigils and showing great faith. The witness of persecuted Christians is producing great results in terms of advancing the Kingdom of God. Young people, the down-and-out, and nearly every people group have Christians reaching out to them. Evangelical Christian faith is slowly but steadily marching across the world. Our sovereign Lord will win, Satan will be thrown into the bottomless pit, and we will see a great multitude from every nation on earth worshiping the Lamb (see Revelation 7:9)!

Art Deyo

Art Deyo is International Liaison Director Asia-Pacific with Youth for Christ International, Denver, Colorado, U.S.A.

Evangelism in a Climate of Social Injustice

Stafford Petersen

What is injustice? Let us explore what the Bible says about injustice and what God expects of us. Ecclesiastes 4:1 says, "Again I looked and saw all the oppression that was taking place under the sun: I saw the tears of the oppressed—and they have no comforter; power was on the side of their oppressors—and they have no comforter" (NIV).

Injustice occurs when power is misused to take control of what God has given others—namely, their life, their dignity, their liberty, the fruit of their love, and their labor. To put it simply, the sin of injustice is the abuse of power.

Amos 5:12 puts it very well: "I know how many are your offenses and how great your sins. You oppress the righteous and take bribes and you deprive the poor of justice in the courts" (NIV). Injustice is not a new thing. The prophet Ezekiel dealt with many issues of social injustice.

God has chosen us to be His hands and His feet and His eyes and His ears here on earth. Isaiah 1:17, says, "Learn to do right! Seek justice, encourage the oppressed. Defend the cause of the fatherless, plead the case of the widow" (NIV). These are doing words: *learn, seek, encourage, defend* and *plead*. These are responsibilities that Scripture places upon our shoulders. Jesus said, "You are the light of the world" (Matthew 5:14, NIV). But sometimes oppressors come under the disguise of "religion."

Galatians 6:9, says, "Let us not become weary in doing good, for at the proper time we will reap a harvest if we do not give up" (NIV). Don't let people's attitudes deter you from doing good. Don't let other people's agendas deter you from following the agenda of Scripture. The Bible says there is to be no respect of persons (see Acts 10:34; Galatians 3:28).

How do we start? We don't sit back and allow injustice to rule. God decided to use you and me to help those who are oppressed. We cultivate "compassion awareness." Hebrews 13:3, says that we are to recall the plight of the mistreated and the imprisoned. This is not a natural inclination. We need to make a concerted effort to reserve a space in our thought life for those who suffer. We need to model a society where justice prevails, as we extend God's Kingdom over one more life, one more family, one more neighborhood.

Every Christian can make a difference in ushering God's justice into the world. Don't think that the contribution you make is too small. In the story of the five loaves and the two fish (see Matthew 14:16–21), Jesus could have fed all of those people. God did so in the wilderness when he rained down manna from heaven (see Exodus 16). But Jesus involved a small boy's lunch. Even though Jesus can wipe out every injustice in this world, He has chosen to use what we have at our disposal and to magnify that to the glory of the Lord.

Each Christian can do something about injustice through three simple acts: Speak up for the oppressed through prayer, and also speak the truth to humans in power. Stand with the oppressed. And ask God to use you to deliver people from spiritual and other oppressions.

Will people ask, as they asked in Malachi 2:17, "Where is the God of justice?" (NIV). The Spirit of God said in Isaiah 59:15–16, "Truth is nowhere to be found. . . . The Lord looked and was displeased that there was no justice. He saw that there was no one, he was appalled that there was no one to intervene" (NIV).

Will God say of our generation, "I am appalled that there is no one to intercede"? Or will God look at our generation and say, "I am pleased that my people have started to intercede to see that justice prevails"?

Stafford Petersen
Stafford Petersen is Senior Pastor of Tabernacle of Life Full Gospel Church of God, Cape Town, South Africa.

The Evangelist and Spiritual Conflict

Philip Steyne

We will never fully appreciate the proclamation of the Word of God, or the ministry of prayer and praise, or the importance of living holy lives until we understand that we are in a spiritual battle. God's Word tells us, "The whole world is in the power of the evil one" (1 John 5:19, RSV). The apostle Paul says, "We are not contending against flesh and blood, but against the principalities, against the powers" (Ephesians 6:12, RSV).

Satan is working to multiply sin in every sphere of life. He is a deceiver who stands against the truth of God. But wherever the Church is alive—a dynamic group of God's people doing what God has called them to do—evil is rolled back. That is why we want to multiply the Church in every people group and nation. The Church's task is to liberate people from Satan's power. It's to deliver captives, to make the blind to see, to release those who are in bondage. We are to declare God's glory; God deserves the worship and praise of every human being. We must model that commitment to God's glory; we have no message if we don't live it.

First, we reveal God's truth so that people understand, "Thus saith the Lord." Second, we expose Satan's deeds of darkness by forcing his corruption into light through the truth of God's Word. Third, we resist the devil's schemes. Prayer is essential. It is also essential that we ourselves stand in truth; otherwise we cannot stand against the onslaughts of the enemy.

Fourth, we overcome the devil's way of influencing our characters. Sometimes we justify things culturally when the Word of God has already said it is sin. We are to recognize sin in our own lives and stand against the enemy. Fifth, we examine our effectiveness and ask why we are not accomplishing what God has gifted us and called us to do.

All over the world syncretism is rife. People practice the old religion along with Christian things. Satan has a hold over people. They must come out of the dominion of Satan, receive forgiveness and become part of the Church of Jesus Christ, an inheritance with the saints. In Acts 26:18, the apostle Paul says, "My task is to open eyes." He says, "I have to help people realize that there is a Kingdom of light and there is a kingdom of darkness." We do have weapons "mighty through God to the pulling down of strong holds" (2 Corinthians 10:4, KJV). People are being delivered today.

To penetrate this world of darkness, remember that Satan is not all-powerful. His kingdom is impressive, but limited. Realize that he has taken people captive and they need to be set free. Know that there should be no arrogance in coming against demonic powers. Jesus disarmed principalities and powers. On the Cross, God was reconciled to us and we to Him; we received forgiveness, our transgressions were paid for; Satan was defeated. If we stay focused on the Cross and the resurrection, then we have a message to proclaim.

Our weapons of warfare are God's truth (we live it; we proclaim it), the ministry of Holy Spirit-directed prayer and praise—walking in a worshipful attitude every day, knowing that God takes sin seriously, and where there is no holiness of life there is no victory against the powers of darkness. God has given us weapons to the pulling down of strongholds. God will triumph!

Philip Steyne
Philip Steyne teaches at Columbia International University in the United States.

Reaching Business and Professional Women

Wilma Tan

More than half of the world's population, 52 percent of the world, is women. In the U.S., 56 percent of university graduates are women. Sixty-five percent graduating from graduate schools are women. Women own a growing number of businesses. They have position, money and the freedom to pursue their interests. This is a great pool of leaders. If we reach these women, they, in turn, can reach their coworkers for Christ.

There are principles to understand about professional women. And there are principles for reaching professional women. First, understand that business/professional women are used to getting things done and making decisions. They are comfortable leading. They're survivors. They want to be treated as adults, not kids. Time is precious to them. These women have schedules. They have meetings to attend. They have projects. They have deadlines.

Many business/professional women wrestle with guilt. They will ask, "Where does God fit in my particular situation?" They may have life partners and/or children or they're dealing with teenage problems. Or they may be single women who put their lives into their careers. Now they realize that they have to fend for themselves for the rest of their lives. They may not know whether what they're doing fits the Christian mold.

Women may be more receptive to the Gospel when they are in transition or are having struggles with issues that they are working through: a death in the family, a son or a daughter going to college, problems in the family. They're hurting; they need the Lord. They want their lives to count, a life that is more than the next paycheck. They may seem to have a different value system such as money, but deep down inside they are looking for values like truth, honesty for their children, and good communication within the family. They want authentic relationships.

What are some principles for reaching business/professional women? First, pray for the women you want to reach. Second, define your target group. Are they young career women or middle-aged career women? It may be a geographic group, that office building or that district in your city. It could be a cultural grouping or an affinity grouping such as lawyers, accountants or teachers. When you know their interests, you're able to address their needs much better. Learn their culture. Try to understand how they view life. Avoid Christian jargon. Speak in a way that a non-Christian can understand.

Last, be willing to sow over the course of a lifetime. Businesswomen can tell if they are only a project. Many times we teach only how to harvest, when the person is ready to pray to receive Christ. But we also need to teach how to prepare the soil and sow in the marketplace. We may be just one of many links for their receiving the Gospel.

Women come to their offices each day with marital issues, parenting concerns, financial burdens, health worries and a thousand other cares that can't be left behind when they leave for work. Address them at their felt needs. When they see God meeting them at their points of need, then they are ready to open their lives to Jesus Christ.

Wilma Tan

Wilma Tan oversees the women's ministry of Global Community Resources, a Campus Crusade ministry. She lives in San Diego, California, U.S.A.

Taking the Gospel to People Where They Are

Shad Williams

There are two kinds of evangelism. There is the "they come to me" model, normally referred to as the crusade model. Then there is the "we go to them" type of evangelism. We call that field evangelism. We're simply finding people in their own world—where they live, work, play—and preaching the Gospel to them.

This can take place in two ways: in institutions such as schools, colleges, prisons, hospitals, offices. There you can get people together and preach the Gospel. The other is public-place evangelism, preaching in bus stations, villages, open-air markets, street corners and beaches. The evangelist finds the places where people gather, then turns a crowd into a listening audience.

Use an attention-getting device that appeals to that crowd. Be Christian but not religious, be friendly but authoritative, be humble and compassionate. Dress to suit the occasion; avoid religious garb. Keep the message simple, relevant, understandable, and call for a verdict. Evangelism is confrontation, communication and invitation.

Confrontation. What attention-getting device can I use to get them to stop? Music? Or maybe a drama team? What's the best time of day to go to this location? What distractions do I need to overcome? Arrive discretely, not with a big Bible tucked under your arm. If they're dressed casually, you do the same. Be friendly, enthusiastic. Know the audience. Who are these people? What is their age? What religion do they have? What is their economic or social situation? What kind of political philosophy do they subscribe to? What are their interests?

Communication. Don't wait for the fish to come to you; put the hook in the water. Use the right language. If I say, "You need to be born again," they don't know what that means. Figure out what communicates in order to present the Gospel in a way that is simple, clear, relevant, and calls for a verdict. Use the right style. Don't condemn. They must hear compassion in your voice. Next, mold the audience together. Use a shared-life experience, something that is common to the entire audience. The central content of the message is simply three things a person has to do to be saved. First, he must face the truth about himself. He's a sinner by birth, by choice. He cannot take himself to heaven. Second, he must face the truth about God's solution. The only solution for sin is the shedding of innocent blood by one who is perfect and sinless. That was Jesus. Third, there are two places in eternity where he can go: a place called hell, a place called heaven. The choice is up to the individual.

Then comes the invitation, giving people an opportunity to receive Christ into their hearts. It's a critical moment. It's like crossing a bridge. Usually I say, "I want to ask everyone to bow your head." They bow their heads. "I'm going to pray for you." I pray for them. And then I say, "Now with your heads bowed, I want you to repeat after me silently," and I lead them in a prayer of repentance and receiving Christ. Then I say, "Now, those of you who prayed that prayer, I want to thank Jesus for coming into your heart. I don't know who you are, so I'm going to ask you to tell me by raising your hand." As people raise their hands, I pray, thanking Jesus for coming into their hearts.

Hopefully, there is a good church nearby where we can send people. If there is not, we attempt to start one. We bring every new believer along as far and as fast as we can.

Shad Williams
Shad Williams is President of Shad Williams Evangelistic Association, Adamsville, Tennessee, U.S.A.

Evangelism Among Refugees

Tom Albinson

R efugees are people in movement. They've been uprooted. As you look at lists of countries where refugees are trying to leave, you'll see that many of these countries are places where missionary work is restricted. That means that we have a unique opportunity among refugees to proclaim Christ. And, since many of our own countries are refugee-receiving countries, each of us has the opportunity to reflect the heart of God to refugees.

The refugee's journey is full of risks. The people offering to transport refugees are not the kinds of people we would want to trust with our family and children. The journey does not always have a happy ending. Refugees face rejection where they are seeking refuge. They are unwanted. The refugee highway is paved with tears and discouragement.

The words *alien, stranger, wanderer* and *foreigner* are used more than 200 times in the Bible. Is it simply coincidence that so many people in the Bible spent part of their lives as refugees? What did David mean by calling God his refuge? He depended upon the protection and provision of God, the redemption of God. He believed God would never forsake him, that God went before him and prepared the way. This is the refuge that God's people can offer the refugees of our world today.

God's Word tells us to take care of the alien, the fatherless and the widow. They have each experienced loss and loneliness. There is no one to protect or provide for them. They often question whether God has forsaken them. They are a burden to society. God expects His people to approach refugees with love. "You and the alien shall be the same before the LORD" (Numbers 15:15, NIV). Love seeks the welfare of others; it includes rather than excludes. "Show your love for the alien, for you were aliens in the land of Egypt" (Deuteronomy 10:19, NASB).

If we fail to demonstrate genuine care for their basic human needs, we will give refugees little reason to trust us with their deepest spiritual need. We have to find them places to sleep and provide food and clothing for them. This kind of ministry is most difficult to get right. It is too easy to offer these things in a way that robs people of their dignity. We honor people when our service flows out of a heart of love.

The presence of refugees in our communities is a great opportunity for mission. Offer refugees a safe place where they feel welcome, where they can share their story with someone who will listen, a place where people will share the Gospel with them and pray with them. Refugees are perhaps the most open people group in our world today. We are to hope that while with us they will hear the Gospel and become worshipers of God, and that their children will become followers of Jesus.

Before a refugee gets on the refugee highway, he is a person with a life, an identity, an education and a profession. Each has an ethnic group, a language and a religion. But when someone becomes a refugee, his identity is stripped away. Jesus Christ offers a new identity upon which he can build a new life. We must take the initiative and find them. They're not going to find us because they're sure we don't want them. We must welcome, invite and include them in our lives and in our churches. Working with refugees requires faith, cooperation and sacrifice.

Tom Albinson
Tom Albinson is an area leader with International Teams in Vienna, Austria.

Evangelism With Interest Groups

Lon Allison

Interest group evangelism is taking the Gospel to where people live. It's proclaiming Christ in settings outside the church to groups gathered around a common need, interest or vocation, even around age groupings and gender kinship. Parents of children with disabilities are a special need group. It can be to a hobby group, such as a meeting with golfers at a country club, or a common vocational group such as teachers. Age groups might be a children's meeting, a junior high or senior high meeting or a university meeting. It can be gender kinship—women's meetings, men's meetings, etc. There are endless possibilities.

Take the Gospel to where people live. Go to restaurants, sports bars, country clubs and city parks. Occasionally you can meet in a church building. But make the topic relevant enough so that pre-churched, pre-Christian persons will feel the freedom to attend. Understand the reticence that pre-Christians have of stepping through the doors of a church.

Look at how many times Jesus focused on different interest groups. When Jesus sent out His disciples to the villages, they were bringing the Good News to people where they lived. With interest group evangelism, we go where we can reach a percentage of people who are not going to hear the Gospel in another way. We want an environment free from barriers, user-friendly, comfortable and safe to the person who is being brought to that interest group meeting.

Encourage Christians to build bridges to their unsaved neighbors and friends. If you're bringing a friend to an interest group meeting and that friend does respond to the presentation of the Gospel, you are the natural bridge to follow-up because you were there at the spiritual birthing process. 1 Thessalonians 2:8 says, "We loved you so much that we were delighted to share with you not only the gospel of God but our lives as well, because you had become so dear to us" (NIV). This verse shows an ongoing involvement in somebody's life: and not just in those who respond to the Gospel, but also in those who continue to seek.

Taking the Gospel to their turf, not asking them to come to ours, is the first element, but it's not enough. The design of the meeting, and especially the communication of the evangelist, has to be relevant. You don't have to be an expert to deal with the people you're talking to, you just have to show some level of affinity. Each message begins differently, according to the type of audience, but each one ends at the Cross. Each one confronts human sin and promises the gift of eternal life through Jesus Christ, if people will turn from their darkness to light.

Interest group evangelism is flexible. It's also affordable financially. Is it effective? We've never seen less than a 15 percent response rate. In interest group evangelism you can narrow the focus of the message. It helps people say, "This evangelist knows where I'm living."

Interest group evangelism takes careful preparation. If you're a large church, give yourself 10 months to a year in the planning phase; a smaller church, five to six months. Choose an interest group chairperson to put together a task force. You need somebody to handle prayer preparation, public relations and promotion, a team to find the facility, and make sure it's available. There should also be a finance committee and follow-up chair.

In follow-up, contact the people who responded. See that they are truly converted to Christ, not just decisions. We want them grounded in the faith, disciples of the Lord Jesus. And we want to build a solid bridge back to the local church.

Lon Allison

Lon Allison is Director of the Billy Graham Center at Wheaton College, Wheaton, Illinois, U.S.A.

Reaching the Secular Mind Through Christian Evidences

Don Bierle

Christian evidences are commanded in Scripture. 1 Peter 3:15 uses the word *apologia*. Apologia, from which we get apologetics, means reason in support of the Christian faith. The use of Christian evidence was practiced in the New Testament Church. When Paul was persuading people, he was using evidence. Matthew, Mark, Luke and John were being sensitive to the audiences that they wanted to reach. Their Gospels, under the guidance of the Holy Spirit, are apologetic.

The role of the apologist in evangelism is to help a person make an informed commitment to follow Jesus Christ. People have different learning styles and are persuaded by God's Spirit differently. One person is moved by a personal testimony, but thinks historical and archaeological evidence is boring. Another person is just the opposite, getting excited about archaeology and history, but having little interest in testimony. A third person is struggling with love, forgiveness and acceptance. The community evidence for faith—lived out, embracing them, showing them that there's a new beginning—is the most persuasive evidence. To reach a broad spectrum of people, evangelists should use a variety of Christian evidences.

Christianity's claim puts God where He can be investigated, where He can be tested to see whether or not He is legitimate or valid. How would we investigate that? We have to check Him out by records. The only records that are complete enough to check out the person of Jesus are Matthew, Mark, Luke and John. The secular mind says, "They are myths."

How would we demonstrate that the Gospels of Matthew, Mark, Luke and John are not myths? We find the first manuscripts of the New Testament in the second century about 20 years after John himself died. Fragments of Matthew, Mark and Luke have been found that are dated around A.D. 50 to 70. We can trace these documents all the way back to the eyewitnesses. People were alive who could have known Jesus personally. The evidence simply would not allow a legend to start in the eyewitness generation itself. Yet we do not have to prove that the Bible is the Word of God in order to talk about Jesus. We need only demonstrate that the Gospels are a reliable source in order to confront people with the person of Christ.

There is evidence of a crucifixion victim found by archaeologists in Jerusalem in which a nail went through the ankle. Yet one of the arguments that the crucifixion story is false is the erroneous claim that they did not have nails at the time of Jesus. The eyewitnesses got it right in the Gospels!

Why do we care? We have faith. We care because if we cannot demonstrate that Jesus is who He claims to be, then it is very difficult to communicate to the secular person. I'm a Ph.D. biologist. I love to talk about the origin of life. Instead of "In the beginning matter," we have "In the beginning God" (Genesis 1:1, KJV). We have intelligence in the universe! And it's the evangelist's job to link the evidence of the design to the Designer.

I must live out the Gospel, not just defend it with evidence. So my testimony that I have been transformed by the power of the resurrected Jesus is another form of apologetics. Evangelistic preaching can be more effective if the presentation includes more than one of the evidences for the Christian faith. Use different people who can speak on an area of apologetics at different points. Not everybody can do everything. In order to reach the secular mind, find people in the church who are capable of doing what others cannot do; use their gifts to convince your audience!

Don Bierle

Don Bierle is Executive Director of Faith Studies International, Chanhassen, Minnesota, U.S.A.

Using Mass Media to Penetrate Cultures for Evangelism

William Brown and Benson Fraser

One of the great opportunities we have in the Church today is to use media to fulfill the Great Commission. We're going to talk about media trends, effects of mass media, and the task of the Church in using media as a powerful communication strategy. We're going to see how we can combine entertainment and education.

Television audiences are rapidly expanding around the globe. Between India and China alone there are now 1.5 billion television viewers. Television is not only multiplying, but the amount of different programs is increasing. In many countries, governments intended media to be an educational tool. But entertainment programming is pushing out educational programming. That's true for television, radio, print, film and theater. We must deal with this as the Church.

First, God is a God who speaks. His stories communicate to us about His design and purpose for the world, and for our lives. To tell the Gospel is to tell the story of God, who has entered human history. Second, we are to have a communication relationship with others. We are beings who communicate through stories. That's ultimately what the media does. It tells stories—good stories, entertaining stories that capture the imagination. It's impossible really to become a Christian without imagining the fact that you are a sinner, that the God of the universe loves you, and that there is hope for you.

Third, we need to understand the nature of communication and our culture if we want to use the mass media for the Kingdom of God. Culture collects and represents our attitudes, our values, our beliefs and our norms. It also includes the symbolic areas of life such as language, music and the arts. The stories that are told within a culture help shape our moral and ethical life and our worldview. At the very heart of evangelism is an understanding of the culture to which we speak and in which we tell our stories.

In producing a film, a video or a television spot, 25 percent of our work is research. Research means listening. We listen to our audiences so that we can present the right answer to the right question. We're making sure that we are addressing people in entertaining and informative ways so that individuals can make a decision to accept Christ. Fifty percent of our work is the development of the product in order to answer the questions that are there. The final 25 percent is production and implementation.

For too long the church has seen entertainment as something negative. But the division between entertainment and education is a false division. Every entertainment program has a message. It is used to promote values, beliefs and behavior. Not only are we educating audiences, we are entertaining audiences.

If we don't capture people's attention and imagination, they will not stay and watch our program, read what we have written or watch our film. Evangelism encounters the whole person, not just the mind. Tell stories that capture the imagination so that people will be turned to the Lord.

William Brown   Benson Fraser

William Brown and Benson Fraser
William Brown is dean of the College of Communication and the Arts at Regent University. Benson Fraser is a professor in the College of Communication and the Arts, and director of the Center for Faith and Culture at Regent University, Virginia, U.S.A.

How to Reach an Audience in Terms They Understand

Michael Cassidy

What a privilege we have in sharing the message of our Lord Jesus! And how important that we do it well, effectively, and in ways people can understand. Ultimately, the One who helps us reach our audience is the Holy Spirit. Unless He works to open and illuminate minds, people aren't going to grasp what we are saying.

A number of factors come into the equation when we talk about communication: the communicator, the audience, the content, the aim or purpose, and the result. Here's a little formula to use the next time you preach: "When does who say what, with what purpose, by what means, to whom, in what situation, with what effect?"

First, when are you delivering this message? If you are delivering your message at noonday in the burning heat, it will affect how long you speak and probably how you speak. The attention span in the heat of a day in a marketplace is not going to be the same as in an auditorium in the evening. Is it to be a three-minute message or a 40-minute message?

Second, who is the communicator? You and I may not be right for a given audience. If there is a meeting of teenagers, an elderly pensioner might not be the right person to take the meeting. If it is a meeting in the marketplace, a churchman in full regalia with a miter and long dress may not be the right person to identify with the masses. Think of age, educational level, cultural background, race and so on. It will determine if you are the right person.

Third, the "what" is the Gospel. We talk about forgiveness and salvation. Whereas Acts 2:38 is very clear, there are two Gospel offers: forgiveness, which deals with the past; and the gift of the Holy Spirit, who is the power for living. Don't just tell them how the past gets dealt with. Tell them about the gift of the Spirit for living in the present. The Gospel's demands are repent, believe and follow. But we haven't always taught about following and Kingdom living, where a new set of rules governs our politics, sexuality, relationships, family life, agriculture, economics and civics. They cannot come to Jesus Christ on Sunday and be sleeping with their girlfriend or crooking in business the rest of the week. We have to explain the full implications of following.

Fourth, what is the purpose? In evangelism, the purpose is to persuade, convince and encourage people to respond to Jesus Christ. You are moving for a verdict. Begin the appeal at the beginning, alerting people that you're going to be asking them to do something at the end. Be clear about it.

Fifth, what is the means? Preaching is not always the best means of getting the message across. In some situations another means is better: a film, a video, a book, a tract, television, the Internet, group study, person to person. We need to ask, "What is the best means?"

Sixth, who is our audience? We preach differently to different audiences—children, teenagers, young adults, businesspeople, politicians, educated, uneducated. Research the audience. Find out who they are and how they think. Seventh, what is the situation you're in? We root the message in the context. We take the timeless message and put it down in a specific moment at a specific place. Eighth, what is the effect? What do we want to see take place in the context where we minister?

We want people to come to Christ. So ask these questions about every bit of communication.

Michael Cassidy
Dr. Michael Cassidy is an international evangelist and founder of African Enterprise, South Africa.

The Use of Television in Evangelism

Steve Chalke

Television provides a bigger platform than a pulpit. Forty years ago the evangelical church in the United Kingdom said, "Avoid the media." We now find ourselves in a situation where there are few Christians effectively engaged in the media. Unless the church starts thinking hard about TV and evangelism, we will not get anywhere. We must engage.

But always we need to be guided by biblical principles. If we're pushed into any course of action simply because it fits the culture, without first taking stock of what the Bible says, we end up doing things that are ineffective.

The apostle Paul had a twofold "come and go" evangelistic strategy. When he arrived in Athens, he went straight to the synagogue and reasoned with the Jews and the God-fearing Greeks, the people who were interested enough in this message to listen. That was his "come" strategy. But it was only half of his strategy.

Then Paul went to the marketplace: "He reasoned in the synagogue with the Jews and the God-fearing Greeks, as well as in the marketplace day by day with those who happened to be there" (Acts 17:17, NIV). When he went to the marketplace he was on their ground where their ideas were formed.

Evangelism in the marketplace is rough. But the New Testament church did well because it was forced to work through its opinions on the anvil of opposition. The problem with evangelism of the "come" variety—on our turf, in our language, where we control the microphone—is that there's no debate; it's not interactive. Paul went on their turf and spoke their language. He didn't start by quoting the Bible. He started where the people were.

TV is the marketplace of today where worldviews are peddled, where people gossip, where thoughts and opinions are shaped. We must be there, be involved and speak the language of the people. We must not abandon the Cross. But we must explain it in language that people use. TV gives those opportunities.

Should we be looking at Christian programming, services, sermons, worship? Or should we be a Christian voice in the everyday programming, the news programs, the debate programs, the chat shows? When religion is segmented from the rest of life, it dies. Christianity has to do with education, marriage, parenting, community, housing and jobs. It has to do with the intellect. It has to do with the emotions. We need an incarnational Christianity that's integrated into the whole of life.

How do you do it? Go and serve. Get involved in a local TV station. Do the slot broadcasting halfway through the night. Sweep the floor. If you serve people, eventually you'll get a break. Most of the producers and the program editors in the United Kingdom served for many years where there is no limelight. It's a long-term calling.

Do non-Christians ever watch a television preacher? Of course they do. But the most biblical approach is to be in the marketplace where other people's ideas are peddled. New Testament evangelism is about debate, dialogue and questioning. We need to get involved as salt and light.

Steve Chalke
Steve Chalke is an evangelist and founder of Oasis Trust in London, England.

Building Bridges to Share Christ

Peter Chao

The chief task of the communicator is to create understanding. It is not enough just to transmit the message, because transmission is when the message reaches the ears alone. We want to create understanding. But we need to go even beyond that. Communication of the Gospel takes place when there is acceptance, when there is change, when there is transformation, when there is obedience to follow Christ. We have to think about how to bring this about.

Whenever we're attempting to reach people for Christ, there are at least four hurdles that we need to cross. First, we need to get the attention of the people. What interests them will always get their attention. If we do not have their attention, we cannot share the Gospel.

The second hurdle is acceptance. The person needs to accept us. The bearer of the message is both the messenger and the message. If we offend people, then what we say will be of no consequence to them. But if they accept us and like us, then there is a chance that what we say will be heard.

The third hurdle is interpretation. What is in their minds as they listen to us? People are never just a group of passive recipients with empty heads waiting to be filled. They perceive things selectively according to their background, upbringing and prejudices. Communication is successful only if you receive in your mind what is in my mind. I'm using words that have meaning to me, but you are interpreting, translating, according to the frame of reference that you have. Approach people on the basis of their needs. Remember the cardinal communication principle is that what interests them will grab their attention.

The fourth hurdle in communication is the disposition, the mood, the attitude, the feelings of people. If a person is hostile to the Gospel, we can argue but the person will remain adamant. It is extremely difficult to turn a hostile heart to Christ. Also there is the disposition of the communicator. If the communicator is disgruntled or unhappy, there will be dissonance between the message and the messenger. Nonverbals always speak louder than verbals.

People are at different levels of understanding and receptivity of the Christian Gospel. We are involved in evangelism as long as we are attempting to move people from one level of understanding to the next, from being resistant to being receptive.

In communicating the Christian Gospel, we have to build bridges. The apostle Peter reminds us that we are "a royal priesthood" (1 Peter 2:9, NIV). In Latin the word for *priest* is the word for *bridge*. If we are priests of God, then we are building bridges, earning the right to be heard with the Gospel message.

Peter Chao
Peter Chao is the leader of Eagles Ministries, Singapore.

Reaching the Disabled

Joni Eareckson Tada

Our heartbeat is to make the Gospel accessible to people affected by disabilities and to help churches include people with disabilities. World Health Organization statistics tell us that more than 10 percent of a country's population includes people with disabilities. In the world there are 650 million disabled people. That means every community has someone with a disability. But often these disabled people are hidden away.

Because of the rejection that so many disabled people experience all through their life, they're often the most receptive to the Good News of the Gospel. The Gospel is about inclusion and acceptance. As we preach the message of acceptance and reconciliation of mankind to God through Jesus Christ, disabled people embrace it readily. They find God in their brokenness as they seek to make sense of the difficult situations in which their disability places them.

Society pushes disabled people to the margins and rejects them, because society likes to feel comfortable. Society likes beautiful people. Any disabled person will say that it's people's attitudes that affect them the most. As the Church, we must model inclusion and pull them in. Look at the priority that Jesus gave to ministry with disabled people. We should look at our own ministry and see the priority that we give them. Jesus gave us the pattern to follow when He told the story of the great banquet (Luke 14:12–14). Jesus is talking to the Church. Reach out to disabled people. These people are indispensable. The body of Christ will never be complete until they are a part of our congregations.

Here are a few practical suggestions: If you encounter someone who is nonverbal, feel free to ask, "What is your sign for yes?" Then learn the sign for no. Once you learn the signs for yes and no, you can have a conversation with that individual just by phrasing your questions in such a way that they can be adequately answered with yes or no. If this person is so nonverbal that you cannot understand any speech at all, then break the alphabet up into parts and simply go through the alphabet. It's a great way to learn someone's name.

What about greeting somebody with a disability? I often extend my hand. It's a gesture saying, "You're welcome to shake my hand," but a lot of people draw back. Other people go through physical gymnastics trying to intertwine their hands around mine in a classic handshake. Don't even worry about doing all of that. Do what you normally do with any person. If you usually shake hands, then reach out and shake my elbow or touch my wrist or squeeze my shoulder gently. Just bridge that distance.

If somebody is deaf and you do not know sign language, a smile communicates so much. Have good eye contact as well. Find a piece of paper and a pencil and jot down a few words of greeting. Then hand the pencil and paper to your deaf friend and let him respond to you. Feel confident to share the Gospel in simple terms with people who have mental impairments. Try to reach them through a medium they can understand. Love them into God's Kingdom. God can give us a love like that. To reach blind people for the Lord Jesus, provide the Bible in Braille or audiotape. Invite them to your meeting so they can hear the Gospel.

The grace of God is so wonderful that He can use a person in a wheelchair to help men and women walk with God; He can use deaf people so that the world can hear the Gospel; He can use a blind person so that others may see.

Joni Eareckson Tada
Joni Eareckson Tada directs the ministry Joni and Friends.

Proclaiming the Gospel With Passion

H. Eddie Fox

How can we more effectively preach the Gospel with persuasion and passion? If you have no passion, your audience will have no passion about what you're saying. If you lose heart, the passion goes and your effectiveness as a communicator of the Gospel is greatly diminished. Testimony and preaching are the expectation of God and a desperate need in today's world. We join our voices with the Psalmist and cry out, "Let the redeemed of the LORD say so" (Psalm 107:2, KJV). We must proclaim the Gospel with passion!

First, we preach and testify because Jesus our Lord preached, taught and testified. Read Mark 1:14-15. Jesus came into Galilee proclaiming, or preaching, the Good News of the Kingdom of God. Second, we preach and testify because Jesus has commanded us to do so. Look at the Acts of the Apostles; you will find the words *preaching* and *testifying* side by side. To fail to preach and give testimony is symptomatic of being ashamed of the Gospel. And to be ashamed of the Gospel is to be ashamed of the Christ who has called us with a holy calling.

Third, something happens when the preaching of the Gospel takes place. There is an intersection in the lives of people as they hear the Gospel being proclaimed. An event takes place. Preaching lifts up the risen, resurrected Christ Jesus so that people may encounter Him. Fourth, when we preach, we are giving the sound teachings of Jesus. The Holy Spirit gives gifts to believers for the ministry of teaching, testifying and preaching.

Fifth, preaching and testifying are the primary ways through which the church gives witness. The word *witness* is found more than 200 times in the New Testament and stresses two points: First, the historical foundation of Christianity—what God has done. And second is the emphasis on the important place of sound teaching or doctrine in a skeptical age. Finally, preaching and testifying are a means of initiating the hearer into the reign of God. We preach, teach and testify with passion because they are our primary means of initiating people into the Kingdom of God.

Preaching matters! It is of eternal significance. It proclaims the biography of the deeds of God—God's story, God's deeds—in light of my autobiography, my own story. If you preach as if this biography has never touched your life, the passion will not be there. People have a right to ask, "How is it with you? Tell us about your relationship with the living Christ."

Here are three foundation stones for preaching with passion. First, preaching is God's idea. Second, preaching is a ministry of the church. Preachers are not freelance artists who just float around. We're accountable. We preach from within the community of faith. Third, preaching is by the power of the Holy Spirit. Our message is Jesus—Christ the creative Word of God, Christ the redeeming Word of God, and Christ the ultimate Word of God. Christ has died, Christ has risen and Christ will come again. We tell the story of the deeds of God in the birth, the life, the death, the resurrection, the glorification, the ascension, the power of Christ Jesus our Lord.

Listen to your sermons and ask the question, "Where is Good News announced to the people today?" No Holy Spirit, no witness. No Holy Spirit, no power. No Holy Spirit, no preaching with passion. The Holy Spirit works in the preacher, and the Holy Spirit works in the people to be receptive to that Gospel message. Doesn't that give us encouragement?

H. Eddie Fox

H. Eddie Fox is the World Director of Evangelism for the World Methodist Council, Nashville, Tennessee, U.S.A.

Models and Resources for Internet Evangelism

Sterling Huston

There are organizations that have done a good job of being creative on the Internet. They are thinking through: What's my target audience? What's my purpose? How am I going to communicate the Good News of Jesus Christ? There are missionaries on the Internet who go into chat rooms and spread the Word. Be creative and think through your own context. Don't look at models and say, "I have to do it this way." Meet the needs that are real in your target group in your country.

The Internet is expensive. Stay away from capital-intensive investments. Ministries need to set aside resources that are focused on the Internet only. Also, ministries should be working together to reduce their costs because they have the same goal. Be sure to plan and staff properly. Analyze. Look at a lot of different ways of doing things. For areas without even a basic knowledge of computers, there are organizations that have tutorials which teach what a computer is, how you browse the Internet and so forth. Gospelcom.net was started to help Christians have impact on the Internet. They have the infrastructure, the servers, the hosts and the technicians so ministries can design their own sites and put their resources into creating impactful content.

E-mail is still probably the most valuable application. It's a great tool for staying in touch with people in two different ways. First, it offers communication that doesn't have to take place at the same time. You can read and respond to e-mail hours or days after it is sent. It also works for direct ministry to Christians, for example, sermon illustrations that a pastor can download, or helps on how to witness, or help if you're struggling with temptation or loneliness.

Second, the Internet is a great way to reach out to non-Christians. You can go onto a chat site and answer questions such as "Why am I here?" "How do I overcome loneliness?" "What makes my life so hard?" People are not necessarily looking for Christian material. They're looking for answers. We can be there with *the* answer and present the Gospel. You have to target an audience, but you also go beyond the target because this is a worldwide Web—not just a local thing for your church. On the Web you are going to the world!

A lot of sites present the Gospel and give an opportunity to respond. That's a key. The other key is to find a way to follow up in order to get people into face-to-face contact with other Christians. There are people who will not talk to another person face-to-face but will, with anonymity, read Christian material. But ultimately our goal is not to keep people in a virtual community. It's to put them in a real community, a local church that can disciple them.

The Internet as a tool is exploding in its use around the world. But we have to be careful that we don't focus on the tool. We keep our focus on the job we have to preach the Gospel and make disciples (see Matthew 28:19). This tool can help us accomplish that goal. But it is not an end in itself. Make sure that you're doing what makes sense for you. Evaluate your approach as to how you want to do things. Don't just do it because you can.

Sterling Huston
Dr. Sterling Huston works with Billy Graham's North American Crusades and is chair for the Internet Evangelism Coalition.

Evangelism Through Conflict Resolution

Emmanuel Kopwe

Because there are conflicts, it is naïve to go on doing evangelistic work without considering conflict resolution. Conflict resolution is a fulfilling ministry. Actually, it shouldn't be evangelism through conflict resolution. Instead, it should be conflict resolution through evangelism, because you cannot resolve a conflict before you work with what has caused that conflict. If you do evangelism first, in the process you find yourself having done conflict resolution. Scripture says, "All this is from God, who reconciled us to himself through Christ and gave us the ministry of reconciliation: that God was reconciling the world to himself in Christ, not counting men's sins against them. And he has committed to us the message of reconciliation" (2 Corinthians 5:18–19, NIV).

The model is Jesus. God took the initiative in the alienation, the estrangement between God and us. In Christ, God left heaven and came down to earth, offering a hand of reconciliation to us. He emptied Himself, and in the process gave us this reconciliation ministry. There is a proverb that says, "The peacemaker gets two-thirds of the blows." If you look at Jesus, He got a lot of blows. He really suffered. He was trying to make peace between God and us.

The Bible indicates that a broken relationship is the root cause of conflict. The task of dealing with a conflict is not just to end the fighting. Nor is it merely to get enemies to be friends. It is to recreate the broken relationship. Until Jesus comes into our lives, we cannot get harmony. There cannot be peace. Therefore, He took the initiative to come down; One who is righteousness took upon Himself the wrong that was done to Him. He took a sacrificial step to recreate a relationship that was broken. He has given us a model that we need to emulate.

The process of conflict resolution brings us to a point where we're taking a sacrificial step based on the love that we have for the other person. We take the initiative because many times the person who is wronged is the one who should be told, "I am sorry." But Jesus Christ—who should hear from us, "We are sorry"—comes to the person who did the wrong. Therefore, the initiative needs to come from the person who understands that there is something wrong.

Somebody needs to go out; that's an evangelistic activity. In peacemaking, we acknowledge first that there is alienation. Until we come to know our problem, we cannot find solutions to it. Second, we need to help people talk together and listen to each other. Third, we do not resist revengefully but take transformation initiatives. Instead of hitting back, the Scriptures say, give the other cheek (see Matthew 5:39).

Fourth, the Word of God asks us to invest in delivering justice, help people to identify themselves with the lowly, to share with the needy. Fifth, love your enemies and help them to understand why you love them. Sixth, pray for your enemies and bless them. Persevere in prayer. And, finally, we make peace in the situations where we find ourselves.

God has given the responsibility of reconciliation to His Church. It is we who have the mind of the Lord. It is we who should portray the love that God portrayed. It is we who know the hearts of men and women and why they fight. It is we who should go out of our way to hold the hand of one who is fighting with another, to be in the middle and not take sides. May God help us to see that He is appealing through us to those in conflict.

Emmanuel Kopwe

Emmanuel Kopwe is Executive Director, Reconciliation and Leadership Ministries of African Evangelistic Enterprise, based in Nairobi, Kenya.

The Becoming a Contagious Christian Course

Mark Mittelberg

How can we get more people mobilized and trained and confident and skilled at sharing their faith, and doing it boldly and clearly and under the power of the Holy Spirit? How can we help each person in our church become a contagious Christian?

It takes all kinds of Christians, and all kinds of evangelistic styles, to reach all kinds of non-Christians. Here are some approaches that we can teach in order to liberate the whole body of Christ for evangelism.

One is the confrontational style of evangelism. It's get-to-the-point evangelism. The apostle Peter was like that, but it was Peter's God-given personality. Some people have personalities like Peter—direct, hard hitting, impatient with small talk. We need to unleash this powerful style of evangelism.

A second style is the intellectual style of evangelism. When Paul was in Athens, he reasoned with people: "Could I tell you about the God you don't know?" He clearly explained the God of the universe who made us and then became one of us and lived among us and taught us and died for us and rose from the dead to give us life. He explained it point by point, very logically. This fits Paul's personality—and it happens to fit mine, as well.

A third style is the testimonial style. The blind man healed by Jesus said, "Here's what I know: I used to be blind; now I can see." He used his story effectively. All of us can use our testimony. It doesn't have to be dramatic.

A fourth style is the interpersonal style of evangelism. Matthew, the former tax collector, threw a great banquet at his house. He invited all the tax collectors that he had been working with. Then he invited Jesus and the disciples. He strategically got them together in that social setting. In a world where people are skeptical about religious institutions, one of the best ways we can reach them is through friendships. We need to follow Matthew's example and have a party with a purpose. When trust is built, you can talk about spiritual matters.

A fifth style of evangelism is the invitational style: "Come with me." The woman at the well met Jesus, realized He was the Messiah, ran to her friends, and said, "You've got to come and hear Him for yourself." She just invited them. People with this style invite others to a Christian event or to a dinner. It's worth the effort to provide these kinds of opportunities for people in our congregations.

Sixth is the service style of evangelism. Dorcas made clothing as an act of loving service, done in the name of Christ. She served with her hands in ways that made heads turn heavenward. There's an unbeatable combination when Christians serve tangibly and combine that with the spoken Gospel message.

Many of these people are shy; they're behind-the-scenes types. But they often reach the hardest-to-reach people. They love the downtrodden and the outcast in ways that tangibly express who Christ is and what He can do for them.

Personal evangelism really can look like you! You do not have to become something you're not. And when we unleash the broader body of Christ, we will see an incredible wave of fruitful, contagious Christianity that spreads from person to person to person.

Mark Mittelberg

Mark Mittelberg is Executive Vice President of the Willow Creek Association, Barrington, Illinois, U.S.A., and coauthor with Lee Strobel and Bill Hybels of the Becoming a Contagious Christian training course.

Evangelism in the Military

Laurence New

The Gospel compels us to preach the Good News to everyone, and that includes the military. In Acts 10:44, we read this, "While Peter was still speaking these words, the Holy Spirit came on all who heard the message. The circumcised believers who had come with Peter were astonished that the gift of the Holy Spirit had been poured out even on the Gentiles" (NIV). This was not only the first time that Gentiles heard the Gospel, but it was in a military officer's quarters. Captain Cornelius was serving in what was called the Italian regiment. We have a right to claim military people for the Lord!

I'd like to list three main evangelistic areas. First is military to military. In many ways this is the easiest platform. In this I include military chaplains, because they already have earned the right to speak to other people in uniform. The second area is the civilian working with the military in a civilian setting. A third category is the civilian minister or evangelist being given permission to come into barracks to minister in a military setting.

Here are some principles that can help in evangelism of the military. First, if we do not have a clear calling to work with the military in evangelism, we may find it pretty hard going. Maybe the Lord wants us to do something else. A clear call is a prerequisite to this work.

Second, believe passionately in prayer. We strongly urge that when you go into this hard-to-reach group, the military, you have organized and requested strong prayer support. Third, have the backing of the church community, not only in prayer, not only financially, but in accountability and advice. Also, if you are working as a civilian in a military context, it helps to have a military contact, especially the chaplain or the commander. They want to know what's going on inside their command. Unity among Christian workers is a necessity. If there is disunity, or any sign of competition, our ministry and the other ministries will be dishonored.

Next is the how-to part. First, pray before you plan. When you pray and plan and seek the Lord's way, it is far more exciting and effective than anything you could have chosen on your own. Second, look for like-minded people. The Christian chaplain will look for believers in his group. The civilian will look for a Christian chaplain and maybe an officer who is committed to Christ.

Third, if you want to evangelize the military, it is an advantage to be military yourself or to have someone on your team who is. If you are military or have been in the military, people recognize that you know what you are talking about and you know their particular difficulties.

You can evangelize through fellowship, conferences, prayer groups, Bible studies and discipleship programs. If you hold men's breakfasts, that's an opportunity for evangelism. Ethics seminars are successful because many people who might be frightened off by a straight evangelistic message will come to discuss ethics. Of course, all ethics lead to the Lord, so it is not difficult to finish up an ethics seminar with a straight evangelistic message. Special events dealing with drugs and suicide are another opportunity for evangelism.

The greatest privilege in the world is to be an evangelist for the Lord! You don't have to work alone. There are many organizations to help. Pray for one another, encourage one another, support one another, communicate with one another, coordinate with one another, cooperate with one another and, above all, love one another.

Laurence New

Sir Laurence New is President of the Association of Military Christian Fellowships and lives on the Isle of Man, U.K.

Reaching Nonbelievers Through Small Groups

Garry Poole

You've never looked into the eyes of a person who didn't matter to God. That person may be skeptical, cynical, neutral or searching. Here are three principles for starting seeker small groups.

First, a group needs to be a safe place for seekers to be themselves, to be accepted, to feel free to voice their objections without feeling like they're going to be judged. Second, a seeker group is an extension of your own personal evangelistic effort. The group provides an opportunity in which you can get together with somebody on a one-to-one basis and talk more specifically about the issues that person is facing. Third, small groups can fit any setting. We've started small groups in neighborhoods, in the marketplace, on job sites and in the church. They work in all kinds of situations.

Here are principles for inviting non-Christians to your group. First, intentionally nurture relationships with non-Christians. One obstacle to evangelism is that we spend time with our Christian friends and isolate ourselves from non-Christians. Do something socially with non-Christians. Then you will have earned the right to invite them to your group.

Second, non-Christians are going to have lots of fears about getting into a group: "I'm going to be the most ignorant person in your group," or "I don't know the Bible and I'm going to look stupid." If you dispel that fear, they might come. Some people have a fear that you're going to try to recruit them to become a member of your church. You have to tell them, "I'm not trying to recruit you." Others have a fear of being locked into a group forever. I tell them, "Come one time. If you don't like it, you don't have to come back." Your friend is going to have lots of fears, hesitations and reservations. Dispel those fears in the invitation process.

Third, be sure to communicate that they can invite their friends. Seekers are the best bringers of other seekers. Never close the door to new people. If the group gets too big to manage discussion, you may have to split into two groups.

Next, here are three principles for leading discussions. First, use icebreakers, lighthearted, non-threatening questions to help generate discussion. These help people feel safe with one another and enable them to talk at a deeper level later about spiritual things. Second, ask lots of questions. You're not lecturing, you're helping them discover spiritual truths on their own. Third, listen well. If you do a lot of good listening to what people are saying, in time they'll turn to you and ask, "What do you think?" You've earned the right to be heard.

Now here are three principles for launching a seeker small-group ministry in your church. First, start a group yourself. That sets the pace for the rest of the church. Model how to do it. Second, recruit other leaders and show how they can be reaching seekers through these kinds of groups themselves. Look for people who have a passion for lost people. Third, train people. Teach what you've learned and some of the do's and don'ts to getting started.

Our calling is to be with non-Christians. It's going to get a little messy sometimes, and there are going to be some habits and words that are not the best. But that's who these people are. Seekers act like seekers. What is going to change them is an encounter with Christ. Be willing to be with them so that eventually they can accept Christ. You don't have to clean the fish before you catch them!

Garry Poole
Garry Poole serves on staff at Willow Creek Community Church, South Barrington, Illinois, U.S.A.

Evangelism and Compassion

Ross Rhoads

There are two aspects to the ministry of Christ. There's the Word of Christ and there's the work of Christ. In the Christian life there should be both.

Christian ministry has to be verbal and it has to be vital. It has to be done as well as said. Many times you'll find you can do something verbal in only a small way, but the work that you can do has a larger impact. Other times you can verbalize by preaching or telling the Gospel, but you can't do something that will help people in a tangible way.

Samaritan's Purse is an evangelical Christian organization. The paragraph that defines us, our mission statement, says that we are an evangelistic organization meeting emergency needs in crisis areas of famine or war or disaster, with the help and the partnership of other organizations, so that people will believe, trust and follow our living Lord.

To couple the work of God with the words of God is a winner. The Gospel needs to be twofold: word and work. There are many ways that we can do the work of God. Think about an aspect of ministry that could be done. A vision is something that is not yet but could be. A vision doesn't necessarily have all the resources yet, but you've got to be able to see it. What does God want you to see that you're not seeing now?

Here are several things for you to think about. First, think about your world. Describe your world. What is your Jerusalem? Who's in your neighborhood? Next, think about the harvest possibilities. Think about the people in your church's community. What are the people like? What are their needs? Find out how you can help to meet those needs. Next, begin to chart each need; break it up into parts. Try to reach that area of need with the compassion of Jesus.

You can't do everything yourself. Try to find people who can help you in that mission. People have time, they have money and they have wisdom to meet that need. Some people may not have any money, but they've got a good idea. There are people with money to give; you accept it. There are people with time to give; you use it. There are people with wisdom; apply it. Everybody has something.

Describe the need, chart it and pray for it. Everybody in your church can pray for something. Then communicate that need. Tell people about it and communicate the Gospel through it. Samaritan's Purse will not go anywhere unless we can share the Gospel. That's the responsibility of the Gospel. Words and the works go together.

Brothers and sisters, don't go through life struggling with what you can't do;

find out what you can do. There's so much need in the world. You can help in the name of Jesus. That's our opportunity.

Ross Rhoads

Ross Rhoads is vice-chairman of the board of Samaritan's Purse, Boone, North Carolina, U.S.A.

"Stone Age" People Learn "High Tech" Skills for Evangelism

Steve Saint

We can't convert people to God's system. That's what the Holy Spirit does. What we can do is say as the Waodani say, "I used to live badly, badly, my heart being dark and sick with sin, but then, seeing God's carvings, His Holy Spirit came, and with Jesus' blood dripping and dripping, He washed my heart as clean as the sky when it has no clouds in it. Now clearly seeing God's trail and following it, I'm going to come to God's place." That's evangelism.

The purpose of missions is not to evangelize the world; that's the purpose of the Church. The purpose of missions is to plant the Church so that it exists where it didn't exist before, so that it can evangelize the world. As stewards of God's Good News, it's incumbent upon us to look for ways that are effective and efficient to share His Gospel.

We forget how much technology we use (faxes, telephone, radio, television, computers, sound systems, books, writing paper). Our lives are so full of technology, we don't even think about it anymore. But when we go down to the jungles, we have no electricity, no stores or tools. My concern is for the people in frontier areas where high technology doesn't exist yet, where Christ's commission is just as real to them as it is to us. How are they going to share the Good News effectively and efficiently? They can't use the same technologies that we use because they don't have the foundation for it or the infrastructure to keep it going.

But if they had appropriate tools, they could be much more effective in sharing the Gospel. The Waodani say, "You teaching us; we will do it." I realized that we needed to reinvent the tools that we are familiar with so that our brothers and sisters on the frontiers of the world and the frontiers of technology could use them too. Technology as an end in itself becomes an idol. But technology as a means to an end is good stewardship in sharing the Gospel. Sometimes it is difficult to transfer the technology because our standards and our priorities are so different.

We've been trying to give the Waodani what they ask for. When they asked me to get them an airplane, I said, "Guys, this is too much." You need several steps from the stone age to top rating your own aircraft. In Ecuador you can't even begin to do pilot training until you have a high school diploma. But in six hours one of the men was able to start, taxi, take off, fly and land a Cessna 172—in six hours! Then he had to start learning what all those round things are that have needles that move; some have two needles. And I was trying to explain the points of the compass. So we decided to go back to something more basic. We took a kit and built a plane.

We have black and white television powered by a solar panel. This is designed for two hundred people to be able to watch at once. Do you know how exciting this is for the people to see on video that Jesus really lived and was baptized just like we should be baptized when we want to follow His trail? This will play for three hours without a charge, and then, during the day when we're not using it, we just stick the solar panel on top for the recharge.

A lot of high-tech people think these people can't do it; they don't have what it takes. But they're wrong!

Steve Saint

Steve Saint, missionary, is the son of martyred missionary Nate Saint. He works with the Waodani (Auca) people in Ecuador.

Multiplying Your Ministry Through the Use of Tracts

Daniel Southern

One tool surpasses all others in terms of reaching people with the Gospel. That's an evangelistic tract. What is a tract? Here are five points to remember.

First, a Gospel tract must be brief and to the point. We don't know how long we have to offer the Gospel to a person. We have to be concise. Second, a tract needs to be relevant. We need to make a relevant connection between the Gospel truth and the heart of the individual that we're speaking to. Third, a tract gets people's attention. We want a tract to be excellent, not only in appearance but also in the message it conveys.

Fourth, a tract must invite people to step closer to Christ. We will not always see a decision to receive Christ as Lord and Savior, but a good tract always has an invitation to receive Christ. Fifth, a tract must contain the Gospel. If a tract does not present the Gospel, it's not a good tract.

Why do tracts work? First, a tract is affordable. It's one of the least expensive ways that you can communicate the Gospel. Second, a tract lasts longer than many other forms of communication. In my country, an average of three people read a tract before it is set aside. In other parts of the world, it could be many times that.

Third, a tract is easy to use. Some people don't evangelize because they don't know how. Yet most people have never met the person who gave out the tract. They found a tract and it spoke to them and they prayed to receive Christ. Fourth, tracts can say it better. I'm not very good with words compared to Billy Graham. How would you like to have Billy Graham with you when you present the Gospel? We have a tract written by Billy Graham. We can take him with us when we go out into the streets. A tract is a pocket evangelist.

Fifth, nothing works harder than a tract. It will give itself away. Sixth, tracts are patient. They will wait until people are ready to read them. Seventh, people can read a tract when they're alone without feeling the pressure of their friends. Eighth, tracts understand how the human psyche works. They're nonthreatening.

How do we use tracts? First, bathe your tract giving in prayer. The Holy Spirit is released in our lives through prayer. Second, rely on the Holy Spirit who wins people to Christ. Third, be sure that your tracts are based on the Word of God. Fourth, match your personal testimony to the tract you are giving. Fifth, be obedient. None of the previous suggestions will work if you are not obedient to God in your personal life and witness.

Nothing has been used more widely in the world to reach people for Christ than a Gospel tract. The tract is a tool that you can use to multiply effectiveness in your ministry.

Daniel Southern
Daniel Southern is the President of the American Tract Society and International Tract Society, Garland, Texas, U.S.A.

Evangelism Through Pastoral Counseling

Modupe Taylor-Pearce

When something traumatic happens to our church members, do they come to us as pastors? Do they see us as relevant? How useful are we in relieving the hurts and needs of our people? People have needs that can be handled in a lasting way only by the Lord Jesus Christ. When these needs are unmet, it brings frustration, despair, violence and suicide. But when people's needs are met, they have satisfaction and joy.

I've discovered that when I preach, people come to me for spiritual counseling and advice. I recommend that our preaching be concrete, not abstract, relevant to the needs, the hurts or the triumphs of people. People will ask, "What is God saying to me in my distress or in my problem or in my success?" We can talk to them about Christ.

Here are the kinds of problems that I have been dealing with: poor relationship with spouse or with children, people convinced that they are the victims of witchcraft, bitterness, unemployment, demonic influences, feelings of guilt, fears, disobedient or wayward children, money problems, the sense of being unjustly treated by spiritual leaders, people who want to marry, business problems, parents concerned over the welfare of adult children.

In each situation I give them the assurance that the Holy Spirit has an answer. I relate the problem to a biblical solution. I give them hope. And almost always I give them homework assignments based on Scripture. The whole point is to develop reliance on the Word of God.

When people come for counseling, there are three questions that I try to answer: What is your problem? What have you done about it? What do you want me to do?

It is very important for the counselee and me to agree on what I should do. If what the counselee wants is unbiblical, then it is my responsibility to lead that person to understand that. Sometimes all that people want you to do is to listen to them. That is good because you are an evangelist as well as a counselor. You are leading them to find out the best that God wants for them. As early as possible, I bring the Gospel to them to see how one can have joy and peace. They need Christ for a satisfying life both on this earth and after death.

A person comes to you as an evangelist and a counselor. Let people know that crisis is part of life. We all go through problems, but Jesus is the answer to our problems. Let your preaching be biblical. Equip yourself with counseling skills. Be deeply versed in the Word of God, and have compassion for your people. Use every opportunity to lead people to Christ.

We are God's servants to help meet people's needs. We lead people to faith and to obey the Word of God. We lead people from darkness to light, from the power of Satan to God. We are called, chosen and faithful. We are truly blessed.

Modupe Taylor-Pearce

Modupe Taylor-Pearce is Director of Diakonia Interdenominational Services for Counseling, Evangelism and Teaching in Sierra Leone.

Evangelism Through Training on the Family

Gerard van der Schee

As parents, we need the help of God. That's why we can have evangelism training in the family and evangelism of non-Christians through the family. Family life is a marvelous opportunity to give a taste of the Kingdom of God to our children, because our purpose is to have them be children of God too. At home, have joy with your family and let non-Christians around you look at your life. People around us want to know, is it relevant to believe in Jesus? Does it work out in daily life? As parents, talk about life issues in relationship to faith in Jesus Christ. In your home discuss opportunities to introduce friends to God's Kingdom. Be honest about what you are afraid of. That's the first point—your family life as a natural place for evangelism.

The next point is evangelism through training parents. Most parents feel guilty because they know they should do better. When we come together with other parents, our values and feelings come to the surface. So, as a church we offer a course on parenthood. We don't preach at them, but we can have wonderful evenings of communication. Here are some subjects that are attractive to non-Christian parents in a course on parenthood: parent-child relationships, knowing your child, how to build your children's trust, how to handle teenagers, conflict of interest between parents and children, launching children into life, how to discipline, how to stay together, protection for the family from negative influences.

We ask people to meet with each other because people like to discuss with each other how they are working with their children. We invite parents who have children around the same ages. So we have one course for parents of very little children, another for parents of children four to 12 years, and another for parents of teenagers. You can meet at your church or in a home.

As you welcome people the first evening, try to have a creative introduction so that people feel at ease. We always explain our meeting rules. What we talk about in the group we won't talk about outside the group. The other rule is that we won't compare with each other. When you have introduced the theme, give them a small group task around the discussion idea. We show a tableau of family life and then say, "Discuss in small groups what you are feeling about it. Does it look like your family?" Give them a picture, an illustration, and get questions coming. After 20 or 30 minutes you can summarize some of the ideas and identify some principles. After a coffee break, you can go on with the same theme, have another group discussion and then illustrate the theme telling a story or using a specific verse from the Bible. You can say, "I want to share something from the

Bible because the Bible gives good ideas too." Then, after questions and answers and remarks at the end, ask to be allowed to pray for them, because God wants to bless them. Make it a short prayer from your heart.

Our meetings last four evenings. Better to have a short timetable and then go on when they like it. Have a firm stopping time because they may have a baby-sitter at home or other appointments. When they know they can leave, they feel served and you have a good relationship. Be clear that you are Christian. As Christians, we are not better parents. Rather, we trust our lives to the Lord because we have reflected on our lives and think, "Well, it must go better, but we can't do it the way we would like to do it." So we say, "Lord, help us." They don't have the idea yet to say, "Lord, help me." That's the best prayer and the shortest prayer we can pray in our lives. That's what we offer to non-Christians.

Gerard van der Schee

Gerard van der Schee is on staff with the Dutch Evangelical Alliance and the author of a book on fatherhood.

Strategy for Reaching a City

Galo Vasquez

Some of us are thinking not only of reaching our neighborhood, but the whole city. No less than 65 percent of the world's population is concentrated in large cities. If we want to reach the largest number of people with the Gospel, we go where the people are. These great centers of culture, entertainment, art and communications are also the places where people experience the most unjust, inhuman and violent events that exist today. People experience loneliness even while surrounded by millions of inhabitants. They live in confusion and stress, and they are constantly in search of a new identity.

To reach a city, we must first know our city. Nehemiah went to Jerusalem. He spent time there meditating, thinking, investigating before starting to organize the people of God. As we looked at our city, Mexico City, we discovered that the tendency of missionaries and denominations was to work with certain types of people in the same geographical zones, so there were social strata, geographical regions, more than 2,000 neighborhoods that weren't being touched. We have to know our city, our reality.

Second, pray for the city. There is a great difference between praying in general and praying specifically and strategically. See the reality of your city by praying for the people arriving at the bus terminals, the people milling around hospitals, people transported by taxis and the subway systems. When one begins to pray specifically for these persons, suddenly the Holy Spirit gives ideas on how to focus on ministry. You will discover that you cannot simply have one method to reach the people. There has to be diversity. This generates creativity. Find a high place from where you can look down on the city and let the Holy Spirit give you a burden for the city. When you do that, you won't be the same person. Your commitment to the cause of Christ for the city will deepen when you go outside the church and pray for the people who aren't in the church.

Third, we reach the city by planning. We cannot minister in isolation; we must cooperate. Without underestimating the importance of the local church, in order to establish the Kingdom of God in the hearts of the urbanites and plant new churches accessible to them, we need to work as a body. We ask questions such as: What do we want to achieve? What is our vision, our goal? With whom will we work? What resources do we have? How can we reach the marginal areas? How can we reach the youth?

In Mexico City a group of us used big maps of the city, and over several months we went to all the areas of the city, and we put on the maps the locations of the established churches and the preaching points, as well as the home Bible study groups. When we discovered thousands of neighborhoods without any testimony, our vision was geographic multiplication of churches, new cells,

Bible studies in homes, preaching centers, new ways to make the Gospel present. The strategy was to motivate, train and mobilize all of the church, to establish growth goals. The evangelical leaders began a wonderful plan—"10,000 for 2000." They wanted 10,000 new churches by the end of the year 2000. Thousands of churches and Christian meeting points are being started in every area of our great city!

Jesus said, "O Jerusalem, Jerusalem . . . how often I have longed to gather your children together, as a hen gathers her chicks under her wings, but you were not willing" (Matthew 23:37, NIV). We must have the same burden as Jesus. It wasn't a single attempt. He said, "How often I have longed." Jesus cried, but He also died for the city. My sister, my brother, when was the last time that you cried for your city?

Galo Vasquez

Galo Vasquez is Founder and President of VELA Ministries, Mexico City, Mexico, and Latin American Director of the International Bible Society.

Using Tomorrow's Technology for Today's Evangelism

Marcus Vegh

We have an unprecedented opportunity today to use digital media for evangelism. We have technology to deliver the Gospel in places not possible before because of the limitations of electricity or because of the durability or portability of technology. A mission's planner should be asking—"Into which countries is technology going, and how can we prepare tools to take advantage of the technology in these countries and cultures?"

Look at the people we're trying to reach. How can we communicate the Gospel in a manner that they can understand? We need to understand a people's educational level, the cultural framework and the political situation, as well as their traditional, historical background. What tools already exist? Do they exist in an international context or do they need to be adapted to a culture? If we create new content, can that content be shared internationally? Should we develop an indigenous tool that will minister in one context much more effectively than it would if simply adapted or translated from a culture which is very different?

In developing content, first we need to understand what our mission is. That requires research, prayer, mapping, field analysis—all the things that need to be done in a pre-evangelism context. The second stage is the actual proclamation of the Gospel. The third stage is equipping emerging shepherds and thought leaders. Fourth is strategic church planting. By using technology we can train a great number of people and mobilize them to share the faith.

In looking at the content, first start with the scriptural idea that is going to penetrate the heart and mind of the persons in that group. Second is application. If it's worth believing, it is worth applying to my own life. Third is reproduction. If it's worth believing and worth applying to my own life, it's worth reproducing in another person's life. The fourth stage is reinforcement; telling the idea in a graphic way for them to remember. The fifth stage is accountability; to hold one another accountable to whatever the commitment might be. The last stage is feedback, when we intentionally ask questions about what is working or not working.

There is VCD, video compact disk, a technology widely used within the house church networks in China. CD is inexpensive for distributing audio material. MP3 is a pen-like instrument that holds twelve hours of audio. The CD-ROM is a powerful tool particularly for doing leadership development. You can create a portable radio station by modifying a boom box, putting a transmitter card inside and turning the boom box from a receiver to a transmitter. DVD has the capability of holding eight audio channels. Another technology is a GPS receiver, a global positioning system for tracking resources being used in the world.

We try to get content on the Web before we produce it in a portable media—just to test it out. People who will be using the material suggest improvements. Then we do video production. Next we assign it to translation, and the graphics are produced. Then voice-over recordings are done. We test it to see if this is going to work. Then we determine the appropriate media platforms for a target region. The final steps are replication and deployment—getting it to the audience that needs it.

Marcus Vegh
Marcus Vegh is President of Progressive Vision, Laguna Hills, California, U.S.A.

KidsGames and Major Sports Events Evangelism

Eddie Waxer

There are hundreds of organizations that are part of sports networks. The International Sports Leadership School is open to any leader in sports ministry in any country of the world. It's a three-month school that takes place near Capetown, South Africa. People who lead sports ministries from all over the world come to train the next generation of leaders on the biblical basis of sports ministry, on major events sports ministry, on working with elite athletes, on using recreation and sports, on the KidsGames.

Through www.sportsoutreach.org, you can find most of the sports ministries in 150–160 countries. A second address is www.thegoal.com. That is the Web site of all the agencies in the world that work together to put the life story, the testimony, of every Christian national-level athlete, every Christian Olympic-level athlete on that Web site. Eventually about 26,000 athletes' testimonies will be on that site in the native language of the athlete and in English.

There is also the Major Sports Event Partnership, which focuses on two events: the summer Olympic games and the men's World Cup of soccer. It's a partnership of all the international agencies that see these events as an opportunity to share the message of the life, death and resurrection of Jesus Christ with 3 to 3.5 billion people, a little more than half of the world's population, who follow these two events. The key is creating culturally relevant resources for churches and ministries to reach athletes, children and the public.

In many countries Olympic video parties have been very powerful, with big crowds coming out to watch the Olympics or the World Cup on television together, then having an Olympic athlete's testimony and action footage on video. Ask if a resource is available in your country and in your language, and if it is culturally relevant. Every church in every country can have an outreach to every person who can be touched through the Olympics or the World Cup. It's not local to where the event is; it's global to the opportunity.

Another strategy is the KidsGames. For the ten-week program, each participating church provides Bible teaching and games for the children representing their church. The children paint the game flag of their own church. When all the churches meet for the final day, the children parade behind the flags they painted.

KidsGames is made up of three major components: an opening ceremony, a ten-week program in which once a week for three hours children meet in their local church for a high-quality sports program and biblical teaching program both for evangelism and discipleship and, finally, a huge sports festival where the whole city comes together for the event. There is a special KidsGames Bible, trading cards of different athletes with their testimonies and favorite Scriptures, and a KidsGames medal that each child receives. Creativity? It's unlimited!

Kids and sports; sports and kids. The curriculum is a solid, Bible-based program designed for teaching at the local church level so that no one is excluded, and which becomes a gigantic festival to celebrate together and to lift up the kids of our cities.

Eddie Waxer
Eddie Waxer is President of World Sports, Bonita Springs, Florida, U.S.A.

Using Films in Evangelism

J. R. Whitby

Christian films, videos, Internet Web sites and other media are some of the most effective tools available to introduce lost souls to the Lord Jesus Christ. First, films are effective because we learn 11 percent by hearing, but 83 percent by seeing. Second, films can be understood by almost anyone. About half the world's population cannot read. But films can be used to reach people in the language that they understand. Third, almost anyone can learn to operate a film projector. Fourth, films can draw large crowds, people who would normally never set foot in a church to hear a sermon. Fifth, the message of the film is always the same.

Here are keys to an effective film showing. First is the planning stage. The most important thing in planning is to spend time in prayer. Ask God to help you with your film showing, to give you a vision to see the lost come to Christ. Pray about how you will invite the lost to receive Christ. We recommend that you show the film in two sections. Find a critical point in the film where you stop the film, so they want to know what happens next. At that point, springboard from what you have just seen in the film to your Gospel presentation. Make that presentation brief and to the point.

Second, decide how counselors will be used and what literature will be distributed. Seek the help of Christian leaders about how follow-up will be performed and how to place new believers in the churches. Third, decide when to show the film, which night of the week will allow you to reach the greatest number of people. Consider festivals and holidays when a crowd may already be gathered.

Fourth, find a neutral site, perhaps an open-air auditorium or a town square. Make sure you have legal permission before you set up in a public location. In tribal settings, talk to the chief of the village to get his blessing on the film showing. You might even ask to have the town criers go about the village and invite people to the film showing.

While films can be used by one evangelist, it's often more effective if a film team is created. The team's responsibilities include maintenance of the film and equipment, inviting people to attend, advertising, setting up and tearing down equipment, preparing counselors to talk with new converts, providing follow-up materials, planning how the film will be shown and determining whether or not music or any other entertainment should be included with the film showing.

Counselors deal directly with the people by answering questions, witnessing and praying with them. When gathering counselors, always get believers from a local church. They'll help new believers be discipled and placed in a local church. The key to successful evangelism is to be filled with the Holy Spirit. Allow Him to work through you, but leave the results to God. You cannot change a person's heart; only the Holy Spirit can do that. Even if people don't accept Christ or come to church, be thankful that you were able to plant a seed with that film showing. When the church and mass media are linked together under the leadership of the Holy Spirit, the task not only becomes possible but also successful!

J. R. Whitby

J. R. Whitby is Vice-President of Gospel Communications International.

The Use of Drama in Evangelism

Willow Creek Drama Team

Our services are designed to reach the unchurched. We try to portray life in all its realness. It's called truth-driven drama, truth based on real life and the truth of Scripture. Drama should not be limited to movies, to television and to plays as the world knows them. Drama belongs on the stage of our Christian services. But for years the Church has shied away from doing courageous dramas in ministry. We want people engaged and involved. Drama has the potential of doing that. It's a tool to pull people in and help them respond to God.

When drama is done well it opens up people's hearts to the truth of God's Word and to the potential of the Holy Spirit in their lives. There are three guiding principles that we follow when we're bringing drama to our services. The first is to know our audience. We need to know their average age, what their struggles are, what is important to them, their interests and what they do for a living. We need to tell stories and show life in a way that people can identify with.

The second principle is to be real. It's absolutely crucial that people be able to identify with what they are seeing and hearing. We must respect our audience and try not to gloss over the difficulties of life. When people see themselves portrayed in a drama, they realize that here is a place that understands them, that won't reject them. Then a trust begins to develop between the persons in the spectator seat and the church. Of course, our ultimate goal is that trust be built between the person coming to the service and God Himself.

The third guiding principle in bringing drama to our services is to not preach. We don't want drama to give the moral of the day. We just want to raise the question or show the conflict. Drama engages people. It gets them to look at their own lives. Our number-one goal in bringing drama to a service is not to entertain—although it can be entertaining. Our goal is to help open the hearts of the people to a place where they begin to feel understood, accepted and safe, maybe for the first time in their lives, so that we can hand them over to the preacher for the wonderful saving message of Jesus Christ. So in our drama preparation, we work closely with the preacher to raise questions in people's minds that he or she will answer, or to provide a life illustration that the preacher can refer to.

There are two groups in our congregation: the nonbeliever and the believer. Nonbelievers are tough to reach. They come to watch, sitting in the spectator seats with arms crossed. We're challenged to be authentic and real with this group, to show them that we are all struggling. We want to relate to their concerns, their lives, and challenge their value system without preaching at them or insulting them.

The second group is made up of believers. Many Christians are hurting. They need to be loved, accepted and assured that no matter what is going on in their lives, here is a group of loving people who will stay by their side and see them through these very tough times. No sin is too awful. We are not there to judge and reject; we are there to love and embrace.

All our dramas are available. For a description of each drama, how many characters are needed for each drama and the various topics, it's www.willowcreek.org/wca. Drama is one of the God-designed tools to reach people today!

Willow Creek Drama Team, Willow Creek Community Church, North Barrington, Illinois, U.S.A.

Mobilizing Prayer for Evangelism

Isaac Ababio

Every evangelist, indeed every preacher, first must develop the habit of serious prayer. It is in the prayer closet that a person's life is transformed into the likeness of Jesus. Second, the evangelist must be an intercessor for the people he or she has reached for Christ and those yet to be reached. Third, the evangelist needs the intensive prayer support of other people. Fourth, prayer is the evangelist's indispensable weapon in spiritual warfare.

Number one is prayer in the life of the evangelist. Prayer is the simplest act a creature of God can perform. It is divine communion with our heavenly Father. Prayer gives vision to the believer. It gives eyes to our faith. In prayer we see beyond ourselves and focus on God's infinite power. Prayer is a gift God has given to us.

Prayer is the mightiest weapon in the evangelist's arsenal. There are certain things that will never happen unless we ask God to bring them to pass. We align our faith to cooperate with Him. In Jeremiah 29:13, God says, "You will seek me and find me when you seek me with all your heart" (NIV). God is wooing us to seek Him. Prayer delights the heart of God.

Number two, the preacher as an intercessor. We live in a world of instant everything. But sometimes the Lord delays in bringing the answer. Persevere, never give up; keep on praying until the answer comes. We need to pray for all those we've led to Christ and also for areas that we intend to reach. God is able to do extraordinary things when we trust Him.

Number three is marshaling prayer support of others. The preacher must desire the prayers of God's people. Teach new converts that they, too, have authority to pray. Affirm them in their faith and let them experience answers to prayer on their own. If you're planning a crusade, part of your preparation is to organize prayer backing for that crusade. Once people are prayerfully involved they will be able to effectively follow up those who come to Christ.

Number four is spiritual warfare. James says, "Submit yourselves, then, to God. Resist the devil, and he will flee from you" (James 4:7, NIV). He gives basic steps for spiritual warfare: one, submitting to God; two, drawing near to God; and, three, cleansing your hands and purifying your hearts. Submission calls for obedience. It means listening to what God has to say and then doing it. The spiritual warrior must develop a life of holiness to succeed in the war against sin and Satan. Put your life in order. Get disobedience dealt with and learn to walk in holiness with the Lord.

Give yourself to seasons of fasting and prayer. Spiritual warfare is done on our knees and involves targeting specific strongholds of Satan. The Lord told the prophet Jeremiah: "See, today I appoint you over nations and kingdoms to uproot and tear down to destroy and overthrow, to build and to plant" (Jeremiah 1:10, NIV). We are to demolish the strongholds of Satan; we are to establish the Kingdom of almighty God.

How have you fared at the battlefront? Have you sometimes felt discouraged? Remember, the Bible says, "They that wait upon the LORD shall renew their strength; they shall mount up with wings as eagles; they shall run, and not be weary; and they shall walk, and not faint," Isaiah 40:31 (KJV). Take hold of the Lord and His Word. He will give you victory!

Isaac Ababio

Isaac Ababio is Executive Director of Hour of Visitation Ministries, Accra, Ghana.

Evangelism Through Explaining the Trinity

Paul Blackham

The heart of the Gospel is that the one true and living God is Father, Son and Holy Spirit. Nothing we say about Jesus Christ makes sense unless we are articulating the doctrine of the Trinity. Jesus of Nazareth is not an agent of God. He's not an addition to God. He is the eternal Son of the Father.

There are three ways *not* to explain the Trinity. First, avoid philosophical arguments. If we deliver a philosophical proof for God, we have not proved the God of the Bible revealed in and through Jesus Christ. Second, avoid analogies. There is no analogy for God. He's not like anything; there is nothing that He can be compared to.

Water can be in three forms: liquid, ice or steam. Is this a good analogy? No, because water is never all three at once. And it isn't personal. God's not just a substance that can be in three different forms. He is three persons all at once. A man can be a husband, a father and a son. But the man is just one person who has three different roles. God is not one person who has three different roles. He is three persons at the same time.

Third, avoid doctrinal definitions. There are excellent descriptions of God in the creeds of the Christian church. But it isn't good to give them to non-Christians, for two reasons. First, we want people to study the Bible rather than church documents. We don't want them to say, "Yes, I believe what the church has taught." We want people to say, "I believe what the Bible says." Second, there is a level of abstract language in the creeds that requires explanation. We will inevitably be drawn into further discussion about why that kind of language is used in the creeds. Then the presentation of the Gospel will not happen. Later, when someone becomes a Christian, these creeds will be invaluable as a guide to understanding the Bible. But in evangelism they can be a distraction.

What should we do to articulate the Trinity? It's important that we understand the way that God is revealed in the Bible. First, the Trinitarian God is not confined to the New Testament. The Trinitarian God is living and active as all three persons throughout the Bible.

In Exodus 33–35, Moses is summoned up the mountain to talk to the Lord. But he also meets with the Lord at the bottom of the mountain in a tent and speaks to Him face to face. He sees Him, and He is God. Yet there is someone else called Yahweh, hidden in thick darkness on top of the mountain, whose voice only is heard. He says, "No one may see my face and live." Now Moses has no crisis of faith. He doesn't think, "How am I going to cope with the person I meet in the tent of meeting and the person I see at the top?" He has no problem with that. He's comfortable for God to be God and present Himself in the way He presents Himself.

If you want to talk about the Holy Spirit, Exodus 33, 34 and 35 is a good place to start because it shows us how there is a person called the Lord who is seen and whom people can meet with face to face. But there is another person called the Lord who cannot be seen. And then we see that there is another person who lives within His people. There is the unseen person, the seen person who meets directly with His people, and there is the Spirit who lives within His people. This is comprehensible only because God is three persons.

If we show this from the Old Testament, then when we see the Son become one of us in the Gospels, the identity and significance of Jesus is clear right away. He is the seen person. He is God, seen from the beginning of the world.

"No one has ever seen God at any time, but the only begotten God, who is from the Father's side, He has made Him known" (see John 1:18). That is Jesus. He has made Him known in all those occasions. He is there from the very first. So in Genesis 32:24–30, we see Jacob wrestling with a man who is God. We know exactly who it is.

There are lots of references to the Holy Spirit also, for example, Nehemiah 9:19–20. The Holy Spirit is a person, a teacher who instructs the people of Israel in the truth. Another is Isaiah 63:9–14. The Holy Spirit doesn't appear on the day of Pentecost from nowhere. He has been with the people of God, teaching them, equipping them, instructing them, being grieved by them, since the beginning.

If we explain the Trinity in this way, we show the living God in action, not in abstract words or philosophical concepts. God never gave us neat little definitions of Himself. He has done something much better than that. He has shown Himself to us in the way that He has created, revealed and redeemed from the beginning.

Also, we are telling the Gospel of Jesus in the way that the Bible does. Christ has been the mediator between God and humanity since the beginning of the world. The birth of Jesus comes as no surprise. When we get to Jesus of Nazareth, we say, "There He is, acting just as He's always acted."

Will we ultimately be able to see the unseen God? Yes. Jesus said, "Blessed are the pure in heart, for they will see God" (Matthew 5:8, NIV). When He comes out of heaven to earth to make His dwelling with us, we'll see Him. Then we'll see Him forever!

Paul Blackham
Paul Blackham is Associate Minister (Theology) at All Souls Church, London, England.

The Master Plan of Evangelism

Robert Coleman

The basic directive of the Great Commission is to make disciples of all nations. We are sent. We are witnesses. The objective is very clear in Matthew 28:19–20: make disciples. Disciples do not stop with conversion. They keep moving on with Christ. To understand what this means, we must look closely at the way Jesus made disciples.

I want to mention nine principles, all of which flow together. First, Jesus came to serve. When He saw a need, He was moved with compassion; He reached out to help. And through it all He held forth the Word of life, proclaiming the Gospel of the Kingdom. People always respond to love when it finds practical expression in ministry.

Second is selection. Jesus looked for disciples. People not only must hear the Gospel, they must follow Christ in a totally new lifestyle of supernatural grace. Jesus wants coworkers, redeemed men and women with the heart of a shepherd, to multiply His ministry.

The third principle is association. Stay with these learners. As the disciples grew, Jesus appointed 12 to be with Him. Jesus deliberately proportioned His life to persons in training. Disciples must have spiritual guardians to help them develop.

The fourth principle is consecration. Jesus said, "Follow me." Obedience to Christ was the means by which those with Him learned more truth. Just as Jesus found His happiness in doing the Father's will, so He wants His followers to find the same. Instill into followers the meaning of obedience.

The fifth principle is demonstration. Following Christ, the disciples observed the way He planned for His people to live. His life was the object lesson of His doctrine. By practicing before them what He wanted them to learn, they could see its relevance in application. We too are the demonstration of Christ's teaching. Disciples of Christ will do those things they see and hear in us.

The sixth principle is delegation. The disciples' first duties were small tasks. After a while their work assignments increased with their developing self-confidence and skill. Whatever form ministry takes, structured or informal, whether in the church or out in the marketplace, it fits into God's plan for making disciples.

Seventh is the principle of supervision. Jesus kept check on their progress. He was building in His disciples a sense of accountability. He asked them how things were going. Experiences the disciples were having in their work became opportunities for Him to teach some new deeper truth. It was on-the-job training all the time.

Eighth is the principle of impartation. Jesus entrusted His disciples to the

Holy Spirit. The Spirit directed Jesus during the days of His incarnate life, and Jesus taught that by this same mighty power persons who believed on Him would partake of His life and ministry. The Spirit calls us to ministry and dispenses the gifts for service.

The ninth principle is enduement. Just as those disciples needed a heavenly enduement, so do we. The sanctifying power from on high must be a reality in our lives. In complete dependence upon the Spirit of Christ, we must let Him have His way in our lives. If we produce this lifestyle in a few, others will follow.

In generations to come, our witness will still be bearing fruit! There will be an ever-widening circle of disciple-makers to the ends of the earth and unto the end of time.

Robert Coleman

Robert Coleman is Director of the School of World Mission and Evangelism at Trinity International University in Deerfield, Illinois, U.S.A.

Three-Story Evangelism

Geoff Cragg and Bill Muir

If you were to reduce post-modern thought to one idea, it is skepticism—being skeptical of everything. When people become skeptical of everybody and everything, then that changes the way we communicate. One of the shifts in post-modernism is that kids don't suffer from guilt, because guilt is "I did something wrong." To do something wrong implies that there's something right, a higher standard. Young people don't feel guilt because there's no standard that they believe is always right. Yet we are ministering to kids who feel shame. The difference between guilt and shame is this: Guilt is "I did something wrong." Shame is "I am wrong. There's something in me that causes me not to like who I am."

What does evangelism look like when we try to communicate what we believe to be true to young people who don't believe in truth? Or, if there is a truth bigger than all of us, then each of us can touch only one part of that truth. This leads back to relativism, because truth is wherever I'm standing. When we come along and say, "Let us tell you about God," most young people don't believe that we can know God. God is much bigger than us, and all we're describing is some part of God, our perspective of God.

The apostle Peter helps us. He says, "Be ready always to give an answer to every man that asketh you a reason of the hope that is in you" (1 Peter 3:15, KJV). The answer to post-modernism is that we can communicate to somebody our hope and our experience with truth. In post-modern thought, nobody can tell you that what you believe or have experienced is not true. You say, "I've experienced Jesus in my life, and He's given me peace and hope and love—things that I've never experienced apart from Him." They can't say, "That's not true."

Three-story evangelism is simply this: There are three stories that we have to connect—God's story, my story and the other person's story. The Gospel moves us from three separate, isolated stories to three stories that overlap. The fact that I've put my faith in Jesus Christ says that His story and my story are connected. But for this lost person, his or her story is disconnected. We want the lost person's story to connect with God's story. In three-story evangelism, the more I can take God's story and allow it to become my story, and the more that I can build a relationship with a nonbeliever, the more I can take that nonbeliever's life and, through his or her story, introduce that nonbeliever to God.

Here's what the apostle Paul says, "We . . . share with you not only the gospel of God but our [very] lives as well" (1 Thessalonians 2:8, NIV). Paul recognized that our relationship with God and our relationship with another person must intersect. The more God's story, my story and their stories intersect, the more likely others will put their faith in Jesus Christ. When you share your story, you're sharing your struggles. People don't want to hear that you've got it all together. They want to hear that you need Jesus. They're willing to hear about Jesus once they see your need. Let God's love flow through you because of His love for you.

People listen to people who listen. So in three-story evangelism, it isn't me coming to tell them something. It's me coming to love them, to listen to them, to discover their story so that I can connect their story to God's story. The more of their story I know, the more I know how to connect their story to God's story. The power of the Gospel is this: Jesus brings an answer to every person's need.

Geoff Cragg and Bill Muir

Geoff Cragg works with Impact Ministries, Wilmore, Kentucky, U.S.A. Bill Muir serves with Youth for Christ, Denver, Colorado, U.S.A.

Bill Muir

Evangelism and Revival

Lewis Drummond

Nothing is more vital than a genuine spiritual awakening in our day. With the population explosion, with conflicts culturally, sociologically, politically, economically, the only answer is for God's mighty moving in your country and in the whole world. Never does evangelism flourish, with more people genuinely converted and the Church coming alive, as it does during a great revival, or spiritual awakening.

What is revival? What is a spiritual awakening? When the Church is revived, then awakening comes. Seven principles outline spiritual awakening. I have gleaned them from James Burns in his book *Revivals, Their Laws and Leaders.*

Number one, the principle of the fullness of time. God's sovereignty rules. It is so easy to say, "Well, if we do one, two, three and four, God is bound to bring it all together with five." No. It's not that God doesn't use human instrumentality, but revival comes from the sovereignty of God in the fullness of God's own timing.

Number two, the principle of the emergence of the prophet. In great revival moments God raises up leaders. They don't precipitate the revival. They embody it because they are revived themselves.

Number three, the principle of spiritual progress. Revival generates new spiritual life as it surges through the Church and the community. The Holy Spirit comes in deep convicting power as people see God for who He is. The seraphim didn't cry, "Isn't God good? He'll solve your problems." They cried "Holy, holy, holy, is the LORD of hosts" (Isaiah 6:3, KJV).

Number four, the principle of variety. Revivals usually differ in many respects. The Reformation of the 16th century was a great spiritual awakening, but it was basically theological, recapturing the Gospel once again. The Great Revival of 1858 was a revival of prayer that brought the power of God. In the Welsh Revival of 1904, Evan Roberts was the prophet. But he didn't do a lot of preaching. People just sang and testified. And the churches were jam-packed with people, with hundreds of thousands saved. Revivals vary; they meet the immediate need of the moment. Wait on the Lord and find out just how He wants to do it.

Number five, the principle of recoil. Revivals end. God's people get down in the valley, then we get desperate, we cry out, and God once again takes the Church, His people, to the height. Are we on the mountaintop or in the valley?

Number six, the principle of theology. When revival comes, God brings the Church, His people, back to a solid, biblical, evangelical, apostolic norm. People come from the extremes into biblical balance.

Number seven, the principle of consistency. There's variety but there are some consistent things such as new life for the Church, great evangelism, social action and concern.

In a spiritual awakening God uses a platform of fervent intercessory prayer. God wants Spirit-filled praying people. Pray, intercede; beg God for revival.

Lewis Drummond

Lewis Drummond is a professor at Beeson Divinity School, Samford University, Birmingham, Alabama, U.S.A.

How to Use Apologetics

Frank Harber

When I was an atheist, trying to disprove Christianity, I read the Bible looking for loopholes. But the more I tried to prove that the Bible was not the truth, the more it kept ringing true. I wasn't a Christian at the time that I read John 14:6, but it dawned on me that if you love truth you're going to love Jesus Christ because He is "the way, the truth, and the life" (KJV).

Apologetics is the Greek word *apologia,* defense. "Always be prepared to make a defense to any one who calls you to account for the hope that is in you" (1 Peter 3:15, RSV).

There are four basic reasons why people reject Jesus Christ. The first is ignorance. How we see Jesus determines how we respond to Him. People make statements about Jesus based on hearsay information. Very few have rejected Christianity on intellectual grounds.

The second reason people reject Jesus is because of the love of sin. Becoming a Christian is not an intellectual question. It's a willingness question. There's a big difference between an honest seeker and a dishonest seeker. Some people who try to prove that Christianity is not true are going to do it no matter what evidence they find. Our wisdom is not going to convert anybody. It is the Holy Spirit working in people, showing them that they have a sin problem.

A third reason people reject Jesus is because of a closed mind. God has given incredible evidence, but many people want to change the evidence. The fourth reason is the faith barrier. God requires faith. We walk not by sight, but by faith (see 2 Corinthians 5:7). God can be approached only through faith.

In our post-modern world, people still believe in truth. But they believe in *their* truth. In a world that embraces many different truths, we help people understand that Jesus is God.

What if a person says, "I don't believe the Bible. I don't believe in God"? We want to be careful that we don't try to tear that person down. The Bible is true because Jesus is true. When we convince somebody that Jesus is true, they won't have any trouble accepting the Bible.

God has given evidence to help launch faith. A ramp helps us clear obstacles that we could never otherwise overcome. RAMP: resurrection, archaeology, miracles and prophecy.

First, "R" is the resurrection. It is the greatest miracle of all time. Many infallible proofs and secular evidences describe the resurrection. "A" stands for archaeology. The people and the places of the Bible are real. There's incredible empirical evidence from archaeology, from history, which demonstrates that Christianity is true.

The "M" stands for miracles. No first-century eyewitness ever denied the fact that Jesus could do miracles. People didn't discuss whether or not Jesus could do miracles. They met to see how they could stop Him from doing any more. No one ever denied His power. The "P" is prophecy. The Bible is the only book that uses supernatural prophecy to confirm itself.

Christianity is a not a leap into the darkness. It is a step into the light. Many people want to know all the answers, "Then I'll have faith." But when we exercise faith, faith produces assurance.

Frank Harber

Frank Harber is president of the Institute for Christian Defense in Fort Worth, Texas, U.S.A.

Maintaining the Biblical Message While Using Modern Methods

Rick Marshall

To communicate the Gospel effectively we need to understand the audience. The world around us is changing rapidly, and we must be like the men of Issachar who understood the times and knew what should be done (see 1 Chronicles 12:32).

In evangelism, the challenge is to add modern ingredients without losing the old flavor. Leadership is the key to moving people from the old to the new, from the security of the past to the insecurity of the future. Prayer will make us open for God to do in and through us what we cannot do for ourselves.

Do we know what communicates today? Number one, don't fear relevant media. There are two kinds of media. First is interpersonal media, and the key word here is *friendship*. We need to release the people of God to have relationships with those outside the church. Fear can prevent the body of Christ from being salt against decay and light in a dark place. We say, "The world is a dangerous place. The devil is on the rampage. Listen to the music; look at the way people dress; watch the films. The culture is in upheaval. What should we do? Pull up the drawbridge, hunker down in safety until Jesus comes back." I don't see that in the Bible.

Second is relevant electronic and print media. Our media must be cutting edge and compelling. We use media to get the attention of those outside the church and outside of Christ, so that interpersonal media can invite them to hear the message. Today for someone under age 40, if nothing moves, nothing can be seen. Today we live in a culture not of the orator, but of the artist. Music and visuals are the voice of our culture. Programming needs to move from the dull and the boring to the attractive, from presentation to participation, from static to visual.

Old and new work together. We reach back and we reach forward. We're not wavering one iota from the spiritual disciplines. We're rooted and grounded in Christ. But we present a program that uses modern methodology—lighting, video, drama and all genres of music. These forms work together. The artists authenticate the communicator by setting up the preaching of the Gospel. The artists open the heart to hear the Word. When people know we understand their world, they will stay to hear the communicator open the Word of God, in language they can understand.

In using modern methods, there may be resistance from the church culture.

Our upbringing and our culture can grab us so firmly that it becomes difficult to make objective decisions. This can lead to the idea that legitimate conversion occurs only through our familiar experiences. We face the danger of being judgmental. Leaders may be unable to see the Spirit's work in each generation or may even attribute the work of God to the devil. But when the heart is soft, the mind is open to change.

As leaders and communicators, we may be out of touch with the culture and modern methods of communication. Sometimes we face concerns that new methods are excessive and too expensive. You have to find the resources for your particular ministry, and stay within your budget! Other times, as we reach out to unchanged people we feel raw fear. Dr. John Stott said, "Failure to move and adapt with the culture will ensure death."

There's a great chasm. The church is on one side entrusted with the message of the Gospel of Jesus Christ; the generation without Jesus is on the other side. The chasm is getting wider and deeper—somebody has to go to the edge to get the attention of the other side. Ask yourself, "Am I in touch with people—their ideas, their hurts and their hopes? Do I know what people are feeling? Have I become tradition-bound? Have I lost my zeal? Am I still willing to take risks?"

What is the nature of the criticism you may face? Is it based on Scripture or is it rooted in culture? The apostle Paul said, "I have become all things to all men so that by all possible means I might save some" (1 Corinthians 9:22, NIV). That is the lifestyle and the communication style of an effective evangelist in the year 2000 and beyond.

Rick Marshall
Rick Marshall is Director of Billy Graham Crusades for the Billy Graham Evangelistic Association.

Amsterdam 2000
Documents

The Amsterdam Declaration is presented as a joint report of the three Task Groups of mission strategists, church leaders and theologians gathered at Amsterdam 2000. It has been reviewed by hundreds of Christian leaders and evangelists from around the world. It is commended to God's people everywhere as an expression of evangelical commitment and as a resource for study, reflection, prayer and evangelistic outreach.

The Amsterdam Declaration

A Charter for Evangelism in the 21st Century

Preamble

As a renewal movement within historic Christian orthodoxy, transdenominational evangelicalism became a distinct global reality in the second half of the 20th century. Evangelicals come from many churches, languages and cultures, but we hold in common a shared understanding of the Gospel of Jesus Christ, of the Church's mission and of the Christian commitment to evangelism. Recent documents that express this understanding include the Berlin Statement (1966), the Lausanne Covenant (1974), the Amsterdam Affirmations (1983), the Manila Manifesto (1989) and The Gospel of Jesus Christ: An Evangelical Celebration (1999).

At the invitation of Dr. Billy Graham, over 11,000 evangelists, theologians, mission strategists and church leaders from more than 200 countries have assembled in Amsterdam in the year 2000 to listen, pray, worship and discern the wisdom of the Holy Spirit for the unfinished task of world evangelization. We are stirred and encouraged by the challenges we have heard and the fellowship we have shared with so many brothers and sisters in Christ. More than ever, we are resolved to make Christ known to all persons everywhere.

This Amsterdam Declaration has been developed as a framework to surround the many action plans that are being made for the evangelization of the world. It is based on the principles set forth in the documents referred to above and includes these three parts: a charter of commitments, definitions of key theological terms used in the charter, and a prayer of supplication to our heavenly Father.

Charter of Commitments

This charter is a statement of tasks, goals and ideals for evangelism in the 21st century. The order of topics reflects the range of our concerns, not the priority of these themes.

1. *Mission Strategy and Evangelism.* The mission of the Church has at its heart world evangelization. We have from our Lord a mandate to proclaim   Matthew 28:19

the Good News of God's love and forgiveness to everyone, making disciples, baptizing and teaching all peoples. Jesus made it clear in His last teachings that the scope of this work of evangelism demands that we give attention not only to those around us but also to the despised and neglected of society and to those at the ends of the earth. To do anything less is disobedience. In addition, we affirm the need to encourage new initiatives to reach and disciple youth and children worldwide; to make fuller use of media and technology in evangelism; and to stay involved personally in grass-roots evangelism so that our presentations of the biblical Gospel are fully relevant and contextualized. We think it urgent to work toward the evangelization of every remaining unreached people group.

Acts 1:8

> *We pledge ourselves* **to work so that all persons on earth may have an opportunity to hear the Gospel in a language they understand, near where they live. We further pledge to establish healthy, reproducing, indigenous churches among every people, in every place, that will seek to bring to spiritual maturity those who respond to the Gospel message.**

2. *Leadership and Evangelism.* We affirm that leadership is one of Christ's gifts to the church. It does not exist for itself; it exists to lead the people of God in obedience to our heavenly Father. Leaders must submit themselves in humility to Christ, the head of the Church, and to one another. This submission involves the acceptance of the supreme authority of Scripture by which Christ rules in His Church through His Spirit. The leaders' first task is to preserve the biblical integrity of the proclamation of the church and serve as vision carriers of its evangelistic vocation. They are responsible to see that vocation implemented by teaching, training, empowering and inspiring others. We must give special attention to encouraging women and young leaders in their work of evangelism. Leaders must always be careful not to block what God is doing as they exercise their strategic stewardship of the resources which Christ supplies to His body.

Ephesians 4:11–13

Mark 10:42–45

Colossians 1:18

> *We pledge ourselves* **to seek and uphold this model of biblical servant-leadership in our churches. We who are leaders commit ourselves afresh to this pattern of leadership.**

3. *Theology and Evangelism.* Christian theology is the task of careful thinking and ordering of life in the presence of the triune God. In one sense, all Christians are theologians and must labor to be good ones rather than bad ones. This means that everyone's theology must be measured by biblical teaching, from which alone we learn God's mind and will. Those called to the special vocations of evangelism, theology and pastoral ministry must

Mark 7:13

2 Timothy 2:15; 3:16

work together in the spread of the Gospel throughout the world. Evangelists and pastors can help theologians maintain an evangelistic motivation, reminding them that true theology is always done in the service of the church. Theologians can help to clarify and safeguard God's revealed truth, providing resources for the training of evangelists and the grounding of new believers in the faith.

1 Timothy 6:20
2 Timothy 1:14

> *We pledge ourselves* **to labor constantly in learning and teaching the faith according to the Scriptures, and in seeking to ensure (1) that all who preach the Gospel are theologically equipped and resourced in adequate ways for the work they have in hand, and (2) that all professional teachers of the faith share a common concern for evangelism.**

4. *Truth and Evangelism.* Under the influence of modern rationalism, secularism and humanism (modernity), the Western intellectual establishment has largely reacted into a relativistic denial that there is any global and absolute truth (post-modernity). This is influencing popular culture throughout the world. By contrast the Gospel, which is the authoritative Word of the one, true and living God, comes to everyone everywhere at all times as truth in three senses: its affirmations are factually true, as opposed to false; it confronts us at every point with reality, as opposed to illusion; and it sets before us Jesus Christ, the co-Creator, Redeemer and Lord of the world, as the Truth (that is, the one universally real, accessible, authoritative, truth-telling, trustworthy person) for all to acknowledge. There is a suspicion that any grand claim that there is one truth for everyone is inevitably oppressive and violent. But the Gospel sets before us one who, though He was God, became man and identified with those under the bondage of sin to set them free from its enslavement. This Gospel of God is both true for everyone and truly sets people free. It is therefore to be received in trust, not suspicion.

Romans 15:16
Galatians 1:7; 2:14

1 Corinthians 9:12
2 Thessalonians 1:8

John 8:31–32

> *We pledge ourselves* **to present and proclaim the biblical Gospel and its Christ, always and everywhere, as fully sufficient and effective for the salvation of believers. Therefore, we oppose all skeptical and relativizing or syncretizing trends, whether rationalist or irrationalist, that treat that Gospel as not fully true, and so as unable to lead believers into the new divine life that it promises them. We oppose all oppressive and destructive uses of God's wonderful truth.**

5. *Human Need and Evangelism.* Both the law and the Gospel uncover a lost human condition that goes beyond any feelings of pain, misery, frustration, bondage, powerlessness and discontent with life. The Bible reveals that all human beings are constitutionally in a state of rebellion against the God

Romans 1:18–32;
5:12, 18
1 Corinthians 15:22

who made them, and of whom they remain dimly aware; they are alienated from Him and cut off from all the enjoyment of knowing and serving Him that is the true fulfillment of human nature. We humans were made to bear God's image in an endless life of love to God and to other people, but the self-centeredness of our fallen and sinful hearts makes that impossible. Often our dishonesty leads us to use even the observance of religion to keep God at a distance, so that we can avoid having Him deal with us about our ungodly self-worship. Therefore all human beings now face final condemnation by Christ the Judge and eternal destruction, separated from the presence of the Lord.

Genesis 1:26

2 Thessalonians 1:9

> **We pledge ourselves to be faithful and compassionate in sharing with people the truth about their present spiritual state, warning them of judgment and hell that the impenitent face, and extolling the love of God who gave His Son to save us.**

6. *Religious Pluralism and Evangelism.* Today's evangelist is called to proclaim the Gospel in an increasingly pluralistic world. In this global village of competing faiths and many world religions, it is important that our evangelism be marked both by faithfulness to the Good News of Christ and humility in our delivery of it. Because God's general revelation extends to all points of His creation, there may well be traces of truth, beauty and goodness in many non-Christian belief systems. But we have no warrant for regarding any of these as alternative gospels or separate roads to salvation. The only way to know God in peace, love and joy is through the reconciling death of Jesus Christ the risen Lord. As we share this message with others, we must do so with love and humility, shunning all arrogance, hostility and disrespect. As we enter into dialogue with adherents of other religions, we must be courteous and kind. But such dialogue must not be a substitute for proclamation. Yet because all persons are made in the image of God, we must advocate religious liberty and human rights for all.

Romans 1:18–20

John 14:6

Acts 4:12

Mark 10:41–45

James 1:20

Genesis 1:26

> **We pledge ourselves to treat those of other faiths with respect and faithfully and humbly serve the nations in which God has placed us, while affirming that Christ is the one and only Savior of the world.**

7. *Culture and Evangelism.* By the Blood of the Lamb, God has purchased saints from every tribe and language and people and nation. He saves people in their own culture. World evangelization aims to see the rise of churches that are both deeply rooted in Christ and closely related to their culture. Therefore, following the example of Jesus and Paul, those who proclaim Christ must use their freedom in Christ to become all things to all people. This means appropriate cultural identification while guarding against equating the

Revelation 5:9

1 Corinthians 6:19

1 Corinthians 9:19–23

Gospel with any particular culture. Since all human cultures are shaped in part by sin, the Bible and its Christ are at key points counter-cultural to every one of them.

> *We pledge ourselves* **to be culturally sensitive in our evangelism. We will aim to preach Christ in a way that is appropriate for the people among whom we witness and which will enrich that culture in all appropriate ways. Further, as salt and light we will seek the transforming of culture in ways that affirm Gospel values.**

8. *Scripture and Evangelism.* The Bible is indispensable to true evangelism. The Word of God itself provides both the content and authority for all evangelism. Without it there is no message to preach to the lost. People must be brought to an understanding of at least some of the basic truths contained in the Scriptures before they can make a meaningful response to the Gospel. Thus we must proclaim and disseminate the Holy Scriptures in the heart language of all those whom we are called to evangelize and disciple.

1 Thessalonians 2:13

Acts 2:14–39; 13:16–41

> *We pledge ourselves* **to keep the Scriptures at the very heart of our evangelistic outreach and message, and to remove all known language and cultural barriers to a clear understanding of the Gospel on the part of our hearers.**

9. *The Church and Evangelism.* There is no dispute that in established congregations regular teaching for believers at all stages in their pilgrimage must be given, and appropriate pastoral care must be provided. But these concerns must not displace ongoing concern for mission, which involves treating evangelistic outreach as a continuing priority. Pastors in conjunction with other qualified persons should lead their congregations in the work of evangelism. Further, we affirm that the formation of godly, witnessing disciples is at the heart of the church's responsibility to prepare its members for their work of service. We affirm that the church must be made a welcoming place for new believers.

1 Corinthians 14:13–17

Matthew 28:19

2 Timothy 2:2

> *We pledge ourselves* **to urge all congregations in and with which we serve to treat evangelism as a matter of priority at all times, and so to make it a focus of congregational praying, planning, training and funding.**

10. *Prayer and Evangelism.* God has given us the gift of prayer so that in His sovereignty He may respond in blessing and power to the cries of His children. Prayer is an essential means that God has appointed for the awakening of the Church and the carrying of the Gospel throughout the world. From the

Acts 1:14; 2:42; 6:4

Acts 4:23–30; 12:5

Ephesians 6:18

first days of the New Testament church, God has used the fervent, persistent praying of His people to empower their witness in the Spirit, overcome opposition to the Lord's work, and open the minds and hearts of those who hear the message of Christ. At special times in the history of the Church, revivals and spiritual breakthroughs have been preceded by the explicit agreement and union of God's people in seasons of repentance, prayer and fasting. Today, as we seek to carry the Gospel to unreached people groups in all the world, we need a deeper dependence upon God and a greater unity in prayer.

Matthew 9:37–38

***We pledge ourselves* to pray faithfully to the Lord of the harvest to send out workers for His harvest field. We also pray for all those engaged in world evangelization and to encourage the call to prayer in families, local churches, special assemblies, mission agencies and trans-denominational ministries.**

11. *Social Responsibility and Evangelism.* Although evangelism is not advocacy of any social program, it does entail social responsibility for at least two reasons.

Psalm 47:7

1 Timothy 6:16

Revelation 17:14

Galatians 6:10

Matthew 5:45

Deuteronomy 24:10–15

Luke 1:52–53; 4:18–19

James 5:1–6

First, the Gospel proclaims the kingship of the loving Creator who is committed to justice, human life and the welfare of His creation. So evangelism will need to be accompanied by obedience to God's command to work for the good of all in a way that is fitting for the children of the Father who makes His sun shine on the evil and the good and sends His rain on the righteous and the unrighteous alike. Second, when our evangelism is linked with concern to alleviate poverty, uphold justice, oppose abuses of secular and economic power, stand against racism, and advance responsible stewardship of the global environment, it reflects the compassion of Christ and may gain an acceptance it would not otherwise receive.

***We pledge ourselves* to follow the way of justice in our family and social life, and to keep personal, social and environmental values in view as we evangelize.**

12. *Holiness and Evangelism.* The servant of God must adorn the Gospel through

1 Timothy 3:2–13

Titus 1:6–9

1 Corinthians 5:1–13

2 Thessalonians 3:14–15

1 Timothy 5:11–13, 19–20

a holy life. But in recent times God's name has been greatly dishonored and the Gospel discredited because of unholy living by Christians in leadership roles. Evangelists seem particularly exposed to temptations relating to money, sex, pride, power, neglect of family, and lack of integrity. The Church should foster structures to hold evangelists accountable for their lives, doctrine and ministries. The Church should also ensure that those whose lives dishonor God and the Gospel will not be permitted to serve as its evangelists. The holiness and humility of evangelists gives credibility to their ministries and leads to genuine power from God and lasting fruit.

We pledge ourselves to be accountable to the community of faith for our lives, doctrines and ministries; to flee from sin; and to walk in holiness and humility.

1 Corinthians 6:18

2 Timothy 2:22

13. *Conflict, Suffering and Evangelism.* The records of evangelism from the apostolic age, the state of the world around us today, and the knowledge of Satan's opposition at all times to the spread of the Gospel, combine to assure us that evangelistic outreach in the twenty-first century will be an advance in the midst of opposition. Current forms of opposition, which Satan evidently exploits, include secular ideologies that see Christian faith as a hindrance to human development; political power structures that see the primacy of Christians' loyalty to their Lord as a threat to the regime; and militant expressions of non-Christian religions that are hostile to Christians for being different. We must expect, and be prepared for, many kinds of suffering as we struggle not against enemies of blood and flesh, but against the spiritual forces of evil in the heavenly places.

Acts 13:6–12

Ephesians 6:11–13

Ephesians 6:14–18

We pledge ourselves ever to seek to move forward wisely in personal evangelism, family evangelism, local church evangelism and cooperative evangelism in its various forms, and to persevere in this despite the opposition we may encounter. We will stand in solidarity with our brothers and sisters in Christ who suffer persecution and even martyrdom for their faithful Gospel witness.

14. *Christian Unity and Evangelism.* Jesus prayed to the heavenly Father that His disciples would be one so that the world might believe. One of the great hindrances to evangelism worldwide is the lack of unity among Christ's people, a condition made worse when Christians compete and fight with one another rather than seeking together the mind of Christ. We cannot resolve all differences among Christians because we do not yet understand perfectly all that God has revealed to us. But in all ways that do not violate our consciences, we should pursue cooperation and partnerships with other believers in the task of evangelism, practicing the well-tested rule of Christian fellowship: "In necessary things, unity; in non-essential things, liberty; in all things, charity."

Ephesians 4:1–6

John 17:21–23

Romans 11:34

2 Peter 3:15

Romans 14:14, 23

We pledge ourselves to pray and work for unity in truth among all true believers in Jesus and to cooperate as fully as possible in evangelism with other brothers and sisters in Christ so that the whole Church may take the whole Gospel to the whole world.

Definitions of Key Terms

The message we proclaim has both a propositional and an incarnational dimension—"the Word became flesh." To deny either one is to bear false witness to Christ. Because the relation between language and reality is much debated today, it is important to state clearly what we mean by what we say. To avoid confusion and misunderstanding, then, we here define the following key words used in this declaration. The definitions are all Trinitarian, Christocentric and Bible based.

1. *God.* The God of whom this declaration speaks is the self-revealed Creator, Upholder, Governor and Lord of the universe. This God is eternal in His self-existence and unchanging in His holy love, goodness, justice, wisdom and faithfulness to His promises. God in His own being is a community of three coequal and coeternal persons, who are revealed to us in the Bible as the Father, the Son and the Holy Spirit. Together they are involved in an unvarying cooperative pattern in all God's relationships to and within this world. God is Lord of history, where He blesses His own people, overcomes and judges human and angelic rebels against His rule, and will finally renew the whole created order.

2. *Jesus Christ.* The declaration takes the view of Jesus that the canonical New Testament sets forth and the historic Christian creeds and confessions attest. He was, and is, the second person of the triune Godhead, now and forever incarnate. He was virgin-born, lived a life of perfect godliness, died on the Cross as the substitutionary sacrifice for our sins, was raised bodily from the dead, ascended into heaven, reigns now over the universe, and will personally return for judgment and the renewal of all things. As the God-man, once crucified, now enthroned, He is the Lord and Savior who in love fulfills toward us the threefold mediational ministry of prophet, priest and king. His title, "Christ," proclaims Him the anointed servant of God who fulfills all the messianic hopes of the canonical Old Testament.

3. *Holy Spirit.* Shown by the words of Jesus to be the third divine person, whose name, "Spirit," pictures the energy of breath and wind, the Holy Spirit is the dynamic personal presence of the Trinity in the processes of the created world, in the communication of divine truth, in the attesting of Jesus Christ, in the new creation through Him of believers and of the Church, and in ongoing fellowship and service. The fullness of the ministry of the Holy Spirit in relation to the knowledge of Christ and the enjoyment of new life in Him dates from the Pentecostal outpouring recorded in Acts 2. As the divine inspirer and interpreter of the Bible, the Spirit empowers God's people to set forth accurate, searching, life-transforming presentations of the Gospel of Jesus Christ, and makes their communication a fruitful

means of grace to their hearers. The New Testament shows us the supernatural power of the Spirit working miracles, signs and wonders; bestowing gifts of many kinds; and overcoming the power of Satan in human lives for the advancement of the Gospel. Christians agree that the power of the Holy Spirit is vitally necessary for evangelism and that openness to His ministry should mark all believers.

Acts 2:43; 5:12; 6:8; 14:3; 15:12

4. *Bible.* The 66 books of the Old and New Testaments constitute the written Word of God. As the inspired revelation of God in writing, the Scriptures are totally true and trustworthy and the only infallible rule of faith and practice. In every age and every place, this authoritative Bible, by the Spirit's power, is efficacious for salvation through its witness to Jesus Christ.

2 Timothy 3:16
2 Peter 1:21

Luke 1:1–4

John 14:26
1 John 1:3

5. *Kingdom.* The Kingdom of God is His gracious rule through Jesus Christ over human lives, the course of history, and all reality. Jesus is Lord of past, present and future and sovereign ruler of everything. The salvation Jesus brings and the community of faith He calls forth are signs of His Kingdom's presence here and now, though we wait for its complete fulfillment when He comes again in glory. In the meantime, wherever Christ's standards of peace and justice are observed to any degree, to that degree the Kingdom is anticipated, and to that extent God's ideal for human society is displayed.

Daniel 7:14

Luke 11:20

Hebrews 13:8

Luke 22:29

Luke 6:20

Matthew 5:3

6. *Gospel.* The Gospel is the Good News of the Creator's eternal plan to share His life and love with fallen human beings through the sending of His Son, Jesus Christ, the one and only Savior of the world. As the power of God for salvation, the Gospel centers on the life, death, resurrection and return of Jesus and leads to a life of holiness, growth in grace, and hope-filled though costly discipleship in the fellowship of the Church. The Gospel includes the announcement of Jesus' triumph over the powers of darkness and of His supreme lordship over the universe.

Romans 1:16–17
1 Corinthians 15:2
Acts 2:14–39;
13:16–41
Romans 1:1–5

Colossians: 2:15
1 Peter 3:22

7. *Salvation.* This word means rescue from the guilt, defilement, spiritual blindness and deadness, alienation from God, and certainty of eternal punishment in hell, that is everyone's condition while under sin's dominion. This deliverance involves present justification, reconciliation to God, and adoption into His family, with regeneration and the sanctifying gift of the Holy Spirit leading to works of righteousness and service here and now and a promise of full glorification in fellowship with God in the future. This involves in the present life joy, peace, freedom and the transformation of character and relationships and the guarantee of complete healing at the future resurrection of the body. We are justified by faith alone, and the salvation faith brings is by grace alone, through Christ alone, for the glory of God alone.

Ephesians 2:8–9
Romans 5:9
Romans 3:21–26; 8:30
Ephesians 2:10
Philippians 2:12–13; 3:21
1 Corinthians 15:43

2 Thessalonians 1:9–10

Romans 4:4–6
Ephesians 2:8–9
Titus 3:4–7

Romans 11:36; 15:9
Philippians 1:11

8. *Christian.* A Christian is a believer in God who is enabled by the Holy Spirit to submit to Jesus Christ as Lord and Savior in a personal relationship of disciple to master and to live the life of God's Kingdom. The word *Christian* should not be equated with any particular cultural, ethnic, political or ideological tradition or group. Those who know and love Jesus are also called Christ-followers, believers and disciples.

Acts 11:26; 26:28
1 Peter 4:16

9. *Church.* The Church is the people of God, the body and the bride of Christ, and the temple of the Holy Spirit. The one, universal Church is a transnational, transcultural, transdenominational and multi-ethnic family, the household of faith. In the widest sense, the Church includes all the redeemed of all the ages, being the one body of Christ extended throughout time as well as space. Here in the world, the Church becomes visible in all local congregations that meet to do together the things that according to Scripture the Church does. Christ is the head of the Church. Everyone who is personally united to Christ by faith belongs to His body and by the Spirit is united with every other true believer in Jesus.

1 Corinthians 12:27
Ephesians 5:25–27, 32

Matthew 28:19
Romans 3:27–30
Revelation 7:9–10

1 Corinthians 1:2

10. *Mission.* Formed from *missio,* the Latin word for "sending," this term is used both of the Father's sending of the Son into the world to become its Savior and of the Son's sending the Church into the world to spread the Gospel, perform works of love and justice, and seek to disciple everyone to Himself.

John 17:18; 20:21

11. *Evangelism.* Derived from the Greek word *euangelizesthai,* "to tell glad tidings," this word signifies making known the Gospel of Jesus Christ so that people may trust in God through Him, receiving Him as their Savior and serving Him as their Lord in the fellowship of His Church. Evangelism involves declaring what God has done for our salvation and calling on the hearers to become disciples of Jesus through repentance from sin and personal faith in Him.

Isaiah 61:1
Romans 1:15–17

12. *Evangelist.* All Christians are called to play their part in fulfilling Jesus' Great Commission, but some believers have a special call to and a spiritual gift for communicating Christ and leading others to Him. These we call evangelists, as does the New Testament.

2 Timothy 4:5
Ephesians 4:11

Prayer

Gracious God, our heavenly Father, we praise You for the great love that You have shown to us through the redeeming death and triumphant resurrection of Your Son, our Lord Jesus Christ. We pray that You would enable us by the power of Your Holy Spirit to proclaim faithfully the Good News of Your Kingdom and Your love. Forgive us for failing to take the Gospel to all the peoples of the world. Deliver us from ignorance, error, lovelessness, pride, selfishness, impurity and cowardice. Enable us to be truthful, kind, humble, sympathetic, pure and courageous. Salvation belongs to You, O God, who sits on the throne, and to the Lamb. We ask You to make our Gospel witness effective. Anoint our proclamation with the Holy Spirit; use it to gather that great multitude from all nations which will one day stand before You and the Lamb giving praise. This we ask by the merits of our Lord Jesus Christ. Amen.

Revelation 7:9–10

A Covenant for Evangelists

As a company of evangelists called and gifted by God to share the Good News of Jesus Christ throughout the world, we earnestly pledge ourselves to:

Worship the one true and living God: Father, Son and Holy Spirit (Deuteronomy 6:4);

Submit to the Holy Scriptures, the infallible Word of God, as the basis for our life and message (2 Timothy 3:16–17);

Proclaim the Gospel of Jesus Christ, God's Son and our redeemer, the one and only Savior of the world (Acts 4:12);

Seek always to preach and minister in the power of the Holy Spirit (Acts 4:29–31);

Live a life of constant personal prayer, Bible study and devotion to God, and also be part of a local fellowship of believers (James 4:10; Hebrews 10:25);

Pray that all persons of all languages and cultures may have access to the Gospel and the Bible (Acts 1:8);

Practice purity in both singleness and marriage, caring for our family and bringing up our children in the nurture of the Lord (Ephesians 5:25, 6:1–4);

Walk humbly before God and our fellow human beings, renouncing arrogance, pride and boastful self-promotion (Micah 6:8; Ephesians 4:1–2);

Maintain financial integrity and accountability in all of our activities, so that the cause of Christ may not be discredited (1 Timothy 6:10–11);

Serve the needy and oppressed, remembering the mercy and compassion of Jesus (James 2:14–17);

Encourage the discipling and nurturing ministry of local churches (Matthew 28:19–20);

Work together in unity with our brothers and sisters in Christ (John 17:23);

Equip others for the practice of evangelism, giving special care to involve new believers in the sharing of their faith (Ephesians 4:11–13);

Stand in solidarity with our brothers and sisters in Christ who suffer persecution and even martyrdom for their faithful Gospel witness (2 Corinthians 1:8–11).

Knowing that apart from Jesus Christ we can do nothing, we make these pledges with prayerful reliance on His help. As we do so, we ask for the prayer and support of all Christ's followers so that world evangelization may be advanced, the Church built up and God glorified in ever-increasing measure.

Church Leaders Task Group Report

R.H. Goodhew, Convener

An integral part of Amsterdam 2000 has been the calling together of theologians, church leaders and church strategists in special Task Groups. The work of each group is designed to assist the Church and evangelists in proclaiming the Gospel faithfully and effectively in order that all peoples in all nations may hear of Jesus Christ.

Church leaders have a vital role in assisting God's people to fulfill their evangelistic responsibilities and in encouraging and promoting the work of evangelists.

The Church Leaders Task Group was composed of some 200 church leaders from approximately 100 countries. What follows is a summary of the issues they discussed and the ideas generated. We pray that God will use our work to stimulate church leaders to a fresh commitment to the task of proclaiming the Gospel to all who have not heard.

1. CHURCH LEADERSHIP AND EVANGELISM

We have endeavored to identify the barriers church leaders encounter in seeking to advance evangelism. The following were identified:

Internal Barriers
- The quality and character of church leaders
    - Lack of vision
    - Lack of focus on evangelism due to other commitments
- Internal church politics and divisions
- An inward rather than outward orientation
- Churches influenced by pluralism that relativizes the Gospel, thereby undermining the motivation
- Dominated by a mentality of maintenance rather than a wholehearted commitment to winning new converts
- Mistrust of and resentment toward evangelists in some regions because of "sheep stealing" and diversion of funds
- Evangelists not recognized as part of the church's normal life and activity
- No proper appreciation of the role and goals of the evangelist
- Churches self-absorbed and confused, failing to understand the Great Commission
- Constrained by traditions
- Lacking in the flexibility which is required to be evangelistically relevant
- Insecure and therefore unnecessarily defensive
- Lack of a comprehensive theology of and vision for evangelism

- A tendency to leave evangelism to the work of specialists
- The evangelistic imperative has been lost
- A lack of appropriate training and specific teaching on evangelism in the church
- The promotion of impractical or outmoded models of evangelism
- The currency of false stereotypes of what an evangelist is—"self-promoting and money-grabbing"
- Failure to provide adequate financial resources
- Evangelists raising doctrinal issues that have caused confusion

External Barriers

- Active persecution of varying degrees of intensity
- Debilitating circumstances such as war, poverty, illiteracy
- Government opposition
- The pressure of other religions and syncretism, and the influence they exert over members
- Secularism
- Language and cultural barriers
- Influences spread by the New Age movement, post-modernism, etc.
- Parental restraints
- Extensive areas with low density population

Appropriate Responses to Overcome These Barriers

- Training of both leaders and people
- Leaders must set a clear understanding of biblical theology, vision and focus on evangelism through Bible teaching
- Prayer that acknowledges the primary role and work of the Spirit of God in winning people to Christ
- Greater cooperation between Christian communities and agencies with a greater unity of purpose and action
- The Gospel to be proclaimed with a concern for social conditions and the recognition of human dignity

2. RESTORING THE PRIORITY OF EVANGELISM

- The primary importance of prayer and the power of the Holy Spirit as indispensable factors in effective evangelism
- The practiced priority of evangelism is high in some churches, but not in all
- Leaders must create an evangelism culture in the church
- Churches with a greater number of new converts give the highest priority to evangelism
- Liberal theology undermines real commitment to evangelistic outreach
- Leaders fulfill a key role in
  Providing Bible-based motivation, effective training and appropriate strategies,

Encouraging prayerful reliance upon the Holy Spirit,
Therefore selecting, training and deploying appropriate leadership
- Leaders give priority in allocating budgets for evangelism

3. RESTORING THE PRACTICE OF EVANGELISM
- All Christians must witness to others about Christ and His saving work
- Christ has given His Church the gift of the evangelist
  - Identify
  - Train
  - Resource
  - Develop accountability
- All Christians need adequate training and mobilization
- Leaders should model evangelism both personally and corporately
- Encouraging creative approaches to evangelism, e.g., theater, literature distribution, etc.

4. INTEGRATING NEW BELIEVERS INTO THE CHURCH

Hindrances
The following barriers to new converts being integrated into the church were identified:
- External pressures from family or community which provide sanctions against church involvement
- The requirements and demands of church involvement—some of these are the costly implications of the Gospel, but others are no more than a particular church subculture
- The lack of welcoming by the existing church members
- Disillusionment with substandard Christian life in the church, or the inevitable imperfection of any Christian congregation
- The failure of the evangelist or organization to help a person into the church
- The lack of availability of a local church
- No church sufficiently close to the culture or socio-economic ethos of the convert—feels out of place
- Apprehension of the unfamiliar on the part of new believers and church members
- Lack of clear steps to join
- No proper follow-up and monitoring of new believers
- Services not designed with new believers in mind

Ways of overcoming these barriers include the following:
- The provision of small groups and/or one-to-one relationships in which a new member can make friends and be personally supported
- Provision of educational materials for systematic follow-up and incorporation into the local church

- The motivating and training of existing members to welcome and include new members
- The provision of special welcoming activities or celebrations that validate new members
- The provision of pastoral support and, where necessary, professional counseling and help for those with special needs
- Early involvement in ministry and contributing to the church
- Creating a variety of points of entry, e.g., drama, music, caring
- In some cultures where individual decisions are not as important as corporate decisions, the need to work with the whole family or other significant group rather than with an individual
- Worshiping together

The church leader, especially the congregational leader, has a significant role in modeling acceptance and ensuring that appropriate mechanisms are in place.

On the question of the role of pulpit ministry in assisting the new convert, the following points were made:
- Good preaching dealing with real-life issues and the full range of Christian teaching
- The preacher keeping in contact with new converts and understanding their needs and issues
- The provision of some kind of post-sermon or follow-up for further teaching—this can be done in a way in which the older members are being fed while the newer converts are being taught
- The preacher should encourage a system of feedback from the congregation

5. THE CHURCH AND THE PREACHING EVANGELIST

Helping Pastors in Their Evangelistic Preaching
- Evangelistic preaching must be required in seminary training
- Ensure evangelistic preaching is biblically based
- Many Christian leaders require ongoing training in evangelistic preaching, evangelistic activities and events
- Congregations need to commit to prayer for the evangelistic preaching
- Develop ways of preaching and calling for response that are both effective in communicating Christ to the society and appropriate to the style and ethos of the particular church
- Pastors need to team with and work alongside evangelists who model good examples of evangelistic preaching
- Those who are good at evangelistic preaching should take responsibility to mentor pastors to help them fulfill more effectively their evangelistic role
- Providing resources to equip pastors in their evangelistic ministry and in equipping those within their congregations who are gifted and called as evangelists

Written material
Videos/cassettes
Peer group
   Internet
    Small group
Conferences

- Renewing spiritual vitality, so that pastors may preach the Gospel motivated by the love of Christ and compassion for lost and broken people, in the power and anointing of the Holy Spirit
- Part of the pastor's role is to ensure that effective evangelism is taking place in the church with which they are actively involved
- Preaching should be for a genuine verdict leading to life transformation

The Evangelist

All Christian believers share a responsibility to make Christ known. However, the Bible speaks about Christ's special gift to the Church, the evangelist, who will communicate the Gospel in a wide variety of ways. "The gifts he gave were that some would be . . . evangelists" (see Ephesians 4:11).

Some evangelists are local church and denominationally based and have the oversight, support and restrictions of these structures. Others are independent and not directly accountable to any church body. However, they need to relate to a local church from which they receive pastoral care.

In order for the office of evangelist to be promoted, the Church itself must give high priority to the ministry of evangelism in all its forms, both local and denominational. Within such a context individuals need to be identified and given opportunity to develop their God-given calling. As one of the essential ministries of Christ, the office of evangelist should have the support and encouragement of the Church. This will involve all the levels and avenues of support that a church gives to its recognized ministries.

For those evangelists who stand outside the church structure, there are tensions that develop between them and the churches. They are often seen as "sheep stealers" and irresponsibly drawing off resources from the local church. These evangelists find church leaders resistant to them and unwilling to receive their ministry. It was proposed that efforts be made by both sides to form better relationships. Pastors and evangelists need to understand each other's concerns and work toward a more fruitful partnership. Such evangelists need to make a conscious effort to hold themselves accountable to persons or groups for financial, pastoral and spiritual guidance.

6. NEW APPROACHES TO DISCIPLESHIP

The goal of evangelism is that men and women become Jesus' disciples (that is, people learning together from Jesus on the basis of their prior commitment to Him as Lord and Savior). This is more than a short course for initial believers—

it is a commitment for a life of obedience that Christ requires of us. It is not simply to grow bigger churches in order to feed the egos of pastors or to fulfill denominational growth goals.

The cell group principle provides an ideal setting in which all the elements of Christian discipleship can be taught, modeled and practiced. For cell groups to be effective the following elements need to be present: mutual support, life transformation, ministry identification and development, evangelistic commitment.

Discipleship should include:

    Belonging

    Teaching

    Modeling

    Involvement in ministry

Evangelists should do all that they can to see that those who make responses to their preaching are linked to a church that will nurture these new converts. It is difficult to disciple both literate and nonliterate people if our strategies are only academic or course-oriented. It must also involve more mature Christians acting as sponsors.

People who present a particular challenge include the following: those who see the church as a club, people who have been churchgoers for a long time, occasional attendees, busy people, those who have been converted through evangelistic strategies which were not rooted in the life of the church, those who want to remain as secret believers because of the dangers they face in identifying with the Christian community, the very affluent, those with biblically inappropriate and deviant lifestyles, and the poorest of the poor who are despised members of our community. In some cases, discipleship may need to be undertaken through retreats, camps and extension courses.

Recognizing the strengths of the cell model, leaders should be open to alternative approaches.

7. COOPERATIVE EFFORTS IN EVANGELISM

Difficulties

- Suspicion among believers, pastors and denominational leaders
- Difficulty in building relations between leaders
- Following personalities
- Denominational exclusivism
- Churches that cling to their theological distinctives
- Leadership struggles between traditional denominations and new revivalist churches
- Small churches feeling inferior when working alongside large churches
- Disagreement on purpose
- Poor handling of new converts and inquirers
- Racial and language barriers

- The danger of too high a profile in politically sensitive environments
- Issues in financial cooperation and accountability
- Internal denominational struggles

Benefits
- We learn from others and are enriched by their gifts
- Removes distrust
- More resources are mobilized
- Civil authorities take notice
- A more diverse audience is reached for the Gospel
- It takes the collective resources of the churches to reach some areas
- It expands and deepens the understanding of the Gospel
- It helps us understand that the Kingdom of God is far greater than one Christian community
- When we all get together to make a coordinated and concerted effort, the urgency of the task is underlined
- Can stimulate a more strategic approach to evangelism over large areas such as a country, state or metropolitan area
- Combined efforts can attract media attention
- It is a visible expression of unity and a sign of reconciliation
- God is glorified by cooperative activities and Christian unity
- Cooperation is itself a testimony to the unbelieving world of the unity of the Church

Principles and Practices
- Need to model servant-leadership as leaders learn to walk alongside other leaders and to serve the greater community
- Demonstrate respect for authority, rather than taking independent action
- No hidden agendas to subvert the main goal or to promote one's own interest
- Agreement with the evangelist's message
- As a basis for participation, determine what are the essentials upon which there must be agreement and those things on which we agree to differ and still work together in love
- Establish rules and protocol to follow before the event and require participation in all phases
- Have integrity and be above reproach in the areas of finance and sexual morality
- Agreed-upon procedures for follow-up which need to be emphasized from the outset
- Clearly establish purpose
- Kingdom building not empire building
- Praying together

• Equitable and open sharing of resources and publicity

8. SPECIAL OPPORTUNITIES IN EVANGELISM

Unreached peoples are defined by certain barriers. They can be barriers caused by isolation or by resistance. Some examples are:

- Language
- Demographics
- Socio-economic level
- Caste system
- Professional groups
- Recreational groups
- Lifestyle options
- Education level (intelligentsia)
- Occult groups
- Other religions
- Institutionalized persons (e.g., prisons, army, fire fighters)
- Geographic remoteness
- Immigrant communities
- Age (youth cultures which are electronically alienated)
- Disabilities
- Tribal groups/nomadic peoples
- The power brokers (bankers, governments, royalty, media)
- Homeless/disadvantaged
- Homosexual practice and heterosexual promiscuity
- Gated/high-rise communities
- Shift workers
- Long-distance truck/bus/taxi drivers
- Traveling entertainment groups (circus, orchestras)

Barriers that exist within the life of the church

- Fear of confronting people in authority
- The attitude of the Christian community toward people living in deviant lifestyles
- Educational barriers
- Lack of insight into the worldviews of groups that the church is endeavoring to reach
- Spiritual powerlessness of the churches to confront demonic forces and address the lifestyle issues of the unreached
- Prejudice that keeps us from seeing how people of bad reputation can become part of the church
- Lack of commitment to witness to these groups
- Church facilities are not accessible for disabled or other-able
- Bad testimony among long-standing Christians

- Negative publicity about Western culture which is mistakenly identified as Christian
- Church culture which does not easily accommodate converts from non-Christian religions/backgrounds
- Fear that openness to new believers who come out of lifestyles antithetical to the Gospel will bring about compromise of Christian standards within the church (Acts 18:10; 1 Corinthians 6:9–11)

What we learn from the DAWN (Discipling A Whole Nation) Model

The impressive implementation of this model in the Philippines proved an inspiration to many of the church leaders assembled at Amsterdam 2000. The transferable elements were identified as follows:
- Principle of networking as a good example of mobilization
- The strategic goal of a church for every community
- The importance of research to reveal the magnitude and the resources available
- Experience shows that where attempts have been made to develop strategy with no vision for its implementation, the attempts have proved abortive
- The model requires long-term commitment to united implementation
- Ongoing united prayer both promotes the vision and provides encouragement

Some Principles of Reaching the Unreached

- Identify the unreached
- Plant congregations within each group
- Discover representatives of the group who are receptive
- Provide mentors, consultants and prayer partners to those planting churches within the unreached people groups
- Identify and empower emerging indigenous leadership as soon as possible
- Budget for the outreach
- Use appropriate, innovative and accessible technology
- Identify which section of the Christian community you represent in communicating the Gospel
- Prepare churches to respond to the social and physical needs of new believers

The Role of the Preaching Evangelist

- The evangelist must have cross-cultural abilities and training
- The evangelist must be at home in the marketplace and not confined to nor domesticated by the local church
- The role of the evangelist must be upgraded in how it is perceived by the Church. The public image of the evangelist needs to be refurbished in the light of highly publicized scandals. There is need in some situations to

improve the education and training of the evangelists to relate to the context in which they are called to minister.
• The evangelist must have an unprejudiced attitude toward those he is seeking to reach

The Role of Church Leaders in Lifting Vision and Implementing Programs

• Capture a strategic vision for reaching the nation
• Develop a sense of ownership of the program
• Cooperate with other church leaders
• Consider forming a national association for evangelists (as in the DAWN program)
• Ensure that necessary research is being carried out
• Commit to the implementation of agreed goals
• Extend formal invitations to diverse church groups to involve them early in the process rather than expecting them to come on board when plans have already been finalized
• Inspire the vision, and then continue to keep the vision before the membership
• Facilitate planning and networking among denominations in reaching out
• Train lay workers in every aspect for the implementation of the vision

Strategists Task Group Report

Paul Eshleman, Convener

During the Amsterdam 2000 event, 520 strategists in world evangelization from 122 countries gathered to discuss one penetrating question: "What must we do differently in the coming decade to complete the task of world evangelization?"

The results of the consultation were far beyond our prayers and expectations. The Lord met with us in a wonderful way. Leaders from throughout the world were energized with the opportunity to work together with one another to help set a global agenda for evangelization in the coming decades.

Outcomes

As a result of our 15-hour consultation, much was accomplished for the Kingdom. The following are just a few of the developments.

A. The remaining 253 unreached people groups among whom there is presently no effort to plant a church were subscribed for by members of the group who committed to launch a church-planting effort within the next two years.

On Friday, August 4, Bruce Wilkinson, president of Walk Thru the Bible, spoke on "A Vision for the Whole World." He stressed the fact that many of us would like to see the whole world reached but have never really accepted the responsibility to be personally involved in helping to get the Gospel to the ends of the earth. At the conclusion of the session, he asked the strategists, organizational leaders and denominational executives to come forward and shake my hand if they were willing to make that commitment personally. At least 150 came forward to make the commitment—many of them sobbing, with great tears, as the Holy Spirit gripped their hearts to care about every part of the world.

At the beginning of that session we had distributed a listing of the 253 people groups of more than 10,000 people in which there has been no attempt to plant a church. I asked if the strategists would commit to taking the responsibility for one or more of these groups. Some began to shout out the particular groups they would take. However, in the end, we simply asked them to commit to the number of groups they would attempt to reach and indicate how many they would be responsible for. All over the room people began to raise their hands showing with one, two, three or more fingers how many they would take. When we got to 170 and it looked as if there would be no more commitments, three leaders representing Campus Crusade for Christ, The DAWN Movement and Youth With A Mission walked forward. They told me very quietly that they would take the responsibility for the remaining groups. At almost the same time, several people from India came up to say there were more unreached groups than were included on the list for India. The three mission leaders from Table 71 indicated they would include the extra groups from India as well.

SUMMARY: As a result of this session, for the first time in the history of the Church, its leaders have taken the responsibility of giving every major people group in the world access to the Gospel through evangelization and the planting of churches. This may stand as one of the great landmarks to come out of the Amsterdam event.

B. The Establishment of a Network of Strategists
    The entire Amsterdam Strategists Task Group was seen from the beginning as part of a process of bringing together in an informal fellowship those people that are continually involved in planning strategy for evangelism—particularly on a regional or global level. Paul Eshleman was asked by BGEA to serve as the initial coordinator of the network. Marcus Vegh of Progressive Vision; Jon Lewis of Mission Aviation Fellowship; Rick Warren, pastor of Saddleback Church in California; and Greg Parsons of the US Center for World Missions were asked to begin the recruitment process to secure representation from each continent of the world for the Steering Committee. E-mail addresses were collected from the participants in the Task Group so that they might receive continued updates on the suggestions compiled in Amsterdam.

C. A new Web site was launched, called www.evangelismstrategists.net. This site is intended to gather the best models of evangelization, as well as the key strategies that are being found to be effective in various parts of the world. The site was previewed during the sessions. An explanation was given as to how to use it and how to submit material. This site is intended to be the primary means of communication for the network of strategists.

D. The presentations of 130 strategists were video recorded. Two taping crews worked tirelessly during the week to record the best ideas, suggestions and models of evangelism being used around the world. These edited tapes will be part of the Internet site and will be useable for both instruction and motivation in doing evangelism in every area.

E. Resource Distribution. On Tuesday, August 1, we allowed every strategist to bring books, videotapes and strategy materials to share with one another. In the one and a half hour resource fair more than 155 different strategists distributed materials worth more than $25,000.

F. Partnerships. One entire day was given to the establishment of partnerships and alliances. In addition to the regional breakdown, there were functional groups formed for discussions relating to 1) media and technology, 2) church-planting movements, 3) incorporating compassion ministries with evangelism and church planting, 4) evangelization of children, and several others. This gave people an opportunity to meet others with similar passions and interests.

   The consensus of many of those who attended the Strategists Task Group was that the most important outcomes of the track were the many partnerships that were formed during the week. The group was scheduled for two hours every afternoon from 1:45 to 3:45, but many groups could be spotted around the tables several hours after the session ended, still making plans to work together. Just a few of the partnerships launched were:

   1) The Table 71 Group. This partnership between Campus Crusade for Christ (CCC), Youth With A Mission (YWAM) and DAWN Ministries was organized to provide the financial backing and administrative infrastructure that would ensure that all the people group commitments could be carried out. The *JESUS* Film Project pledged to provide video- and audiotapes to help reach each of the 253 groups selected.

   2) DAWN Ministries and a group of compassion ministries formed an alliance in order to develop a mindset in church planters that combines the demonstration of the Gospel with the evangelization of a people group.

   3) Latin America took its first steps in organizing some multi-church efforts in several countries.

   4) A U.S. group consisting of representatives from Mission America, Southern Baptist International Mission Board, Christian Broadcasting Network, CCC, the American Bible Society and several other organizations met to discuss the distribution of Scriptures and *JESUS* films to 110 million homes in the United States.

   5) In addition, there were many other alliances formed that did not want their names published because of security issues in their areas of the world.

G. Discussion and Feedback

   Another of the great outcomes was the collecting of information from each of the 75 tables in answer to specific questions on world evangelization.

   1) What are the biggest obstacles to completing the task of world evangelization?

2) What must the Church do differently in the coming decade to complete the task of world evangelization?

3) What are the best solutions that participants have found for raising the needed financial resources in each country?

4) What are the most important principles for increasing the number of people reached with the Gospel?

5) How can we increase the comprehension of the Gospel? In this regard, there was a tremendous response to a videotape presentation by a young woman representing Generation X in which she talked about their values, fears and search for God. She began the presentation by saying, "We use the same words but speak a different language," and finished with a plea for those doing evangelism not to give up trying to reach her generation, and she spoke very passionately about the need for people to show their commitment to Christ by the life they live.

H. Survey Results. Prior to the conference we sent a survey to everyone invited to the conference. We received back approximately 200 completed surveys. The results were compiled and distributed during the Task Group meetings, along with other helpful materials on the statistical state of the unfinished task and other global overviews in evangelization.

I. Harvest Investors. One of the most significant outcomes of the Strategists Task Group was the new vision given to a group of 60 businessmen and women who were invited to participate in the Task Group. About half of them stayed the entire time and served as recorders at various discussion tables. These men and women represented a number of major foundations in North America and Europe. Though no specific appeals were made for any program, we are aware of a number of commitments they made to various organizations to help fund various projects. Greater than the amount of money pledged, however, was the impact in their personal lives and vision.

The Process

A. Participant Invitations. An invitation committee was formed consisting of leaders from worldwide organizations to help select those people able to contribute to this international forum. In addition, the BGEA added others it felt would make a contribution and ensure geographical representation. Approximately 900 were eventually invited, and 520 attended.

B. Attendance. In our planning we assumed that many of the organizational leaders would drop out after the first day or two and simply conduct personal agendas in the hallways. However, this was not the case. Except for those who had scheduled early flight departures, almost all the participants attended every session right through the final afternoon. In fact, 79 people came begging to be allowed into the session. As people left for one reason or another, we were able to fit them in and the room remained full all week. Leaders of organizations such as Wycliffe Bible Translators, Southern Baptist International Mission Board, Mission Aviation Fellowship, Church of the Nazarene, and many others remained an active part of the discussions.

C. Format. The participants met around tables of eight seats for the purpose of discussing each of the topics. From the beginning of our planning times, the feedback was that they didn't want more plenary sessions. They wanted to talk with one another. Except for the last two sessions, we had no presentations that exceeded 5–10 minutes. These topics included:
1) Global Overview by Luis Bush
2) Technology in the New Millennium by Marcus Vegh
3) The Responsibility of Leaders to Raise Funding by Pat MacMillan
4) The State of Church Evangelization by Peter Brierley
5) The Power of Partnerships by Phil Butler
Also presented were some five-minute presentations of models of evangelization, including:
1) Church-Planting Strategies by Alex Abraham
2) Equipping National Churches for Ministry to Unreached People Groups by Willie Crew
3) Local Church Evangelism by Rick Warren
4) ALPHA Groups by Sandy Millar
5) Biblical Audiotapes by Ramez Attalleh
6) KidsGames by Sami Morris
7) Ports Projects by Henri Aoun
8) Unreached Peoples by Iman Santoso
9) Radio to AIDS Sufferers by Viggo Sogaard (and his guest from Thailand)
The only two plenary talks were given by Bruce Wilkinson on "Developing a Burden" and "The Test of a Vision."

D. Feedback. We had one recorder appointed for each of the 75 tables, and we received more than 300 pages of feedback during the course of the week. We had people from each region of the world share one-minute responses of the best ideas gathered from each table. We placed five microphones at various places in the room for this purpose.

E. Seating. We assigned all of the table facilitators and recorders to specific table numbers, and then estimated the number of tables needed for each region of the world. We then drew up maps of where the various regions of the world should be located, erected regional signs, and prepared handouts for each participant to help him or her locate the tables in the regions where they would sit. As people came in the first day, they were given a seating chart, and we were able to start on time because of the number of stewards and staff who assisted in seating the participants.

F. Interpretation. We provided interpretation in French, Spanish and Russian. We were not aware of our need to find interpreters until the last few days, but God provided sufficient people for this task. However, there was never full participation from these three language groups. The assessment was that there was not full understanding by these language groups of when to move to discussion groups and how to find the meeting rooms.

G. Room setup. In order to enhance the room arrangements we did the following:
   1) Put up colorful banners with scenes from each of the continents.
   2) Hung banners giving the theme of the Strategists Task Group "COMPLETING THE TASK" in four languages.
   3) Hung a banner under each screen with the Web site www.evangelismstrategists.com.
   4) Used PowerPoint graphics on two screens further describing the emphasis of the Strategists Task Group: The Future of World Evangelization.
   5) Prepared PowerPoint support for many of the presentations to aid in interpretation and comprehension by those listening in other languages.
   6) Developed colorful regional signs and table numbers to help people find their places for discussion.

H. Facilitation. Each table had a facilitator that was selected for guiding conversation and ensuring that everyone at the table participated. Regional facilitators were appointed for each region to help replace table facilitators who left or to train alternates in their responsibilities. We conducted a facilitators' briefing conference (two times), but we were only able to pre-train about 60 percent of the facilitators. We met with the facilitators after each session the first two days to evaluate the process. The remaining part of the week we met daily with the regional facilitators to assess the participation. The staff of INTERDEV assisted in the training and direction of the facilitation process.

Report of Theologians Task Group

J. I. Packer, Convener

During Amsterdam 2000 almost 300 theologians from over 100 countries and territories met to discuss the major theological issues which affect the evangelistic outreach of the Church at the beginning of the 21st century. We reaffirmed our commitment to evangelism as the primary calling of the Church, and we acknowledged our responsibility as theologians to encourage and assist all who are called of God to do the work of an evangelist.

Every generation confronts us with new theological trends and challenges, many of which directly influence the Church's understanding of its mission. This generation is no exception. In some parts of the world, for example, post-modernism denies the reality of objective truth and rejects the claims of the Gospel as God's way of salvation. Other parts of the world challenge the evangelist with entrenched religions, idolatries, ideologies and mythologies which create resistance to the Gospel message. To overcome these barriers, the theologian and the evangelist must learn to work together, in the power of the Spirit.

Specifically, the Theologians Task Group identified several areas of need in theology and evangelism, and sought to lay a foundation for further thinking and action. They include the following:

1. The need for clarity and integrity in presenting the Gospel message.

The Gospel is always in danger of compromise or distortion. In a pluralistic, post-modern world one of the theologian's primary tasks must be to reaffirm the central themes of the Gospel message, and especially the uniqueness of Jesus Christ as Lord and Savior. The Bible alone is the source for our understanding of the Gospel, and through it we understand that salvation is found only in Christ, who is unique both in His person and in His power to bring us into a personal relationship with God.

2. The need to present the Gospel without compromise, and yet in ways that are culturally sensitive.

The Gospel is transcultural and yet is always presented within the context of a specific culture. An effective presentation of the Gospel, therefore, needs to take this cultural context into account. Otherwise we may raise unnecessary barriers to belief or unintentionally cause people to misunderstand the Gospel message. However, we must never lapse into syncretism or pluralism, nor must we allow our presentation of the Gospel to be distorted by cultural values that are opposed to the message of Christ.

3. The need to understand the religious beliefs and traditions of those we seek to evangelize.

We live in a multi-faith world, and understanding the religious beliefs of those we seek to evangelize can help us reach out to them with both clarity and sensitivity. Interaction with non-Christians can help us develop this understanding and must involve honest listening, with mutual respect that must be maintained even in debate. (Unfortunately, interfaith discussion has often been marred by the assumption that all religions are equally valid—an assumption evangelicals cannot share.) At the same time, some contexts do not allow for authentic interaction, such as those in which the Church is facing persecution.

As part of this, we must learn to understand and identify the idolatries that non-Christian cultures express. Idolatry takes many forms in the modern world, from traditional paganism to secular materialism and sensualism.

4. The need for theologians to undergird the ministry of those who are called of God to the work of evangelism.

Theology must not become only an academic, ivory tower exercise. Instead, as evangelical theologians we are called to make evangelism the cornerstone of our teaching and writing, working to communicate the truth of the Gospel in ways that will assist and encourage all who are involved in evangelism. By the grace of God, we commit ourselves to this task.